www.wadsworth.com

www.wadsworth.com is the World Wide Web site for Wadsworth and is your direct source to dozens of online resources.

At *www.wadsworth.com* you can find out about supplements, demonstration software, and student resources. You can also send email to many of our authors and preview new publications and exciting new technologies.

www.wadsworth.com
Changing the way the world learns®

RESEARCH METHODS
for
GENERALIST SOCIAL WORK

Fourth Edition

Christine R. Marlow

New Mexico State University

with

Sarah Boone

THOMSON

BROOKS/COLE

Australia · Canada · Mexico · Singapore · Spain · United Kingdom · United States

THOMSON

BROOKS/COLE

Executive Editor: *Lisa Gebo*
Assistant Editor: *Alma Dea Michelena*
Editorial Assistant: *Sheila Walsh*
Technology Project Manager: *Barry Connolly*
Marketing Manager: *Caroline Concilla*
Marketing Assistant: *Mary Ho*
Advertising Project Manager: *Tami Strang*
Project Manager, Editorial Production: *Jennifer Klos*
Print Buyer: *Doreen Suruki*

Permissions Editor: *Bob Kauser*
Production Service: *Hockett Editorial Service*
Copy Editor: *Kathleen Erickson*
Cover Designer: *Denise Davidson*
Cover Image: *Leslie Parr*
Text and Cover Printer: *Webcom Limited*
Compositor: *International Typesetting and
 Composition*

Printed in Canada
2 3 4 5 6 7   08 07 06 05

For more information about our products,
contact us at:
Thomson Learning Academic Resource Center
1-800-423-0563
For permission to use material from this text,
contact us by:
Phone: 1-800-730-2214
Fax: 1-800-730-2215
Web: http://www.thomsonrights.com

Library of Congress Control Number: 2003117033

ISBN 0-534-54159-3

Brooks/Cole—Thomson Learning
10 Davis Drive
Belmont, CA 94002
USA

Asia
Thomson Learning
5 Shenton Way #01-01
UIC Building
Singapore 068808

Australia/New Zealand
Thomson Learning
102 Dodds Street
Southbank, Victoria 3006
Australia

Canada
Nelson
1120 Birchmount Road
Toronto, Ontario M1K 5G4
Canada

Europe/Middle East/Africa
Thomson Learning
High Holborn House
50/51 Bedford Row
London WC1R 4LR
United Kingdom

Latin America
Thomson Learning
Seneca, 53
Colonia Polanco
11560 Mexico D.F.
Mexico

Spain/Portugal
Paraninfo
Calle Magallanes, 25
28015 Madrid, Spain

Contents

3

Deciding on the Question   29

4

The Literature Review and Identifying the Variables   47

5   Designing Needs Assessments   69

8

Selecting the Participants in the Research   135

9

Collecting the Data   163

10

Organizing the Data   203

11

Analysis of Qualitative Data   215
With Colin Collett van Rooyen, M.Soc.Sc.

12

Analysis of Quantitative Data   237

13

Research Writing   267

Appendixes

My reason for writing this text is not unusual. After several years of seeking a social work research methods text and unsuccessfully trying a new text each year, I gave up and started to write. From teaching the same course repeatedly, I developed a number of ideas of what a text needed: more of a focus on the type of research undertaken by social workers rather than academic social scientists; more international content; and presentation of research concepts in such a way that students can see the connection between research and social work practice. These ideas became crystallized through many discussions with students and colleagues and through my experiences with the Council on Social Work Education (CSWE) accreditation process. This text is intended for both undergraduate and graduate students taking a research methods course for the first time.

This fourth edition has a number of new features including updated examples to illustrate the research concepts, greater content on the analysis of qualitative data, and some reorganization of content in response to requests from regular users of this text. In addition, instead of the use of the terms "positivist" and "interpretist," the more commonly adopted terms "quantitative" and "qualitative" are used. Instructors' materials include power point slides; examples of published research articles illustrating research concepts for each chapter; learning objectives; and further reading examples and test questions.

THEMES AND ORGANIZATION

A Focus on Generalist Practice   Undergraduate and foundation graduate courses in social work programs usually are taught from a generalist perspective. Research methods must also be taught within this framework; consequently, the text includes examples from generalist practice. The relevance of research to the rest of the curriculum is thereby increased.

Emphasis on the Practice-Research Link   When the parallels between generalist practice and research are emphasized, research becomes more accessible, because practice is often perceived as more intuitive and understandable. Consequently, the text illustrates these parallels. Throughout the text, examples emphasize the link between research and practice by presenting real-life social work studies.

Discussion of Production and Consumption   The text presents research methods from the perspective that social workers can be both producers and consumers of research. This also ensures compliance with the CSWE accreditation requirements for the research curriculum.

Agency Focus   In line with ensuring the relevance of research methods, the text discusses the application of research methods in agency rather than academic settings, because agencies are where the majority of social work graduates will be employed. The focus of the text is on needs assessments, program evaluation, and evaluating individual practice.

Ethics Content   Ethical issues are included for each stage of the research process; that is they are integrated into each chapter and not viewed as separate, discrete topics.

Human Diversity Content   Similarly, issues concerning human diversity as they relate to research methods are included. Although in part addressed through discussions of alternatives within and to the scientific method, this content (as with the ethics content) is considered for each stage of the research process.

Discussion of the Different Approaches to Research   This text includes coverage of different research approaches: both qualitative and quantitative. A beginning text in research methods cannot engage in complex epistemological debates; what is important for the student to understand is that research can be conducted using different methods and within different paradigms, and that they have a choice.

International Content   As universities become increasingly conscious of internationalizing their curricula, social work programs are also adopting global perspectives. Researchers in the United States are beginning to adopt more participatory approaches, historically a research approach used more extensively in other countries. Many of the examples include research conducted outside of the United States.

This text is written so that each chapter can stand independently if necessary. Key concepts appear in the text in boldface type and are defined there. These terms also are included in the glossary at the back of the text. Each chapter includes a reference section, as well as a summary and study/exercise questions. If possible, students should complete the exercises as a group; a group effort often provides a richer educational experience.

ACKNOWLEDGMENTS

Completion of this new edition depended on many people (too many for me to name them all), but I would like to thank the following specific individuals and groups: First, the reviewers of the manuscript contributed critical comments as the book progressed, and I would like to thank Michael Coconis, Capital University; Adele Crudden, Mississippi State University; Martin Martsch, University of Illinois, Springfield; David Moxley, Wayne State University; Donald Pierson, Idaho State University; Qingwen Xu, San Francisco State University; Diane Young, Syracuse University; and Kimberley Zittel-Palamara, State University of New York at Buffalo. Joe Buenker, reference Librarian at Arizona State University West, provided the extremely thorough and practical Library Appendix. Colin Van Rooyen, previously of the University of Natal, South Africa, contributed to Chapter 11 and helped me move from a U.S.-centric research perspective to one that is more international and inclusive. My thanks go to Rachel Youngman of Hockett Editorial Service, for her coordination of the production process. Lisa Gebo at Brooks/Cole was, as always, wonderfully understanding and supportive. I thank Alma Dea Michelena, also at Brooks/Cole, for her patience. Sarah Boone came to my rescue early in 2003 and found the wonderful "gray box" examples in the literature, and gracefully survived her computer crashing. Leslie Parr, Loyola University, New Orleans, furnished the superb photographs, and I offer many thanks to those who were photographed, several of whom are students and their families at New Mexico State University. Leslie and I have been friends for many years; her photography continually reminds us that social work research has to do with people rather than numbers.

Also many thanks to all the social work students who over the years, in New Mexico, South Africa, Zimbabwe, and Uganda gave me instruction, intentionally and unintentionally, on how research methods should be taught and what should be included in a social work research text.

Finally, to my family—Mike, Sam, and Michael—many thanks for your great patience and support.

Science and Social Work

■■■

"The social work research methods course was the one I dreaded the most. I didn't want to take it."

—*social work student*

INTRODUCTION

The attitude reflected in this student's statement is not unusual in social work classrooms. Social workers often express inherent suspicion, or even a phobia, about research. Have you ever skimmed over articles in social work journals because you were intimidated by the language and the displays of results? Have you ever shuddered at the thought of undertaking a research project? If so, you are not alone. Because research is typically associated with mathematics, you may not be enthusiastic about applying what is perceived as a cold, impersonal approach to human needs and problem solving. After all, most social workers want to work with people, not numbers. Research, however, is simply a means of gaining knowledge, and in social work practice, we need all the knowledge we can muster if we are to be optimally responsible to ourselves, our clients, and our agencies.

Once you understand the research process, you will have access to a vast amount of information in the literature. Articles that once eluded you with discussions of "validity" and "correlation coefficients" not only will become accessible but also will make available information that you can apply to your practice.

When you are equipped with the knowledge and skills to apply research methods, you will also know how to answer many of the questions that arise in your role as a generalist social worker, such as these:

- Are my visits to Mrs. Garcia really helping her cope with the death of her husband? What was her experience with the grief counseling?

- How effective is program X in providing services that support and protect victims of domestic violence? What are the experiences of the clients receiving these services?

- What are the needs of adolescent fathers in City Y? What is it like to be a teenage father in City Y?

This book emphasizes the strong links between the processes of research and practice, helping you to answer these types of questions and to understand social work research. The steps taken in generalist social work practice have their equivalents in social work research.

Thus, the following chapters help you to learn the steps of research in a process similar to the way you learn the steps of practice.

Certain themes of this text will help to explain research methodology and its relevance to your practice as a generalist social worker:

- The research process and generalist practice are connected.

- You may be either a consumer or producer of research.

- Research examples throughout the book are those you will encounter as a generalist researcher.

- Different research approaches may apply depending on the type of question being asked.

- Special issues are involved when you conduct research in agencies.

- Ethical issues are associated with each stage of the research process.

- Human diversity issues are also involved with each stage of the research process.

These overlapping themes support the mission of the book: to present research methods within a generalist social work framework.

Many new concepts are introduced in this book. These terms are boldfaced in the text where they are first defined; they are also listed in the glossary at the end of the book. Each chapter includes an overview, a summary, study/exercise questions, references, and a section called InfoTrac® College Edition.

This chapter will discuss the following topics:

- common types of understanding
- conceptions of science
- the positivist/quantitative approach to science
- the interpretive/qualitative approach to science
- the choice of a scientific approach in social work

COMMON TYPES OF UNDERSTANDING

In our attempt to understand the world, we have developed many different ways of understanding and thinking about human behavior. These types of understanding include using values, intuition, past experience, authority, and the scientific approach. Social work can involve any or all of these types of understanding, and it is important to know about them and the role they play in generalist social work practice.

Values   **Values** are beliefs about what is right and wrong. They are closely tied to our respective cultures. For example, among many cultures, a strong value is placed on children's having respect for their elders. Among some groups, formal education is highly valued, whereas among others education within the family is emphasized.

Values can be institutionalized by religion. For example, certain values characterize Christianity, such as the Protestant value that work is a means to gain societal and individual worth and the Catholic belief in the value of the forgiveness of sins. Buddhists value reincarnation, and this belief affects how they live their present lives. Other religions practice ancestor worship, whereas others strongly value the natural world around them, revering the plants and animals that make up their world.

Although values may be fundamental to a culture's tradition, these traditions can change over time. For example, many cultures now recognize that women should have the same career opportunities as men. This was not the case a hundred years ago, or even ten years ago, in some of those cultures.

Social work as a profession is based on certain values. These include fundamental notions about the most desirable relationships between people and their environment. Social work values include respect for the individual's dignity and uniqueness, recognition of the client's right to self-determination, and confidentiality.

Intuition   **Intuition** can be defined as a form of insight: when we intuitively know something, we understand it without recourse to specialized training or reasoning. Intuition may also be based on past experiences. In some cultures, intuition is a powerful tool for understanding and explaining the world. People with strong intuition may be seen as having magical powers. If they also exhibit experience and skills, they may enjoy special status. An example is the *curandera,* a woman who is perceived to possess healing powers in the Hispanic culture in the Southwest United States and Mexico. Similarly, in South Africa among the Zulu people, the *sangoma* is thought to be able to understand the world using special intuitive powers.

Sometimes we call on intuition in social work practice, and it is a valid source of professional understanding (Allen-Meares and DeRoos, 1994). Although it is unlikely that we would act on intuition alone, we might use it to give ourselves leads to investigate further. For example, we might have an intuition that a child is being sexually abused. It may be hard for us to explain this feeling rationally, but the insight can provide a base or starting point for gathering information, which may or may not support the intuition.

Experience   **Experience** can be defined as firsthand, personal participation in events that provides a basis for knowledge. You often use this experience to guide present and future actions, particularly when the experience had a previous successful outcome (even though you may not understand why it was successful). Clearly, these experiences vary from individual to individual and according to the type of situation. Most cultures value experience highly. Elders are often highly regarded for their experience; employers often use experience as a criterion for assessing job applicants. In the practice of social work, experience is often referred to as practice wisdom. Although highly valuable as a source of knowledge, it is risky to use practice wisdom as the sole guide to practice and as the only resource for making practice judgments.

Authority   Sometimes events and circumstances are understood by referring to outside sources of knowledge or to an **authority** on specific topics. The authority is credited with an understanding and knowledge we do not directly possess. Thus, in lieu of direct understanding—whether obtained through values, intuition, or experience—we accept an explanation by virtue of our confidence in authorities.

Who or what the authority is depends on the nature and context of the problem. In practice, social workers rely on authority in a number of ways. We identify experts in different fields of practice and seek their opinions and knowledge, either by consulting with them personally or by reading their publications. There is vested authority in the social work professional organizations, such as the National Association of Social Workers (NASW) in the United States and the National Institute of Social Work in Great Britain. We use their authority to direct us in different areas, for instance in adhering to a prescribed code of ethics.

Science   Specific characteristics of **science** distinguish it from the other forms of understanding discussed in this section. Science refers to both a system for producing knowledge and the knowledge produced from that system. We can think of science as including the following characteristics (Neuman, 2003).

Universalism   Regardless of who conducts scientific research or where it is conducted, it is judged solely on its scientific merit. If a project adopts the scientific method which is built on systematic objective observation, then the researcher's characteristics, qualifications, national origin, and so on, are not relevant. The research findings are viewed independently of the researcher. This is different from say best-selling novels, where knowledge about the author can be important (previous books written, nationality/ethnicity, gender, experiences, etc.), because novel writing in addition to including craft and skill is generally viewed as an artistic endeavor rather than a scientific one.

Organized Skepticism   All scientific evidence should be challenged and questioned. Scientific research is closely scrutinized to ensure that the scientific method has been followed. There are a number of generally accepted aids for following the scientific method. The first aid is completing a research methods course—students often undertake a research project that is closely scrutinized by the course instructor. Graduate students may complete a thesis or dissertation, which is even more closely scrutinized and subject to questioning by your committee and advisor. Professionals may publish in journals that are "refereed," which means reviewed by scholars anonymously (authors do not know who the referees are) and blindly (referees do not know who the authors are).

Disinterestedness   Scientists should be able to accept other scientific evidence that runs against their position. If you have worked in an agency developing a program that uses behavioral interventions to work with substance abusers, you might read a research report that discloses less than satisfactory results using this type of intervention. You may at first dismiss the study because it runs counter to your beliefs and perhaps even counter to some research you have undertaken. However, the research should be considered on its merits and the findings used to enhance your program, if possible.

Communalism   Scientific knowledge must be shared with the public, including the methods used. Research almost always results in some type of report, available to those who are interested. The search for new knowledge is the primary reason research is undertaken. This may be a class research report shared with your classmates and instructor, it may be an agency evaluation disseminated to the staff and administrators, or it may be a published article in a social work journal. A research report includes a careful description of each step undertaken in the research process (discussed in detail in Chapter 13).

Honesty   Scientists demand honesty in all research. A code of ethics guides how the research is undertaken. In social work the NASW Code of Ethics includes a specific section relating to conducting social research. Throughout the research process the participants must be protected in every way from harm, and the researcher must be scrupulously honest at every step of the research process. Every chapter in this book discusses ethical issues confronted at each of these stages.

One important section in any research report is the limitations section, where the researcher spells out any problems with or limitations to the research method they have undertaken. Although the ultimate in research honesty, the limitations section is often difficult for researchers. A research report or article without a limitations section is subject to question, because as every researcher knows, there are always limitations to all research studies!

As well as being characterized by these norms, science consists of **theories** and **research methods**. Theories attempt to describe or to explain logical relationships among phenomena in our world. Theories help to guide our thinking about many aspects of social work practice and include theories of human behavior, such as developmental theories, and theories of underlying practice, such as systems theories.

Theories are to be distinguished from values, which are concerned with what should be rather than what is. Theories attempt to understand and to explain logical and persistent patterns in phenomena. Theories cannot stand alone in science. They need to be supported by the other component of science: research. The methods of research adhere to the following principles:

1.   Information is collected from *observing* the world. This observation can be carried out in different ways, but it is different from philosophizing or speculating.

2.   The steps of the research process are *systematic,* not random or haphazard.

3.   Studies should be *replicated;* repeating studies a number of times determines whether the same results can be found.

People think about the relationship between research methods and theory in different ways. Just as different types of theories explain different phenomena, so different research methods may apply to different topics. These different methods and ways of conceptualizing science will be discussed in the next section of this chapter.

This text focuses on science because it is the dominant type of understanding today. Many individuals and organizations throughout the world depend on science. For example, the medical profession relies on knowledge derived from the application of science. Businesses use scientifically based theories and strategies. Social work is no exception; the profession has historically recognized the contributions of the scientific approach.

Before proceeding with a more detailed description of the scientific method, it is important to note that although the scientific approach dominates the thinking in many countries, this has not always been the case. For example, Greek rationalism once dominated Western thought, offering logic as the test of truth and not relying on scientific evidence. Even today, scientific thinking is not dominant in all cultures. For example, in some American Indian cultures, direct experience of an event is the primary means of explanation. Among some other groups, including the Zulu, scientific explanations are not always accepted. For example, existence of HIV (the human immunodeficiency virus) in the body is not always seen as evidence of a person's being HIV positive (van Rooyen and Engelbrecht, 1995).

CONCEPTIONS OF SCIENCE

Although science is unified by its shared norms, scientific practice varies. Up until about 25 years ago, this was not the case. One model or approach was used in the social sciences; this model was broadly referred to as **positivism**. (Variations of and other terms for that approach include logical positivism and **empiricism**.) More recently it is also referred to as the **quantitative approach** or **method**. Positivism or the quantitative approach rests on a number of different principles about how science should be done. One central principle is that science depends on the collection of observations that support theories. These observations need to be made objectively. **Objectivity** refers to the condition that, to the greatest extent possible, researchers' values and biases do not interfere with their study of the problem. Another principle is that the theories and observations remain separate. A theory ultimately needs to be supported by independent observations, which can be used to devise laws and rules that help us to make sense of the world.

Over the years, however, the positivist/quantitative approach and its principles have been questioned. Throughout the social sciences, including social work, positivism's claim to be the same thing as the scientific method and empirical science has raised skepticism. The questioning derives from several sources: students of the history of science; those exploring new frontiers in the scientific disciplines, for example the field of quantum physics; and people who traditionally have been excluded from the scientific community, including women and other underrepresented groups.

Thomas Kuhn explores the issue of values in *The Structure of Scientific Revolutions* (1970). From studying the history of science, Kuhn concluded that factors other than specific observations and theoretical necessity lead to the emergence and acceptance of the "best theory." These other factors include values. Kuhn wrote about paradigms, defining a paradigm as "the entire constellation of beliefs, values, techniques, and so on shared by members of a given [scientific] community" (Kuhn, 1970). Paradigms function as maps, giving structure to important problems to address, acceptable theories, and possible procedures to solve the problems. Kuhn proposed that paradigms shift over time. Paradigms reflect changing values, countering the idea that a fixed reality exists out there to be objectively observed. Objective reality appears to change as paradigms change.

An example of a paradigm shift occurred in social work during the last 50 years. In the 1920s and 1930s, the prevailing paradigm or framework for social work practice was psychoanalytic and was tied closely to a medical model. In the 1960s, a more ecological systems framework was adopted. This paradigm shift has important implications not only for how social workers conceptualize their practice but also for how research is conducted. Research questions deriving from a medical model differ substantially from those deriving from a systems perspective.

The views of underrepresented groups, which previously had been virtually denied access to the traditional scientific paradigm, have had an increasing impact on how science is perceived. Many of them argue that the types of questions asked are influenced by the social context of the researcher (Kuhn's point) and that different groups bring different experiences to the research, influencing the types of questions asked.

One example of a group that has questioned how science is viewed is **feminist researchers**. They argue that men and women experience the world differently, and that the objective model of science is more compatible with men's ways of thinking. Because women see the world more in terms of relationships and interaction, feminists think that a relationship is formed between the researcher and subject, which results in the formation of a constructed reality between them. Thus, according to feminist researchers and many others, no facts exist out there that can be objectively observed.

This questioning by many people of the principles underlying the positivist approach to science resulted in the adoption of alternative research models in many disciplines, including in the social sciences. Positivism has not been rejected, but alternatives to positivism also are now considered to be part of scientific inquiry. Just as positivism embraces a number of different variations, for example postpositivism, so several models have also been developed as alternatives to positivism or the completely quantitative approach. **Interpretism** and the **qualitative approach** are the terms used here to denote these alternatives. In the next two sections, the positivist/quantitative and interpretist/qualitative approaches will be examined, and the different principles guiding the two approaches will be discussed.

THE POSITIVIST/QUANTITATIVE APPROACH TO SCIENCE

Positivism and the quantitative approach are traditionally equated with science and is the approach predominantly used in the natural sciences. We described some principles of this approach in the previous section; here they are presented in more detail.

According to the quantitative approach, observations of the world can and must be carried out objectively. Biases and values must be eliminated as much as possible. Positivist research methods are designed for this purpose. Many of these methods rely on a clear distinction between the researcher and the subject, with any contact between the two being strictly formalized. In quantitative research, the subject actually becomes the object of study. The science is researcher-driven (Guba, 1990); the subjects have little say about how the research is carried out.

The goal of the quantitative approach to science is to search for causes of phenomena. Such a search is possible because it is assumed that the world has an order that can be discovered, such that you can explain and predict what happens. In other words, positivist researchers strive to identify factors that lead to certain events. For example, if a family lives in a rural area, has more than four children, and is headed by a single parent, there is a greater likelihood that there will be parental involvement with the children's school system. Obviously these kinds of research findings can be useful to social work practice.

Causality means that changes in some factor or factors (A) produce variations in another factor or factors (B). The following conditions have to exist to infer the existence of a causal relationship:

- A statistical association has to exist between the factors. (The intricacies of statistical association will be explained later.)
- Factor or factors A must occur prior to factor or factors B.
- The relationship between the factors A and B must not be spurious. In other words, the relationship must not disappear when the effects of other factors are taken into consideration.

The quantitative researcher uses a deductive approach to build knowledge. **Deduction** involves drawing conclusions from the general to the particular. A theory generates questions; these questions are then compared with observations. For example, various researchers have investigated whether Piaget's theory of child cognitive development is valid across different cultures, testing through observation whether Piaget's theory describes what occurs in different cultures. The results are then fed back into the theory.

Quantitative data are usually collected. To gather quantitative data, categories of the phenomena under study are created prior to investigation. Numbers are assigned to these categories, which are then statistically analyzed.

The quantitative approach requires studying large numbers of subjects, because a central concern is that one should be able to **generalize** the results of the research to as large a group as possible. Findings from a study can be generalized if they can be applied to other groups rather than being specific to those in a specific research sample. For the findings to be generalized, the subjects being studied need to be representative of the groups to which the researcher wants to generalize the findings. Certain techniques in positivist research ensure this representation. Large groups are also needed because the statistical tests used to analyze the quantitative information usually gathered by positivist research are designed for large numbers of subjects.

A Quantitative Study

Kulis, Napoli, and Marsiglia (2002) examined the relation of strength of ethnic identity, multiethnic identity, and other indicators of biculturalism to the drug use norms of 434 American Indian middle school students. The sample was randomly selected. The 45-minute questionnaire administered to the sample of students consisted of Likert-type items to capture students' norms in use of alcohol, tobacco, marijuana, and other drugs along with the strength of their ethnic self-identities. Statistical analysis of the results indicated that students who maintained a strong sense of ethnic identity had possessed a higher level of antidrug norms than students without the same sense of ethnic identity.

As discussed earlier, the quantitative approach has come under increasing criticism, particularly in the social sciences. In general, critics have questioned whether using this approach to the exclusion of others is appropriate when studying human beings. One main group of alternative approaches to science is offered in the next section.

THE INTERPRETIVE/QUALITATIVE APPROACH TO SCIENCE

There are several branches of interpretive science, including hermeneutics, ethnomethodology, constructionism, phenomenology, naturalistic inquiry, and qualitative methods. Here we need not be concerned about the distinctions among these approaches (see Patton, 2001, for a good discussion), but rather with their overall assumptions and methods of interpretation.

For the interpretive/qualitative researcher, reality is based on people's definitions of it, rather than on something externally present. The **subjective** experience is what needs to be studied, rather than the objective one. For the qualitative researcher, observation takes on a different quality than it does for the quantitative researcher. People's behavior cannot be observed objectively; instead, the researcher and subject create a reality through their interaction. Because reality is perceived as interactive and constructed, the subject's role in the research process is more active. Instead of being researcher-driven as in the positivist/quantitative approach, the research process is subject-driven. Subjects or rather participants become partners with the researchers and are empowered in the process. In addition, the qualitative researcher explicitly acknowledges the researcher's biases and values. These are stated explicitly rather than ignored.

Qualitative researchers are primarily interested in description rather than explanation. Because of the assumption that reality is socially constructed and is in a state of being mutually shaped, causes cannot always be definitively established. Instead the interactive reality is discovered and described.

Qualitative Research in Social Work

Zaidu (2002) conducted a nonprobability convenience sample of 20 single, Pakistani Muslim females to explore their perceived attitudes toward arranged marriages. Five themes, including attitudes toward romantic love in marriage, preferred method of mate selection, redefining arranged marriages, reasons for engaging in an arranged marriage, and breaking the silence were investigated through interviews with Pakistani women. The researcher used an unstructured interview. Two distinct groups based on perceptions of arranged marriages emerged from the interviews. The first group which included 15 interviewees was against the system of arranged marriages, and the second group of 4 interviewees expressed favor toward the arranged marriage system.

Qualitative researchers usually build knowledge inductively. Research by **induction** uses observation to examine the particulars of a phenomenon and then develops generalizations to explain or to describe relationships among the particulars. Inductive reasoning involves finding patterns common to separate phenomena. For example, certain similarities may be seen in children with behavioral problems in school. After collecting case examples, a theory is developed that states the children have other characteristics in common in addition to the behavior problems. The majority may be found to be new immigrants whose parents do not speak English, and their behavioral problems may result from teachers' failures to appreciate the children's difficulty in making the transition from home to school. Thus, a theory is built from observations, rather than developed through generating questions that are then answered through observations.

A qualitative approach or qualitative researchers usually collect **qualitative** data. Qualitative information involves the nonnumerical examination of phenomena, using words instead of numbers, and focuses on the underlying meanings and patterns of relationships. Often these underlying patterns are disguised if categories are formed before numerical observations are made. Analysis of qualitative information consists of creating categories after the verbal material has been collected. When qualitative information is collected, the number of participants in the study is often small, because the focus is on collecting in-depth information from each participant to understand the participant's subjective experience of the phenomena under study.

See Figure 1.1 for an illustration of the relationship between the interpretist/qualitative and positivist/quantitative approaches. Remember that the distinction made between the two approaches here is a fairly crude one. As mentioned earlier, different terms are often used in different ways, and what they denote is subject to considerable debate. The complex field of the philosophy of science is beyond the scope of this book.

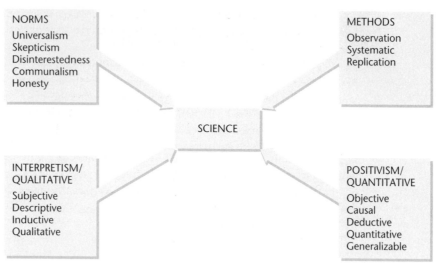

NORMS
Universalism
Skepticism
Disinterestedness
Communalism
Honesty

METHODS
Observation
Systematic
Replication

SCIENCE

INTERPRETISM/
QUALITATIVE
Subjective
Descriptive
Inductive
Qualitative

POSITIVISM/
QUANTITATIVE
Objective
Causal
Deductive
Quantitative
Generalizable

Figure 1.1   ***Different approaches to science***

THE CHOICE OF A SCIENTIFIC APPROACH IN SOCIAL WORK

Having described two basic approaches to science, how do you reach a decision about which one to use for social work? There has been debate in social work about this question. Some professionals argue that social work will lose its credibility as a social science if it abandons the positivist or quantitative approach, and that this is the only method that develops sound knowledge on which to base social work practice (Schinke and Nugent, 1994). Others defend and promote alternative perspectives, arguing that only they can capture the essence and meaning of social work (Heineman-Pieper, Tyson, and Pieper, 2002; Gilchrist and Goldstein, 1994), reminding us that human behavior is complex and not always observable and measurable. They argue that the basic principles underlying the interpretive, alternative approaches are more compatible with social work in that they empower the subjects and reflect more accurately the diversity of opinions and perspectives within the field.

The position behind this book is that both positivism and interpretism offer the potential to build knowledge in social work, and this idea is supported in the literature (Boland and Atherton, 2002). Just as different models exist to guide practice, each offering its strengths and weaknesses, so in research different methods have advantages and disadvantages. Each method is a response to different perceptions of reality. Neither the quantitative nor the qualitative approach can offer the ultimate "truth."

Because both approaches offer advantages, the question becomes which one to use when. The decision depends on the type of inquiry. Some problems are more suited to a quantitative research method and some to a qualitative one. Take the three sets of questions at the beginning of this chapter. The first part of each question is asking for information that goes beyond the particular to the general. The answers need to be as generalizable as possible. The focus, at least in the first two questions, is on explanation—in other words, whether and how the programs and interventions are working. The intent of these questions is to produce information that is as objective as possible so that funding decisions can be made and programs developed.

The second part of each question focuses more on the subjects' experiences, and the goal is to understand rather than to explain. These questions are less concerned with objectivity and the ability to generalize the findings.

Sometimes the type of question to ask and subsequently the type of approach to use depend on the level of knowledge we have about the area under study. For example, suppose the phenomenon under study is battered women. Initially, Walker's (1979) theory that "learned helplessness" can explain why battered women stay in violent relationships was developed using a qualitative approach. It was only after the theory was developed through close observation that the theory was tested using a more quantitative approach. Thus the generation of knowledge can be seen to be cyclical, with both approaches integral to the development of concepts and theories.

In this book, both approaches will be described, and you will be given guidance about when one might be more appropriate than the other. Both approaches require specific skills, experience, and planning. The appropriate choice depends on the question under study and the overall purpose of the research. As with practice—where, for example, behavioral interventions require a different knowledge base and are appropriate to different circumstances from psychodynamic interventions—no one approach is always better or right.

SUMMARY

This chapter introduces the themes in this book. Different types of knowledge and understanding are based on different sources of knowledge, including values, intuition, experience, authority, and science. The positivist/quantitative and interpretist/qualitative approaches to science can both offer advantages in addressing the different types of research questions asked in generalist social work.

STUDY/EXERCISE QUESTIONS

1. List the five different types of understanding presented in this chapter and discuss how you use each of them in your practice.

2. Go to a public place and observe people for 15 minutes. Report back to your class. Note the similarities and differences in what each student observed. Discuss the implications of these observations for the concept of objectivity.

INFOTRAC COLLEGE EDITION

1. Search for *qualitative method* and examine how the articles refer to and use this term.

2. Search for *feminist research* and discuss this concept in class and its use in social work research.

REFERENCES

Allen-Meares, P., & DeRoos, Y. S. (1994). Are practitioner intuition and empirical evidence equally valid sources of professional knowledge? In W. W. Hudson & P. S. Nurius (Eds.), *Controversial issues in social work research.* Boston: Allyn and Bacon.

Boland, K., & Atherton, C. (2002). Heuristics versus logical positivism: Solving the wrong problem. *Families in Society, 83* (1), 7–13.

Gilchrist, L. D., & Goldstein, H. (1994). Is research training important to the development of analytic reasoning and critical judgment in social work? In W. W. Hudson & P. S. Nurius (Eds.), *Controversial issues in social work research.* Boston: Allyn and Bacon.

Guba, E. G. (Ed.) (1990). *The paradigm dialog.* Newbury Park, CA: Sage.

Heineman-Pieper, J., Tyson, K., & Pieper, M. H. (2002). Doing good science without sacrificing good values: Why the heuristic paradigm is the best choice for social work. *Families in Society: The Journal of Contemporary Human Services, 83* (1), 15–35.

Kuhn, T. (1970). *The structure of scientific revolutions.* Chicago: University of Chicago Press.

Kulis, S., Napoli, M., & Marsiglia, F. F. (2002). Ethnic pride biculturalism, and drug use norms of urban American Indian adolescents. *Social Work Research, 26* (2).

Neuman, W. L. (2003). *Social research methods: Qualitative and quantitative approaches.* Boston: Allyn and Bacon.

Patton, M. Q. (2001). *Qualitative research and evaluation methods.* Thousand Oaks, CA: Sage.

Schinke, S. P., & Nugent, W. R. (1994). Are some research methodologies inherently more worthy of professional endorsement than others? In W. W. Hudson & P. S. Nurius (Eds.), *Controversial issues in social work research.* Boston: Allyn and Bacon.

van Rooyen, C., & Engelbrecht, B. (1995). The impact of culture on HIV/AIDS social work service delivery: Emerging themes from a study in progress. *Social Work Practice, 3.95,* 2–8.

Walker, L. (1979). *The battered woman.* New York: Harper & Row.

Zaidu, A. U. (2002). Perceptions of arranged marriages by young Pakistani Muslim women living in a western society. *Journal of Comparative Family Studies, 33* (4), 495–514.

Research and Generalist Social Work Practice

One problem in understanding the research process is that it is often viewed in isolation rather than being closely linked to practice. In this chapter the link between research and practice will be explored, and close parallels between the practice process and the research process will be examined. This chapter discusses the following:

- generalist practice
- the purpose of research in generalist social work practice
- research roles in generalist practice
- research and generalist practice processes
- values and ethics in research and practice
- research and human diversity

GENERALIST PRACTICE

Before discussing how research is linked to generalist practice, we need to explain what is meant by **generalist social work practice**. From its inception social work has been committed to addressing individual competencies and implementing social change. Today generalist practice is the form of social work practice taught in undergraduate programs in the United States and in other parts of the world as a basis for professional social work education.

Over the years various views have developed about what constitutes generalist practice. Several writers have tried to clarify its components and have proposed different conceptualizations. Miley, O'Melia, and DuBois (1998) suggest that the generalist approach rests on four major premises:

1. Human behavior is closely connected to the physical and social environments.

2. Enhancing human functioning depends upon changing the system itself and altering other systems.

3. Work on either the macro or micro level involves similar social work processes.

4. Generalist social workers have a responsibility to work for just social policies and to conduct and to apply research.

THE PURPOSE OF RESEARCH IN GENERALIST SOCIAL WORK PRACTICE

As generalist social workers, why do we need to be concerned with research? Given that the dominant way of understanding the world is through science, building a strong research base for practice helps legitimize and give credibility to the profession. Relying on research, however, does not mean dismissing other forms of understanding.

Beyond its legitimizing role, research fulfills a number of other functions by promoting a strong knowledge base and fiscal and ethical responsibility, and by empowering clients. Each of these will be discussed in turn.

1. Scientific Knowledge

Scientific knowledge is built by using research methods to develop and refine theories. In the last chapter two different research approaches were discussed. Each builds knowledge rather differently from the other. The positivist approach generally uses the deductive method of building theory, deducing premises from the theory and testing those premises. The interpretist approach uses the inductive method, in which systematic observations are used to make generalizations and build theories.

The development of knowledge through research is a central function of research in social work. Knowledge about the extent, nature, and causes of social problems, and about the effectiveness of various interventions and programs, significantly enhances social work practice. Without this research-based knowledge, social workers would have to rely on the other sources of understanding described in the last chapter. Although each of those sources has its own contributions to make to the generalist practice, social work would suffer without scientifically based knowledge.

For example, if you were employed in Child Protective Services as an investigator, a critical part of decisions made about family intervention would be based on assessment tools. These tools, such as Structured Decision Making (Myers, 1999), are based on previous research and are tested using scientific methods. Without such tools, your decision might be based on your authority as an investigator, your intuition, your values, or your past experience with similar situations—all important components in the final decision but weakened by an absence of the scientific component.

Entire programs are developed on the basis of research. For example, early intervention programs for new parents are based on research that indicates that parent training and support can help reduce the incidence of child abuse and neglect. The training itself is based on theories of child development that are supported by research.

On a larger scale, major welfare reform decisions need to be based on information gathered from previous studies. For example, Chilman (1995) critically reviewed studies concerning the working poor. As a result of this review, she proposed further legislation to help move welfare recipients from economic dependency to self-sufficiency through employment.

2. Ethical Issues

Social workers need to be knowledgeable about research for ethical reasons. Social workers are ethically responsible for providing the best possible services to their clients. In the United States, the NASW (1999) Code of Ethics specifically addresses this issue.

Ensuring Fiscal Responsibility through Research

Giardino, Montoya, Richardson, and Leventhal (1999) used a 16-item question-naire to examine staffing, funding sources, reimbursement, and financing of medically oriented child protection teams. Questionnaires were mailed to a sample of 118 child protection teams. Results indicated that even though more than 50% of the teams identified funding as important, they demonstrated vary-ing levels of awareness of budget and reimbursement issues. Additionally, one-third of the teams reported that funding was unstable. The researchers concluded that team leaders need to increase their knowledge of fiscal issues so that they may be more effective advocates at the institutional level for continued team support.

Code of
Ethics

- Social workers should educate themselves, their students, and their col-leagues about responsible research practices.

- Social workers should monitor and evaluate policies, the implementation of programs, and practice interventions.

- Social workers should promote and facilitate evaluation and research to con-tribute to the development of knowledge.

- Social workers should critically examine and keep current with emerging knowledge relevant to social work and fully use evaluation and research evi-dence in their professional practice.

To abide by the NASW Code of Ethics, the social worker needs to be proficient in social work research methods.

3. Fiscal Accountability

As long as social work practice is predominantly funded by government and charitable contributions, accountability will be a critical issue in the field. In recent years, fiscal accountability has become even more important. Funds allocated to the human services are decreasing rapidly, and different organizations must compete for smaller and smaller pools of money.

Two aspects of social accountability must be considered. First, social workers are expected to demonstrate that they are spending money responsibly—this includes the assurance that a social program's goals are being met and that funds are being distributed in the most efficient way to meet those goals. The agency or the individual practitioner may be responsible for this accountability. Second, generalist social workers are often called upon to establish new services and pro-grams, particularly in rural areas. To do so, and to solicit funds for this purpose, they need to substantiate their claim by providing clear evidence of need and a strong basis in research for the proposed program.

4. Empowering Clients

Research can be indirectly empowering to clients—through building knowledge and ensuring fiscal and ethical accountability—and certain research methods can be directly empowering, too. Subjects (often clients) can be directly involved in the research process from planning to implementation. Some research strategies involve clients more than others. We discussed in the last chapter how the interpretive approach tends to be more subject-driven than researcher-driven. This tendency derives in part from the assumption that meaning emerges from the interaction of subject and researcher rather than from the researcher's objective observations alone. Through use of the interpretive approach, clients become empowered because they are not being used as subjects but instead as direct participants in the research.

Another opportunity for clients' involvement in research, and subsequent empowerment, is through **participatory action research**. This approach to research has three aims, all intended to empower clients. The first is to produce knowledge and action directly useful to groups of people. A second aim is to encourage people to construct and to use their own knowledge for self-empowerment. The third aim is to promote collaboration throughout the research process. Participatory action research originated and grew in developing countries, where it continues to be a standard approach to research. In the United States, participatory research historically was restricted in its use to motivate workers to adopt new productivity strategies. For example, in a case study of Xerox Corporation, White (1991) demonstrated how labor, management, and the researcher worked as a team to help increase productivity, instead of the researcher simply going in with a plan and recommendations from management's perspective. Participatory action research (or PAR) is used much more extensively (Hick, 1997) now in the United States. Participatory action research is particularly compatible with generalist social work in that the approach emphasizes empowering systems of different sizes, from individuals to whole communities. Usually, the people under study participate actively with the researcher throughout the research process, from the initial design to the final presentation and dissemination of results. Note that a number of different research methods can be used within the participatory action research framework, including either the positivist or interpretist approach.

RESEARCH ROLES IN GENERALIST PRACTICE

As we have seen, generalist social work practice is based in research, and practitioners must be able to assess or examine their own practice in terms of research. To accomplish this goal, the generalist social worker needs to adopt two roles with respect to research: the consumer and the producer.

The Consumer

As was discussed earlier, the scientific approach is essential in building a knowledge base for social work. To use this knowledge in an informed manner, social workers need to understand research methods so that they can evaluate the extent of a theory's research base. Even if the theory has apparently been validated and supported by research, there is no guarantee this research is of high quality. A social worker who is knowledgeable about research can better evaluate the quality of that research base. In their users' guide to social science research, Cook, Crouch, and Katzer (1997) point out that many mistakes and errors occur even in published research. Your research instructor can undoubtedly confirm this statement.

Critical analysis of research is also essential in the social worker's assessment of specific practice techniques. For example, home-based services are commonly provided by generalist practitioners, and there exists a whole body of literature and research about these services. The practitioner informed about research can turn to this research for practice guidelines. A social work approach known as "empirically based practice" is gaining recognition and is built on the ability of the practitioner to consume research (Briggs & Rzepnicki, 2004).

The Producer

The second reason social workers need to know about research methods is the most obvious one. Armed with this knowledge, social workers can then use the methods directly in their own practice to answer questions that arise. This ability to use research methods is vital whenever answers cannot be found in the existing literature, as is frequent in social work, whether or not the social worker is engaged in generalist practice. Social workers often need to carry out their own research on the effectiveness of interventions they use. In addition, generalist social workers are often required to demonstrate the need to provide new services or to improve existing services. Clearly, these types of inquiries demand knowledge and implementation of research methods.

In sum, generalist social workers, acting as producers of research, can begin to build new knowledge for practice. Though such a task may seem overwhelming to you at this point, this book will describe how to produce research step by step. You will be provided with the tools to become not only a producer of research, but also a critical and intelligent consumer.

Remember that social workers use many of the skills and techniques described in this book routinely, without formal research training or education.

Social workers act as consumers of the literature, for example, when they read reports and gather relevant information. As producers, social workers gather data from multiple sources. In addition, they document progress toward clients' goals, write reports, and engage in many other activities that, as we will see, are all included in the larger activity of research.

RESEARCH AND GENERALIST PRACTICE PROCESSES

Social workers are often intimidated by research, in part because they think it involves types of knowledge and skills that are different from those of practice. In fact, as we are about to see, the processes of practice and research are similar, particularly for generalist social work practice.

Although the generalist perspective is conceptualized in different ways, authors of generalist social work texts are in basic agreement on a general process for practice. This process is usually conceptualized sequentially, as consisting of progressive stages leading to certain goals. This concept originated with one of the founding mothers of social work practice theory, Helen Harris Perlman (1957), who proposed "operations" as part of practice process. Others later modified these operations; for example, Pincus and Minahan (1973) described "guideposts for the process"; Schulman (1992) and Egan (1994) proposed "stages" or "phases"; and Hull and Kirst-Ashman (2004) wrote about "planned change steps." One approach to generalist practice is to reframe it from a problem-solving process to an *empowerment-based practice* (Miley, O'Melia, and DuBois, 1998) that focuses on strengths rather than on problems. However, it still involves steps, and we will see that they follow closely those of research.

Forming Partnerships

A critical step in social work practice is the building of the relationship between the social worker and the client, a relationship that respects the uniqueness of the client. Miley, O'Melia, and DuBois (1998) state that forming partnerships is "the process whereby a worker and client system define their working relationship in ways which reflect the purposes of social work and standards of ethical codes. For the process to be empowering, social workers and client systems resolve power and authority dilemmas by defining their relationship in an egalitarian way, maximizing their respective contributions" (pp. 101–102). This establishment of a relationship is also critical in social work research. As stated earlier, one of the purposes of research is to empower clients, and one way of accomplishing this is to involve clients directly through participatory action research. Participatory action research is rapidly becoming the preferred approach to social work research. For example, if your agency wants to assess some of the problems and difficulties faced by children with AIDS, an important first step is to establish relationships with some of the professionals and family members who work and live with these children. In this way they can become partners in your research.

Articulating Challenges

Social workers used to refer to the preliminary statement of the problem, but now we tend to conceptualize problems in social work as "challenges." At this stage of the practice process, clients and social workers develop a mutual understanding of the situations that bring the clients to seek help. Similarly, in research, the first step after developing a relationship with the client is to *decide on the question*. For example, consider the issue of children with AIDS. Instead of simply conceptualizing the question as "the problem of children living with AIDS," seek greater clarity. For example, the question might be stated: "To what extent are the needs of children living with AIDS being met?" And then (framing it from a strengths perspective,) "What are some of the strengths of this population?" For example, they could be resiliency and emotional maturity.

As we proceed with the research, new insights occur and new information is gathered, which in turn may lead to a reformulation of the challenge. For example, the question may change to focus on evaluating the services of a specific agency: "To what extent is program X serving the needs of children living with AIDS?" This question may then become even more specific: "How effective is program X in advocating for children living with AIDS?" Or, from more of a strengths perspective: "What are some of the characteristics of programs that successfully serve children with AIDS?" This issue of deciding on the question to be asked is discussed further in Chapter 3.

Defining Directions

The next step in practice is for the worker and client to "orient their work together toward a specific purpose" (Miley, O'Melia, and DuBois, 1998, p. 102). This helps to establish a specific direction for their work together. The process of definition also occurs in research and is known as writing the literature review and identifying the variables stage. Clear definitions of terms and explicit statements of the assumptions that underlie the research question help reduce bias. This is an important consideration whether one is adopting the objective stance of positivism or the empathic neutrality of interpretism. Many of these defnitions are contained in the research literature. Although assumptions can be made at all stages of the research process, clearly stating what is assumed during the initial stages of the research is particularly useful. One strategy is to state carefully the nature of the question and to identify its different components. In our example on children living with AIDS, we would need to define the term *advocating*. We may have a number of different assumptions about this function of social work, but how does the agency see this role and how can it be defined so that all concerned are in agreement? What do we mean by effective or successful? That all children living with AIDS referred to the agency receive advocacy services? Half the children? How are children living with AIDS defined? Are we concerned with children who are infected with the HIV virus or those with AIDS symptoms? What ages will be included in this study? This issue of identifying the variables will be further discussed in Chapter 4.

Identifying Strengths

In practice, the social worker collects information, recognizing that the identification of client strengths is critical if change is to occur. Strengths can be found in interpersonal relationships, culture, organizational networks, and community connections. In research the collecting of the information is also critical. It consists of three tasks: *data collection, sampling,* and *design.* For the project concerning children with AIDS, data collection might include interviewing or administering questionnaires to the children's caretakers. The sample might be relatively small, perhaps only ten or so caretakers, and thus their selection will need careful consideration. The research design might include a comparison group of caretakers of children with AIDS who do not receive services from program X, which provides services specifically to those with AIDS, but instead receive services from a more generic type of agency. Each of these research steps will be discussed further in Chapters 5, 6, 7, 8, and 9.

Analyzing Resource Capabilities

In practice, this stage is often known as assessment and includes examining the information or data collected. Workers and clients jointly assess personal, interpersonal, familial, group, organizational, community, societal, and political systems looking at the interrelationships within an environment. Miley, O'Melia, and DuBois (1998) state: "This analysis transforms the abundant information generated through assessment into a coherent, organized foundation of information on which to construct a plan of action" (p. 103).

The next step in research is known as *analysis* and involves a process similar to that undertaken in practice. If quantitative data are collected, statistical techniques are used. However, with qualitative data, the information is sorted and categorized so that meanings will emerge. As in practice, the analysis step needs to be carried out systematically and conscientiously to avoid misinterpreting the results. Specific techniques are used to ensure bias-free results. Results often generate new questions and issues much as plans are generated in practice.

Analysis of the data about children with AIDS may reveal that those in program X thought they had received more advocacy services than those from the comparison program Y, but that those in program X were less satisfied with the types of medical services available to them. Another phase of the research might include examining the source of this dissatisfaction and investigating whether this dissatisfaction extends to the adults with AIDS who receive services from program X. Organization of data and data analysis will be further discussed in Chapters 10, 11, and 12.

Framing Solutions

In practice, the social worker takes the results of the assessment and develops a plan of action that often involves the formulation of goals.

The comparable step in research is the writing of the report, which formally presents the analyzed results along with a description of the research method. The research report includes recommendations for further research, a logical extension of the process in which analysis of results generates new questions. An important section of a social work research report is the one on the implications of the research for practice: How can the findings help social workers in the field?

The researcher may recommend further research into reasons for the dissatisfaction with medical services, and, more specifically, into the medical needs of children with AIDS. Report writing is further discussed in Chapter 13.

Activating Resources, Creating Alliances, and Expanding Opportunities

This stage in practice is often known as *intervention* or *implementation of the plan*. Implementation is the "action" part of social work practice. This process includes developing alliances through collaboration with clients and between the clients themselves. Also, the worker continues to create opportunities at the macro level, including creating resources that address social justice. Unfortunately, this step tends to be downplayed in research, although research findings are of little use unless they are implemented in some way. In research this stage is known as *utilization of research.*

Ideally, going back to our example, workers in program X would take the findings from the research and try to monitor more closely their medical referrals for the children, perhaps undertaking a more thorough follow-up with the families to ensure that the children's medical needs are being met.

Recognizing Success and Integrating Gains

The last step in practice is often known as *evaluation* and *termination*. Miley, O'Melia, and DuBois (1998) refer to it as recognition of success and integrating gains. Perhaps because it comes last, this stage is often given little attention. We may find ourselves simply moving on to the next case instead. In research this step involves evaluating the research by discussing its limitations and generally assessing its overall quality.

For example, one problem with the project concerning children and AIDS might have been that the caretakers in one program group were influenced in their questionnaire answers about satisfaction with medical treatment. Wanting to please the researcher, the caretakers might have covered up some of the problems they experienced in caring for the children. Thus the answers might have been biased, making the program appear to be more effective than it was. See Table 2.1 for a comparison of these steps of research and practice.

VALUES AND ETHICS IN RESEARCH AND PRACTICE

In addition to the similarities in the processes of research and practice, there is a similarity in their values and ethics. Values relating to social workers' conduct and responsibilities to their clients, colleagues, employers, profession, and society all are reflected in social workers' ethical codes. In the United States, the NASW Code of Ethics (1999) includes ethical standards that apply to research. Many of these ethical standards are directly related to the values that underlie practice,

Table 2.1   **The relationship between research and practice**

Practice	Research
Forming partnerships	Using participatory methods
Articulating challenges	Deciding on the question
Defining directions	Writing the literature review and identifying the variables
Identifying strengths	Collecting the data, sampling, and design
Analyzing resource capabilities	Organizing and analyzing the data
Framing solutions	Research writing
Activating resources, creating alliances, and expanding opportunities	Utilization of research findings
Recognizing success and integrating gains	Evaluation of research

values such as confidentiality, privacy, and self-determination. Some of these standards were listed earlier in this chapter. Here are the remaining standards with reference to the chapters where they will be considered in more detail:

- Social workers engaged in evaluation or research should carefully consider possible consequences and should follow guidelines developed for the protection of evaluation and research participants. Appropriate institutional review boards should be consulted. (See Chapter 9.)

- Social workers engaged in evaluation or research should obtain voluntary and written informed consent from participants, when appropriate, without any implied or actual deprivation or penalty for refusal to participate; without undue inducement to participate; and with due regard for participants' well-being, privacy, and dignity. Informed consent should include information about the nature, extent, and duration of the participation requested and disclosure of the risks and benefits of participation in the research. (See Chapters 6 and 8.)

- When evaluation or research participants are incapable of giving informed consent, social workers should provide an appropriate explanation to the participants, obtain the participants' assent to the extent they are able, and obtain written consent from an appropriate proxy. (See Chapters 6 and 8.)

- Social workers should never design or conduct evaluation or research that does not use consent procedures, such as certain forms of naturalistic observation and archival research, unless rigorous and responsible review of the research has found it to be justified because of its prospective scientific, educational, or applied value and unless equally effective alternative procedures that do not involve waiver of consent are not feasible. (See Chapters 6 and 8.)

■ Social workers should inform participants of their right to withdraw from evaluation and research at any time without penalty. (See Chapters 6 and 8.)

■ Social workers should take appropriate steps to ensure that participants in evaluation and research have access to appropriate supportive services. (See Chapter 9.)

■ Social workers engaged in evaluation or research should protect participants from unwarranted physical or mental distress, harm, danger, or deprivation. (See Chapter 9.)

■ Social workers engaged in the evaluation of services should discuss collected information only for professional purposes and only with people professionally concerned with this information. (See Chapter 9.)

■ Social workers engaged in evaluation or research should ensure the anonymity or confidentiality of participants and of the data obtained from them. Social workers should inform participants of any limits of confidentiality, the measures that will be taken to ensure confidentiality, and when any records containing research data will be destroyed. (See Chapter 9.)

■ Social workers who report evaluation and research results should protect participants' confidentiality by omitting identifying information unless proper consent has been obtained authorizing disclosure. (See Chapters 9 and 13.)

■ Social workers should report evaluation and research findings accurately. They should not fabricate or falsify results, and they should take steps to correct any errors later found in published data by using standard publication methods. (See Chapters 11 and 12.)

■ Social workers engaged in evaluation or research should be alert to and avoid conflicts of interest and dual relationships with participants, should inform participants when a real or potential conflict of interest arises, and should take steps to resolve the issue in a manner that makes participants' interests primary. (See Chapter 5).

These values and ethics guiding research will be discussed throughout the book. Each chapter will include a section on ethics and how ethical standards relate to the topic being discussed in that chapter.

RESEARCH AND HUMAN DIVERSITY

By human diversity we mean the whole spectrum of differences among populations, including but not limited to gender, ethnicity, age, and sexual orientation. In practice we recognize the importance of understanding and appreciating group differences so we will not impose inappropriate expectations; we must also account for these differences in research. We discussed earlier that an important step in both research and practice is to clarify our assumptions. If we are not aware of our assumptions regarding certain groups, these assumptions can be disguised and undisclosed, causing biases in the research itself. Clarifying assumptions is only one way in which human diversity issues should be considered in the research process. As with ethics, each chapter in this book will discuss human diversity issues as they relate to research.

SUMMARY

In conclusion, research and practice follow parallel processes in approaching problems. When research methods are viewed in this way, they appear far less intimidating. We all know that practice can be frustrating; in truth, so can research. Just as practice has its great rewards, however, so does research. The road at times is a rocky one, but ultimately we all benefit.

STUDY/EXERCISE QUESTIONS

1. Discuss some of the ways you may find yourself engaged in research as a generalist social worker.

2. Select a research article from a social work journal. How could the findings from this research help you in your practice?

3. Select a research article from a social work journal. How would you change the research to make it more participatory?

4. Imagine you were asked to evaluate the program in which you were working (use your field placement as an example). How would you justify the importance of this research to a fellow student?

INFOTRAC COLLEGE EDITION

1. Search for *participatory action research* and describe the advantages to both the researcher and the participant in conducting this type of research.

REFERENCES

Chilman, C. (1995). Programs and policies for working poor families: Major trends and some research issues. *Social Service Review, 69* (3), 515–544.

Cook, K., Crouch, W. W., & Katzer, J. (1997). *Evaluating information: A guide for users of social science research.* New York: McGraw-Hill.

Egan, G. (1994). *The skilled helper: A problem management approach to helping.* Pacific Grove, CA: Brooks/Cole.

Giardino, A. P., Montoya, L. A., Richardson, A. C., & Leventhal, J. M. (1999). Funding realities: Child abuse diagnostic evaluations in the health care setting. *Child Abuse & Neglect, 23* (6), 531–538.

Hick, S. (1997). Participatory research: An approach for structural social workers. *Journal of Progressive Human Services, 8* (2), 63–78.

Hull, G. H., & Kirst-Ashman, K. K. (2004). *The generalist model of human services practice*. Belmont, CA: Thomson Brooks/Cole.

Marlow, C. (2004). The evidence based practitioner: Assessing the cultural responsiveness of research. In Briggs, H. E., and Rzepnicki, T. (Eds.). *Using evidence in social work practice*. Chicago: Lyceum Books.

Miley, K., O'Melia, M., & Dubois, B. (1998). *Generalist social work practice*. Boston: Allyn and Bacon.

Myers, B. (1999). Implementing actuarial risk assessment: Policy decisions and field practice in New Mexico. Proceedings from the Twelfth National Round Table of CPS Child Risk Assessment. American Humane Association, Boulder, Colorado. *Research and Generalist Social Work Practice, 27.*

National Association of Social Workers (1999). NASW Code of Ethics. *NASW News, 25,* 24–25.

Perlman, H. H. (1957). *Social casework: A problem solving process*. Chicago: University of Chicago Press.

Pincus, A., & Minahan, A. (1973). *Social work practice: Model and method*. Itasca, IL: Peacock.

Schulman, L. (1992). *The skills of helping individuals, families, and groups*. Itasca, IL: Peacock.

White, W. (1991). *Participatory action research*. Thousand Oaks, CA: Sage Publications.

Deciding on the Question

■

"How do I know whether this is a *real* research question? Is this what a research question should look like? I can't quite pin down what it is I need to find out." You will find yourself asking these kinds of questions when you are first confronted with the task of deciding on the research question. As a generalist social worker, you may not always participate in deciding on the question; this decision is often made within the agency prior to your involvement in the research. You need to be familiar with the procedure involved in deciding the question, however, so that you can understand how one step in the process leads to the next (as in practice). You also need to learn about this research stage so that you can evaluate your own practice, a process that is described later in this chapter.

As discussed in Chapter 2, one of the early steps in the research process—deciding on the question—is equivalent to one of the first steps in practice, articulating challenges. This step, in research as in practice, is one of the most challenging. Often, this step is ongoing and involves continuously reworking and reevaluating the process. This chapter will discuss the following topics:

- sources of questions
- research strategies
- types of questions
- the agency and deciding on the question
- ethical issues in deciding on the question
- human diversity issues in deciding on the question

SOURCES OF QUESTIONS

For generalist social workers, research problems or questions usually are determined by their agencies; these questions are directed at solving problems that arise in practice and are intended to produce practical outcomes. This type of research is known as **applied research**. When research is instead aimed at satisfying our intellectual curiosity, even if the results eventually will be applied to help solve practice problems, it is known as **pure research**.

An example will help to clarify these definitions. You are employed in an agency where a large proportion of the clients are victims of spousal abuse, and you see this as a growing problem. A pure research question would concern the causes of spousal abuse per se. As a generalist social worker employed in the agency, however, you would also ask applied research questions, such as how well your agency serves the victims or what other services are needed by this client population.

If this distinction between pure and applied research still seems difficult to understand, some would argue that it is because the distinction does not really exist in social work. Social work is in itself an applied field, so any question related to social work in any way will be some type of applied question. Some research, though, is more immediately applicable to social work practice than other research is. Rothman and Thomas (1994) actively promote forms of social work research called developmental research (also called intervention research). This type of research focuses on developing innovative interventions; research is used to design the interventions, test their effectiveness, and modify them based on recommendations that emerge from testing.

Personal experiences also can come into play in the formulation of research questions. For example, you may find yourself working with a number of physically challenged young adults in the agency in which you are employed. You become aware that some specialized type of housing needs to be established for these clients, and after consulting with your supervisor, you decide that it would make sense to carry out a needs assessment to determine the extent and type of need in the community. Your interest may also have stemmed in part from the fact that a member of your family is physically challenged.

The following is a checklist you can use to test whether the question you are thinking about can be successfully answered.

> Does this topic really interest me? For example, am I choosing this topic to please someone else or do I have a genuine interest in it?

> Do I think that this is a problem that is appropriate for scientific inquiry? For instance, if the question is along the lines of whether child abuse is morally wrong, the question may not be a suitable topic for scientific inquiry, as we discussed in Chapter 1.

> Do I have enough resources available to investigate this topic? For example, will the topic require large samples that will be costly to access or many time-consuming interviews? Do I or other people have the time and money to pursue the topic appropriately?

> Will this topic raise ethical problems? For instance, will the questions to be asked of participants arouse potentially harmful emotions? Will the subjects feel coerced to participate?

> Will I be able to secure permission—from the agency, community, clients, and so on—to carry out this research?

> Are the results of the research going to be useful and have implications for the practice of social work?

Note that research questions are constantly under review and can change at any time given the availability of new knowledge or new resources. For example, it might be that a local politician becomes interested in housing for the physically challenged and is asking about community support for the development of special facilities. Hence the focus of your research might shift to community attitudes. Alternatively, you read in an issue of *Social Work* that a study was carried out identifying some of the housing difficulties confronting the physically challenged. This, too, may change the focus of your research.

Developmental Research (Intervention Research)

Dore, Nelson-Zlupko, and Kaufmann (1999) stated that they could not find any school-based interventions aimed at latency-aged children from drug-abusing families, so they designed and tested a model curriculum to use with children in schools located in high drug-use communities. The authors found that the children needed strategies and skills for working with their environment. The group participants responded well to structure, predictability, and affirmation, and their classroom behavior improved and measures of self-worth increased.

RESEARCH STRATEGIES

Before you embark on the actual formulation of a research question, you need to identify the general research strategy that the question will adopt. The research strategy is determined by three factors: (1) the intent or goal of the research; (2) the amount of information we already have on the topic to be investigated; and (3) the intended audience. Two main strategies can be identified: descriptive and explanatory. Each of these will now be examined.

Descriptive Research

Descriptive research describes, records, and reports phenomena. Descriptive research can provide important fundamental information for establishing and developing social programs, but it is not primarily concerned with causes. Many surveys trying to determine the extent of a particular social problem—for example, the extent of child sexual abuse—are descriptive. In fact, an entire approach to research, called **survey research**, focuses on describing the characteristics of a group; this type of research will be discussed further in Chapter 5. Descriptive research can use either the quantitative or qualitative approach.

Using the qualitative approach, rich descriptions of phenomena can be produced. Often these descriptions emerge after carefully selecting the participants in the research—perhaps those who are best informed about the phenomenon being described. If the intention, however, is for the results to be generalized to wider populations and to be used as the justification for new or expanded services, the quantitative approach would probably be more suitable. Here it would be more useful to collect relatively objective quantitative data describing the phenomena (rather than seeking people's subjective experiences) and to select the participants in the research according to how well they represent the population under study.

You will encounter descriptive research in social work journals. A considerable amount of policy evaluation and analysis is of this type. As a generalist practitioner, you may also be engaged in descriptive research. You could be asked to present some descriptive data relating to your agency (number of clients served, types of problems, and so forth) or to your community (the proportion of the

Quantitative Descriptive Research

Moon and Benton (2000) studied the tolerance of elder abuse and attitudes toward third-party intervention among African-American, Korean-American, and White elderly. Data were collected using structured interviews with elders aged 60 or older living in Los Angeles County, California. Eighteen statements were used to measure the respondent's tolerance of and attitudes toward elder abuse: the respondents were asked whether they agreed or disagreed with the statements. The results were then presented for each group. The results suggested that the African-American and White elderly are similar in their responses, but Korean-Americans differed significantly from those two groups.

Qualitative Descriptive Research

Alaggia (2002) conducted an exploratory study to identify factors that contributed to maternal response to children sexually abused by the mother's intimate partner. Ten mothers were interviewed based on evolving variables such as level of maternal support, maternal history of abuse, nature of relationship with perpetrating partner, ethnic affiliation, and other factors. Alaggia posits that more detailed dimensions of support could prove useful to clinicians when working with clients. The mothers' narratives can assist in developing guidelines for more comprehensive assessments for professionals to utilize after a child sexual abuse disclosure.

population living below the poverty line, for example). Your supervisor may also require you to keep a journal describing your activities in the agency.

Explanatory Research

Explanatory research aims at providing explanations of events to identify causes rather than simply to describe phenomena. For example, a descriptive study might examine the extent of self-mutilating behavior among teenage girls, whereas an explanatory study would try to identify the factors associated with the causes of this phenomenon. Explanatory research requires the formulation of a **hypothesis** which is a statement about the relationships between certain factors. Hypotheses usually have an "if *x*, then *y*" structure: for example, "if the ethnicity of the group leader is the same as the client, then success in the group will be more likely." Or, "if a teenage girl's mother experiences major health problems, then the girl is more likely to engage in self-mutilating behavior."

As discussed in Chapter 1, certain conditions need to be met to establish causality, which is central to explanatory research. These conditions are: First, *two factors must be associated with one another.* Usually this association is established

Explanatory Research

Rittner and Dozier (2000) studied the effects of court-ordered substance abuse treatment in the cases of 447 children in kinship care while under child protective services supervision. The effects of court orders on the duration of service and on numbers of placements were studied. Results were mixed and indicated that levels of compliance with the mandated treatment did not influence rates of re-abuse or duration of service. Court orders affected the number of caretakers and placement experienced by the children.

Hypothesis: Hodge (2003) examined the degree of value similarity between social workers and consumers. Hodge used the "new-class" theory to propose two hypotheses. The first hypothesis was that graduate social workers affirm value positions more liberal than those of working class and middle class clients. Hodge also hypothesized that bachelor's level social workers hold value positions somewhere between the value positions of graduate workers and clients. Data analysis indicated that both hypotheses were supported.

empirically. For example, you might determine that there is a relationship between the grade B.S.W. students received in their practice class and their grade in the field. That relationship, however, does not necessarily mean that the practice grade caused the success in the field. The other conditions of causality also need to be met. The second condition is that *the cause precedes the effect in time.* In our example, you would need to demonstrate that students completed their practice courses prior to entering the field. The third element of causality is that *the relationship between the factors cannot be explained by other factors.* In our example, it is possible that other factors, such as past experience, had as much impact on field performance as the practice course grade.

In each step of the research process, explanatory research tries to address these conditions of causality. In reality, meeting all three conditions is often extremely difficult; the best we can expect is that only one or two of the conditions will be met. A positivist approach is often most appropriate to use when testing hypotheses and carrying out explanatory research. Qualitative data, however, can often be used to add depth and detail to the findings and so assist in the acceptance or rejection of the hypothesis.

Explanatory research is found in the social work literature, and as generalist practitioners, you may be directly involved in such research. Usually, you would not undertake such research alone but would participate as a member of a team—for example, in determining the effectiveness of a particular program or agency.

Exploratory Research

Beyond the strategies of explanatory and descriptive research, another strategy, **exploratory research**, deserves mention. This strategy is undertaken when

Exploratory Research

Hyde and Ruth (2002) used an exploratory study to examine class participation and student self-censorship. From survey and focus group data, the authors studied student discomfort in social work courses, reasons for self-censorship, and solutions to self-censorship. Surveys were distributed to all sections of the first-year MSW HBSE course and to the second-year Social Work Ethics course students to yield the greatest number of responses. All students in the program were enrolled in one of these two courses. The survey comprised three sections, including a section on demographics, one on self-expression in class, and a third section focusing on solutions. The researchers included the open-ended questions in the survey to provide students with the opportunity to express their own reasons for class participation. Students self-selected to be members of focus groups ranging in size from four to seven students. Results from the surveys and focus groups revealed that general classroom factors such as shyness and lack of preparation rather than political correctness were the reasons for self-censorship.

little is known about the topic under study. Such studies can adopt either an explanatory or a descriptive strategy. Either a qualitative or quantitative approach is appropriate with exploratory research, although exploratory research is often associated with the former. Exploratory research often determines a study's feasibility and raises questions to be investigated by more extensive studies using either the descriptive or the explanatory strategy.

For example, you might suspect that the ethnicity of a group leader is important for success in the support group you have organized for children of alcoholics. The group leader is Puerto Rican. After interviewing some of the clients in the group to get their opinions, you find that the Puerto Rican clients were more likely than the others to state that the group was successful. Based on these results from the exploratory study, you plan to undertake more extensive research to evaluate the impact of the group leader's ethnicity on clients' perceptions of success.

TYPES OF QUESTIONS

This section will explore the different types of applied research questions that are asked in generalist practice. The following questions from Chapter 1 provide examples of these different types of questions.

The following questions evaluate the effectiveness of individual practice and are known as **practice evaluations**.

1. How effective is the grief counseling I am providing to Mrs. Garcia in helping her to cope with the death of her husband?

2. How is Mrs. Garcia experiencing the grief counseling I have been providing?

The following questions evaluate the effectiveness of a program and are known as **program evaluations**.

1.   How effective is program X in providing services that support and protect victims of domestic violence?

2.   What are the experiences of the clients who receive services from program X?

The following questions describe the extent of a social problem and are known as **needs assessments**.

1.   What are the needs of adolescent fathers in city Y?

2.   What is it like to be a teenage father in city Y?

Note that two examples are offered for each type of question. As we discussed in Chapter 1, the first example for each type of question is asked in a way that is more appropriate for the quantitative approach—for example, "Program X received additional funding for next year. How can we show our program is effective and deserves more money?" The second example for each type of question is more appropriate for the qualitative approach—for example, "In what areas could our program be improved and what are our clients' experiences with the program?" The choice of which type of question to ask depends on the level of knowledge that already exists for the topic under study and on the overall purpose of the research.

These types of questions, practice evaluations, program evaluations, and needs assessments represent the different types of applied research encountered by generalist social workers in their practice. Of course, other types and forms of research can be undertaken, but as discussed earlier in this chapter, they are less applied. For example, a more "pure" social science research question might ask: "What are the factors associated with (or the causes of) teenage fatherhood?" This inquiry can generate important new knowledge, but generally it is not the type of research question a generalist social worker would undertake research to answer. This might be the type of question you would ask if you were writing a thesis or a dissertation in social work.

We will now discuss the different types of questions in more detail.

Practice Evaluations

One type of research question that often occurs in social work practice is concerned with the effectiveness of an individual social worker's practice. Practice evaluations usually involve only one case, subject, or client system and require social workers to use specific criteria and methods in monitoring their own practice cases. For the generalist social worker, these cases include individuals, families, groups, or communities. Whatever the type of client system, only one is evaluated in a practice evaluation. This type of research can be either descriptive or explanatory, and either quantitative or qualitative.

Increasingly, practice evaluations are being recognized as an integral element of social work practice. In part, this recognition has resulted from social

A Practice Evaluation

Pandya and Gingerich (2002) conducted a multi-ethnographic practice evalua-tion study of group therapy for male batterers. The researchers described the change processes in abusers. Additionally, the researchers offered insight into the dynamics of unsuccessful processes. Data collection for this study used passive participant observation in one group treatment program. The researchers utilized ethnographic domain and theme analysis to answer the research questions focusing on the discovery of the change process.

workers' seeking a method of evaluation that could be integrated into their prac-tice relatively easily. In addition to being easily integrated into practice, practice evaluations offer the generalist practitioner the advantages of low cost and immediate feedback (to the client, too). Practice evaluations will be discussed more fully in Chapter 7.

Program Evaluations

Program evaluation research questions are asked extensively in generalist social work practice and involve assessing a program's overall functioning rather than an individual practitioner's effectiveness. This type of question relates directly to the generalist social work function of promoting the effective and humane oper-ation of the systems that provide resources.

Program evaluations play an increasing role in today's social work practice. During the federal government's War on Poverty of the 1960s and early 1970s, funding for social programs was high. Unfortunately, however, there was little accountability to funding sources regarding social programs' effectiveness in meeting client needs. Fischer (1976) conducted a review of casework practice in social work. He concluded that approximately half of the clients receiving case-work services either deteriorated to a greater degree or improved at a slower rate than did subjects who did not participate in the programs. Fischer's study jolted social workers and others into the awareness that adequate funding did not ensure a program's effectiveness. Fischer's work also disclosed that many of the studies he reviewed contained various methodological problems. As a result, the profession realized the necessity for more sophisticated research methods to assess service effectiveness and to conduct program evaluations so that findings—positive or negative—would be reliable.

Program evaluation is primarily concerned with determining a program's effectiveness, which can be accomplished using any of three different strategies: formative, summative, or cost-benefit approaches. First, the **formative pro-gram evaluation** approach, or **process analysis**, examines a program's plan-ning, development, and implementation. This type of evaluation is often performed as an initial evaluative step and is generally descriptive. Often the

A Formative Program Evaluation

Onyskiw, Harrison, Spady, and McConnan (1999) conducted a formative evaluation of a program focusing on client and team member views of project implementation. The program, *Together for Kids,* was a child abuse prevention project which involved the collaboration of various agencies in the health, social services, and law enforcement sectors. The evaluation strategy employed was primarily qualitative using in-person interviews by an external evaluator to identify the elements of the program that appeared to be beneficial. The sample size included 17 clients who were purposely chosen to represent the demographic characteristics of the community. Results indicated that the community-based approach, the multidisciplinary composition of the teams, the immediacy of the response time, and several other factors made the project beneficial. The researchers concluded that multidisciplinary, community-based service models prove to be effective and compassionate responses to vulnerable families.

Summative Program Evaluation

Whipple (1999) researched the effectiveness of a community-based parent education and support program that was aimed at reducing the risk factors for child physical abuse. Based on previous research, selected risk factors were examined in this study. Three unstructured programs and one ongoing support group, which differed in duration and intensity, were assessed. The researchers collected quantitative data using three types of measuring instruments: self-report questionnaires, staff assessments, and observational home visits over a 15-month period. Administration of the three instruments to the participating parents took place both before and after the parents participated in the program. Results revealed that parents who participated in the more intensive program made the strongest gains.

interpretive approach is used because it allows for a fuller understanding of the processes at work within the agencies and can address these processes from multiple perspectives—those of the client, the worker, and the administrator.

The **summative program evaluation** approach, or **outcome analysis**, determines whether goals and objectives have been met and the extent to which program effects are generalizable to other settings and populations. This type of research is usually explanatory. The quantitative approach is generally more appropriate with summative evaluations, because the purpose is to establish causality (the program's effect). Often these types of evaluations are required by funding organizations, which are more interested in the kind of research evidence (generally quantitative) produced by quantitative studies.

A Needs Assessment

Fredriksen (1999) studied the variety of family-care responsibilities experienced among lesbians and gay men. Thirty-two percent of the participants in the study provided some time of caregiving assistance. Lesbians were more likely to be caring for children and elders, whereas gay men were more likely to be assisting working-age adults with a disability. The author suggested that these findings have important implications for the development of family-responsive services and policies.

Needs Assessments

Needs assessment questions are concerned with discovering the characteristics and extent of a particular social problem to determine the most appropriate response. This type of research is usually descriptive and, as previously mentioned, is also known as survey research. This kind of question is related to the practice function of linking people with systems.

An example of this type of needs assessment is the following: "I have talked to a couple of clients who need an alternative living situation for their adult developmentally delayed children. I wonder if there is a great enough need in the community to start a group home for the adult developmentally delayed?"

Reporting hearsay, citing individual cases, or simply acting on a hunch does not provide enough evidence for funding sources. Usually a funding source, whether a voluntary organization, a private foundation, or state government, requires documentation of the need for the program with evidence that the needs assessment has been performed scientifically. Generally, a quantitative approach is used for a needs assessment, because most needs assessments are concerned with generalizability of results rather than in-depth understanding of how people experience social problems. Sometimes, however, a qualitative approach can provide some important insights and new directions for assessing the needs of certain populations. Needs assessments can be designed in different ways; these design issues are discussed in Chapter 5.

Although these three types of research questions appear to be quite different, they all follow essentially similar research steps and strategies. Differences in approach are sometimes required, particularly in the design stage. Thus, a separate chapter is devoted to each of the three main types of research questions: needs assessment, program evaluation, and practice (Chapters 5, 6, and 7, respectively).

The three types of research questions described here are not the only types of research questions social workers ask. If you look through any social work journal, you will find other types of research questions. You may find some pure research questions or historical studies. In addition, some articles may be theoretical and conceptual rather than empirical in nature.

In this book we focus upon practice evaluation, program evaluation, and needs assessment questions simply because these are the types of research questions you will be most likely to encounter as generalist social workers. Remember, though, that many other types of questions are possible in social work.

THE AGENCY AND DECIDING ON THE QUESTION

As we discussed earlier, except when conducting practice evaluations, you may have little or no choice in the research you will be doing as a generalist social worker. The question may have already been decided, and your task instead may be to conduct a needs assessment to help build a case for developing a new program in your community. Or perhaps your program's funding source demands that an evaluation be undertaken for funding to continue. You may find that you often have little opportunity to decide on research strategies or types of questions.

Despite this tendency for low opportunity to choose the research, in many respects you are in an ideal position for conducting applied research. As an agency-based generalist social worker who is knowledgeable about research and familiar with the agency's workings and the community's concerns, you are well situated to conduct relevant research. You can also act as a resource person for outside researchers; when the opportunity arises, you may assist them in conducting research that is beyond the scope of your immediate responsibilities in the agency.

If you are asked to initiate a research study from the ground up, however, you must recognize that research is almost always a team effort, particularly at the stage of deciding on the question. Consult with agency staff, clients, and community to determine what they want from the evaluation or needs assessment. Don't forget to confer with those who are providing the funding for the project.

One strategy for ensuring that those who are affected by the research or its findings participate more fully in the research implementation is the use of **focus groups**. A focus group is a special group formed to help decide on the research question and the research method. A focus group is composed of people who are informed about the topic or will be affected by it in some way. A focus group can be used at any stage of the research process, but is particularly useful in the beginning stages.

The focus group is informal. The researcher asks participants focused questions with the emphasis on sharing information. The empowerment or action approach to research often uses focus groups, because a focus group enables clients to become directly involved in the research. For example, focus groups are an excellent way of involving community members in developing the research. The focus groups can themselves help identify other stakeholders and so expand the potential input.

In addition to focus groups, agencies often use task forces to help formulate research questions. Task forces are usually made up of representatives of the agency and sometimes representatives from the community, including clients. They often are charged with assessing needs or developing strategic plans, these activities often being the starting point for the development of research questions that are of concern to the agency.

Collaboration Between a Researcher and a Practitioner

Carise, Cornely, and Gurel (2002) discussed factors that contribute to effective research-practice collaborations. A successful partnership between a group of treatment researchers and a group of substance abuse recovery houses operated by Fresh Start was examined. The study showed that factors such as adequate advance preparation of clinical and research staff to utilize the new system and overcoming bilateral biases were critical to success. The researchers noted that Fresh Start's treatment completion rates prior to participation in the project were 45%, but increased to 70% after becoming part of the collaborative project.

The Use of Focus Groups

Kruzich, Friesen, Williams-Murphy, and Longley (2002) used an exploratory study to examine families' perceptions about involvement in residential treatment from the viewpoints of African-American and non-African-American family members. While the use of focus group interviews demonstrated that all family members shared some positive and negative experiences, unique issues were presented for African-American caregivers. Four focus groups were held. Several themes were cited during the focus group process.

Task Force

Pine, Warsh, and Maluccio (1998) developed a model to evaluate and improve an agency's family reunification services. The model included a task force comprising administrators, supervisors, line staff, trainers, attorneys, staff members with financial responsibilities, foster parents, collateral providers, and birth parents. The goal of the task force was to conduct a self-assessment of the agency's service delivery systems and to develop an action plan for change. A positive impact that resulted was a set of 65 recommendations to improve family reunification services.

ETHICAL ISSUES IN DECIDING ON THE QUESTION

Two ethical issues are central to the stage of the research process concerned with deciding on the question: the question's applicability to social work practice and the availability of funding.

Participatory Action Research

Crabtree, Wong, and Mas'ud (2001) formed a participatory research project to study dengue prevention in Sarawak, Malaysia. Objectives of the study included a reduction in the high *Aedes* mosquito index and associated risk of dengue in two coastal Malay villages. The researchers used behavior modification strategies and a participatory approach. The participatory action research approach enabled the community to plan, act, monitor, and evaluate the program, resulting in community "ownership" of the program. The behavior modification approach accomplished a reduced *Aedes* mosquito index for the communities, and benefits included improved physical well-being of the community and reduction of health risks in addition to more successful networking with government agencies and the larger community.

Applicability of the Question to Social Work Practice

One concern when you are deciding on a research question is whether and how the answer to the question is going to contribute to the field of social work. Usually applicability to practice is not much of an issue, particularly for generalist social workers, because most questions derive directly from our practice in an agency. If your question has evolved from your personal experiences, however, you must ask whether answering the question is going to assist the clients you serve. To determine the appropriateness of the question, discuss it with colleagues.

This issue presents another reason for adopting more participatory action research—it is rooted directly in clients' concerns, and they can become active contributors to the research process.

Another strategy to ensure that the research is applicable to social work practice is to use a developmental or intervention approach to research. This approach, which was discussed earlier in the chapter, uses research to help design and develop interventions. A number of different ways of conducting developmental research have emerged, but the basic principle is that effective interventions must be built systematically using the stages of design, continued testing, feedback, and modification. The focus is on using research to test and improve interventions—hence the alternative label *intervention research.*

Availability of Funding

In agencies, research projects may be conducted because funding is available for these projects. Certain issues may be a priority at the local, state, or federal level, and funds consequently become available. You should be aware of the reason you are conducting research on these particular issues—namely, at least in part, the availability of funds. Presumably, it has already been established that this topic is a deserving one, but you need to realize that other issues are probably equally deserving and should not be ignored because of the convenience of funding. In other words, you should continue to act as advocates for all important issues, regardless of the extent to which they are receiving fiscal support.

In addition, you may sometimes want to confirm for yourself whether a research program deserves an investment of time and money. Again, the best source for this type of information is the literature and colleagues.

HUMAN DIVERSITY ISSUES IN DECIDING ON THE QUESTION

Characteristics of the Researchers

During the stage of deciding on the question, you need to pay attention to human diversity issues. You should be aware that researchers' characteristics can influence their research and that agencies may also promote biases. Researcher characteristics can be key factors in conducting culturally responsive research. In the past most social work research was conducted by a fairly homogeneous group, resulting in an inherent bias in the types of questions being asked and in the research methods used (Davis, 1986). Now there is greater diversity among those undertaking research and a corresponding diversity of topics and methods. However, it is important to note that the problem of "researcher identity bias" exists. The discussion of the characteristics of those undertaking the research tends to focus on either ethnic/racial diversity or gender diversity, relatively ignoring another important source of researcher bias: socioeconomic status. Hodge (2003) points out this potential discrepancy between client and social worker, but a similar social class and subsequent value disparity can also exist between researcher and subject. Although socioeconomic status is interrelated to other aspects of diversity, particularly race/ethnicity, almost certainly the researcher will be well educated and middle class, introducing a whole set of socioeconomic values that will drive the research from the initial research question through to the interpretation of the findings.

One strategy for addressing this diversity issue is for the researcher to undertake a participatory approach, discussed in Chapter 1. If the research participants are directly involved in planning, designing, implementing, and disseminating the results of the research, the identity of the researchers and their associated biases become less influential in the research itself. Instead, it is the "subjects" who drive the direction of the research, a research philosophy that is directly compatible with the empowering approach of social work in general.

A final point concerning who conducts the research relates to the potential problem of people studying themselves—an issue when members of an organization or agency evaluate their own performance. Although the input and participation of organization members are essential, these evaluations do need to be counterbalanced by outsiders' evaluations.

Bias in the Agencies

Most of our research questions derive from practice in agencies. We need to be aware that bias can also exist in agencies and that this bias can influence decisions about research questions.

Including Participants in the Research Design

Stevens (1998) used a participatory research approach to examine consultation in South African schools, with the intention of making consultations more relevant. Social workers were involved from the outset in planning the research, identifying what needed to be studied, and planning a workshop on consultation. They were also involved in the resulting evaluation. Focus groups were used in which the social workers were able to start thinking critically about what they were doing.

For example, an agency's homophobic attitudes may result in ignoring the needs of lesbian clients, even though that group may require substantial social support. Your supervisor may dismiss your request to carry out a needs assessment of this particular group. Watch for these biases; be aware that your agency's operation may be influenced by presuppositions and prejudices.

SUMMARY

This chapter described two main research strategies, descriptive and explanatory, and a third strategy, exploratory, and noted that research can be divided into two kinds: applied research and pure research. Generalist social workers usually engage in three types of applied research: practice evaluations, program evaluations, and needs assessments.

Usually agencies decide research questions, but it is important to ensure maximum input from those affected by the research and by the resulting services. Focus groups are useful in ensuring this input, and participatory action research is recommended. Ethical issues in deciding on the research question include assessing the question's applicability to social work practice and the availability of funding. Human diversity issues include the researcher's characteristics and the agency's biases.

STUDY/EXERCISE QUESTIONS

1. Look through a social work journal such as *Social Work Research and Abstracts* or *Affilia* and identify studies that adopt the research strategies described in this chapter (descriptive or explanatory) and the type of question that was decided on (practice evaluations, program evaluations, or needs assessments). Discuss in class the reasons for your decisions.

2. If you are enrolled in a practicum or field placement, ask your supervisor about any program evaluations or needs assessments carried out by the agency. Find out why the evaluation or needs assessment was carried out.

Who suggested it? Who was involved in the decisions? Present the results of this discussion in class.

INFOTRAC COLLEGE EDITION

1. Search for *exploratory* research studies and identify the purpose of these studies, explaining why they are exploratory (rather than descriptive or explanatory).
2. Find a *program evaluation* and identify it as summative or formative.

REFERENCES

Alaggia, R. (2002). Balancing acts: Reconceptualizing support in maternal response to intra-familial child sexual abuse. *Clinical Social Work Journal, 30* (1), 41–56.

Carise, D., Cornely, W., & Gurel, O. (2002). A successful researcher-practitioner collaboration in substance abuse treatment. *Journal of Substance Abuse Treatment, 23,* 157–162.

Crabtree, S. A., Wong, C. M., & Mas'ud, F. (2001). Community participatory approaches to dengue prevention in Sarawak, Malaysia. *Human Organization, 60* (3), 281–290.

Davis, L. (1986). A feminist approach to social work research. *Affilia, 1,* 32–47.

Dore, M. M., Nelson-Zlupko, L., & Kaufmann, E. (1999). "Friends in need." Designing and implementing a psychoeducational group for school children from drug-involved families. *Social Work, 44* (2), 179–190.

Fischer, J. (1976). *The effectiveness of social casework.* Springfield, IL: Charles C. Thomas.

Fredriksen, K. I. (1999). Family caregiving responsibilities among lesbians and gay men. *Social Work, 44* (2), 142–155.

Hodge, D. R. (2003). Value differences between social workers and members of the working and middle classes. *Social Work, 48* (1), 107–120.

Hyde, C. A., & Ruth, B. J. (2002). Multicultural content and class participation: Do students self-censor? *Journal of Social Work Education, 38* (2), 241–257.

Kruzich, J. M., Friesen, B. J., Williams-Murphy, T., & Longley, M. J. (2002). Voices of African American families: Perspectives on residential treatment. *Social Work, 47* (4), 461–471.

Moon, A., & Benton, D. (2000). Tolerance of elder abuse and attitudes toward third party intervention among African-American, Korean American and White elderly. *Journal of Multicultural Social Work, 8* (3/4), 283–303.

Onyskiw, J. E., Harrison, M. J., Spady, D., & McConnan, L. (1999). Formative evaluation of a collaborative community-based child abuse prevention project. *Child Abuse & Neglect, 23* (11), 1069–1081.

Pandya, V., & Gingerich, W. J. (2002). Group therapy intervention for male bat-terers: A microethnographic study. *Health and Social Work, 27* (1), 47–56.

Pine, B. A., Warsh, R., & Maluccio, A. N. (1998). Participatory management in a child welfare agency. A key to effective change. *Administration in Social Work, 22* (1), 19–31.

Rittner, B., & Dozier, D. C. (2000). Effects of court-ordered substance abuse treatment in child protective services cases. *Social Work, 45* (2), 131–140.

Rothman, J., & Thomas, E. (1994). *Intervention research.* New York: Haworth Press.

Stevens, L. A. (1998). Consultation as a social work method. In M. Gray (Ed.), *Developmental social work in South Africa: Theory and practice.* Cape Town: David Philip Publishers.

Whipple, E. E. (1999). Reaching families with preschoolers at risk of physical child abuse: What works? *Families in Society,* March/April, 148–159.

Writing the Literature Review and Identifying the Variables

■

Suppose your supervisor asked you to carry out a needs assessment to establish a health promotion program for a local business. You have some implicit assumptions about what the program will include—namely, seminars and information dispersal on wellness. After consulting with the staff of the business, however, you find that they are defining a health promotion program more broadly. Their idea of a health promotion program includes other services, such as revising the business's health insurance coverage and providing discounts to local health clubs, counseling information and referral, and so forth.

This chapter will describe the research stage of writing the literature review and identifying the variables, which is equivalent to the practice stage of defining directions. This stage involves consulting the literature and clarifying the research question once it has been initially formulated. This clarification can help us make explicit some initial assumptions inherent in research, in much the same way as is necessary in practice.

Here developing the question will be examined more closely. The following will be discussed:

- the literature review
- units of analysis
- levels of measurement
- naming the variables and values
- the relationship of variables
- defining and operationalizing the variable
- the agency and writing the literature review and identifying the variables
- ethical issues in writing the literature review and identifying the variables
- human diversity issues in writing the literature review and identifying the variables

As discussed in the last chapter on deciding on the question, the research question often has been decided prior to your involvement. For example, the agency may have been asked by one of their funding sources to carry out an evaluation of services, and you are asked to help with planning and implementing the study. Similarly, many of the stages discussed in this chapter may already have been completed by the time you are involved. It is still important for you as a participant in the project to understand the rationale behind these stages and, if you have the opportunity, to develop them yourself.

Note that often the central assignment in a beginning social work research methods course is to write a research proposal. This text takes you through that process step by step. At this point you may want to refer to Chapter 13 where there is a full discussion of research writing, from the research proposal through to the final report.

THE LITERATURE REVIEW

When conducting applied research—whether a program evaluation, a needs assessment, or single system study—we need to consult other sources of information. Sometimes information can come from colleagues who have had experience with the questions we are trying to answer. Our usual source of other information, however, is published material, and surveying these sources is referred to as the literature review.

Undertaking a **literature review** means consulting the written material relevant to a research problem. This written material can be found in a variety of places including libraries, public and private; city, state, and federal buildings; social agencies; private collections; and political, professional, social, and interest group organizations such as the NASW.

In this section we will discuss the specific uses of the literature review, accessing the information, and writing the literature review report.

Using the Literature Review

The literature review assists with developing the question in the following ways:

- connecting the research question to theory
- identifying previous research
- giving direction to the research project

Consulting the literature is useful in conducting research and in guiding practice, particularly if the literature is based on research.

Connecting the Research Question to Theory

As discussed in Chapter 1, science consists of both theories and research methods. Consequently, in any research, the connection to theory has to be made clear. In pure research, connecting a question to theory is a fairly obvious step. For example, if you are investigating the causes of spousal abuse, you need to be apprised of the human behavior theories that attempt to explain spousal abuse. This theoretical base can be found in the existing literature.

In applied research, however, this connection between the research question and the theory is not so obvious and can be easily bypassed. This connection will be clarified by giving illustrations on the use of the literature review for linking different types of social work research questions to theory.

Practice Evaluations   When evaluating your own practice, you need to understand the theoretical base underlying your use of a particular intervention. For example, if you are using positive reinforcement to help a parent learn disciplining skills, you need to be familiar with the theory behind positive reinforcement—namely, behavior theory. The literature on behavior theory can then be consulted.

Connecting the Research Question to Theory: Program Evaluation

Washington (2002) evaluated the comprehensive services offered at Estival Place, a transitional housing program, through the eyes of former residents. The author stated that programs serving homeless populations use the systems approach with a focus on the person in situation. Data for the research were gathered through face-to-face, in-depth interviews using an instrument that began and ended with general questions about the participant's family size, current employment status, current living conditions, and how each service offered at Estival Place was used to achieve self-sufficiency. Findings demonstrate that Estival Place can serve as a model of service to homeless families, as the program provides life skills classes, job development, counseling, and resources and referrals to promote and maintain self-sufficiency.

In addition, you need to understand the theoretical link between the use of positive reinforcement in disciplining children and its appropriateness and effectiveness for this purpose, again turning to the literature for this information.

Program Evaluations   You recall that program evaluation can take several forms: summative, formative, or cost-benefit analyses. For each form, we need to consider how the research question links to theory. For example, you may be examining whether the agency in which you are employed is meeting one of its goals in providing support services to homebound elderly. You consult the literature to ascertain the theoretical basis for this type of care and examine studies of this type that have already been carried out. You may also find some of this material in the initial program proposal.

Needs Assessments   When assessing the need for a program, the literature can also be consulted to provide some theoretical substance. For example, in conducting a needs assessment to determine the number of homeless women and children in your community, a theoretical perspective and context can be gained by consulting the literature and determining the risk factors and problems experienced by homeless women and children.

Identifying Previous Research

When you choose or are assigned a research question, it is useful to find out whether a similar or identical question has already been answered. If it has, you may wish to reconceptualize the research question. For example, in conducting your needs assessment, you may find a report on a survey conducted in your community two years ago. This information will probably be useful because the survey was done recently. If the survey had been conducted ten years ago, however, you would need to replicate or repeat the study. Similarly, in a program evaluation, you may find that other evaluations of comparable programs have already been conducted and thus your evaluation might not necessarily contribute new and useful knowledge. Alternatively, you may find that the evaluations were conducted in communities different from the one your agency serves, which would suggest that your evaluation would fulfill a useful purpose.

Note that a thesis paper requires a section with a clear discussion of the relationship between your research topic and its theoretical framework.

Giving Direction to the Research Project

Although the concern here is primarily with the role of the literature review in developing the research question, you should also note that the literature review can give overall direction and guidance to the entire research project. You can, for example, review the literature to find out how researchers set up comparison groups in similar projects or to get ideas about how samples can be selected. Using the literature review in this way, particularly in the early step of developing the question, can save considerable time later on and prevents "reinventing the wheel."

Accessing Information

As we discussed previously, several literature sources are available to the social worker. Libraries have always housed the most wide-ranging and extensive collection of these materials. Government agencies along with public and private organizations often maintain specialized collections of materials, and they are increasingly making their own publications available on the World Wide Web. The Web allows the researcher access to a seemingly endless supply of information.

Libraries

Academic libraries have traditionally provided research literature and the tools (indexes, abstracts, databases) for accessing the literature. Although the Web has begun to transform the process of identifying and acquiring information, libraries still play an important role for researchers. To begin with, contrary to popular belief, all information on the Web is not free. Web-based indexes, reference materials, and journals to which the library once subscribed in print (or, in some cases, in CD-ROM format) are still paid subscriptions, made available through license agreements to authorized library users, through the library's Web site. The enormity of the Web gives the illusion that all information is available online (somewhere). However, a print source is often still the only way to satisfy an information need. In addition, libraries can provide effective navigation through the Web wilderness.

Library Catalogs   Computerized library catalogs, which show what is available in a particular library, can usually be searched on the Web. They also provide direct links to the full text of information that is available to the library's users, in both online books and journals. Although different libraries have different systems, the general principles are similar. You can enter an author's name, a title, or subject words, or a combination of terms, and you can usually limit or modify a search by publication date or other criteria. The computer will retrieve a list of potential sources of information. One way to retrieve more relevant information when searching a library catalog is to limit your search to the "subject headings" category. First, do a more general "keyword" search. If you find a good source among your results, use the subject headings, which have been assigned to that source to conduct another search. Through the library catalog you can find journals, books, dictionaries, encyclopedias, and bibliographies that will lead to more information.

Government Documents   Government documents are a great resource for social work researchers; these documents include census data, congressional proceedings, agency information, and statistics. Although some library catalogs include listings for the government documents that are held in that library, other libraries provide a separate online system for finding them. Certain libraries are depositories for all published U.S. government information, but an increasing amount of government information is being disseminated only on the Web. Gateway sites for Web-based government information are listed in Appendix A.

Indexes and Databases   Indexes and abstracts, whether available on the Web or in the library in print or CD-ROM format, will help you identify specific articles, dissertations, chapters in books, or books and documents that will not necessarily be held in your library. You will usually need to use such an index to locate literature in your area of research. The list of references will lead you to further relevant resources.

Some of these indexes or databases are quite specific, defined by a subject area or type of material to which they provide access. Some databases provide "citations" or information about the resources that you will then need to locate them in the library or obtain them through interlibrary loan. Some databases will provide access to the full text of the actual articles or documents, and others include some citations, perhaps abstracts and some full text, or links to full text. Searching an electronic database involves using keywords or subject terms and limiting the search by other various parameters. Relevant indexes and abstracting databases are listed in Appendix A.

Access to Web-based Library Resources   When a library subscribes to electronic books or journals, a license agreement usually limits the access to authorized members of the community served by the library, such as university faculty, staff, and students. Just as it is necessary to have a library card to check out a book, often that same library card will enable you to have remote access to Web resources that are provided by the university or public library. Computers within the domain served by the library (such as those in the library building or on a university network) will usually have barrier-free access and, in most cases, anyone walking into a library can have free access to the library's Web-based subscriptions using computers provided by the library.

Interlibrary Loan   Indexes and databases often provide information about resources that are not available on the Web or in your local library. To access those books or articles, it is necessary to use your library's interlibrary loan or document delivery service. Libraries can borrow books or obtain photocopies of articles from other libraries or from a commercial supplier. Some libraries will subsidize all or part of the cost of this service, whereas others will pass along all or part of the cost to the borrower. Interlibrary loan can take days or, in some cases, even weeks. Start your search early so that you will have time to receive articles and books that are not available locally.

Library Staff   When trying to access information, do not forget to consult with the library staff. They are professionally trained in every aspect of information management and can be a tremendous resource. They will save you time in the library and on the Web, and with their help you should find better resources.

The World Wide Web

More and more of the types of information social work researchers need is being made available only on the Web, which also provides unprecedented access to international information. However, it can be time-consuming to wade through this vast amount of information, most of which is of little use to the researcher. Search engines lack precision, and many hierarchical sites are designed with commercial interests in mind. It is sometimes difficult to evaluate the currency, authority, or accuracy of the information you retrieve. Your Web-searching efficiency and success will increase with practice, and the tools for information retrieval improve and become more precise. For example, the Google search engine (http://www.google.com) ranks results based on how many other Web sites are linked to the sites listed in your search results.

When you find a site that suits your needs, bookmark it for later use. It is often impossible to recreate a search or remember a circuitous path that led to good results. However, keep in mind that Web sites get reorganized, and URLs (Web addresses) change. Make use of gateway sites that provide organized and well-maintained access to Web sites of interest to a specialized audience. Social work gateways have been developed and maintained by schools and departments of social work, libraries that support them, and organizations of social workers. Some of these sites are listed in Appendix A. Also refer to Vernon and Lynch (2000) for guidance in using the Web in research and in other aspects of social work practice.

A literature review places the current research in its historical and theoretical context. It describes the background to the study and the relationship between the present study and previous studies conducted in the same area. It also identifies trends and debates in the existing literature.

The following are a few issues to consider when constructing a literature review (van Rooyen, 1996).

- Cite only research that you find specifically pertinent to the current study; be selective. Avoid reviewing or referring to sections of articles or texts that are not related to your study.

- Discuss and evaluate the literature you have selected.

- Show the logical continuity between existing literature and your study.

- Identify controversial issues or differences in the literature and your study.

- If there is a choice, cite the more recent literature, unless the older citations are needed for additional perspective.

- Write the literature review in the past tense.

- Refer to published studies for examples of literature reviews.

Figure 4.1   **Checklist for writing the literature review**

Summary

1. State the topic, limit the range, and list all the relevant synonyms and keywords. Use background sources in Appendix A for help with terminology and scope.

2. Using the computer catalog in your library, use the keywords to access potential sources of information.

3. When you access a relevant item, look at its subject headings and use these words in the subject headings category to find similar items.

4. If relevant, locate other materials in government documents.

5. Use your keywords to search the online databases available through your library.

6. Use a print index if you have not found enough results in databases.

7. From your results, try to develop a literature review on your research topic. Consult the list of references for further resources.

8. Use gateway sites on the Web to track down other materials. Verify the source of Web-based information and evaluate it for accuracy, currency, and integrity.

9. If material that you have identified is not available locally or on the Web, use interlibrary loan through your local library.

10. Ask a reference librarian for other ideas and help, if you need it, for each of these steps.

Writing the Literature Review

Although writing up your research, including the literature review, is discussed in Chapter 13, some guidelines for writing the literature review will be given here. The literature review is usually the first section of the research to be completed and written. It should be completed before other stages of the research are undertaken. The literature review places the current research in its historical and theoretical context. It describes the background to the study and the relationship between the present study and previous studies on the same topic. The literature review should also identify trends and debates in the existing literature. It provides a link between past, present, and future, in addition to providing a context for the discussion of the results from the study. See Figure 4.1 for a checklist for writing the literature review (van Rooyen, 1996).

UNITS OF ANALYSIS

After conducting the literature review, which as we discussed earlier connects the research to theory, identifies previous research, and gives direction to the research project, it is important to further develop the question by "breaking it down" into smaller components. This is all part of engaging in the *systematic* steps of the research process discussed in Chapter 1. Such a breaking down process helps us to focus the question and ensures that the area of research is not too broad and that there is a shared understanding about what is being investigated. Ultimately this produces more useful research and it allows the *replication* of the research (also discussed in Chapter 1).

One of the first steps is to determine the **unit of analysis**. The unit of analysis refers to what or who is being studied. Three types of units of analysis are used in social work research: individuals, groups, and social artifacts.

Individuals   These are the most common units of analysis. Descriptions of individuals are often aggregated to explain social group functioning. For example, in conducting a needs assessment for a community youth center, you may interview individual youths to assess their needs. This information would then be aggregated to document the needs of the group.

Groups   Groups can also be the unit of analysis. Groups are of different types and include families, organizations, and communities. Families are often the unit of analysis in social work. For example, in an evaluation investigating the impact of a program on family cohesion, although individuals will be studied, the family group would make up the unit of analysis.

Social Artifacts   These are behaviors or products resulting from human activity. In social work, social artifacts may include books, divorces, birth practices, or ethical violations. For example, you are asked by your state NASW chapter to investigate unethical social work practice behavior. In the study, you look at the characteristics of those charged with such behavior: whether they are B.S.W.s or M.S.W.s, the field of practice in which they are employed, and so on. Here the unit of analysis is unethical social work practice.

LEVELS OF MEASUREMENT

Another step in developing the research question, and one that is also concerned with ensuring that the research is focused and is carried out systematically, is considering the **level of measurement**. The level of measurement is the extent to which a variable can be quantified and subsequently subjected to certain mathematical or statistical procedures and is an important step in positivist/quantitative studies. Quantification involves assigning a number to a variable; it depends, as you might guess, on how the variable is being operationalized. To measure depression, for example, we could count the number of hours the client sleeps each night, use an already developed measure such as the Generalized Contentment Scale, or have the client simply note each day whether she was depressed. Each measure involves assigning numbers in different ways, and consequently they result in different levels of measurement. Four different levels of measurement can be identified: nominal, ordinal, interval, and ratio (see Table 4.1).

   Nominal measures classify observations into mutually exclusive categories, with no ordering to the categories. Phenomena are assigned to categories based on some similarity or difference (for example, ethnicity, gender, marital status). Numbers are assigned to nominal categories, but the numbers themselves have no inherent meaning. For example, 1 is assigned to Hispanic and 2 to African American, but the numbers could be reversed and no meaning would be lost. The use of numbers with nominal data is arbitrary. In the example of depression, the client recording the absence (no) or presence (yes) of depression each day would result in a nominal level of measurement, as would other yes/no responses to questions.

   Ordinal measures classify observations into mutually exclusive categories that have an inherent order to them. An ordinal level of measurement can often be used when we are examining attitudes. Respondents to a survey might be asked whether they agree with a particular statement, with the alternatives as follows: strongly agree, agree, disagree, disagree strongly. These responses are ordered in sequence from strongly agree to strongly disagree (or vice versa) and numbered 1 to 4. Nevertheless, although these values are placed in sequence and

Table 4.1   **Levels of measurement**

Level of measurement	Definition	Example
Nominal	Data are assigned to categories based on similarity or difference.	Ethnicity, marital status, yes/no response
Ordinal	Data are sequenced in some order.	Many attitude and opinion questions
Interval	Data are sequenced in some order, and the distances between the different points are equal.	IQ, GRE scores
Ratio	Data are sequenced in some order, the distances between the different points are equal, and each value reflects an absolute magnitude. The zero point reflects an absence of the value.	Years of age, number of children, miles to place of employment

are meaningful in that sense, the distance between each of the values is not necessarily equal and may be somewhat arbitrary.

Interval measures classify observations into mutually exclusive categories with an inherent order and equal spacing between the categories. This equal distance differentiates the interval level from the ordinal level of measurement. A good example of an interval scale is the IQ test: The difference between an IQ of 120 and 130 is the same as between 110 and 120. Nevertheless, the interval level of measurement does not allow one to make any statements about the magnitude of one value in relation to another. It is not possible to claim that someone with an IQ of 160 has twice the IQ of someone with an IQ of 80.

Ratio measures possess all the characteristics of the interval level of measurement and reflect the absolute magnitude of the value. Put another way, at the zero point, the value is absent, or did not occur. Measurements of income, years of education, the number of times a behavior occurs—all are examples of ratio levels of measurement. In the depression example, counting the number of hours of sleep each night would result in a ratio level of measurement. Note that most variables can be defined to allow different levels of measurement.

Our example of depression is one case; anger is another. For example, a variable like anger can be measured at various levels. If the question "Do you think your child is angry?" is posed, and possible responses are yes and no, this constitutes a nominal level of measurement. But say the question is "To what extent do you think your child is angry?" and the respondent is offered the following scale: very aggressive, aggressive, not aggressive. This would be an ordinal level of measurement. If anger is measured as one component in a personality test such as the Minnesota Multiphasic Personality Inventory (MMPI), the resulting level of measurement would be interval. Finally, if anger is defined in behavioral components, for example, the number of times the child hit another in an hour, it would be possible to use a ratio level of measurement.

These levels of measurement have important implications for the statistical analysis of research results. These implications will be examined in Chapter 12.

NAMING THE VARIABLES AND VALUES

After specifying the unit of analysis and the level of measurement, the next research step is to identify the factors that are of central interest in the research. These factors are known as the **variables**.

A variable is a characteristic of a phenomenon, and it is something that varies. Some common examples of variables often seen in social work research are income, ethnicity, and stress level. These characteristics vary or have different quantities, and these different quantities of variables are referred to as *values*. Note that our use of *value* in this context is not the usual meaning we assign to that term in social work practice, such as the social work value of self-determination. You can also think about values as being the potential answers to questions, on a questionnaire for example.

Using the examples just given, possible values of income might include the following:

under $15,000/year

$15,000–$19,999/year

$20,000–$24,999/year

$25,000–$29,999/year

$30,000 and over/year

Ethnicity attributes might include the following:

white (non-Hispanic)

Hispanic

African American

Native American

Other

Stress level values might include the following:

high

medium

low

Both the variables and the values that are used in research studies differ from study to study. In conducting a survey to assess the need for a day care center for developmentally delayed preschoolers, one variable might be income, so that you could assess the extent to which parents could pay for such a service. If you were carrying out the needs assessment in rural Kentucky, you might anticipate that incomes would be low. Consequently, the values included on the survey instrument would also be low; the levels presented in the above example might be too high. However, if the needs assessment were being performed in Santa Barbara, California, this categorization might be too low, and we would need to add much higher income levels.

In the same survey, ethnicity might also be considered a factor that would influence service need and consequently should be included in the study. As a variable, ethnicity is restricted in terms of the values that may be included, but there are still some choices. For example, if the study was carried out in New Mexico, the values for ethnicity listed earlier would need to be included. Alternatively, if the study was conducted in South Africa, completely different values would be used. Again, the values included depend on the purpose and context of the study.

One of the problems with naming values in this way is that information is lost in the process. For example, clustering all individuals in a category such as "Native American" leads to the loss of potentially critical information: the differences between different tribes, places of residence (on or off the reservation, rural or urban areas), and so on. This problem points to the importance of using the interpretist approach when appropriate, particularly when you are unsure about the nature of the values to be included in the study.

In interpretive studies the variables and values are not necessarily named prior to the research, but instead emerge from the study. For example, in the study identifying factors that contributed to the maternal response to children sexually abused by the mother's intimate partner, the researcher did not know what they were prior to undertaking the research. Instead, the variables—level of maternal support, maternal history of abuse, nature of the relationship with the partner, and ethnic affiliation—appeared to be important in understanding this phenomenon. Even in interpretive studies, however, you need to have some idea of what variables are to be studied, even if other variables and their values are to be added later. In this example, the major variable studied was pregnancy.

One note of caution is in order about deciding variables to include in a study: Beware of what is called **reductionism**, or the extreme limitation of the kinds and numbers of variables that might explain or account for broad types of behavior. Reductionism is particularly problematic when using the quantitative approach, in which all the variables are named prior to the study and little allowance is made for the discovery of additional variables. For example, in a study on spousal abuse you may try many perspectives to explain this phenomenon. You might focus on economic factors, biological factors, family dynamics factors, or psychological factors, to name a few. According to the literature, all appear to play some role in spousal abuse. Incidentally, the literature review is helpful in the selection of these variables. Time and money constraints, however, often force us to consider only one group of factors. In this case, you may opt for the economic factors because the literature review disclosed these as being in need of further investigation. Choosing economic factors above the others is not, in itself, necessarily a problem; however, if you then suggest that these are the *only* factors in explaining spousal abuse, you would be guilty of reductionism. When you select the variables for a study, these variables may represent only one perspective on the explanation; in discussing your results, you need to acknowledge this. Social workers study human behavior, and human behavior is complex. You cannot expect to come up with a complete explanation; you need to be aware of this limitation from the early stages of the research process.

THE RELATIONSHIP OF VARIABLES

The next step in identifying the variables is to focus on the relationships between the variables and to think about what functions and roles the variables have in the research. The major distinction is between the roles of the independent and dependent variables. Independent and dependent variables are of primary concern in an explanatory study where specific variables are identified as contributing to specific outcomes—in other words, the study attempts to establish causality. In descriptive studies, such as a needs assessment, independent and dependent variables are often not identified as such.

The **independent variable** is the variable that can affect other factors in the research. If you were studying the impact of social isolation on child sexual abuse, the independent variable would be social isolation. In a program evaluation, the independent variable is the program itself.

You can think of the **dependent variable** as the outcome variable that has presumably been affected by the independent variable. In a summative program evaluation where you are interested in whether a program's goals are being met, the dependent variable would be those goals. In the example of the study attempting to identify the factors leading to child sexual abuse in a community, child sexual abuse would be the dependent variable. For each study, there may be a number of independent and dependent variables. In the study of child sexual abuse, income level (in addition to social isolation) may be another independent variable, and different types of child sexual abuse might be identified as different dependent variables.

As with the identification of variables and values, the literature review is extremely important in identifying the dependent and independent variables. In the study of child sexual abuse, any related theories need to be found in the literature and additional variables identified.

As in the case of different values, variables are not fixed as dependent or independent; the nomenclature depends on the study's purpose and context. Although child abuse is identified as a dependent variable in the example just given, in a study examining the factors that determine teenage pregnancy, child sexual abuse might well be identified as an independent variable.

Independent and Dependent Variables

Elze (2002) recruited 169 self-identified lesbian, gay, and bisexual (LGB) youths, ages 13 to 18, in northern New England to investigate the risk factors associated with internalizing and externalizing problems. Dependent variables for the study included emotional and behavioral problems which were assessed with the Youth Self-Report (YSR) to self-report feelings, behaviors, problems, and emotional difficulties. The identified independent variables included risk factors unrelated to sexual orientation such as demographics, family mental health problems, stressful life events, and family functioning. Additional independent variables included risk factors related to sexual orientation such as ages of awareness and self labeling, discomfort with sexual orientation, stressful events related to sexual orientation, family attitudes about sexual orientation, victimization, perceived stigmatization, and perceived negative community environment. Elze utilized a number of standardized tests to assess the independent and dependent variables. The youths did not differ on internalizing and externalizing problems in terms of gender or sexual orientation. Findings suggest that adolescent service providers should assess LGB youths for concerns related as well as not directly related to sexual orientation or identity.

DEFINING AND OPERATIONALIZING THE VARIABLES

Variables need to be defined in a clear and unambiguous manner, in much the same way we need to define concepts in practice.

A central tenet of the quantitative approach is that variables must be clearly defined so they can be measured. Definition is less of a priority when using the qualitative approach, in which the definitions of concepts or variables emerge as the topic of inquiry is explored. Nevertheless, the focus of a qualitative study still must be clearly defined. In a study exploring people's beliefs about mental illness, the researcher would have to be clear about defining *mental illness,* even if the study itself ultimately explores and expands this definition.

Many variables used in social work practice tend to be vague; they may seem open to a number of different interpretations depending on who is using them. In my first field practicum in a psychiatric hospital in Chicago, I was confused by such terms as *ego strength, depression,* and *independent living skills.* The definitions of these terms either were not provided or varied depending on who was doing the defining. In social work practice, we have to be careful that we clearly define our terms; otherwise confusion can result. A worker and client may think they both know what they mean by *independent living*: The client may have in mind "living in my own apartment with no supervision," whereas the worker may mean "living in her own apartment with close supervision." In this example, no matter which definition is accepted, the term *supervision* will also need to be defined—perhaps as "the client's reporting to the social worker twice a week."

Defining Variables in a Qualitative Study

Patterson and Marsiglia's (2000) study strived to gain a beginning understanding of the phenomenon of natural helping among Mexican Americans to facilitate comparisons with other groups, recognizing that the Mexican-American community is heterogeneous in the southwest. This was an exploratory study with six males and six females in the sample, and the researchers used interviews to collect qualitative data. The findings indicated that friends, relatives, and neighbors were helpers, the boundaries of extended family were open and included friends, and that helping involved both teaching and learning. Some gender differences were also identified; women were motivated to help from a sense of caring and men from a sense of moral obligation.

One danger of defining variables is that a definition appropriate in one culture may be inappropriate in another. So you have to be particularly careful about using definitions cross-culturally. Be especially careful with definitions when studying people in an unfamiliar culture (with *culture* not limited to describing nationality or ethnicity but also including groups of diverse types, such as single fathers or children of alcoholics). A more qualitative approach might even be advisable so that definitions can emerge from the research.

As you did when *naming* the variables earlier, use the literature when *defining* variables. Consult both the previous research and the theoretical writings on the topic for approaches to definitions. This can save considerable time. It also is sound research practice and facilitates any future replication of the research.

Operationalizations

When using a quantitative approach, the next step after defining the variables is to **operationalize** them—this means specifying how the variables are to be measured. This process is central to the positivist or quantitative approach, where measuring and quantifying the study's variables are important. An interpretist or qualitative approach is not concerned with this step because the purpose of the study is to understand different dimensions of the variable.

Operationalizing becomes easier once variables have been formally defined. Even after definitions have been accepted, however, some ambiguities remain. For example, measuring the extent to which a client's independent living has been achieved would involve clarifying the issue of supervision. Would the client report by means of a telephone call or a face-to-face visit? How long would the client need to live independently to be considered successful? What kind of financial status would qualify as independent living? These are only a few of the questions that need to be answered before a satisfactory operational definition of the variable is achieved.

Operationalization

Cabassa (2003) examines prominent theoretical models and assumptions that direct acculturation measures. The strengths and limitations of the Bidimensional Acculturation Scale for Hispanics (BAS) and the Acculturation Rating Scale for Mexican Americans—Revised (ARSMA-II) are studied. Cabassa suggests that improvement of the operationalization of acculturation indicators is a key to enhancing the measures of acculturation. Further, Cabassa advocates for a move toward more basic measures of cultural change and the need to move beyond language-based indicators to basic attitudes, beliefs, and behaviors.

Measuring a variable could entail simply recording the presence or absence of a phenomenon. If reporting is defined as a telephone contact, either the contact was made or it was not. Or measurement might involve more elaboration, such as specifying the nature of the telephone contact. For example, if a prior arrangement was made regarding the time of the call and who was to initiate it, were these conditions fulfilled?

Operationalizing variables can be a challenge. Measuring a concept such as depression may seem overwhelming to the social worker. A useful strategy in operationalizing a variable is to look in the literature and determine how others operationalized this concept. We refer to many variables in social work research over and over. Depression is a good example; many measures of depression are available in the literature. Many of these measures can be adopted by social workers for evaluating their own practices.

Nevertheless, perhaps none of these measuring instruments is appropriate for the aspect of depression you are interested in examining. *Depression* is generally a label applied to specific behaviors being exhibited; to operationalize a variable such as depression often we must consider the behaviors that led to the label's original application. These behaviors might include excessive sleeping, loss of appetite, and so forth. A person's excessive sleeping is easier to measure than the person's level of depression. Excessive sleeping could be measured by the time spent sleeping.

The processes of defining and operationalizing the variables are closely related and can become circular. After defining a variable, the social worker may find that it is still difficult to operationalize the variable, and consequently the variable needs to be redefined. In fact, this circular process characterizes the entire research process, in the same way as it characterizes social work practice.

Defining and Operationalizing Goals and Activities

One type of defining and operationalizing that demands a separate discussion is when the generalist social worker conducts a summative program evaluation to determine whether a program has met its goals. As mentioned previously, using the quantitative approach might be most appropriate for this purpose, and the program's goals and activities need to be defined and operationalized.

First, you need to specify what is meant by *goal* and *activity*. People use these terms in different ways, which confuses the matter. Occasionally, people use the terms *goal* and *objective* synonymously, or they use *goal* to refer to a long-term end product and *objective* to refer to a short-term end. *Activity,* in this context, refers to the means by which the goal is achieved.

The goals of a program called Adolescent Family Life might be to reduce the rate of high-risk babies born to adolescents and the rate of child abuse and neglect among teenage parents. The activities might include providing prenatal care and parenting classes to teenage parents.

The next step is to define and operationalize these goals and activities. The first goal, reducing the rate of high-risk babies born to adolescents, requires us to define *adolescents* and *high risk*. We might decide to define *adolescents* as those 18 years and under, and *high-risk babies* as low birth weight or premature infants. Of course, we would then need to operationalize these last two terms—*low birth weight* perhaps as under 5.5 pounds at birth and *premature* as born after a pregnancy lasting 32 weeks or less. We would continue defining and operationalizing the other goals and the activities in a similar manner.

THE AGENCY AND WRITING THE LITERATURE REVIEW AND IDENTIFYING THE VARIABLES

Much of the development of the research question occurs before the social worker becomes involved. Variables may have already been named, defined, and operationalized by those who initially conceived of the research question: supervisors, agency administrators, funding organization, or individuals or groups in the community.

Don't be discouraged about not having had a role in this step of the research. Work with what you have, and remember that you are at the beginning of the research. Often you can enhance the future development of the project through your research knowledge and your skills as an agency-based generalist practitioner. Don't forget that research is a team endeavor.

ETHICAL ISSUES IN WRITING THE LITERATURE REVIEW AND IDENTIFYING THE VARIABLES

Giving Credit to Contributors

When drawing on information generated by others (for example, using a literature review or consulting with colleagues), you need to give credit to these sources of information when you write the research report. How to do this is discussed in Chapter 13. If you refer to someone else's ideas and do not give him or her credit, particularly if they are written ideas, you may be guilty of plagiarism.

Including Relevant Variables

The major ethical issue at this stage of the research process is determining what variables and values to include in the research question. You need to be certain you included all the important variables. In a needs assessment, it might be tempting to leave out some factors that you think may not support the need you are trying to document. In surveying a community to assess the need for an elder day care center, you might want to leave out variables such as transportation needs because, if such needs are great, the eventual funding of the project might be jeopardized. All variables perceived as important to the study should be included, however. Completeness is particularly critical when conducting positivist research, in which the variables are clearly defined before the research is undertaken. Including relevant variables is less of a problem with the interpretist approach, when the variables are often identified as part of the study.

Avoiding Reductionism

An associated issue to relevant variables that we discussed previously is reductionism. You need to avoid looking at only one type of variable (for instance, economic factors) and claiming, if an association is found, that this variable alone is responsible for the particular outcome. Reductionism can be a danger when carrying out program evaluations because you are tempted to look only at the variables associated with the program, rather than considering others. For example, if you are evaluating a program that is intended to enhance self-esteem among high school dropouts, you would undoubtedly include program-related variables such as length of time in the program. You may not be considering measuring outside factors that could also influence self-esteem, however, such as involvement in a local sports activity. These other factors may turn out to have far more impact than the program itself, but you may be reluctant to include them because they jeopardize the demonstrated efficacy of the program. Again, this problem of reductionism is more apparent in positivist research. In fact, a tendency to reductionism is one of the major drawbacks of this research approach and provides one of the rationales for social work to use more interpretive studies when attempting to answer many of the questions confronting social workers.

HUMAN DIVERSITY ISSUES IN WRITING THE LITERATURE REVIEW AND IDENTIFYING THE VARIABLES

In this stage of the research, you must look carefully at human diversity issues to ensure that you are not building in biases against certain groups. The last chapter described the possible bias that exists when only certain groups undertake research in social work. Here we discuss the potential bias in the literature.

Before you use materials to help guide a particular research project, you need to be aware of bias in the literature. Literature relating to human diversity issues has been scarce, although in recent years it has grown rapidly. For example, one

Bias in the Literature

McLaughlin and Braun (1998) discussed the differences between individualist and collectivist orientations in health care decisions. Americans tend to have individualist orientations, whereas Asians and Pacific Islanders tend to have collectivist orientations, meaning that many decisions are made by families and groups rather than by the individual. This is especially true concerning health care decisions. The authors note that the collectivist orientation is not well represented in the research and literature. They recommend that universities and health care organizations provide education and training to promote cross-cultural practice and sensitivity.

social work journal is specifically devoted to human diversity issues: the *Journal of Multicultural Social Work*. Generally, though, we need to remember when consulting the literature that most social science research has been conducted by white, middle-class men; even when women have contributed, they have tended to be white, middle-class women. Overrepresentation of the views of these segments of the population, to the exclusion of others, constitutes a clear bias. Research questions developed by other groups may take a rather different course. For example, until relatively recently, few studies had been conducted on the relationship between women's work and family lives, particularly those of minority women and their families. Studies of family functioning often did not examine women's experiences but instead focused on role relationships or parenting practices.

Another human diversity issue in this stage of the research is the influence of cultural factors on each of the processes presented in this chapter. For example, how a variable is defined is influenced heavily by the culture in which the definition occurs. One of the examples discussed earlier, *independent living*, is a culturally laden term. In some cultures, independence may refer to the individual's marital status, or their employment status, or even whether the person is living alone or with his or her family of origin. The possible different definitions are as diverse as the number of cultures. See the Patterson and Marsiglia (2000) example of their attempt to describe natural helping systems among diverse Mexican-American populations in the southwest United States.

SUMMARY

A critical step in the research process is the literature review, which assists in the generation of questions, connecting the question to theory, identifying previous research, and giving direction to the project. The unit of analysis needs to be determined at this stage in the research process. Variables and values must be distinguished. The definition and operationalization of variables includes defining goals and activities. Another step in developing the question involves determining the level of measurement: nominal, ordinal, interval, or ratio.

Often the generalist social worker does not have much influer stage of the research. Ethical issues include ensuring the identification ᴏɪ ɪᴄɪᴄ vant variables and avoiding reductionism. Human diversity issues in the development of the question include identifying potential bias in the literature and understanding different cultural definitions.

STUDY/EXERCISE QUESTIONS

1. Look at research articles in *Social Work* and identify the unit of analysis used in the study. Also identify the independent and dependent variables when appropriate.

2. You are involved in an evaluation of a support group for parents of children with developmental disabilities.

   a. Identify some possible goals and activities of the group.

   b. Name at least five variables you would need to include in the evaluation.

   c. Define and operationalize these variables.

3. You have been asked to help design and implement a needs assessment for an elder day care facility in your community. Whom would you consult in the early stages of developing the assessment?

4. If you are in a field placement, talk to your supervisor; if not, talk to someone who is employed in a supervisory position in an agency in your community. Discuss with that person who they have involved in research projects at the agency and how they have involved them.

5. At your university library, meet with the social work reference librarian. Practice searching for a specific topic.

INFOTRAC COLLEGE EDITION

1. Identify three research articles that examine different aspects of domestic violence and compare the literature review sections. How are these reviews similar to and different from one another?

2. In these same articles, identify the independent and dependent variables.

REFERENCES

Cabassa, L. J. (2003). Measuring acculturation: Where we are and where we need to go. *Hispanic Journal of Behavioral Sciences, 25* (2), 127–147.

Elze, D. E. (2002). Risk factors for internalizing and externalizing problems among gay, lesbian, and bisexual adolescents. *Social Work Research, 26* (2), 89–101.

McLaughlin, L. A., & Braun, K. L. (1998). Asian and Pacific Islander cultural values. *Health and Social Work, 23* (2), 116–126.

Patterson, S. L., Marsiglia, F. F. (2000). "Mi casa es su casa": Beginning exploration of Mexican Americans' natural helping. *Families in Society, 81* (1), 22–31.

van Rooyen, C. (1996). *Taking the leap: A guide to higher degree research study in the Department of Social Work at the University of Natal.* Durban, South Africa: The University of Natal, Department of Social Work.

Vernon, R., & Lynch, D. (2000). *Social Work and the Internet.* Pacific Grove, CA: Brooks/Cole Publishing.

Washington, T. A. (2002). The homeless need more than just a pillow, they need a pillar: An evaluation of a transitional housing program. *Families in Society, 83* (2), 183–189.

Leslie Parr

Designing Needs Assessments

■

This chapter will examine needs assessments, one of the three major types of research questions undertaken in generalist social work and first described in Chapter 3. Needs assessments are concerned with discovering the characteristics and extent of a particular social situation to determine the most appropriate response.

Needs assessments are also known as **feasibility studies, front-end analyses**, or **strengths assessments**. Needs assessments were introduced in Chapter 3 as an important research strategy in social work. Social workers carry out needs assessments prior to designing a program, and for generalist social workers the needs assessment is probably the most common type of research undertaken.

Needs assessments are often thought of as a type of survey research. Surveys measure people's attitudes, behaviors, or beliefs at one point in time; data are usually collected using questionnaires. In this chapter we will see that the survey is only one type of needs assessment design. This chapter will not include all the information you need to complete a needs assessment, so you can refer to Chapter 9 where there is information on different data collection methods that you will require to conduct an effective needs assessment.

This chapter will include the following topics:

■ reasons for conducting needs assessments

■ types of designs for needs assessments

■ the agency and designing needs assessments

■ ethical issues in designing needs assessments

■ human diversity issues in designing needs assessments

REASONS FOR CONDUCTING NEEDS ASSESSMENTS

Sometimes it may seem unnecessary to conduct a needs assessment, because it seems obvious that a particular program is needed. For example, a social worker working with families of children with developmental challenges has heard parents for the last year maintaining that increased respite care would help considerably to relieve some of the stress for themselves and their families. So why not just go ahead and develop a program? The answer is that when writing program proposals you will usually be competing with many other prospective program developers, and one way of strengthening your proposal is to add a well-designed and well-implemented needs assessment. Thus, although you think you know what the needs are, this presumed knowledge is only subjective opinion and will not carry much weight with your proposed program's potential funders. In addition, and perhaps more important, it will result in a sounder and ultimately more effective program because it will be responsive to clearly identified needs.

There are a number of different types of needs assessments that can be designed. Each one has a different purpose or reason. Being clear about the reason for conducting the study is important because that can help you more accurately plan, design, and implement the needs assessment. Five different reasons can be identified (Royse and Thyer, 1996):

1. To determine whether services exist in the community
2. To determine whether there are enough clients
3. To determine who uses existing services
4. To determine what barriers prevent clients from accessing services
5. To document the existence of an ongoing social problem

Needs assessments may be conducted for only one of these reasons, or for several. Each will be described in turn using the example of respite care for the parents of mentally retarded children as an illustration.

Determining Whether Services Exist in the Community

Just because you do not know of an intervention or program does not mean that it does not exist. Obviously this is more likely to be the case if you work in a large metropolitan area than if you are employed in a rural setting.

To make this determination, use your networking skills, the Internet, or other resources to search for programs. If your community does not already have a directory of social service agencies and programs, create one. Use your research skills to put together a directory of available services on computerized databases. This can be either a community-wide resource, or one specifically addressing the needs and concerns of the client population with which you work. In our example, this step would involve documenting services that are already available for families with developmentally challenged children in your community.

Determining Whether There Are Enough Clients

One of the more common reasons for conducting a needs assessment is to find out whether enough clients have a particular problem to justify a new program. You may hear the need expressed for respite care from the majority of your clients, but your clients may not constitute enough of a need to start a new program. Perhaps your clients are not representative of clients of other agencies or other workers; in other words, your clients may be a nonrepresentative sample. The extent of the need should be systematically documented.

Determining Who Uses Existing Services

Just because an agency or community runs a certain program does not mean that those who could benefit from it use the program. Respite services may be available, but parents may think they are ineligible or may simply not have heard of the program. Certain parents may use the program, but others may not; for example, older parents may use the services more than younger parents.

A Needs Assessment Determining the Number of Clients with a Particular Problem

Given that the elderly continue to face problems of undernutrition, Quandt and Rao (1999) assessed the level of food insecurity and identified predictors among 192 residents 65 years old or older in rural Appalachia. Data were collected from the participants using a structured questionnaire in face-to-face interviews to determine the number of elderly in rural Appalachia who had the problems of undernutrition and food insecurity. Results of this research yielded important implications for policies aimed to reduce nutrition problems for elders and general problems in supplying a sufficient amount of food for the rural elderly.

A Needs Assessment Determining Who Uses Existing Services

Noting that the number of grandparent-maintained families is increasing, Burnette (1999) examined the pattern of service use and predictors of unmet needs among seventy-four Latino grandparent caregivers in New York City. A significant sociodemographic predictor of unmet need was level of education. Additionally, stressful life events had the strongest effect on unmet needs of grandparent caregivers. Burnette reported that close examination of services used and reasons for nonuse provide important information for targeted planning, programming, and policy.

Determining What Barriers Prevent Clients from Accessing Services

Sometimes clients know about services and may be referred to them by social workers but for various reasons do not use the services. Identifying these barriers can start the process of redesigning services or developing supplementary services. Often factors such as transportation and child care work as barriers. In the example of parents of children with developmental challenges, one barrier might be parents' feeling of guilt concerning their children, in which case counseling and support to the families might be necessary before the families would actually use respite care.

Documenting the Existence of an Ongoing Social Problem

Sometimes it is not clear what problems people are confronting. This is a more fundamental question than documenting how many people need a service (which assumes the nature of the problem is already known) and focuses on the

A Needs Assessment Determining the Existence of Barriers to Use of Services

Weathers et al. (2003) used a survey to assess the use of health services among migrant children. Additionally, the researchers sought to evaluate the association between the childrens' health status and their use of health services. Participants were selected from four counties in eastern North Carolina through a five-part multistage sampling procedure. Face-to-face interviews were conducted with a 40-item questionnaire, available in Spanish or English. The researchers found that migrant children of first and second generation immigrants are a vulnerable population with a number of resource barriers such as lack of insurance, mobility issues, or having an illegal caretaker. The findings demonstrate that continued efforts need to be made to improve access of care for migrant children.

A Needs Assessment Assessing the Nature of a Social Problem

Kwong-Lai Poon, Trung-Thu Ho, and Pui-Hing Wong (2001) conducted a survey to assess the needs of men who have sex with men (MSM) who visit bars and/or bath houses in Toronto, Canada. The sample groups of men were of East Asian and Southeast Asian descent. The questionnaire addressed reasons for visiting bars and bath houses, sexual practices, condom use, HIV testing, and information respondents would like to receive from safe-sex educators. The two subgroups of MSM of East Asian and Southeast Asian descent under 39 years of age and bisexual men of East Asian and Southeast Asian descent were identified as needing greater outreach. Findings suggested that HIV-testing and information about HIV and sexually transmitted infections need to be more accessible to the aforementioned populations.

characteristics of the social problem.) In the respite care example, it was not until the parents started speaking out and expressing their need for support and assistance in the care of their children that the need for respite was recognized.

TYPES OF DESIGNS FOR NEEDS ASSESSMENTS

A needs assessment is (usually conceptualized as a descriptive survey) and as discussed in Chapter 3 does not require the types of explanatory designs needed for program evaluations. Some choices in design do need to be made, however. The first step is to understand why the study is being conducted. Use the options

Assessing an Organization's Need

Hall, Amodeo, Shaffer, and Bilt (2000) conducted a study on the training needs of social workers in selected substance abuse facilities in New England. To better serve the clients and the needs of the agency, clinical supervision for the social workers was determined to be a vital priority. The researchers used a needs assessment survey instrument to administer to responding social workers. While the social workers demonstrated high levels of knowledge and skill, they reported a need for the organization to provide additional training.

outlined in the previous section as a guide. Regardless of which of these questions is being addressed (with the exception of determining whether services already exist), almost all surveys, including needs assessments, rely on a probability sample from which results can be generalized. Because the primary purpose of a needs assessment is to document the need for services as accurately as possible, selecting the sample is critical. Refer to Chapter 8 for a full discussion of this aspect of the study.

The next step in deciding what type of design to use is to pose a number of questions.

1. Whose need is being assessed?
2. Who will have input into the design of the needs assessment?
3. When will the needs assessment be carried out?
4. What type of understanding of the need is required?
5. What level of description is useful?

Each of these questions will be discussed next. (See Figure 5.1 for a chart depicting the different reasons for conducting a needs assessment and the different types of designs.)

Whose Need Is Being Assessed?

The first question, whose need the assessment is addressing, should be answered early on, because it determines who will be selected as participants in the research. Four different levels of needs can be studied: individual, organizational, community, and societal. Most needs assessments are concerned with individual needs of clients or potential clients, including basic needs such as food and shelter and needs for social services. A significant proportion of needs assessments carried out by social workers are concerned with organizational needs, the need for technical assistance or training of some type—for example, the need for an employee assistance program.

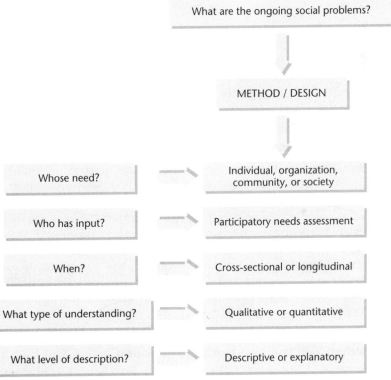

Figure 5.1   *Designing a needs assessment*

Participatory Action Needs Assessment

Reese, Ahern, Nair, O'Faire, and Warren (1999) conducted a participatory action research project to address the issue of African-American access to and use of hospice. The research involved an ongoing collaboration with respondents and practitioners, and included several meetings with the ministerial association and local health care providers to discuss the research. Qualitative interviews were conducted to identify major themes for the development of a scale to measure barriers to hospice. This effort was followed with a subsequent quantitative study documenting these barriers. The results indicated that institutional barriers, such as lack of knowledge of services, economic factors, lack of trust by African Americans in the health care system, and lack of diversity among health care staff, are significant impediments for African Americans to access hospice services. Additionally, the results of both studies led to additional social action efforts in the community.

Needs assessments are also carried out in communities, assessing the community's need for neighborhood development or services—for example, a community's need for a youth program. Societal needs are assessed at an even broader level—for instance, assessing the need for revisions in Social Security or in national policies related to services to the very old.

Who Will Have Input into the Design of the Needs Assessment?

As with program evaluations, early on you need to determine who will be involved in designing and implementing the needs assessment. Clearly, this determination is partly related to the answer to the previous question about whose need is being assessed. The decision then becomes whether and to what extent participants will have input into planning the project. This book stresses the importance of participatory or action research. Involving the participants in the study design ensures their "ownership" of the results. If participants are involved in designing and implementing a needs assessment, the results not only will have greater validity and relevance but also will be much more likely to be heard.

When Will the Needs Assessment Be Carried Out?

Two main choices exist about the timing of the data collection. The assessment may be cross-sectional or longitudinal. With a **cross-sectional design**, a survey is carried out at one point in time. For example, parents are asked about their need for a respite care program. Although it may take a few months to collect the data, whether through a questionnaire or interview, data are collected from each parent just once. This is the most common type of design for a needs assessment.

A **longitudinal design** might sometimes be necessary. Longitudinal studies are surveys conducted on multiple occasions over an extended period of

A Cross-Sectional Study

Slanger, Snow, and Okonofua (2002) conducted a cross-sectional study with 1,107 women at three hospitals in Edo State, Nigeria. The women reported on their first-delivery experiences. Evidence of genital cutting in childhood was reported among 56% of the sample. Multivariate analysis which controlled for sociodemographic factors and delivery setting showed no difference between women who had suffered genital cutting and women who had not in terms of one's likelihood of first-delivery complications or procedures. Researchers suggest that in settings such as southwest Nigeria, further attention needs to be paid to widespread issues threatening the health of women, for example sexually transmitted diseases, in addition to the act of female genital cutting.

A Trend Study

Hoffman, Barnes, Welte, and Dintcheff (2000) studied trends in combinational use of alcohol and marijuana or alcohol and cocaine by students in grades 7–12 in New York State. The surveys were conducted in 1983, 1990, and 1994. The samples were diverse, allowing for analysis of trends in various adolescent subgroups such as gender, grade level, and race/ethnicity. Analyses showed a sharp drop in use from 1983 to 1990, but use increased or remained stable from 1990 to 1994. Of particular importance was the finding that both forms of combinational use increased in the 1990s more among younger adolescents than among older adolescents. Implications from this study include a need for prevention programs that target younger adolescents and convey the dangers of combinational use.

time. There are three types of longitudinal studies: trend surveys, cohort surveys, and panel surveys.

Trend studies require multiple samplings from the same population over months or years to monitor changes or trends. For example, a trend study might examine how the characteristics of clients, or their problems that are served by a program, change over time, with the goal of changing the focus of the program to meet any changing needs.

Cohort studies examine specific subgroups as they change over time. These subgroups have specific characteristics in common; often this characteristic is age. For example, a cohort study may study the changing needs of families over time. In 1985 a group of families with parents in their early twenties were interviewed; in 1990 a different group in their late twenties; and in 1995 families with parents in their early thirties. An analysis of changing needs could then be made. Cohort studies differ from trend studies in that they examine changes

A Panel Study

Caputo (2001) examined depression and health of grandmothers who co-resided with grandchildren in 1997 using two cohorts of women. The study data were from the National Longitudinal Surveys of Labor Market Experience (NLS), Young and Mature Women's cohorts. The Young Women's cohort was a nationally representative sample of 5,159 women age 14–24 in 1968. The Mature Women's Cohort was a comparable sample of 5,083 women age 30–44 in 1967. The respondents were interviewed on a continuing basis between their start dates and 1997. Co-resident grandmothers in both cohorts were more likely than other mothers to have higher levels of depression, and about one-fifth had depression levels high enough to place them in "at-risk" categories.

over time of a *specific subgroup,* whereas trend studies look at changes in a *population* over time.

Panel studies, unlike trend and cohort studies, study the *same set of people* over time. For example, graduates of a B.S.W. program might be asked about their further education needs two years, four years, and six years after graduation. In the cohort sample above, it would also be possible that the same families could be studied over a period of ten years.

What Type of Understanding of the Need Is Required?

As with other types of research strategies, the decision about whether a positivist/quantitative or interpretist/qualitative approach is appropriate needs to be made.

Generally needs assessments adopt primarily a quantitative approach. The goal after all is to provide documentation of need that will withstand the critical review of a funding organization or other monitoring body. As such, needs assessments usually involve either collecting new data through questionnaires (either mailed or face-to-face) or using secondary or already existing data, which could be from government or nongovernmental sources. (See Chapter 9 for a discussion of these data collection methods.)

Sometimes, however, a more in-depth understanding of a need is required. In such cases it may be necessary to use a qualitative approach. For example, you may be interested in finding out more detail about what parents of mentally retarded children have in mind when they express the need for respite care. What is their definition of respite care? What have been their experiences of respite care in the past?

Qualitative data collection methods often include interviewing key informants, using focus groups, a community forum, and observation, all of which are discussed in detail in Chapter 9. These types of needs assessments are less

A Needs Assessment Using Qualitative Data

Strug, Rabb, and Nanton (2002) conducted a needs assessment regarding the service needs of male primary caretakers (MPCs) of HIV/AIDS-infected and HIV/AIDS-affected children. The researchers studied 34 service providers involved in the Title IV programs of the Ryan White Comprehensive AIDS Resources Emergency (CARE) Act. Qualitative data included the answers to questions such as "What particular concerns do you or does your staff have about these male caregivers?" The service providers identified emotional support, networking, child care, and parenting skills as needs that must be addressed with MPCs. Findings suggest that additional programs that gear services toward MPCs are needed to help these caretakers best serve children infected and affected by HIV/AIDS.

dependent on probability sampling because of the different type of understanding sought.

What Level of Description Is Useful?

You need to determine whether it is necessary to go beyond basic description and examine the relationship between certain variables in the study. These types of designs that include variable relationships are often used in program evaluations and will be described in the next chapter. However, in some needs assessments (unlike program evaluations, where the program itself is the independent variable and can be changed), the independent variable is fixed and cannot be changed in any way. For example, you might be interested in the relationship between the level of the developmental challenge in the child and the expressed need of the parents for respite care. Here the level of developmental challenge cannot be changed as the participants in the study already possess this factor (level of developmental challenge) before the study begins. This type of study is known as **ex post facto design** (meaning "after the fact"). Common variables in ex post facto designs include gender, ethnicity, age, living situation, and type of problem.

A number of problems are associated with ex post facto design, and it is important to note that this is not a form of experimental design. (See Chapter 6 for a full discussion of experimental designs). The independent variable is simply an attribute, not an experimental manipulation such as random assignment to a program or to the group that is not in the program. In addition, any difference in the dependent variable could be due to many other factors for which this design does not control. Thus the relationship between the variables is simply an association. Statements about causality cannot be made with ex post facto designs. In other words, although there may be a relationship between parents' requesting respite care less frequently and parents' having less severely developmentally

An Ex Post Facto Needs Assessment

Hulme (2000), using an ex post facto needs assessment, sought to determine the symptomatology of women primary care patients who experienced childhood sexual abuse. Hulme used both a self-report survey and chart review. Additionally, the study sought to determine the health care utilization patterns, using chart and information system reviews. A random sample of participants was recruited from a large primary care clinic. Women primary care patients who reported childhood sexual abuse (CSA) were compared to women who had not reported CSA. Twenty-three percent of the women who participated in the study reported CSA on their survey. Women who reported CSA experienced 44 out of 55 physical and psychosocial symptoms more frequently than their counterparts. Findings from the study demonstrated that women who experienced CSA encounter multiple symptoms that are not reflected in their charts.

challenged children, it cannot be said that being a parent of a less severely developmentally challenged child *causes* the need for less frequent respite care.

THE AGENCY AND DESIGNING NEEDS ASSESSMENTS

A needs assessment is the type of research most often carried out by generalist social workers. The designs and variations offered in this chapter offer only a glimpse of what can be accomplished with needs assessments. When you need to carry out this type of research, be creative in your attempt to document need. Instead of just a mailed survey, think about some alternative strategies for collecting the data. Involve the participants as much as possible; remember, they are the ones who will be receiving the services.

ETHICAL ISSUES IN DESIGNING NEEDS ASSESSMENTS

A key ethical issue with needs assessments is ensuring that the needs documented in your report are those expressed by the participants in the research, rather than the needs the agency or administration would like to see met. Agencies do have their own agendas; sometimes there is a temptation to respond more to these agendas rather than to the "true" needs of the community. This temptation cannot be underestimated. After all, you are employed (as a student or a regular employee) in that organization and must be responsive to your supervisors; it is a dilemma that must be acknowledged and dealt with responsibly.

There is also the temptation to pursue funding sources and to have those sources guide your research rather than the needs of the potential or actual clients. Obviously, with limited funding sources, you must be somewhat responsive to any

An Empowering (and Participatory) Needs Assessment

Larson, Poswa, and van Rooyen (1997) described how a group of students in Kwa Zulu Natal, South Africa, were placed for their field practicum in a community called Bhambayi, a model community established by Gandhi. Now it is primarily a squatters' settlement, with few formal services and extremely high unemployment. The students, in consultation with the community, wanted to assess the needs of the youth in Bhambayi. After interviewing 60 youths, all of whom were officially unemployed, more than half were found to have never attended high school. One of the questions asked about their skills. Their responses included carpentry, needlework, shoemaking, and mechanics. It was also disclosed that many held informal jobs. The students and the community built on these skills by developing income-generating projects such as food production, concrete block making, and mechanical repairs. The research itself gave motivation and a sense of hope to the residents of Bhambayi—many of them commented that until asked about their skills, they had felt they did not possess skills that could be used to create income.

available funds, but not to the point that you move away dramatically from your original interest. For example, a prominent foundation in your state is interested in funding programs for the visually impaired and your initial interest was in programs for sexual offenders. Such a radical shift of focus in response to the source of funds may not be advisable; ultimately the overall quality of the research will suffer. However, sometimes you can shift the emphasis of your research, say from visually impaired children to adults, to respond to a financial source.

Again, as with ethical issues raised previously in this book, some of these issues can be ameliorated by ensuring that clients have input into the research. They must direct and design it as much as possible, with the result that they, rather than the agency, come to own it. This approach not only ensures an appropriate focus for the research but also can empower the participants in the study.

HUMAN DIVERSITY ISSUES IN DESIGNING NEEDS ASSESSMENTS

The primary purpose of a needs assessment is to identify "deficits" or problems so that they can be addressed through new programs or modifications to existing programs. Identifying needs, while obviously a necessary step, can lead to certain groups being stigmatized as consistently being associated with certain problems. For example, inner-city African-American youths may be associated with crime, adolescent parents with inadequate parenting skills, refugee groups with acculturation problems, and so on. It is important to remember that needs assessments can also assess the strengths of the participants in the research and often should do this in addition to presenting the needs.

A "Strengths" Needs Assessment

Acosto and Toro (2000) included a probability sample of 301 homeless adults followed over six months to document their utilization of community services, examine services desired, and identify factors associated with service utilization, preference, and satisfaction. Using a strengths needs assessment, this study involved asking homeless individuals directly to identify their needs, rather than using the opinions of service providers and policy analysts to determine needs. The needs assessment measure was constructed based on needs empirically identified by homeless adults themselves. A significant finding of this needs assessment was that younger adults, persons of color, those with dependent children, and persons with fewer social supports reported less service utilization and less satisfaction with services received.

SUMMARY

Designing needs assessments is a central research activity for generalist social workers. There are five reasons for carrying out needs assessments: to determine whether services exist; to determine whether there are enough clients to justify a program; to assess who uses the existing services; to assess the barriers that prevent clients from accessing existing services; and to document the existence of an ongoing social problem. The type of design adopted depends on the reason for conducting the needs assessment; whose need is being assessed; who will have input into the design (that is whether a participatory design will be used); when the assessment will be carried out (that is whether it will be a longitudinal or cross-sectional study); what type of understanding is needed (interpretive or positivist); and what type of description is required.

Ethical issues include ensuring that participants have maximum input into the design of the needs assessment. Human diversity issues include the importance of addressing strengths as well as deficits in the documentation of needs.

STUDY/EXERCISE QUESTIONS

1. Find an article in a social work journal and identify
    a. limitations in the methodology
    b. how you would have designed it differently
2. Talk with your fellow students about a service/program need that seems to exist at your university. Design a needs assessment for this issue.
    a. Design one using the positivist approach.
    b. Design one using the interpretist approach.

INFOTRAC COLLEGE EDITION

1. Search for a *needs assessment* study and describe whose need was assessed, who had input, when it was carried out, what type of understanding was required, and what level of description occurred.

2. In the needs assessment found as a result of the above search, what recommendations for services or programs were made as a result of the research?

REFERENCES

Acosto, O., & Toro, P. A. (2000). Let's ask the homeless people themselves: A needs assessment based on a probability sample of adults. *American Journal of Community Psychology, 28* (3), 343–355.

Burnette, D. (1999). Custodial grandparents in Latino families: Patterns of service use and predictors of unmet needs. *Social Work, 44* (1), 22–34.

Caputo, R. (2001). Depression and health among grandmothers co-residing with grandchildren in two cohorts of women. *Families in Society, 82* (5), 473–483.

Hall, M. N., Amodeo, M., Shaffer, H. J., & Bilt, J. V. (2000). Social workers employed in substance abuse treatment agencies: A training needs assessment. *Social Work, 45* (2), 141–162.

Hoffman, J. H., Barnes, G. M., Welte, J. W., & Dintcheff, B. A. (2000). Trends in combinational use of alcohol and illicit drugs among minority adolescents, 1983–1994. *Journal of Drug & Alcohol Abuse, 26* (2), 311–324.

Hulme, P. A. (2000). Symptomology and health care utilization of women primary care patients who experienced childhood sexual abuse. *Child Abuse & Neglect, 24* (11), 1471–1484.

Kwong-Lai Poon, M., Trung-Thu Ho, P., & Pui-Hing Wong, J. (2001). Developing a comprehensive AIDS prevention outreach program: A needs assessment survey of MSM of east and southeast Asian descent who visit bars and/or bath houses in Toronto. *The Canadian Journal of Human Sexuality,* 25–40.

Larson, B. K., Poswa, T., & van Rooyen, C. (1997). Youth unemployment—A study in an informal settlement in Kwa-Zulu-Natal. *Social Work, 33* (2), 165–177.

Quandt, S. A., & Rao, P. (1999). Hunger and food security among older adults in a rural community. *Human Organization, 58* (1), 28–35.

Reese, D. J., Ahern, R. E., Nair, S., O'Faire, J. D., & Warren, C. (1999). Hospice access and use by African Americans: Addressing cultural and institutional barriers through participatory action research, *Social Work, 44* (6), 549–559.

Royse, D., & Thyer, B. A. (1996). *Program evaluation,* 2nd ed. Chicago: Nelson Hall.

Slanger, T. E., Snow, R. C., Okonofua, F. E. (2002). The impact of female genital cutting on first delivery in southwest Nigeria. *Studies in Family Planning, 33* (2), 173–185.

Strug, D., Rabb, L., & Nanton, R. (2002). Provider views of the support service needs of male primary caretakers of HIV/AIDS-infected and -affected children: A needs assessment. *Families in Society: The Journal of Contemporary Human Services, 83* (3), 303–314.

Weathers, A., Minkovitz, C., O'Campo, P., & Diener-West, M. (2003). Health services use by children of migratory agricultural workers: Exploring the role of need for care. *Pediatrics, 111* (5), 956–964.

Leslie Parr

Designing Program Evaluations

■

This chapter will discuss the design of program evaluations, a type of research question asked by generalist social workers, first introduced in Chapter 3. As with needs assessments (discussed in the last chapter), understanding how to design and implement a program evaluation is critical to ensuring an effective intervention or organization. With the needs assessment, the goal is to establish the need for the program and to help guide an appropriate response. Program evaluations assess the program itself and determine how well it is functioning.

There are two different types of program evaluations: formative and summative. These were discussed briefly in Chapter 3. A formative program evaluation focuses on description rather than on causality. For these types of evaluations, the interpretive or qualitative approach is sometimes more appropriate. A summative program evaluation is used in determining the extent to which the goals of the program were met—in other words, assessing the extent to which the program caused a specific outcome. Usually a positivist or quantitative approach is adopted with this type of research. Causality demands that three basic conditions be met, as set out in Chapter 1. First, the cause precedes the effect in time. Second, the cause and the effect are related to one another. Third, this relationship cannot be accounted for by other factors.

These three conditions of causality are established by aspects of the summative research design, which includes the timing of the data collection and the formation of comparison groups. These types of research designs are referred to as group designs because they assess the relationship of the program to a group of client systems rather than just one client system (referred to as evaluating individual practice, a topic that will be discussed in Chapter 7).

Both formative and summative program evaluations are critical to assessing programs. A summative program evaluation, however, is usually required by a funding source, and the establishment of causality can present a major challenge. The focus in this chapter will be upon these summative group evaluation designs.

As with other steps of the research process, you may not be directly involved in designing the research for a program evaluation. At some point, however, your agency will undertake such an evaluation, and it is important that you understand the implications of selecting one type of design over another. In some cases, you may find yourself with the responsibility of initiating an evaluation.

Throughout this chapter a case example will be used to demonstrate the pros and cons of different designs. Assume you are employed by a program that offers high-risk adolescents a series of six birth control classes to increase knowledge of birth control practices. You are asked to evaluate the effectiveness of the program. During this process you will need to consider different types of designs. This chapter will discuss the following:

■ formative program evaluations

■ summative program evaluations

■ types of summative program evaluation designs

■ the agency and program evaluation design

A Formative Program Evaluation

Weissman and LaRue (1998) explored a program that serves students whose parents are incarcerated. The authors looked at the outreach and programmatic approaches that were implemented to address the special needs of the population being served by the program. They found that the holistic, multifaceted, and open approach that the program used to identify, assess, and meet the needs of the students was beneficial.

- ethical issues in program evaluation design
- human diversity issues in program evaluation design

FORMATIVE PROGRAM EVALUATIONS

Formative evaluations are generally descriptive and provide detail about a program's strengths and weaknesses. Interpretive approaches using qualitative data are particularly useful with these types of evaluations.

In the adolescent birth control program, a formative evaluation would be undertaken if you were interested in finding out how the adolescents experienced the program: What did they perceive as its limitations and strengths? Alternately, a formative evaluation might examine how the parenting classes were being conducted, how the syllabus was developed, and whether the syllabus was being followed.

Formative evaluations make no attempt to establish any type of causality—in other words, no claim is made that the program resulted in specific outcomes. Also, no attempt is made to generalize the findings. Consequently, there are no dependent and independent variables and the sampling is generally purposive, rather than random. The focus is on in-depth description and analysis as a means of improving and strengthening the program. Thus, much of the emphasis in a formative program evaluation is in assessing quality.

In understanding the adolescents' experiences with the birth control classes, in-depth interviews might be conducted to try to elicit the youths' reactions to the program. The classes could be observed and the facilitator interviewed in an attempt to understand how the classes were being implemented and to identify areas in need of development.

Often, formative evaluations can be strengthened by comparing various factors, such as males and females, ethnic groups, socioeconomic groups, and so on.

Formative evaluations are extremely useful in the first year or so of a program's implementation, because findings from such a study can provide immediate feedback for improvement and growth. Thorough formative evaluations can lay the groundwork for later summative evaluations.

SUMMATIVE PROGRAM EVALUATIONS

Summative program evaluations and their associated group designs are primarily concerned with causality. As such, validity is a central issue. When considering the validity of a research design, two different validity issues are considered: internal validity and external validity.

Internal validity is the extent to which the changes in the dependent variable(s) are a result of the introduction of the independent variable(s) and not some other factor(s). For example, was the knowledge of birth control a result of the adolescents' participation in the birth control classes, or were other factors responsible for this increase in knowledge? This is an attempt to establish causality. To ensure internal validity in the birth control question, the three aspects of causality described in the previous section need to be addressed.

The first two conditions—that the cause precedes the effect and that there is a relationship between cause and effect—can be met by one aspect of the research design: the data collection time. With the adolescents, you can measure their level of knowledge about birth control before and after the classes. If you find that their knowledge level is low prior to the classes and high after the classes, this establishes that the classes preceded the increase in knowledge level.

The two measures also allow you to assess the extent of the relationship between a change in knowledge levels and participation in the classes. For example, 80% of those in the classes had a high level of knowledge after their participation. To decide whether this is a significant or important relationship, statistical tests are used (these will be discussed in Chapter 12). Even if you do determine that the relationship is significant, however, you still cannot say the classes caused a change in knowledge level because the relationship could be explained by other factors.

For example, the adolescents may have received some instruction at school on birth control at the same time as you were collecting data, which contributed to the change in knowledge level. This is where the second aspect of research design, **comparison groups**, as it relates to causality becomes so important. Comparison groups either go through another type of program or else receive no type of bona fide intervention. These comparison groups can help strengthen causality claims. If the increase in knowledge level is greater among those who attended the classes than among those who were in the comparison group, you can begin to narrow down the factors responsible for that change to the classes. See Figure 6.1 for an illustration of internal validity.

It is important that the comparison groups be otherwise equivalent to the group involved in the program being studied. The most reliable way of ensuring equivalence of the groups is to use random assignment of subjects into an **experimental group** (the group that receives the intervention being evaluated) and a **control group** (the group that does not receive the intervention being evaluated). **Random assignment** means that every subject has an equal chance of being assigned to either group. Equivalency of the groups is important because without it you cannot determine whether the disparity in outcome between the two groups is because of the treatment or a difference between the two groups. Later in this

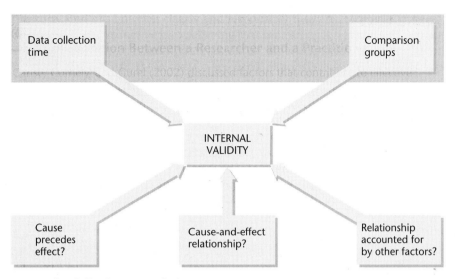

Figure 6.1 **Internal validity in group design**

chapter some problems associated with random assignment and some alternative strategies for setting up comparison groups will be discussed.

Do not confuse random assignment with random sampling. Random sampling and random assignment may or may not be used in the same study. They are independent procedures and have different implications for the findings. Random sampling involves creating a sample from a population and is concerned with the representativeness of the sample. In other words, to what extent does the sample reflect all the characteristics of the population? This is important to know when you want to generalize the research results gained from the sample to the entire population. There are a number of different ways you can select a random sample and these will be discussed in detail in Chapter 8. Random assignment, on the other hand, is concerned with the equivalence of the experimental and control groups and with establishing causality.

External validity is the other type of validity of concern in group design; and as with the type of sampling method selected (random or not) it is concerned with the generalizability of the research results to the wider population. (See Chapter 1 for a more detailed discussion of generalizability.) In other words, how effective is the birth control program with adolescents in general? In addition to generalizability being affected by the type of sampling method, generalizability depends on two other conditions: first, ensuring the equivalency of the groups, and second, ensuring that nothing happens during the course of the evaluation to jeopardize the equivalence of the groups or the representativeness of the sample.

The first condition for external validity is to ensure the *equivalency of the groups* being compared. You may decide that randomly assigning the comparison

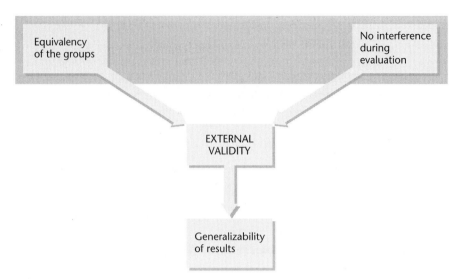

Figure 6.2 **External validity in group design**

group is not feasible and that the comparison group should be made up of adolescents who are not eligible for the classes. This type of comparison group is problematic, however, because individuals in the comparison group might possess different characteristics from those who entered group therapy. Consequently, not only would any outcome showing differences between the two groups have a lower internal validity than it might otherwise (that is, the causality would be questionable), but in addition the population to which the results could be generalized would be limited. The results could only be generalized to those eligible for the classes.

The second condition influenced by the research design that affects external validity is ensuring that *no interference* occurs during the course of the evaluation that may decrease the distinction between the experimental and control group. Interference of this kind is sometimes called **treatment diffusion**. It can occur in three ways. First, the adolescents may discuss the class with their peers, some of whom may be in the comparison group. Then comparison between the two groups becomes problematic. Second, when the program is not clearly defined, the distinction between the program group and the comparison group can be difficult. (This often points to the need for a formative evaluation to define the program components more clearly.) Finally, treatment diffusion can result from reactivity effects. Changes occur when people are aware they are participants in a study that blurs the distinction between the program group and the comparison group. Treatment diffusion leads to problems in generalizing the initial results to the wider population. See Figure 6.2 for an illustration of external validity.

TYPES OF SUMMATIVE PROGRAM EVALUATION DESIGNS

In this section, different types of research designs, with their relative validity problems or threats, will be examined. Three main types of design can be distinguished: the **preexperimental design**, the **quasi-experimental design**, and the **experimental design**. The experimental designs are the strongest in that they have the fewest threats to external and internal validity.

Preexperimental Designs

A preexperimental design is a group design that often is the only feasible design to adopt for practical reasons. It uses comparison groups rather than control groups or no type of comparison or control group, and thus, as we will see, has limited internal and external validity. Hence, it is named "preexperimental."

One-Group Posttest-Only Design

The one-group posttest-only design consists of one group (there is no comparison group) with only one point of data collection (after the intervention). Figure 6.3 shows how this design might be visualized. Sometimes this design is referred to as a one-shot case study. Note that although the term *test* is used in the name of this design, this is simply a way of talking about the point at which data collection occurs. The data collection method may be any of the types discussed in Chapter 9, such as observing a behavior or administering a questionnaire.

The one-group posttest-only design can be useful in gathering information about how a program is functioning. This design can answer several questions: For example, how well are participants functioning at the end of the program? Are minimum standards for outcomes being achieved? This type of design is

A One-Group Posttest-Only Design

Denby, Rindfleisch, and Bean (1999) studied predictors of foster parents' satisfaction and intent to continue to foster. A sample of 539 foster parents in a specific state completed a questionnaire on the factors that influence the satisfaction of foster parents and the factors that influence the intent of foster parents to continue to foster. The researchers found that efforts to increase the supply of foster homes through recruitment is insufficient and that foster parents need greater support, training, and professional regard after they have begun fostering.

Figure 6.3   ***One-group posttest-only design***

often used for **client satisfaction surveys**, in which clients are asked about how they experienced or perceived the program.

The one-group posttest-only design is limited in its ability to explain or make statements about whether a program caused particular outcomes for clients and about whether the results can be generalized to other client populations. Consequently, this design is viewed as having numerous threats to its validity—both internal and external.

Threats to Internal Validity

Remember that internal validity refers to whether it can be determined if the program caused a particular outcome. With the case example, we need to ask whether it was, in fact, the provision of birth control information that led to any increase in the knowledge.

Using the one-group posttest-only design results in the following threats to internal validity.

Selection   The kinds of people selected for one group may differ from the kinds selected for another. It may be that the clients who enrolled in the program were already highly motivated to learn about birth control. There was no pretest to measure this potential predisposition of the clients, so this possibility of **selection** threatens internal validity.

History   **History** involves those events—other than the program—that could affect the outcome. Participants' high levels of knowledge about birth control may result from classes held in school or from some other factor. Without a comparison group, this possibility cannot be assessed.

Mortality   Subjects may drop out of the groups so that the resulting groups are no longer equivalent; this possibility is called **mortality**. Some adolescents may have attended one class on birth control and then dropped out; however, they are still considered to be members of the experimental group. As a result, the group that ultimately receives the posttest is biased and perhaps shows a higher success rate than would be the case if the success rates of those who dropped out were also monitored. Consequently, the outcome of *all* participants must be assessed, which cannot be done without some type of pretest.

Note that mortality and selection are a little like mirror images. Selection is the bias involved when people initially choose to participate in the program. Mortality is the bias introduced by those who drop out of the program after they have begun.

As in our case example, because the data collection occurs only once (after the intervention) and because of the lack of a comparison group, the extent to which it can be stated that the program caused a change in birth control knowledge is limited with the one-group posttest-only design.

Threats to External Validity

The one-group posttest-only design poses some threats to external validity and generalizability of results. Possible problems include the following.

Pre-test/Post-test

A One-Group Pretest/Posttest Design

A study conducted by Boyle, Nackerud, and Kilpatrick (1999) provided an innovative approach to increasing the number of bilingual, culturally competent social work professionals in the southeastern U.S. The project included an educational exchange project with the University of Veracruz, Mexico, and a group of social work students, practitioners, and social work educators from the University of Georgia (UGA), U.S. The objectives of the exchange program were operationalized by the School of Social Work team from UGA. To meet their objectives, participants engaged in cultural immersion whereby they stayed in the homes of local people in the city of Xalapa; spoke only Spanish in the daily language school sessions; visited social service agencies in Xalapa; attended cultural events; visited local places of historical and cultural significance; and developed collaborative academic, scholarly projects with Mexican faculty members, social work professionals, and students. To measure the efficacy of the project, the participants completed the Multi-cultural Counseling Awareness Scale (MCAS), form B, before and after their stay in Mexico. Data from the pretest and posttest indicated a positive gain in total score for the participants.

Figure 6.4 ***One-group pretest/posttest design***

Selection-Treatment Interaction **Selection-treatment interaction** occurs when the ability to generalize is limited because the sample is not randomly selected or there is no pretest, so you cannot determine how typical the clients are. In our example, the adolescents may all be highly motivated to learn about birth control prior to enrolling in the program so that whether they complete the classes is irrelevant.

History-Treatment Interaction **History-treatment interaction** occurs when other factors may be contributing to the outcome and so might affect the generalizability of the results (for example, if the positive outcomes resulted from a massive media campaign on pregnancy prevention rather than from the program). The program might have a negative outcome if the evaluation were carried out at a different point in time.

One-Group Pretest/Posttest Design

Another preexperimental design, the **one-group pretest/posttest design** (Figure 6.4), is similar to the preceding design except that a pretest is added. In the case example, the pretest might consist of a questionnaire given to all clients that asks about their knowledge of birth control prior to attending the classes. This design helps answer several questions: not only how well participants are functioning at the end of the program, and whether minimum standards of outcome are being achieved, but also how much participants change during their participation in the program. This is a useful design, and certainly one that is often used in program evaluations. It is also a useful design when no comparison group is feasible. Some additional information can be gained from this type of design that can enhance statements of causality. The pretest allows selection to be ruled out as an alternative explanation, because any preexisting information on birth control would be identified. In the long run, however, this design often poses even more threats to validity than the one-group posttest-only design.

Threats to Internal Validity

The one-group pretest/posttest design poses the following threats to internal validity.

History   Because there is no comparison group, there is no way to tell whether other events apart from the birth control classes resulted in increased knowledge.

Maturation   Even though a change may be detected between the pretest and the posttest, this change may be due not to the subjects' participation in the program, but rather to **maturation**. This refers to the participants changing, in this case acquiring knowledge about birth control, over the course of time, because of lifelong learning effects rather than program effects. With adolescents and children, especially, the possibility of maturation is a potentially serious threat to internal validity.

In the case example, the adolescents' level of knowledge would have changed regardless of the program. Maturation is a particularly strong threat if the participants are young, or if there is a long time between the pretest and the posttest. A comparison group helps control for maturation effects.

Testing   The **testing** threat to validity may occur any time the subjects are exposed to a measuring instrument more than once. If the pretest included information that could increase the adolescents' knowledge of birth control, this effect then cannot be separated from the effect of the classes. A comparison group can help control for these testing effects because if they do exist, they exist for both groups; if the knowledge of the clients in the experimental group changed more than those in the comparison group, the researcher would be much more comfortable in concluding that the intervention was responsible for this change, rather than the pretest.

Instrumentation   The way in which the variables are measured, known as **instrumentation**, may change during the course of the evaluation. For example, a questionnaire may change between its first and second administration.

Sometimes these changes are difficult to avoid. For example, the context in which the questionnaire is administered may change, as may the person administering it. This change, rather than the intervention, may account for any difference in the results.

Regression to the Mean   In our example, if eligibility for the birth control classes was determined by a test on birth control knowledge (those with low knowledge levels would be eligible), then a posttest after the classes could exhibit a regression to the mean. This may occur because most people tend to perform close to their averages, but on some days they may score particularly high or low. When they take the test again, they will tend to regress to the mean or be closer to their average score. Thus any change in score between the pretest and the posttest would not necessarily reflect the influence of the program but could simply be **regression to the mean**.

Interaction of Selection and Other Threats   Even if none of these previously discussed threats to internal validity is applicable to the general population, the threats may be relevant for those subjects selected to participate in the study. To take maturation as an example, it may not be the case that women in general become more knowledgeable about birth control as they mature. Adolescents who express a desire to receive more information through counseling, however, may also be more likely to become more knowledgeable just as a function of their age. This represents the interaction of selection and other threats—in this case, maturation.

Threats to External Validity

History-Treatment Interaction   History-treatment interaction may be a problem with the one-group pretest/posttest design.

Reactive Effects   **Reactive effects** can occur when subjects change their behavior because they know they are participating in a study. The resulting outcomes may be distorted and cannot be generalized to a wider population. These reactive effects are difficult to overcome with any design because you cannot ethically engage in research without gaining the participant's consent. Consent will be discussed later in this chapter.

Static-Group Comparison Design

The static-group comparison design is a third type of preexperimental design. An extension of the posttest-only design, it includes a comparison group that also has a posttest (Figure 6.5). In this design, the groups are nonequivalent in that the comparison group was not randomly assigned, and there is no way of knowing how the groups are different or similar. Several strategies can be adopted to achieve some equivalency for the comparison group even if random assignment does not occur. These strategies include baseline comparison, matching, cohort groups, and overflow comparison.

A Static-Group Comparison Design

Umbreit (1999) conducted a study on victim-offender mediation programs in Canada. Phone interviews with victims and offenders were completed approximately two months following each mediation session. Observations of the mediation sessions were also conducted. Findings demonstrate that offenders and victims who participated in mediation programs had a greater degree of satisfaction than similar offenders and victims who did not participate in a mediation program. Additionally, victims who participated in the mediation program showed a lesser degree of fear of revictimization than those in the comparison group.

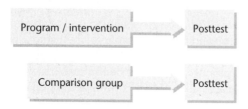

Figure 6.5   ***Static-group comparison design***

Baseline Comparison

Baseline comparison occurs when the comparison group is composed of cases handled prior to the introduction to the program. The problem with this approach is that it is difficult to determine whether cases identified as eligible in the absence of a program actually would have been referred to the program.

Matching

Matching involves selecting certain characteristics that are thought to have an important impact on outcomes—for example, gender or ethnicity—and ensuring that these characteristics are equally represented in each group. In the example, because of previous research and our own experience, you may think that ethnicity—for instance, being Latina—is an important factor in determining the effectiveness of the program. Consequently, you make sure the program group has the same proportion of Latina adolescents as the comparison group.

One drawback to matching is that you need to be sure that the variables you consider in the matching are, in fact, key variables. Often it is difficult to determine the critical variables because of the lack of previous research or other sources of information that could be used to guide these decisions.

Cohort Groups

Cohort groups provide another strategy for compiling comparison groups. A variation on matching, cohort groups are composed of individuals who move

Matching

Manion, Firestone, Cloutier, Ligezinska, McIntyre, and Ensom (1998) matched case families with comparison families on the sex and age of the child (within 6 months) and, where possible, the family constellation (single-parent/two-parent family) to evaluate the emotional and behavioral adjustments of parents and children within three months and one year after the discovery of child extrafamilial sexual abuse. The children in the comparison families had never experienced any form of sexual abuse as reported by the parents and/or the child. The study showed that both parents and children of case families experienced significant effects both initially and one year after the disclosure. For the children, self-blame and guilt for the abuse and the extent of traumatization predicted their symptomology three months and one year postdisclosure. Child age and gender also contributed to the prediction of child outcome measures. For mothers, satisfaction in the parenting role, perceived support, and intrusive symptoms predicted their initial emotional functioning, while longer-term predictors of emotional functioning was predicted by avoidant symptoms, child's internalizing behavior, and mother's initial emotional functioning.

through an organization at the same time as those in the program being evaluated do, but who do not receive the services of the program. For example, you compare adolescents in the same class at school. Some are enrolled in the program—that is, the birth control class—and others are not; or one entire class is enrolled, and another class is not. Cohort groups can also be combined with matching.

Overflow Comparison

Sometimes people are referred to a program, but because the slots are filled, a waiting list is created. The **overflow comparison group** made up of people on the waiting list can then serve as a comparison group. However, the comparison groups are formed in the static-group comparison design; they are all non-equivalent—that is not randomly assigned. This design offers one advantage over single-group designs: The threat from history is eliminated, because external events that may have an effect on the outcome will be occurring in both groups. The static-group comparison design still has other threats to internal and external validity, however.

Threats to Internal Validity

Selection   The major threat to the static-group comparison design's internal validity is selection, which results from not randomly assigning the groups and from having no pretest. Consequently, it is not possible to determine how similar the two groups are to each other. Any difference that occurs in the outcome between the two groups may not be due to the presence or absence of the intervention, but to other differences between the groups.

For example, if the experimental group is made up of adolescents who elected to enroll in the birth control classes and the comparison group is made up of adolescents who did not want to attend the classes, the comparison group may be very different from the experimental group. The experimental group may later have greater birth control knowledge than the comparison group, but this may be less a function of the classes than a function of the experimental group's greater motivation to learn about birth control. The equivalency of the groups is not assured, because of the absence of random assignment and the lack of a pretest.

Mortality   Because of the absence of a pretest and the absence of a randomly assigned comparison group, mortality is also still a problem with the static-group comparison design.

Threats to External Validity

Selection-Treatment Interaction   Selection-treatment interaction is a problem with this design.

Reactive Effects   Reactive effects threaten the external validity of this design.

Quasi-Experimental Designs

These types of designs eliminate more of the threats to internal validity and external validity than preexperimental designs, but they use comparison groups rather than control groups and thus are ultimately not as strong as experimental designs.

Time Series Design

A **time series design** overcomes some of the problems of the designs discussed previously, by measuring several times before the intervention and then several times after the intervention (Figure 6.6). For example, the adolescents might be tested on their knowledge of birth control several times over the course of several months prior to the classes. Then, the same test is given several times after the classes. The test might also be given during the time of the classes.

The advantage of the time series design is its ability to detect trends in the data before and after the intervention. In effect, this discounts the problems of maturation, testing, and instrumentation associated with the single pretest/posttest design because any trends in these effects could be detected. For example, if maturation is having an effect on the adolescents' knowledge of birth control, that effect will be detected in a difference between the pretest scores.

Threats to Internal Validity

History   Because of the absence of any type of comparison group, history is a major threat to internal validity in the time series design. Events external to the evaluation would have to be fairly powerful, however, to confound the effect of the classes.

Time Series

Nugent, Bruley, and Allen (1999) tested the effectiveness of Aggression Replacement Training (ART) on male and female antisocial behavior at a runaway shelter. The case records of 522 adolescent participants who stayed in a runaway shelter were assessed using measures of antisocial behavior for a 310-day period before the implementation of the program and then for a 209-day period after the program. The results suggested that ART may be useful along with other approaches in reducing juvenile antisocial behavior in a short-term residential setting.

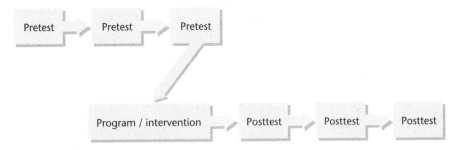

Figure 6.6   ***Time series design***

Threats to External Validity

History-Treatment Interaction   A potential threat to external validity is history treatment interaction, as history interacts with the classes. An intervention that appears to work under some circumstances may not work under others.

Reactive Effects   With repeated testing, reactive effects are also a problem.

Pretest/Posttest Comparison-Group Design

The pretest/posttest comparison-group design is a combination of the static-group comparison and the one-group pretest/posttest design (see Figure 6.7). The comparison group is still not randomly assigned, although this design can adopt any of the various methods used to set up comparison groups that are mentioned for the static-group comparison design. By combining features of both the static-group comparison and the one-group pretest/posttest design, this design becomes less problematic than either of them. History is controlled with the comparison group, and the pretest identifies, to a certain extent, differences or similarities between the groups.

A Pretest/Posttest Comparison-Group Design

Kramer (1998) compared social work students enrolled in a "Grief, Death, Loss, and Life" course to those who were enrolled in other electives to determine students' level of death acceptance and sense of preparedness to respond to personal and professional losses. The author administered a pretest on the first day of class to both groups of students and the posttest on the last day of class. The findings suggested that students who enrolled in the grief course perceived greater competence in their knowledge, skills, and sense of preparation for working with grieving clients. Students enrolled in the grief course also demonstrated increased cognitive and affective dimensions of death acceptance.

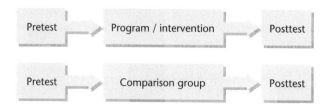

Figure 6.7   ***Pretest/posttest comparison-group design***

Threats to Internal Validity

Selection and Maturation Interaction   In the example, the pretest may indicate that the group that received classes had more knowledge about birth control than the comparison group prior to the intervention. If the posttest also indicates this difference between the groups, maturation may have been the cause of the treatment group's having even greater knowledge over time, whether or not they received the classes. This potential problem with internal validity depends a great deal on how the comparison group is selected and how significant the results are.

Threats to External Validity

Selection-Treatment Interaction   A potential problem is selection-treatment interaction, which can affect generalizability of the results.

Maturation-Treatment Interaction   Another potential problem is maturation-treatment interaction.

Reactive Effects   Reactive effects are also a problem with the pretest/posttest comparison-group design.

A Pretest/Posttest Control-Group Design

Children with learning disabilities are at risk for poor peer relationships even in mainstreamed classrooms. The program to be evaluated was designed to work with fifth-grade learning disabled (LD) children to improve their acceptance by their nonlearning disabled (NLD) fifth-grade peers. The intervention was a cognitive behavioral program. Hepler (1997) compared pretest and posttest scores of both LD and NLD children who had been randomly assigned to a program group and to a no-treatment (control) group. Results provided positive feedback for the implementation of programs that help LD children increase their social skills and acceptance by their peers.

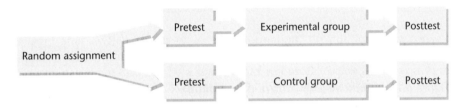

Figure 6.8   *Pretest/posttest control-group design*

Experimental Designs

These designs result in findings that can make the strongest claim for causality and eliminate the majority of the threats to external and internal validity.

Pretest/Posttest Control-Group Design

The difference between the **pretest/posttest control-group design** and the previous design is that the comparison group and experimental groups are randomly assigned. When this occurs, the comparison group is referred to as a control group (see Figure 6.8). In the example, random assignment to either the control or experimental group might be made from high-risk students in a high school class. As a result of a randomly assigned control group, the threats to internal validity of history, maturation, mortality, selection, regression to the mean testing, and instrumentation are virtually eliminated.

Only one potential external validity problem with the pretest/posttest control-group design remains. This involves the possible reactive effect of the pretest. Despite the strength of this design, there are some difficulties in its implementation. Some of these problems are similar to those encountered in setting up nonrandomly assigned comparison groups, including treatment diffusion and nonavailability of a list or pool of clients from which random

A Posttest-Only Control-Group Design

Cunningham, Wild, and Bondy (2001) studied the effects of normative feedback on problem drinking. An intervention pamphlet was mailed to 6,000 randomly selected households; 4,000 households in the region did not receive the pamphlet (the control group). In a month after the mailing, a general population survey was carried out of the 10,000 households. Respondents from the households receiving the normative feedback reported significantly lower alcohol use than those in the control group.

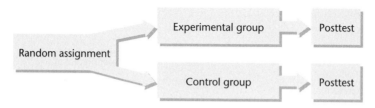

Figure 6.9   ***Posttest-only control-group design***

assignment can occur. Some ethical issues with this design will be discussed later in this chapter.

Posttest-Only Control-Group Design

One way of eliminating the threat to external validity posed by the previous design is simply to eliminate the pretest. In the **posttest-only control-group design** (see Figure 6.9), the two groups are again randomly assigned and consequently should be equivalent, and there should be no need for the pretests. Some researchers, however, are reluctant to eliminate what is essentially a safety measure to ensure the groups' equivalency.

The Solomon Four-Group Design

The **Solomon four-group design** is a combination of the previous two designs and as a result is extremely valid (see Figure 6.10). It is rarely used in social work research, however. It is usually difficult to find enough subjects to make assignments randomly between two groups, and the cost of the design exceeds the budgets of most social work program evaluations.

Table 6.1 summarizes each of the summative group designs and their threats to internal and external validity as discussed in this chapter.

A Solomon Four-Group Design

The Hope Scale is designed to measure hope in terms of effectiveness of treatment in outcome studies. Hope is comprised of two components: (1) the Pathways component, which is an individual's planning strategy to achieve goals, and (2) the Agency component, which is the individual's determination to implement strategies. Westburg (1999) used a Solomon four-group design to evaluate the relationship of the Hope Scale pretest to the posttest scores. Additionally, this study explored the use of humor in elevating total Hope Scale scores. Westburg randomly assigned 80 undergraduate students to one of four groups to take the Hope Scale. Analysis showed that pretest scores were not associated significantly with posttest scores. In addition, humor intervention did not elevate scores on the Hope Scale.

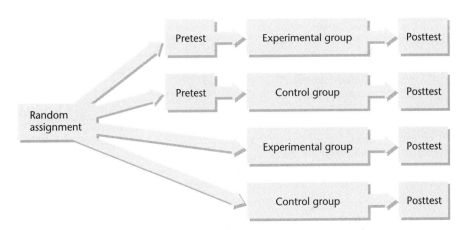

Figure 6.10   ***Solomon four-group design***

THE AGENCY AND PROGRAM EVALUATION DESIGN

It should be clear from this chapter that experimental designs with randomly assigned control groups are preferable to use if you are interested in establishing whether a program or intervention, and not some other factor or factors, was responsible for a specific outcome. As generalist social workers, however, you may find that the textbook research examples are not practical, nor are they necessarily preferred. Don't be discouraged if you can't use a Solomon four-group design or, for that matter, random assignment; it may be that one of the other designs will help you acquire the kind of information you need.

The challenge is to develop designs that are *feasible and appropriate for the research question,* and that is why this chapter includes some practical ideas on, for example, alternative ways of setting up comparison groups. These alternative

Table 6.1   **Group research designs—threats to internal and external validity**

Type of design	Threats to internal validity	Threats to external validity
One-group posttest-only	Selection, history, mortality	Selection-treatment interaction, history-treatment interaction
One-group pretest/posttest	History, maturation, testing, instrumentation, regression to mean, interaction of selection, and other threats	History-treatment interaction, reactive effects
Static-group comparison	Selection and mortality	Selection-treatment interaction
Time series	History	History-treatment interaction, reactive effects
Pretest/posttest comparison	Selection and maturation	Selection-treatment interaction, maturation-treatment interaction, reactive effects
Pretest/posttest control group	None	Reactive effects
Posttest-only control group	None	None
Solomon four-group	None	None

strategies are compatible with agency practice, and if the comparison groups receive services or treatments (including simply part of the intervention being provided to the experimental group) many of these strategies become even more feasible and attractive to agencies. This approach is particularly useful with crisis-oriented or court-ordered services.

Another strategy that may result in the greater participation of agencies involves the use of unbalanced designs with fewer subjects assigned to the comparison or control group. Consequently, clients referred to the agency are more likely to receive services.

Finally, do not overlook the importance of formative program evaluations. They have an important role to play in the development of programs and should be the evaluation of choice for new programs.

Most important is to acknowledge your design's drawbacks and address them in the reporting of the evaluation. If research is conducted in this practical and responsible way, knowledge building in social work can progress with a solid agency-based foundation.

ETHICAL ISSUES IN PROGRAM EVALUATION DESIGN

Two major ethical issues are related to group design, both of them associated with control or comparison groups. First is the issue of whether establishing a comparison or control group involves denying services to clients. Second is the question of whether the subjects' informed consent should be obtained so that a comparison group can be established.

Assignment to the Comparison or Control Group

The NASW Code of Ethics (1999) states that social workers should take appropriate steps to ensure that participants in evaluation and research have access to appropriate supportive services. Participants in the research should always be assured of some services. Whether they will be is an issue when participants are assigned to comparison or control groups.

This research strategy could be viewed as a denial of services, justified in the name of science; it poses an ethical dilemma that can have implications for administration of the evaluation. Personnel may see the creation of comparison or control groups as a way of manipulating clients, which could consequently influence the evaluation. For example, in a situation where the comparison group is receiving a variation of the intervention to be evaluated, the staff—if they disagree with the creation of the comparison group—may not adhere to the guidelines governing this variation in their attempt to bring legitimate services to the subjects in the comparison group. In addition, clients may not be referred to the project at all.

Two arguments that use of comparison or control groups does not always pose a serious ethical problem can be made, however. First, the decision about who receives services in an agency is often arbitrary and political. Program services may run on demand, and the deprivation of services is not uncommon. Second, by suggesting that clients are being denied valuable treatment, we are assuming that the intervention being evaluated is effective. Often enough, that assumption has no empirical basis. In fact, if it did, there would be little reason for carrying out the research in the first place. As in practice, however, the situation in research is often not this clear-cut. Usually some evidence—perhaps a combination of practice wisdom and research findings—indicates that the treatment is helpful to some extent. The purpose of the evaluation is then to determine how helpful it is. Consequently, our concern that we are violating subjects' rights by possibly denying them beneficial treatment involves other factors, such as individual judgments and values about how detrimental the denial could be. This is another example of the important role that values play in the scientific process.

Decisions relating to the establishment of control or comparison groups are probably governed by the seriousness of the problem. Under most circumstances, it would be hard to justify establishing a control group of emotionally disturbed children involved in self-destructive behaviors. In addition, the use of waiting lists and cohort groups, baseline comparison groups, and assignment to other types of interventions or programs can help ameliorate some of the potential ill effects of being assigned to the comparison or control group.

Informed Consent

Informed consent involves informing potential subjects fully of their role and the consequences of their participation in the research and seeking their permission. The NASW Code of Ethics (1999) states:

- Social workers engaged in evaluation or research should obtain voluntary and written informed consent from participants, when appropriate, without any implied or actual deprivation or penalty for refusal to participate; without undue inducement to participate; and with due regard for participants' well-being, privacy, and dignity. Informed consent should include information about the nature, extent, and duration of the participation requested and disclosure of the risks and benefits of participation in the research.

- When evaluation or research participants are incapable of giving informed consent, social workers should provide an appropriate explanation to the participants, obtain the participants' assent to the extent they are able, and obtain written consent from an appropriate proxy.

- Social workers should inform participants of their right to withdraw from evaluation and research at any time without penalty.

Informed consent is an issue, first of all, because of the difficulty of forming comparison groups. In seeking a comparison group, you may be reluctant to fully inform potential participants that they will not be receiving a service. In attempting to ensure their participation, you may justify your failure to inform them on the ground that their consent is not necessary if they are not receiving the service. Informed consent is less of a problem with control groups, in which participants will be randomly assigned to the control and experimental groups and therefore can be told that they may or may not be receiving the service. *Consent must be gained at all times for any participation, however*—whether for the experimental group or for the comparison or control group.

As discussed in the previous section, the effects of being in the control group can be improved somewhat by adopting alternative strategies—waiting lists, alternative programs, and so forth. These strategies can also help with the consent issue. In other words, the researcher will not be so tempted to avoid seeking informed consent in anticipation of the potential subject's refusing to participate, because ultimately the client will receive some type of intervention. The second issue relating to informed consent is the possibility that informing the subjects of the details of the evaluation will jeopardize the validity of the findings.

For example, if the experimental group knows they are the experimental group and the control or comparison group knows that they are the control or comparison group, expectations can be set up that can affect outcomes. The experimental group may expect to change and, regardless of the actual impact of the intervention itself, may show improvement. This threat to validity was discussed earlier in the chapter as a reactive effect. Given the possibility of this threat, it is tempting to avoid giving subjects all the details of their participation. Informed consent should still be obtained, however. One way of dealing with the reactive problem is to inform the subjects that they will be placed either in a control or comparison group or in an experimental group but not told which one to protect the validity of the findings. Of course, this is only an option if the control or comparison group is receiving at least some type of intervention, whether it is a variation of the one being evaluated or another intervention. If such an intervention is not feasible during the study, the researcher needs to acknowledge possible reactive effects rather than not inform the subjects of the research.

HUMAN DIVERSITY ISSUES IN PROGRAM EVALUATION DESIGN

When developing a program evaluation and making decisions about the research design, the major issue relating to human diversity is ensuring that certain groups are not being exploited for the purpose of establishing comparison groups. Sometimes such exploitation can occur unintentionally. In social science research, the tendency is to assign members of disadvantaged groups, such as the poor, minorities, women, and others, to comparison groups. (This is not an issue for control groups when subjects are randomly assigned.)

Parlee (1981) argued that in psychology research (and this argument can be extended to social science research in general) the choice of particular comparison groups demonstrates the scientist's "implicit theoretical framework." She suggested that many of these frameworks are biased against women and that this bias becomes a problem when we engage in matching. "Knowing" what variables to include entails biases that can favor certain groups over others. The choice of the comparison group defines the perspective that will dominate the research and in turn influence the findings.

Parlee (1981) cited a study in which a matched comparison group of women was sought for a 20-year-old/men-only study of aging. One alternative was to match the women according to intelligence, education, and occupation. Another might argue for matching according to physiological similarities, by, for example, including the men's sisters. The former represented the social scientists' perspective while the latter reflected that of biomedical scientists. Clearly, these two alternatives involved two different perspectives on the causality underlying aging and would probably result in different conclusions being drawn from the study.

It is critical to recognize this potential bias in comparison group selection. To counterbalance this problem, we should involve diverse people in conceptualizing the research, particularly if the program evaluation will have impacts on diverse populations. In this way, alternative viewpoints and perspectives can be fully incorporated into the group design.

SUMMARY

There are two main types of program evaluations: formative and summative. Formative evaluations are primarily descriptive, whereas summative evaluations focus on causality. When designing summative program evaluations, it is necessary to select a group design. Each design poses various threats to internal and external validity. Internal validity is the extent to which the changes in the dependent variable are a result of the independent variable. External validity refers to the generalizability of the research findings to a wider population. Research designs may have to be modified in agency settings. A design's drawbacks should be acknowledged in reporting the evaluation.

Ethical issues relating to group design include potentially denying services to clients when establishing comparison or control groups and obtaining informed consent from all clients in a research study. Human diversity issues include not exploiting certain groups for use as comparison groups.

STUDY/EXERCISE QUESTIONS

1. The family service agency in which you are employed is planning to conduct an evaluation of its services. As the leader of a support group of parents of developmentally challenged children, you are asked to design an evaluation of this service.

   a. What design could you develop that would be feasible and would maximize the validity of your findings?

   b. Under what circumstances would a formative evaluation be appropriate and how would you carry this out?

2. Review an issue of *Social Work Research and Abstracts* and select an article that used one of the research designs described in this chapter.

   a. What are the threats to internal and external validity?

   b. Were these threats explicitly discussed?

   c. Propose an alternative design that would be feasible.

INFOTRAC COLLEGE EDITION

1. Search for a *client satisfaction survey* and describe the limitations of the findings.

2. Search for three *program evaluations* and compare the research designs used. Did the authors comment on the limitations of the designs used?

REFERENCES

Boyle, D. P., Nackerud, L., & Kilpatrick, A. (1999). The road less traveled. *International Social Work, 42* (2), 201–214.

Cunningham, J. A., Wild, T.C., Bondy, S. J., & Lin, E. (2001). Impact of normative feedback on problem drinkers: A small area population study. *Journal of Studies in Alcohol, 62* (2), 228–233.

Denby, R., Rindfleisch, N., & Bean, G. (1999). Predictors of foster parents' satisfaction and intent to continue to foster. *Child Abuse & Neglect, 23* (3), 287–303.

Hepler, J. B. (1997). Evaluating a social skills program for children with learning disabilities. *Social Work with Groups, 20* (3), 21–36.

Kramer, B. J. (1998). Preparing social workers for the inevitable: A preliminary investigation of a course on grief, death, and loss. *Journal of Social Work Education, 34* (2), 211–227.

Manion, I., Firestone, P., Cloutier, P., Ligezinski, M., McIntyre, J., & Ensom, R. (1998). Child extrafamilial sexual abuse: Predicting parent and child functioning. *Child Abuse & Neglect, 22* (12), 1285–1304.

National Association of Social Workers. (1999). NASW Code of Ethics. *NASW News, 25,* 24–25.

Nugent, W. R., Bruley, C., & Allen, P. (1999). The effects of aggression replacement training on male and female antisocial behavior in a runaway shelter. *Research on Social Work Practice, 9* (4), 466–482.

Parlee, M. B. (1981). Appropriate control groups in feminist research. *Psychology of Women Quarterly, 5,* 637–644.

Umbreit, M. S. (1999). Victim-offender mediation in Canada: The impact of an emerging social work intervention. *International Social Work, 42* (2), 215–227.

Weissman, M., & LaRue, C. M. (1998). Earning trust from youths with none to spare. *Child Welfare, LXXVII* (5), 579–594.

Westburg, N. G. (1999). Hope and humor: Using the hope scale in outcome studies. *Psychological Reports, 84* (3), 1014–1021.

Leslie Parr

Designing the Evaluation
of Practice

■

D uring the last 20 years, social workers have experienced increased pressure to evaluate their practices. In part, this pressure stems from studies done in the 1960s and early 1970s, which suggested that social work practice was not as effective as many had expected (Fischer, 1973). On closer examination, the research studies themselves were found to have major methodological problems, raising questions about whether the findings from the studies should be viewed seriously and as an accurate reflection of the state of social work practice.

First, the research studies often used no type of comparison group, which led to questions about the internal and external validity of the results. Second, because group designs used in program evaluations pooled the results from both successful and unsuccessful programs to determine average results, they were not able to determine what actually worked with whom and with what kinds of problems. Consequently, the results were often of little use to the practitioner.

Third, the group designs generally relied on only two measures—one before the intervention and one after the intervention. There was no way of knowing what happened between these two measurement points. For example, a posttest may indicate that the target problem has not decreased in severity. It is possible, however, that at some point after the intervention but before the posttest, some decrease did occur. It could not be determined whether and why such an effect might have occurred because of the way many of these studies were designed.

In addition to these methodological problems, other problems relating to ethical and social issues characterized these early studies. First, it was and is often difficult to get the support of agency personnel in assigning clients to control or comparison groups because of the ethical issues discussed in Chapter 6. Second, it was and is also often difficult or impossible for agencies to come up with the funds for a full-scale evaluation of even a moderate-sized program.

As a consequence of these problems and of the continuing demand for accountability of social services, social workers were increasingly required to evaluate their practices. Different ways of implementing these evaluations emerged. At first, the emphasis was on an approach adopted from psychology, a technology known as **single-system** or **single-subject designs** or **studies**. These types of studies tried to assess the impact of interventions on client systems.

Single-system designs relied heavily on the collection of empirical behavioral data and were grounded in the positivist tradition. They grew in popularity as they produced results identifying how specific interventions were effective with specific clients with specific types of problems.

Later, after single-system designs were taught in departments and schools of social work, single-system technology came under criticism. Reasons included the single-system design's inability to produce new knowledge (Wakefield and Kirk, 1997) because of lack of agency support, intrusiveness of the designs (Gorey, 1996), and an unrealistic expectation of the social worker (Marlow, 2003). Alternative approaches to evaluating practice began to emerge. Instead of the single-system design approach of assessing the impact of interventions on client systems (that is explanatory designs), descriptive methods were developed to monitor client progress and to monitor the intervention. Many of these methods used interpretive and qualitative approaches, differing significantly from the positivist approaches associated with single-system studies.

These new ways of evaluating practice give the social worker choices about which approach to use. As stressed in Chapter 1 and throughout this book, the choice in part depends upon the question being asked. Practice evaluation involves three major questions. First, how can the intervention be described? Second, how can the client's progress be monitored? Third, how effective is the intervention in bringing about client change? The first two questions are primarily descriptive, whereas the third question is explanatory. Different types of descriptive and explanatory designs will be presented in this chapter.

This chapter will discuss the following topics:

- descriptive designs for practice evaluation
- explanatory designs for practice evaluation
- analysis of practice evaluation data
- the agency and practice evaluation
- ethical issues in practice evaluation
- human diversity issues in practice evaluation

DESCRIPTIVE DESIGNS FOR PRACTICE EVALUATION

As just discussed, two types of questions in practice evaluation require descriptive designs: questions that focus on the nature of the intervention and questions that focus on monitoring any client change. Each of these will be presented in this section.

Monitoring Interventions

Often it is important to examine and reflect on the intervention being used; this is referred to as **monitoring interventions**. Evaluation then becomes a process of discovery rather than an experiment (as with a formative as opposed to a summative program evaluation). As a student social worker, you may be asked to evaluate how you are applying an intervention and to describe your activities to your supervisor. You can use various strategies to evaluate an intervention. Three methods can be used to monitor interventions: process recordings, practice logs, and case studies.

Process Recordings

Process recordings are written records based on notes or on a transcription of a recording (audio or video) of interactions between the worker and clients. These qualitative data become an important source of information for improving practice.

Suppose you are just beginning your employment with Child Protective Services, and your supervisor has given you the go-ahead to visit a family alone.

Reflecting on Practice

McCormick (1999) reflected on her practice with residents in a halfway house for people recently released from jail or prison:

> Tonight was our second parenting group. About seven of the original members attended along with about three new members. I began by having them pair off—with one person acting as the parent and the other as the child. I gave the "children" two pieces of clay and instructed them to go ask their "parent" to play with them. The dads played for a timed ten-minute period. During this time, I went around the room, modeling how to praise, encouraging creativity and interaction. All except two members participated, and they all were creative and interested. After the ten minutes were up, I talked about "special time" with children and how play benefits children. I encouraged them to spend ten minutes per day with each child as a special time and to make time for play in their visits with their children. Together, the group and I brainstormed ways to play with children. I encouraged storytelling—both with books and orally. I tried to focus on the strengths of their ideas.
>
> I noticed at one point that everyone was talking at once. I asked them to take turns, but it was too late. Next time, I will begin by addressing this issue and asking for agreement. I will ask them to whisper quietly if they need to talk to each other during the group process. I may make a talking stick and bring it to the next group. I think kinetic materials work well with this group.
>
> Many of the parents brought up discipline during our discussion, so I think I'll focus on that next time—maybe the next two times. I think they're ready for that now. Otherwise, I'll put their suggestions (from the list they constructed during the first group) back on the board and ask them to choose what they want to focus on next.
>
> Overall, I think it went well. On the sign-in sheet, some positive comments were made. I'd like to develop a form for them to use that will reflect what they feel they got out of the group for each session.

You are still unsure about whether you are conducting the interview appropriately, however. Consequently, immediately after the home visit you sit down and record the major interactions that occurred. You later share this process recording with your supervisor. This process can help identify the strengths and weaknesses in your interviewing skills; if you continue this type of monitoring for several cases, you may see patterns emerging.

Practice Logs

A variation on the process recording is an ongoing **practice log**, using self-reflection and analysis to understand how you and the client worked together in resolving issues raised. Papell and Skolnick (1992) discuss how practitioners' self-reflection can add to their understanding of practice. Practice logs go beyond a process recording in that the writer self-reflects and comments on his or her use of the intervention and the experience of practice. Practice logs are often required of students in their field practica. As a form of data collection, these will be discussed in Chapter 9.

For example, say you are involved in trying to organize a community center for youths but have never tackled anything like this before. Consequently, you carefully record all your activities, impressions, and thoughts connected with this endeavor, and you share this information with a more experienced community organizer whom you met at a NASW chapter conference the previous year. In this situation, rather than having to rely on anecdotes and your memory, your practice log gives you a systematic record of what occurred. This record can provide potential data for a more explanatory design you might want to attempt at a later date, in which you try to determine whether your strategy resulted in the anticipated outcomes.

These types of evaluations are rarely published because they are used primarily by individual workers and within agencies to enhance practice.

Case Studies

Case studies involve a more complete description of the application of the intervention, and tend to be more "objective" and less self-reflecting than the process recordings or practice logs. Detailed case studies of unusual cases, successful cases, or unsuccessful cases can yield some vital information. The type of information generated may either support existing practice principles or suggest new approaches and principles. Single-case or multiple-case studies can be used.

One major advantage of monitoring interventions using any one of the three approaches described here is that it provides a means for practitioners to reflect on and study their own practice. The reflective method "would encourage practitioners to examine professional activity and the knowledge reflected in that activity against empirically based theory as well as against their practice wisdom and tacit knowledge, using a range of methodologies" (Millstein, 1993, p. 257).

Monitoring Client Progress

You monitor an intervention, and you can also monitor the client's progress. Information is gathered on the client while the intervention is taking place. As a result, decisions can be made about whether the intervention should be continued, modified, or stopped. These data can be either qualitative, in the form of notes and narrative, or quantitative, in the form of behavioral observations or the different rapid assessment instruments described in Chapter 9. Whichever data collection method is used, client goals must be clearly specified (Blythe, Tripodi, and Briar, 1995).

For example, in working with a group of adolescent mothers you may decide to monitor the clients' progress both during the months when the groups are held and after they stop. The change goal was to learn parenting skills, the maintenance goal was to practice those skills, and the prevention goal

Case Study: Support of Practice Principles

Lemieux (2001) used a case study to highlight the application of principles of empowerment-oriented practice to interventions with families headed by mothers with mental retardation. Included in the detailed case study were strategies that supported the social work principles and values of empowerment, inclusion, and self-determination. Lemieux described the value of empowerment and advocacy activities, and she noted that time limitations and expected outcomes of child protective services can put such techniques in conflict with set timelines. Lemieux presented recommendations for social work practice and research to increase knowledge about the experiences of mothers with mental retardation in the child welfare system.

Multiple Case Studies: Suggestions for Innovations in Practice

Pandey (1998) reported on multiple case studies done in various regions of Nepal where women are involved in community forestry programs. The article discussed the factors that inhibited the participation of the rural poor in these programs, including their fear of exploitation and the inaccessibility of resources. To promote sustainable development, the author suggested that social workers advocate for the participation of the poor.

was to reduce or eliminate future child abuse or neglect (measured by reported occurrences). The goals were monitored monthly for two years.

These types of practice evaluations are rarely published, although they are important strategies for evaluating practice. Often, the information gained from descriptive evaluations of individual practice can help to formulate hypotheses for future evaluations of our own practice. Consequently, descriptive studies can be viewed as an inductive mode of knowledge building (as discussed in Chapter 1).

EXPLANATORY DESIGNS FOR PRACTICE EVALUATION

Explanatory designs examine the impact of the intervention on the target behavior. These designs are now also called single-system designs or single-system studies. They involve three elements that help establish causality: a baseline, clear identification of the intervention, and target behaviors that can be operationalized and repeatedly measured.

↘elderly incomes

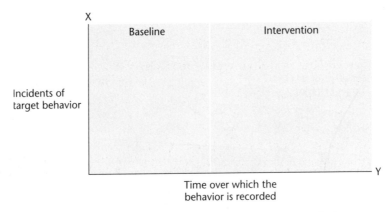

Figure 7.1   ***Displaying the results from explanatory single-system designs***

Baseline

Rather than depending on control or comparison groups in their search for causality, single-system designs rely on the target behavior's being measured multiple times. In effect, the client system serves as its own control. A similar principle is in effect here as that used in the time series designs discussed in Chapter 6; with that group design, however, a group of client systems is monitored, whereas the single-system study monitors only one client system. The repeated measurement prior to the intervention is known as the **baseline**. The baseline allows you to compare target behavior rates before and after the intervention, thus helping you to assess the impact of the intervention on the target behavior. This repeated measurement or baseline can take different forms; it could be the frequency of a behavior, the duration of a behavior, or the intensity of a behavior. The choice depends on the focus of the intervention. Figure 7.1 demonstrates how results from explanatory single-system designs are usually displayed. The X axis records the incidents of the target behavior, and the Y axis shows the time interval over which the behavior is recorded. The vertical line represents the point at which the intervention was introduced.

For the assessment to have some validity, a stable baseline is needed prior to the implementation of the intervention. The baseline consists of an observable pattern between the data points. Fluctuations may occur, but as long as they occur with some regularity they constitute a stable baseline. An unstable baseline makes it difficult to interpret the study's results. A problem with interpreting the findings also occurs when the baseline is stable but is moving in the direction of the desired outcome prior to the intervention's implementation (see Figure 7.2).

Clearly Defined Intervention

Explanatory designs also require a clearly defined intervention, and the point at which it is introduced must be clearly presented.

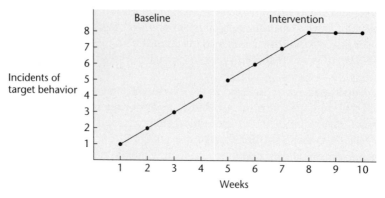

Figure 7.2   ***Example of a baseline moving in the direction of the desired outcome***

Operationalization and Repeated Measure of Target Behavior

Explanatory designs also require that the target behaviors that are the focus of the intervention be clearly defined. For example, rather than a target behavior's being defined as a child's inattentiveness, a clearer definition would be the number of times a question is repeated to a child before he or she answers. In addition to being clearly defined, data about the target behavior need to be collected repeatedly.

Different types of explanatory designs will now be presented.

AB Design

The **AB design** is the simplest of the single-system designs. Data are collected on the target behavior prior to the intervention, and this constitutes the baseline, or phase A of the design. The B phase consists of measurements of the target behavior after the intervention has been introduced. The effectiveness of the intervention is determined by comparing the A measure of the target behavior to the B measure.

Let's look at a case in which the problem is a family's low attendance at a parenting class. The goal or target behavior of the intervention is to increase attendance. The A phase would be the number of times the family attends the class prior to the intervention. The class is held twice a week, and data are already available on the family's attendance over the previous three weeks. These data can be used as a baseline.

The point at which the intervention is introduced marks the beginning of the B phase. The intervention in this case might be to arrange for another family to help with transportation to the class. The frequency of the target behavior is then recorded for several weeks after intervention.

An illustration of how these data might look if charted is given in Figure 7.3. The results can be analyzed by simply viewing the chart. An increase in attendance is clearly evident.

An AB Design

Barrett and Wolfer (2001) undertook an interesting single-system evaluation. Barrett, who was a social work student, provides a personal account of her experiences as a domestic violence victim and her self-evaluation of the intervention that was used to treat her anxiety. She used an AB design, and the intervention involved structured writing. Barrett monitored her anxiety level using a standardized measure (the Clinical Anxiety Scale), a behavior count, and a self-anchored scale. For every method of measurement, anxiety decreased after using the writing intervention.

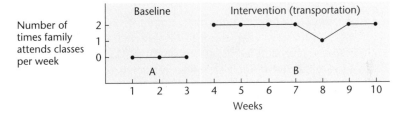

Figure 7.3   ***Example of an AB design***

One of the advantages of the AB design is its simplicity. In addition, the design can easily be integrated into the practice process, giving important information about those interventions that appear to work with particular client systems.

Some problems are associated with the AB design. The major problem is that you do not have any control over extraneous factors or the history threat to internal validity. In our example, it was possible that the classes suddenly became more interesting to the family or that the mother had persuaded the father, who was exhibiting the most resistance to attending, of the benefits of the class. Or, the results might have been effected or affected by a multitude of other factors. Thus the AB design is restricted in the information it can give about causality.

ABC Design

The **ABC design** is also known as the **successive intervention design** because the C phase represents the introduction of another intervention. Other phases can be added on as D or E phases. The ABC design is simply the AB design with the addition of another intervention. With this design, the target behavior continues to be measured after the introduction of each intervention.

The ABC design can be convenient in that it often reflects the reality of practice. We introduce one intervention, and if it seems ineffective, we implement

An ABC Design

Kazi and Wilson (1996) presented several examples of single-case evaluations from a project in Great Britain to train and encourage social workers to apply this type of evaluation to their practice. One is a modification of an ABC design. The A B BC C design collected data on a 15-year-old girl's school attendance and the mother's feelings about her relationship with her daughter. Intervention B was weekly counseling sessions with the 15-year-old girl, her grandmother, her mother, and her boyfriend. These sessions did not improve school attendance, although the mother's feelings about the relationship improved. When intervention C (positive encouragement from teachers) was added to B, both dependent variables improved and remained stable for the C phase.

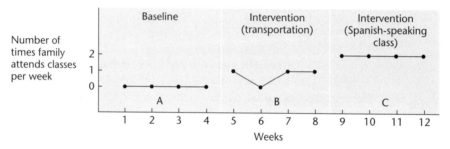

Figure 7.4   ***ABC single-system design***

another intervention. The ABC design adds an empirical element to this common practice.

To continue with the example we have been using, transportation assistance did not increase attendance for another family. After further assessment it was found that the parents—although English-speaking—were native Spanish speakers and were having difficulty following the class. Consequently, a second intervention was the organization of a Spanish-speaking class for a number of Spanish-speaking families in the community. The families' attendance was monitored following this intervention and showed an increase. See Figure 7.4 for an illustration of how these results would be displayed.

Although the ABC design nicely reflects the reality of practice, this design has the same types of problems associated with the AB design. You have no way of knowing whether the intervention or some other factor accounted for any change in the target behavior. This validity issue is complicated in the ABC design by not knowing whether it was the C intervention that resulted in the final outcome or a combination of the B and C interventions. Although you may not know specifically which intervention influenced the outcome, you do know

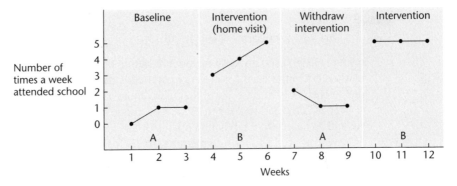

Figure 7.5 **ABAB—reversal single-system design**

about the effect of some combination of the interventions—a finding that in itself can enhance your practice and service to clients.

ABAB Design

The **ABAB design** is also known as the **reversal design** or the **withdrawal design**; it consists of implementing the AB design and then reversing it by withdrawing the intervention and collecting baseline data again before implementing the intervention a second time. Suppose a school social worker works constantly with the problem of absenteeism. In the past, she has made regular home visits to the families involved, and she has a sense that this is working. She decides to test the intervention, starting with one case, that of a 12-year-old boy.

The social worker monitors his attendance at school over a three-week period and then starts the home visits, which include counseling, information, and referral, twice a week. She collects data on attendance for another three weeks and then stops the visits, again monitoring attendance, for another three weeks. Finally, she once again introduces the intervention. The results, displayed in Figure 7.5, indicate that the intervention appears to have some impact on the student's school attendance.

The great advantage of the ABAB design is its ability to tell us about the impact of the intervention versus the impact of other possible factors; in other words, its ability to explain and imply causality is greater than the AB or the ABC designs.

The ABAB design does have a few problems. First, it cannot be applied to all target behaviors and all types of interventions. Some interventions cannot be reversed, particularly those that involve teaching a new behavior. For example, suppose you identify the target behavior as a second grader's tardiness, and you assess the problem as resulting from the mother's not being assertive with the child about getting ready for school. The intervention consists of the social worker's teaching the parent how to be assertive with the child. This would be a difficult intervention to reverse, because the mother now behaves differently.

An ABAB Reversal Design

Soliman (1999) used an ABAB research design to assess treatment processes and measure outcomes from a number of psychiatric cases in Kuwait following the Iraqi aggression. The case illustration highlighted in Soliman's study was of an 11-year-old boy diagnosed with PTSD. The design included two baseline phases (A1 and A2) and two intervention phases (B1 and B2). In all four phases, the social worker used two tools to measure the clients' symptoms. For the first baseline, A1, the client responded to a 20-item, 5-point, Likert-type scale in each session of the assessment period. In addition, the parents maintained a weekly chart to report the number of times the client experienced sleep disturbance. The intervention, B1, included behavioral and cognitive therapeutic activities such as individual counseling, group counseling, and family involvement. During the second baseline phase, A2, the client's symptoms were reassessed with the same techniques used in the previous phases. In A2, the intervention was withdrawn for a period of three weeks. The client continued to meet with the group, although no structured activities were provided. The second intervention phase, B2, continued for four weeks, at which time the client received the same interventions as B1. Using the ABAB design, the social worker was able to determine which interventions effected the desired treatment outcomes.

Even if the intervention seemingly could be reversed, some residues of the intervention might remain. In the example of the 12-year-old boy's absenteeism, the home visits might have resulted in some carryover effects even after they were halted; in fact, this seems to have been the case. The interpretation of the results and the precise impact of the intervention then become more difficult.

With any explanatory single-system study, and particularly with the reversal design, you must spell out the details and possible consequences for the clients before the intervention is instituted. This procedure is similar to obtaining clients' informed consent prior to engaging in a group study.

Multiple Baseline Designs

A **multiple baseline design** involves replicating the AB design by applying the same intervention to two or more target behaviors, to two or more clients, or in two or more settings at different points in time. For example, a child is exhibiting problems at school; the target problem is identified by the teacher's concern that the child is not verbally participating in class. After assessment, it becomes apparent that this behavior is associated with the child's Navajo cultural background, which discourages speaking out. Intervention consists of discussion with the teacher about cross-cultural issues, including suggesting that she use some Navajo examples in teaching. This intervention could be tested *across client systems* by using the intervention with three different Navajo children.

A Multiple Baseline Design

Reamer, Brady, and Hawkins (1998) used a multiple baseline across families with children who have developmental disabilities to assess the effects of video self-modeling. The intervention combined self-assessment, self-modeling, discrimination training, and behavioral rehearsal on parents' interactions with their children during the children's self-care tasks and social play with their siblings. The video intervention was designed to alter parents' assistance patterns and to provide less directive task-related prompts. Results showed increased parental social prompts, altered parental assistance during children's tasks, and an increase in children's social behavior and task completion.

Alternatively, the intervention could be used *across target problems,* in which additional problems such as low grades and low socialization might be identified. These behaviors could be monitored before and after the implementation of the intervention.

The intervention could also be tested *across settings* by, for example, looking at changes in one of the target problems in a day care center, at home, and in the school setting. Often multiple baseline designs are further strengthened by introducing interventions at different points on the baseline. As the intervention is introduced for the first behavior, client, or setting the others are still at the baseline phase. This aspect of the design strengthens the internal validity of the design in that if an external event occurs at the same time as the introduction of the intervention, the potential impact of this event will be picked up by the baseline. However, if the intervention is responsible for the change then this change will occur on each graph at the point that corresponds to the introduction of the intervention.

Figure 7.6 shows how data from a multiple baseline design might be displayed. The multiple baseline design offers a great deal of potential for examining the effectiveness of particular interventions and can allow us to be more confident in our belief that the intervention was responsible for any measured change. In effect, the multiple baseline design involves the principle of comparison groups in group design, using another client, another setting, or another target problem as a comparison. For example, if you find that the same intervention for the same target problem for the same setting was effective for two different clients, you would be more certain of the intervention's effectiveness than if you had simply looked at one client.

Nevertheless, there are some limitations on the extent to which you can hold the intervention responsible for any change in the target problem even with these designs. For example, when applying the multiple baseline design across clients, even if the change in the target problem resulted in a positive outcome for all clients, there is still no guarantee that it was the intervention and the intervention alone that resulted in the specific outcome. In fact, the validity

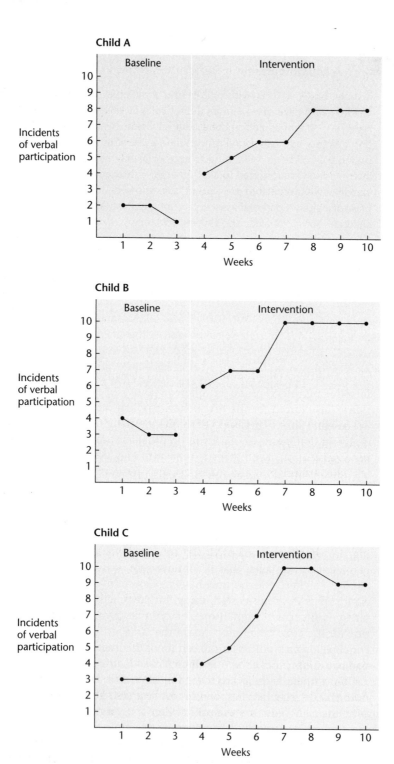

Figure 7.6 **Multiple baseline design**

Multiple Baseline and Program Design

Whitfield (1999) evaluated the effectiveness of anger control training with male adolescents. A multiple baseline design across participants was used to assess matched pairs of students (eight experimental and eight control students). The experimental students significantly improved in their anger control, immediately and at a six-month follow-up assessment. The author concluded that the cognitive/ behavioral approach is more effective at reducing school violence when compared with a nonspecific counseling approach (see Figure 7.7).

limitations are similar to those associated with many of the nonexperimental designs discussed in Chapter 6.

As mentioned earlier in this chapter, it is the multiple baseline design that can be used to evaluate entire programs. The results of a number of these types of designs can be put together to give an overall assessment of a particular intervention's effectiveness.

ANALYSIS OF PRACTICE EVALUATION DATA

After collecting the data using the designs described in this chapter, it then becomes necessary to make sense of the results. In later chapters the analysis of data from group designs will be discussed. When quantitative data are collected from these designs, statistical analysis is required (don't throw away this book quite yet; it's not as painful as you might think). Statistical analysis is discussed in Chapter 12. For qualitative data, methods of data analysis other than statistics are used. Even so, this type of data analysis is challenging and potentially time-consuming. Here we will discuss ways of presenting the results from single-system studies.

The first step is to describe the findings, and this is best done visually. You can think of practice evaluation data charts as possessing certain properties (Bloom, Fischer, and Orme, 1995) including:

Level   The magnitude of data is the level. Differences in levels can occur between the baseline and the intervention. A change in level is called a **discontinuity** (see Figure 7.8).

Stability   Where there is clear predictability from a prior period to a later one, the data are stable. Stability occurs if the data can be easily represented by a mean line. Data lines can still be stable even if they change in magnitude. See Figure 7.9 for two examples of stability of data between baseline and intervention periods.

Trends   Where the data tend in one direction—whether the pattern is increasing or decreasing—a trend is present. Trends are called **slopes** when they occur

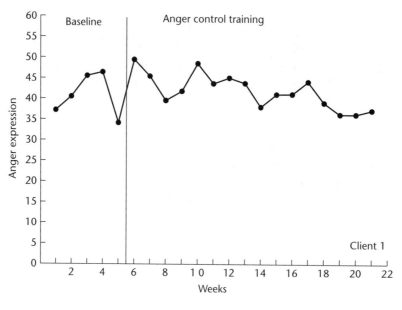

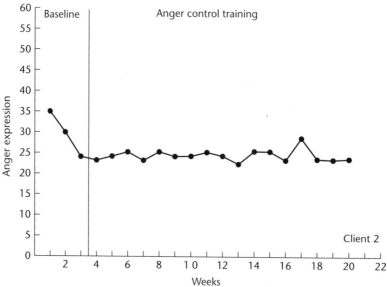

Figure 7.7   **Weekly anger expression scale scores for clients 1 and 2**

Source: From "Validating school social work: An evaluation of a cognitive-behavioral approach to reduce school violence," in G. W. Whitfield, 1999, *Research on Social Work Practice, 9* (4), 399–426. Reprinted with permission of Sage Publications, Inc.

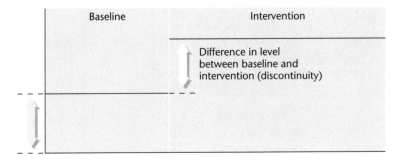

Figure 7.8 **Levels of data**

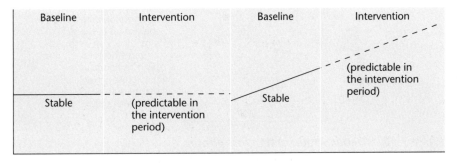

Figure 7.9 **Stability of data between baseline and intervention**

within a given phase and **drifts** when they occur across phases. See Figure 7.10 for variations of trends.

Improvement or Deterioration Specific comparisons between the baseline and intervention periods can show improvement or deterioration in the target behavior. Of course, a determination of what is improvement and what is deterioration depends on whether greater or lesser magnitudes of the behavior are desired. Figure 7.11 illustrates this idea.

Other factors that need to be considered when describing findings from the charts include the following:

The Timing of the Effects Sometimes effects occur immediately after the baseline and sometimes they are delayed (Figure 7.12).

The Stability of the Effects The effect of the intervention may wear off. If so, implementation of a different intervention is indicated (Figure 7.13).

Variability in the Data This often happens but needs to be treated cautiously, particularly when the variability occurs during the baseline period. In both

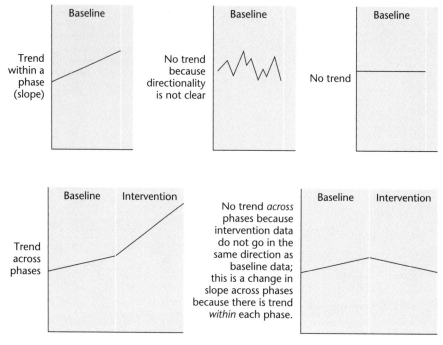

Figure 7.10 **Trends within and across phases**

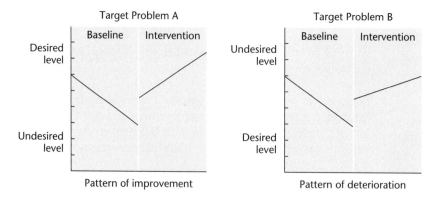

Figure 7.11 **Patterns of improvement and deterioration**

examples in Figure 7.14, it is difficult to interpret the effects because of the variability in the baseline data.

Chapter 12 will discuss how data from single-system studies can be analyzed using specifically designed statistical techniques. These techniques then give you an indication of the data's statistical significance. This is particularly useful when the data are variable, as in Figure 7.14.

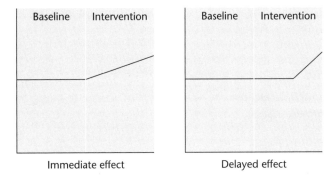

Figure 7.12   **Immediate and delayed effects**

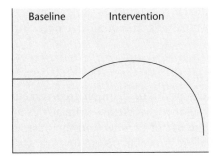

Figure 7.13   **Unstable effects**

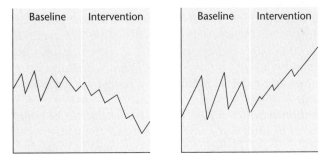

Figure 7.14   **Variability in data**

THE AGENCY AND PRACTICE EVALUATION

The evaluation of individual practice should, of course, be extremely compatible with agency settings, although there seems to be some disagreement on this point. Much has been written about the relative strengths and limitations of practice evaluations and specific designs and about their applicability to practice and agency settings. A good overview is presented in an article by

Corcoran (1993). The strengths and limitations of practice evaluations are described next.

Strengths

Strengths include feedback to the client, knowledge building for practice, and cost and time factors.

Feedback to the Client

One benefit of practice evaluation is that feedback can be provided to the client. The intervention-monitoring and client-monitoring designs provide consistent feedback, and with single-system designs the client is provided with some tangible evidence that the intervention does or does not appear to have an impact on behavior. Feedback can result in longer-term effects and the clients' adopting of self-help measures, lessening the need for further social work intervention.

Knowledge Building for Practice

The activity of monitoring interventions or client progress can enhance workers' knowledge of their practice by allowing workers to critically examine the values and assumptions underlying the use of theories and their associated interventions in practice. Questions that are critical in developing knowledge about practice include these (Millstein, 1993): Am I doing what I think I'm doing? If not, what am I doing? What does my work tell me about how I make meaning of practice? What ways of knowing do I use?

The single-system explanatory studies offer information about the efficacy of specific interventions. Further information can be obtained by replicating or repeating the single-system studies—testing interventions with other clients, on other target behaviors, and in other settings. Replication increases internal validity (it is the intervention and not something else that is affecting the outcome) and external validity (the results are generalizable to a wider population).

As mentioned earlier in this chapter, knowledge can be built through single-system studies by integrating single-system and group approaches in evaluating program effectiveness. Berbenishty (1989) provided an example:

> The basic building blocks of the advocated methodology are single-case evaluation, intentionally designed, selected, and combined to form an assessment on the agency level. For each intervention, data on the characteristics of treatment, therapist, problem, and client are collected. These data from each single-case study are then aggregated to access the overall effectiveness of the group of cases. Further, in order to assess differential effectiveness, subgroups were identified and compared (as to their relative improvement), or certain background or treatment characteristics were correlated with outcome measures. (p. 33)

Time and Cost

Unlike group studies, which often require additional funds, evaluation of individual practice can be easily incorporated into practice with no extra expense or excessive time commitment.

Limitations

Evaluation of individual practice, then, offers some advantages in agency settings, but some arguments are also made against the use of such evaluations in agencies. They do possess some limitations, including limited application, limited validity, and limited data analysis.

Limited Application

Historically, single-system explanatory designs were used almost exclusively for testing the effectiveness of behavioral intervention techniques. In part, their application was limited because of the emphasis in behavior theory on being able to define behaviors clearly so that any changes in the behaviors can be easily recorded. Many social workers, including generalist social workers, are deterred from using single-system studies because they have assumed the design is appropriate only for behavioral intervention and clearly observable and recordable behaviors. Designs that monitor intervention and client progress, however, can be used with a variety of interventions and target behaviors.

In addition, some designs, such as the withdrawal and multiple baseline designs, are often simply not practical. It is rarely possible to withdraw an intervention. Finally, often it is difficult to select a design when just beginning to work with a client; instead, designs are determined as practice evolves. This is less of a problem with the monitoring designs described in this chapter, which are sensitive to the process of practice.

Limited Validity

Internal and external validity are a problem with the explanatory single-system designs, even when results are replicated. Single-system studies simply are not as valid as well-designed group designs used in program evaluations. As discussed in Chapter 6, however, well-designed group studies are rare. More often, less satisfactory designs (in terms of causality) are used, resulting again in internal and external validity problems. Consequently, in many instances single-system studies can be thought of as no worse in terms of validity than many group designs and they are certainly better than no design at all.

Another validity issue is the extent to which the use of self-report instruments, designed to measure subjective aspects of the client's problems, result in therapeutic reactive effects. Some researchers claim that these effects are minimal (Applegate, 1992).

Analysis of Results

Another potential drawback of evaluating practice in agencies is that the analysis of findings is largely a matter of judgment. Therefore, their applicability is limited. Some statistical analyses can be carried out for single-system designs, and these will be discussed in Chapter 12.

ETHICAL ISSUES IN PRACTICE EVALUATION

Issues relevant to other types of social work practice are obviously applicable here, such as issues about confidentiality and informed consent, but two other ethical issues specifically relate to practice evaluation: the use of the reversal design and the issue of the interference with practice.

Reversal Design

One could argue that withdrawing an apparently effective intervention, as discussed in the reversal design section, is unethical. The counterargument is that withdrawal of the intervention will allow us to determine whether the intervention is responsible for any change in the target problem. This determination not only enhances the worker's knowledge of the intervention's effectiveness but also demonstrates its effectiveness to the client. As a result, the intervention may have a longer effect; parent training is a good example.

Interference with Practice

The second issue—the idea that practice evaluation procedures interfere with practice—has been raised consistently over the years. One response to this position is that practice evaluation studies can enhance practice and help direct and inform social workers in their day-to-day contact with client systems. For example, determining the data collection method may offer opportunities for other insights and further exploration with the clients regarding the target problem.

In addition, the client's involvement in the research, particularly in the data collection, can result in the client's being engaged in the change process to a greater extent, simultaneously limiting problems with confidentiality and informed consent. This effect constitutes not so much an interference as an enhancement of practice.

In conclusion, because of the joint participation of worker and client in several of the methods used in this chapter, ethical violations are far less likely than they are in group designs for program evaluations.

HUMAN DIVERSITY ISSUES IN PRACTICE EVALUATION

Throughout the process of evaluating individual practice, you need to pay attention to human diversity issues. This effort includes carrying out more studies on diverse clients, recognizing that what may be effective for one type of client is not necessarily effective for another. In fact, practice evaluations provide an excellent opportunity for exploring the richness of human diversity.

SUMMARY

There are two major approaches to evaluating practice: descriptive and explanatory. Descriptive methods include monitoring interventions and monitoring client progress. Explanatory approaches, or single-system designs, include the AB design, the ABC design, the ABAB design (reversal), or the multiple baseline design. The evaluation of individual practice in agency settings is advantageous because of the opportunity for direct client feedback, knowledge building for practice, and time and cost factors. There are also problems associated with the evaluations, however, including limited analysis, limited validity, and limited application. Because of the partnership required between client and worker, ethical violations are less likely than with group design. Evaluations of individual practice offer many opportunities for exploring the great diversity among groups.

STUDY/EXERCISE QUESTIONS

1. You are working with a family with an adolescent who is not attending school regularly. You want to evaluate your intervention with the adolescent and will collect data on her school attendance. What would be the advantages and disadvantages of the following designs for this evaluation?

    a. AB design   b. ABC design   c. ABAB design

    What would be the ethical issues in this case?

2. You would like to evaluate your practice as a generalist social worker in a hospital, but your supervisor objects, saying it would be too time-consuming. Support your request and address her concerns.

3. Find an article in a social work journal that examines practice evaluation. Summarize the main points.

4. You have been facilitating a support group for teenage parents. The goal is for the group to continue without a facilitator. You will be monitoring attendance at the group as an indicator of its effectiveness. How would you do this?

5. Your supervisor asks you to monitor your practice, focusing on the interventions you use. How would you do this?

INFOTRAC COLLEGE EDITION

1. Search for a *case study* and discuss how this research contributes to our knowledge of social work practice.

2. Search for a *single-system design* or *single-subject study*. What type of design was used?

REFERENCES

Applegate, J. S. (1992). The impact of subjective measures on nonbehavioral practice research: Outcome vs. process. *Families in Society, 73* (2), 100–108.

Barrett, M. D., & Wolfer, T. A. (2001). Reducing anxiety through a structured writing intervention: Single-system evaluation. *Families in Society, 82* (4), 355–62.

Berbenishty, R. (1989). Combining the single-system and group approaches to evaluate treatment effectiveness on the agency level. *Journal of Social Service Research, 12,* 31–48.

Bloom, M., Fischer, J., & Orme, J. (1995). *Evaluating practice: Guidelines for the accountable professional* (2nd ed.). Englewood Cliffs, NJ: Prentice Hall.

Blythe, B., Tripodi, T., & Briar, S. (1995). *Direct practice research in human service agencies.* New York: Columbia University Press.

Corcoran, K. J. (1993). Practice evaluation: Problems and promises of single system designs in clinical practice. *Journal of Social Service Research, 18* (1/2), 147–159.

Fischer, J. (1973). Is casework effective? A review. *Social Work, 18,* 5–20.

Gorey, K. M. (1996). Effectiveness of social work intervention research: Internal versus external evaluations. *Social Work Research, 20* (2), 119–128.

Kazi, M. A., & Wilson, A. F. (1996). Applying single-case evaluation methodology in a British social work agency. *Research on Social Work Practice, 6* (1), 5–26.

Lemieux, C. (2001). The challenge of empowerment in child protective services: A case study of a mother with mental retardation. *Families in Society, 82* (2).

Marlow, C. (2003). Paper presented at the symposium in honor of Elsie Pinkston. School of Social Service Administration, University of Chicago, March 2003.

McCormick, J. (1999). Notes from an MSW student fieldwork journal. New Mexico State University School of Social Work.

Millstein, K. H. (1993). Building knowledge from the study of cases: A reflective model for practitioner self-evaluation. *Journal of Teaching, 8* (1/2), 255–277.

Pandey, J. (1998). Women, environment, and sustainable development. *International Social Work, 41* (3), 339–355.

Papell, C. P., & Skolnick, L. (1992). The reflective practitioner: A contemporary paradigm's relevance for social work education. *Journal of Social Work Education, 28* (1), 18–26.

Reamer, R. B., Brady, M. P., & Hawkins, J. (1998). The effects of video selfmodeling on parents' interactions with children with developmental disabilities. *Education and Training in Mental Retardation and Developmental Disabilities, 33* (2), 131–143.

Soliman, H. H. (1999). Post-traumatic stress disorder: Treatment outcomes for a Kuwaiti child. *International Social Work, 42* (2), 163–175.

Wakefield, J. C., & Kirk, S. A. (1997). Science, dogma, and the scientist-practitioner model. *Social Work Research, 21* (3), 201–205.

Whitfield, G. W. (1999). Validating school social work: An evaluation of a cognitive-behavioral approach to reduce school violence. *Research on Social Work Practice, 9* (4), 399–426

Leslie Parr

Selecting the Participants in the Research

■

ow that you've decided on your research question and the type of design you will be using, who are the participants in your research going to be? In social work research, **sampling** involves choosing the participants in the study. Sampling is necessary because you usually cannot include everyone in the study, just as in practice you cannot interview or meet with all those involved in a situation. For example, you may be interested in determining the need for an after-school program in your community, and you want to identify and get opinions from all the families in the city who have school-age children 12 and under in age. Even in a small-sized city, this could be a large number of families, but you have a limited budget and only two months in which to complete the project. Consequently, you need to select a smaller group of participants, or **sample**, from this large group, or **population**, that is made up of all possible cases that you are ultimately interested in studying (see Figure 8.1). Note that the population is a theoretical construct and refers to people with certain characteristics that the researcher is trying to understand.

Sampling should be a familiar concept to you as a generalist social worker. You often need to collect information relating to a target problem from a large number of people. When, because of time and other constraints, you cannot contact all of the relevant people, you select a sample. In research, there are specific ways to select a sample; the particular method we use depends on the nature and accessibility of the population and the type and purpose of the study we are undertaking.

As with the steps of the research process already discussed, you may not be directly involved in sampling decisions. Knowledge of the process is essential, however, for two reasons: First, sometimes you will be involved in the sampling decision; second, you need to understand how sampling can affect use of the research findings in your practice. This chapter will discuss the following:

- key concepts in sampling
- types of sampling methods
- sample size
- the agency and sampling
- ethical issues in sampling
- human diversity issues in sampling

KEY CONCEPTS IN SAMPLING

One of the key concepts of sampling is the extent to which the sample is representative of the population. A **representative sample** means that the sample has the same distribution of characteristics as the population from which it is selected. For example, in assessing the city's need for an afterschool program, you are interested in making statements applicable to the entire city, so your sample needs to be representative. Thus, in this case it is important that the

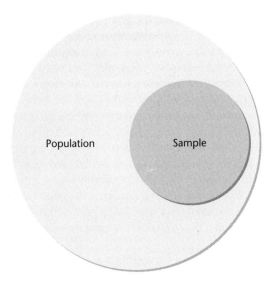

Figure 8.1   ***Population and sample***

sample not be biased in any way. One way bias could occur would be if only one neighborhood was selected.

Neighborhoods tend to have specific socioeconomic and ethnic characteristics—for example, upper-middle-class suburbs, Latino barrios, retirement communities. As a result, they are not usually representative of the entire city population, at least not in terms of socioeconomic and ethnic structure. Neighborhood is only one example of possible bias. Other groupings, such as schools and churches, also may not be representative of the larger community.

If your sample is representative of the population, then you can generalize the findings from your sample to that population. When you **generalize**, you claim that the findings from studying the sample can be applied to the entire population. If you discover in your representative sample of families from your city that 70% express an urgent need for an afterschool program, you then generalize that 70% of the families in your city (that is your population) will also express this need. In needs assessment studies such as this, it is critical that you are able to generalize your findings. Thus, a quantitative approach, which emphasizes generalizability of the findings, is the one taken when conducting many needs assessments.

In other studies, however, generalizability and representativeness are not such important issues. For example, rather than looking at the extent of need for an afterschool program, you instead might be concerned with exploring the experiences of families with children who spend part of the day unsupervised. Here you might use a qualitative approach, where the concern is less with the representativeness of the sample and the generalizability of the findings and more with description and gathering new information. In an interpretive or qualitative study, the key concept is that the sample is **information rich**; that is the sample consists of cases from which you can learn about issues central to the research question.

Before describing different sampling strategies, you need to become familiar with two other general sampling concepts. First, an **element** in sampling refers to the item under study in the population and sample. In generalist social work research, these items or elements may be the different client systems with which we work—individuals, families, groups, organizations, or communities. The element depends upon the unit of analysis. Elements may be more specific than these basic systems. In our example, families with school-age children 12 and under are a more specific element than simply families.

The second concept is the **sampling frame**: a list of all the elements in the population from which the sample is selected. In the above example, the sampling frame would consist of a list of families in the city with school-age children 12 and under.

As you confront the realities of compiling a sampling frame, you may need to redefine the population. For example, you might have decided on families with children 12 and under as your element because the state in which you are conducting the study legally mandates that children of this age cannot be left without adult supervision. When you begin to compile a sampling frame, however, you run into problems because you find it difficult to identify families with children of this age and younger. Instead, you discover that through the school system you can more easily identify families with children in the first through the seventh grade. You may end up with a few 13-year-olds, but this isn't a problem if you redefine your population as families with children in the first through the seventh grades. Remember though that the population and the sampling frame are not the same thing. The population is more of a theoretical construct whereas the sampling frame is a tool to select the sample.

TYPES OF SAMPLING METHODS

The sample can be selected in two major ways: probability and nonprobability sampling. **Probability sampling** allows you to select a sample where each element in the population has a known chance of being selected for the sample. This type of sampling increases the representativeness of the sample and should be striven for when using the quantitative approach to research.

Instead of a probability sampling method, you may choose a **nonprobability sampling** or purposive sampling method. **Purposive sampling** allows the researcher to handpick the sample according to the nature of the research problem and the phenomenon under study. As a sampling method, purposive sampling is limited in terms of representativeness, in that the probability of each element of the population being included in the sample is unknown. It is, however, the sampling method of choice in qualitative studies, where generalizability of results is less important.

Table 8.1   ***Probability sampling methods and generalization of findings***

Sampling method	Generalizability
Simple random	Can generalize; limitations minimal
Systematic random	Can generalize; limitations minimal—note how the elements are listed in the sampling frame
Stratified random	Can generalize; limitations minimal—make sure the strata involved are reflected in the analysis of the data
Cluster	Can generalize, but some limitations possible—note the characteristics of the elements because there is a possibility of sampling error with this type of probability sampling

Probability and nonprobability sampling approaches will be presented in the following sections.

Probability Sampling

Probability sampling occurs when every element in the population has a known chance of being selected; thus, its representativeness is assured. In addition, no subject can be selected more than once in a single sample. There are four major types of probability sampling: (1) simple random sampling; (2) systematic random sampling; (3) stratified random sampling; and (4) cluster sampling. Table 8.1 includes each of the probability sampling methods along with their associated potential generalizability.

Simple Random Sampling

Simple random sampling is the easiest of the sampling methods, where the population is treated as a whole unit and each element has an equal probability of being selected in the sample. Because the sampling is random, each element has the same chance of being selected. When you toss a coin, there is an equal chance of its being heads or tails. In the afterschool program needs assessment example, a simple random sample would involve assigning identification numbers to all the elements (families with children in the first through seventh grades) and then using a table of random numbers that can be generated by a computer. Most software packages for the social sciences have the ability to generate random number tables. If you did not have the random numbers table, you could literally put all the identification numbers of each element in a container and pick your sample from this.

Simple random sampling is the most straightforward probability sampling method. It has some problems, though, which will become apparent as the other types of probability sampling are discussed.

Simple Random Sampling

Rittner and Dozier (2000) examined the effects of court-ordered substance abuse treatment in Child Protective Services cases. The sample consisted of 447 randomly selected children in kinship care while under CPS supervision. The sampling frame consisted of a computerized client information system of the total countrywide pool of cases. Results suggested that court interventions had mixed outcomes.

Systematic Random Sampling

Johnson, Renaud, Schmidt, and Stanek (1998) studied social workers' views of parents of children with mental and emotional disabilities. A systematic random sample (*n* = 570) was taken of the total membership (12,750) from the National Association of Social Workers (NASW) Register of Clinical Social Workers. The authors found that the most prevalent problematic area reported by the social workers was parent-blaming beliefs.

Systematic Random Sampling

Systematic random sampling involves taking the list of elements and choosing every *n*th element on the list. The size of *n* depends upon the size of the sampling frame and the intended size of the sample. For example, if you had 400 elements in your sampling frame and you needed a sample of 100, every fourth element would be selected for the sample. If you needed a sample of 200, every second element would be selected.

Generally, systematic random sampling is as random as simple random sampling. One potential problem with systematic random sampling arises, however, when the ordering of elements in the list being sampled from follows a particular pattern. A distortion of the sample may result. In the afterschool program example, students from the school district may be arranged into class lists of approximately 30 students, and all students who moved to the community within the last six months may be placed at the end of each of these lists. In some communities, these recent additions may be made up primarily of migrant workers. Consequently, if you were to select every 10th, 20th, and 30th element in each class list, your resulting sample would be made up of a disproportionate number of migrant workers, because even though each class has only three or four such students, they are more likely to be the 30th element in a class list.

Problems with the ordering of elements can usually be identified quite easily, and precautions can be taken. When lists are available, systematic random

Stratified Random Sampling (Proportional)

Zimmerman et al. (2001) studied the effect of the Vaccines for Children (VFC) program on the likelihood of physicians to refer children to public vaccine clinics for immunizations. The VFC program is an entitlement program which provides states with free vaccines for disadvantaged children. The researchers selected Minnesota and Pennsylvania primary care physicians through a stratified random sampling technique. Four strata were used: general practitioners; board certified family physicians in urban and suburban areas; family practitioners in rural areas; and pediatricians. Results indicated that physicians' reported referral of Medicaid-insured and uninsured children to public vaccine clinics has decreased because of the implementation of VFC programs in Minnesota and Pennsylvania.

sampling may be easier than simple random sampling because it avoids the step of assigning identification numbers.

Stratified Random Sampling

Stratified random sampling is a modification of the previous two methods; in it the population is divided into strata, and subsamples are randomly selected from each of the strata. Sometimes you need to ensure that a certain proportion of the elements is represented. (Sometimes this sampling method is referred to as **proportional stratified sampling**.) Stratified random sampling provides a greater chance of meeting this goal than either systematic or simple random sampling.

In the afterschool program study, you may be concerned about representation of the different ethnic groups of the families with children in the first through the seventh grades. You identify 10% of the families as Native Americans. With a simple or systematic random sample, your sample should, if it is truly representative, include 10% Native American families. Unfortunately, due to the workings of probability theory, this is not always the result. At this point, we cannot delve into the depths of probability theory, but if we toss a coin 20 times, we might expect to end up with 10 heads and 10 tails. Individual toss results will vary, however. We might end up with 12 heads and 8 tails some of the time, or with any other possible combination.

To ensure that Native American families are representatively included in the sample, you can use proportional stratified random sampling. Stratified random sampling requires two preconditions. First, you must be sure that membership in the group whose representation you are concerned about actually has an impact on the phenomenon you are studying. In our example, do you think that Native American families' viewpoints on afterschool programs will differ from those of other families? If not, their adequate representation in the sample may not be that important. Second, you need to know the proportion of this group relative to the rest of the population. In our example, 10% are Native American.

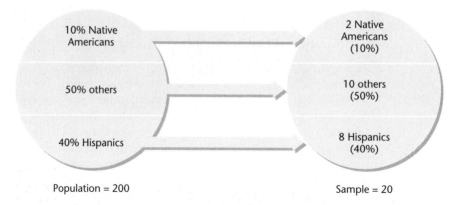

Population = 200   Sample = 20

Figure 8.2   **Stratified random sampling**

Stratified random sampling involves dividing the population into the groups or strata of interest; in this example, you would divide the population into Native Americans and non-Native Americans. (Note that you can create more than two strata if necessary. For example, you might also be concerned that Hispanic families be assured adequate representation in the sample. Knowing they make up 40% of the population, you would then create three strata: Native Americans, Hispanics, and others.) After creating the strata, simple or systematic random sampling is then carried out from each stratum in proportion to the stratum's representation in the population. In our example, to end up with a sample of 40, you would randomly select 4 from the Native American stratum, 16 from the Hispanic stratum, and 20 from the other stratum (see Figure 8.2).

Although under some circumstances stratified random sampling may be an improvement over simple random sampling, the disadvantages are the two preconditions described earlier—that is the certainty that the characteristics with which you are concerned will have an impact on the outcome, and that you know the proportions of these characteristics in the population prior to the sampling. Sometimes it may be necessary to use a variation of stratified random sampling, referred to as disproportionate stratified random sampling. With the proportionate stratified random sampling example discussed earlier, only a small proportion of Native Americans are included in the sample, reflecting their proportion in the population. This is not a problem if we are interested in an overall assessment of the afterschool program. However, you might be interested in comparing the experiences of the different ethnic groups. If that is the case, then you would need to take equal proportions of each ethnic group, 13 from each group for a total sample size of 39.

Cluster Sampling

Cluster sampling involves randomly sampling a larger unit containing the elements of interest, and then sampling from these larger units the elements to be included in the final sample. Cluster sampling is often done in social work

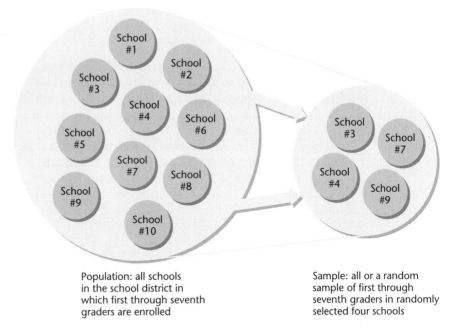

Population: all schools in the school district in which first through seventh graders are enrolled

Sample: all or a random sample of first through seventh graders in randomly selected four schools

Figure 8.3   ***Cluster sampling***

research because it can be used when it is difficult to get a sampling frame, and yet it is still a form of probability sampling. In the afterschool program example, suppose you are required to obtain the lists of students from each school rather than from the school district office. This could present a lengthy undertaking in a large school district with many schools. Or, the lists may not be available either from the schools or from the school district. In these cases, cluster sampling might provide a feasible solution.

In cluster sampling, a random sample of a larger unit is taken; in this case, the schools in which first through seventh graders are enrolled. This random sampling can be simple, systematic, or stratified. In the afterschool program example, you use simple random sampling to select four schools. Then a random sample (again, either simple, systematic, or stratified) of the first through seventh grades in these four schools would be selected (Figure 8.3). Alternatively, if a student list is not available, all first through seventh graders in the four schools would be included in the final sample.

Cluster sampling can be useful in an agency setting, for example when an agency serves a large number of clients over a yearly period (for example, 8,000 clients are referred). Instead of randomly selecting from this large sampling frame, three months (every fourth month) may be systematically randomly sampled from the year, and the clients referred during those three months included in the sample. Each month represents a cluster.

Cluster sampling has one potential problem. When a small number of units is sampled (for example, four schools), there is greater probability of sampling

Cluster Sampling

Biggerstaff, Morris, and Nichols-Casebolt (2002) studied people receiving food assistance services from food pantries and soup kitchens in Virginia. This study of emergency food program participants includes two years of data collection and analysis. A cluster sampling was used to select a sample of individuals who use Virginia's food pantries and soup kitchens. In the first stage of sampling, seven regional food banks produced a list of all food pantries and soup kitchens they served ($N = 2,000$). Then a random sample of the medium to large pantries and kitchens was taken in each of the seven areas. The data revealed that a significant number of individuals and families are seeking assistance from food pantries and soup kitchens. Another noteworthy discovery of the study was that fewer than 40% of respondents received food stamps. The study yielded recommendations and suggestions for future social work interventions to address food security.

error. The four schools may consist of three white middle-class schools, whereas the students' population (in ten schools) is a 50-50 mix socioeconomically. Consequently, the sample would be biased in favor of white middle-class students, and other groups would be underrepresented.

Nonprobability or Purposive Sampling

Purposive sampling allows the researcher to intentionally select those elements that are information rich, which makes it the sampling method of choice in qualitative studies. In the afterschool program example, you may decide you are more interested in learning about the problems and experiences of families who need afterschool care rather than finding out the proportion of families who are in need of afterschool care services.

There are a number of different types of purposive sampling methods. Described here are eight of the most commonly used in social work: typical case, criterion sampling, focus groups, key informants, community forum, quota, snowball, and availability. See Table 8.2 for the different types of purposive sampling methods.

Typical Cases

Typical case sampling is often used as a method of purposive sampling. Typical cases are sought using the literature, previous research, or consultation with relevant groups. For the afterschool program example, families who appear typical in their need for services would be contacted through a local agency or the schools.

Criterion Sampling

Criterion sampling involves picking all cases that meet some criterion—for example, including all families in an agency who meet eligibility criteria to receive services from that agency.

A Typical Case

Ensign (2000) purposely selected a group of homeless adol
the larger homeless population in Seattle, Washington, for
was designed to elicit perspectives of homeless adolescent fe
to health issues, self-care, and fertility control, in addition to lessons learned from
being homeless. Using semistructured interviews and focus groups, Ensign cap-
tured the voices of female youth ages 15–23 years of age. From the interviews, it
was revealed that the youths in this study faced female-specific health issues such
as sexual exploitation and problems with hygiene. Additionally, most participants
related stories of other female youth who had attempted self-induced abortions
through drugs, herbs, and physical abuse. Ensign suggested that health care
providers receive additional training to address issues such as survival sex and
self-induced abortions.

Table 8.2   **Purposive or nonprobability sampling methods**

Method	Characteristics
Typical cases	Those with "typical" characteristics
Criterion	Participants selected according to some eligibility criteria
Focus groups	Those with an interest in the research topic
Key informants	Those with expertise on the research topic
Community forum	Open to a community; some can be purposively invited
Quota	Certain proportions of participants from different groups selected according to specific characteristics
Snowball	Some participants identified; these participants then identify others with certain characteristics
Availability	Those selected because they are available

Focus Groups

Focus groups were discussed in Chapter 3 as a means of helping to formulate a
question and will be discussed further in Chapter 9 as a source of data collection.
Focus groups are picked purposefully—those invited have some type of interest
or expertise in the topic under study. Focus groups are also an excellent way of
ensuring maximum participation and involvement by the community and by
those on whom the research will have the most impact.

Key Informant Sampling

Key informant sampling relies on people in the community identified as
experts in the field of interest.

Pharmasut

Criterion Sampling

Hughes (1997) studied young adult black and Latino males who had been previously involved in crimes, but who were more recently making positive behavioral changes. The author wanted to know what factors facilitated their decisions to make the positive changes. The criteria applied to the sample included: (1) male between the ages of 18 and 28; (2) history of destructive behavior; (3) evidence of effort(s) to make positive life changes; and (4) evidence of positive involvement in the community. Twenty young adult inner city males made up the sample of this exploratory study. Findings indicated that fatherhood was a primary factor in facilitating positive behavioral changes among the young men.

Focus Groups

Linhorst, Hamilton, Young, and Eckert (2002) used the means of focus groups with clients and staff of a public psychiatric hospital to help determine potential barriers to empowerment in treatment planning. Additionally, this study sought to identify conditions necessary for client empowerment in the treatment planning. Between October and December 1998, the researchers conducted focus groups with 17 groups of clients and 15 groups of staff. A moderator used a semistructured interview schedule while leading the focus group discussions. Staff members were not present during the focus group with clients to help increase openness and enhance validity. Findings showed that to achieve empowerment, clients must be psychiatrically stable and able to utilize decision making skills. In addition, findings reflected a need for organizations to promote empowerment by allowing staff enough time to involve clients in treatment planning, providing clients with a range of treatment options, and by designing programs with a strong philosophical commitment to client empowerment.

Community Forum

The **community forum** involves publicizing a meeting or series of meetings at which individuals are briefed on the issues and then asked for input.

Quota Sampling

Quota sampling involves a certain proportion of elements with specific characteristics to be purposively included in the sample. In some respects, quota sampling is similar to stratified random sampling, except that no randomness is involved in selecting the elements. When examining the experiences of families

Key Informants

Artz (1998) used six key informants in her research on violence among teenage girls. All of the informants, identified both as victims and perpetrators of violence, wanted "to do something about violence." The girls' presentations of themselves revealed that they have negative notions of the self and that they believe that women achieve their greatest importance by commanding the attention of men.

A Community Forum

Delgado (1997) reports on the use of a community forum among Puerto Rican elderly to help interpret results of a survey. After responding to a survey examining how ethnicity and social class impact on the disability level and receipt of care among elderly Puerto Ricans in Springfield, a community forum was held. The forum addressed five questions that emerged from the surveys and a specific format was utilized in addressing the questions. This included four parts: (1) a statement of the question posed to elders attending the forum, (2) presentation of the rationale for each question, (3) elder responses at the forum, and (4) consideration of these responses in relation to insights derived from focus groups and key informant interviews. Researchers found the community forum to be invaluable in interpreting the quantitative survey data. The forum participants' responses served as recommendations to develop culturally based constructs for practice with other Latino groups.

with unattended school-age children in a qualitative study, you might be interested in ensuring that you interviewed families from all ethnic groups in the community. Like stratified random sampling, quota sampling requires that you know the proportion of these ethnic groups in the population. The problems associated with this form of sampling, as with stratified random sampling, are that the researcher needs to be sure that the categories or variables selected are important ones and that the proportions of these variables are known in the population. It may be that ethnicity is not a key variable that needs to be included.

Snowball Sampling

Snowball sampling involves identifying some members of the population and then having those individuals contact others in the population. This is a useful strategy to adopt with less accessible populations, for example, the homeless, although it could also be used with the example of families whose children

Quota Sampling

G. D. Johnson et al. (1998) used quota sampling to conduct research on stress and distress among shrimp fishermen in 34 fishing communities along the Gulf of Mexico. "Ports were selected and interview quotas established based on total shrimp landings for the years 1991 through 1993 as reported by the National Marine Fisheries Service" (p. 408). Data were collected from face-to-face interviews with 577 shrimp boat captains. The interviews transpired at ports in all the U.S. Gulf states. G. D. Johnson et al. noted from previous research that shrimp fishing is challenging work which often involves stressors such as work overload, safety issues, and separation from family. The dependent variable of this study included the presence or absence of a diagnosable mental health issue. Results of the study indicated that stressor variables such as work overload and conflict with coworkers can predict a diagnosable disorder.

Snowball Sampling

Prindeville (2002) used a snowball sampling technique to identify participants for a study examining the similarities and differences among grassroots women leaders and women in public office. Sixty political leaders, including 26 indigenous women, 24 Hispanas, 6 Euro-American women, and 4 African-American women participated in this study. The sample of women was established through the snowball technique in which participants identified other women active in New Mexico politics to be included in the study. Prindeville used a semistructured interview style to conduct personal interviews. The interview format of open-ended questions provided the participants with the opportunity to share experiences, thus affording a "rich profile of each of the leaders" (p. 67).

are unsupervised after school. You might identify and contact a few families and then ask them to contact others who they think are having problems.

Availability Sampling

Availability or **convenience sampling** is used extensively in social work research and involves including available or convenient elements in the sample. Sometimes availability sampling is confused with random sampling because superficially it appears random. A typical example of availability sampling is interviewing people in a shopping mall in an attempt to get a sample of the community. Alternately, in an agency you are asked to conduct a program evaluation. The funds for the evaluation are available now, and you have two months

Availability Sampling

Lindsey (1998) mailed surveys to an availability sample of directors of 165 homeless and domestic violence shelters in two southern states. The response rate was 54%. The author wanted to know the directors' perceptions about what helped or hindered homeless, mother-headed families to emerge from homelessness. Respondents believed that mothers' attitudes and motivation were the most important factors in helping their emergence from homelessness, while lack of social supports and relationship difficulties were those problems that hindered emergence the most. Scarce housing within the community was also identified as a factor that hindered the families emerging from homelessness.

to collect the data. Consequently, you decide to include in your sample clients referred to the program during the next 30 days. The population under study is all those referred to the program.

Research findings from availability samples cannot be generalized to the population under study. In the shopping mall example, you are going to be able to include in your sample only people who shop at the mall—maybe a small and unrepresentative sample of the community as a whole. In the program evaluation example, the clients referred to the agency in the month of the sampling may be different from clients referred at other times of the year; December may not be a representative month of the entire year. Consequently, the sample is biased, making it difficult to generalize results to the entire community. Availability sampling is also problematic in that it does not possess the advantages of a purposive sampling method. The elements are not picked for their information richness, but selected on the basis of convenience. Availability samples, however, often present the only feasible way of sampling.

Availability sampling is often the sampling method to use when evaluating your own practice. One case or more is selected and the effectiveness of the intervention assessed. This type of research was discussed in more detail in Chapter 7.

Studying Complete Populations

Sometimes, particularly when conducting program evaluations, it is possible to study the entire population rather than a sample. For example, you could define the population in such a way that you can include all the elements in that population in your study. If the program is relatively small, all the clients served during a certain period (say, six months) could be defined as the population, and all could be studied. (Remember, the definition of the population is in part up to you.) Or if the program is new, it might be quite feasible to study the entire population—namely, all who have been served since the program's inception. It is also possible to study the entire population if the population is quite specific—for example, children with Down's syndrome in a medium-sized city.

Studying an Entire Population

Garcia and Floyd (2002) used nationwide data to examine the mechanisms by which schools of social work assess educational outcomes in addition to how they integrate evaluation data into each respective MSW program and in curriculum development. To study the entire population of accredited MSW programs, the researchers mailed surveys to the 139 MSW programs listed by the Council of Social Work Education (CSWE). The research demonstrated that resources to support program assessment efforts are inadequate and in need of attention.

SAMPLE SIZE

Statisticians devote a considerable amount of energy to determining the size of samples. Some of the kinds of research that generalist social workers usually conduct, such as program or practice evaluations, do not require you to make a decision about sample size because the sample is fixed—namely, a small program or your own practice.

The size of the sample in part depends on its homogeneity, or on the similarity among different elements. If you can be assured that the characteristics of the sample elements are similar on the dimensions you are interested in studying, then the sample can be smaller. In the example of unsupervised children, if all the children are similar in the characteristics in which you are interested—ethnicity, socioeconomic status, and family configuration—then the sample size can be small. If, however, you are interested in comparing the afterschool program needs of different types of families—for example, across family configuration, income, and so on—then you would probably need a larger sample to ensure that you have enough subjects in each category. As we saw in Chapter 3, a minimal number of cases are required in each category to do statistical analyses.

The size of the sample also depends on the research approach used. In quantitative studies using probability samples, sample sizes usually need to be quite large, whereas in interpretive studies the sample size is small, and it is the information richness of the cases that is important. In qualitative studies the size of the sample is no larger than that needed to gather the information of interest.

Also important to consider when deciding on sample size is the issue of sampling error. **Sampling error** is the extent to which the values of the sample differ from those of the population. The **margin of error** refers to the precision needed by the researcher. A margin of error of 5% means the actual findings could vary in either direction by as much as 5%. For example, a client satisfaction survey that finds 55% of clients were "very satisfied" could have actual results anywhere from 50% to 60%. If the sample is large enough, the sampling error and margin of error can be reduced. With 100 tosses of a coin, you are more

Table 8.3   **Size of sample required at 5% margin of error**

Population size	Sample size
50	44
75	63
100	80
150	108
200	132
250	152
300	169
400	196
500	217
750	254
1,000	278
2,000	322
4,000	351
5,000	357
10,000	370
15,000	375
20,000	377
25,000	378
50,000	381
100,000	384
1,000,000	384

Source: From *Educational and Psychological Measurement,* by R. V. Krejcie and D. W. Morgan, pp. 607–610. Copyright © 1970 Sage Publications, Inc. Reprinted by permission of Sage Publications, Inc.

likely to end up with 50% heads and 50% tails than you are with 20 tosses. In reporting the results of large-scale surveys, it is important to report the extent of sampling error.

A number of quite complicated formulas can assist in determining sample size. If you have concerns about the size of your sample, consult with a statistician or refer to a good statistics text.

Table 8.3 gives different sample sizes and their associated margin of error. The margin of error reported in this table is 5%. This means that the actual findings could vary as much as 5% either positively or negatively. Another way to view this is to state that the findings, using the sample sizes in the table, have a 95% **confidence level**, which expresses how often you would expect similar results if the research were repeated. For example, in a sample with a 95% confidence level (or alternatively stated, a 5% margin of error), the findings could be expected to miss the actual values in the population by more than 5%, only 5 times in 100 surveys. Use the table as a guide and not as a strict formula for sample size determination.

A final consideration when deciding on the sample size is to recognize that sample size can have an impact on statistical analysis. This will be discussed more in Chapter 12. Very briefly, the smaller the sample the more likely statistical analysis will yield positive results. This in turn then influences the generalizability of the results. Findings from a large sample are more able to be generalized to the wider population.

THE AGENCY AND SAMPLING

As generalist social workers engaging in research, you may need to use sampling methods that are not textbook examples. Two cases of these modifications are discussed in this section: limited probability sampling and combined sampling methods.

Often, an integral part of a needs assessment is the ability to generalize the findings to an entire community, county, or larger area. Unfortunately, it is often not possible to obtain representative samples because of most agencies' time and money constraints. Sometimes, however, it is possible to obtain a **limited probability sample**—for example, from a neighborhood or agency—and then compare the characteristics of this sample with the characteristics of a sample drawn from a larger population. In this way, some tentative generalizations of the findings can be made. Sometimes similarities are not found between the smaller and larger samples. This method of expanding generalizations suffers from some problems similar to those of stratified random sampling: the assumption that we know what the important characteristics are when comparing a smaller sample with a larger sample. Consequently, this method should be used with caution.

Another often-needed modification of sampling is to combine sampling methods. Sometimes practical constraints do not allow you to proceed with the type of sampling planned; it may be possible to sample one group using a planned method but not another group.

ETHICAL ISSUES IN SAMPLING

Two ethical issues relate to sampling: first, responsible reporting of the sampling method and, second, obtaining the subject's consent to the research.

Combined Sampling Methods

In an effort to study ways to prevent risky sexual behavior, Lackey and Moberg (1998) conducted focus groups and face-to-face survey interviews with youth and parents. The focus groups consisted of 6–10 participants drawn from area community centers, while the cross-sectional survey comprised 593 youth and 95 parents. The latter interviews were completed in the participants' homes. Analysis of the qualitative and quantitative data suggested that sexual meanings and practices are embedded in popular culture and various subculture environments, thus bombarding teens with an over-glamorized view of sex. This study offers important insight into cultural influences on youth sexual activity and particularly in the development of youth sexual activity prevention programs.

Reporting the Sampling Method

It is the researcher's responsibility when reporting research findings—whether in a journal article, a report, or a presentation—to ensure that the research methods used in the study are described as accurately as possible. Details of reporting will be described in Chapter 13. Some discussion is necessary here, however, because inaccuracies and ambiguities in research reports often concern the sampling method.

Sometimes authors write about supposedly random methods of sampling that are really availability or some other form of nonprobability sampling. In reading reports and articles, look for an explicit description of the sampling method along with a frank description of the generalization limitations, particularly if a nonprobability sampling method was used. It is unethical to claim even implicitly that the results of a nonprobability sample are generalizable to a wider population. Such a claim is misleading and can have some serious negative implications. As discussed earlier in this chapter, nonprobability and probability sampling methods have different purposes.

Informed Consent

Whenever any type of social work research is undertaken, it is critical that no coercion is exerted and that subjects voluntarily agree to participate. The subjects or participants must always be told about the purpose and goals of the research. As discussed in Chapter 6, voluntary, informed consent should always be obtained from the participants. Fortunately, the researcher is assisted in the process of gaining informed consent by the existence of Institutional Review Boards (IRBs). All organizations that do research and receive federal funds are required to have an IRB that reviews the procedures adopted in the treatment of human subjects and protects the participants from harm. The IRBs provide guidelines that the researcher should follow and information that needs to be included in a consent form. IRBs will be discussed further in Chapter 9.

Many organizations that support a large number of research studies, for example the National Institutes of Health, have specific guidelines for the content of consent documents. These guidelines include:

- A statement that the study involves research
- An explanation of the purpose of the research, an invitation to participate, an explanation of why the participant was selected, and the expected duration of the participation
- A description of the procedures to be followed and the use of randomization and placebos explained
- A description of any foreseeable risks or discomforts to the participants and the steps to be taken to minimize these
- A description of any benefits to the participant
- A disclosure of any appropriate alternative procedures that might be advantageous to the participant
- A statement describing the extent to which the records will be confidential
- For research involving more than minimal risk, an explanation of any compensations or medical treatments available
- An explanation of whom to contact for questions about the research
- A statement that participation is voluntary and that there will be no penalties for declining to participate
- A statement indicating that the participant is making a decision whether or not to participate

(National Institutes of Health, 2002).

Figure 8.4 is an example of a consent form. Cover letters used in mailed questionnaires, which are discussed in Chapter 9, often also include content on informed consent.

Many ethical guidelines present dilemmas. You may feel that by disclosing information about the research project to the participant, you will jeopardize the research results. For example, if you are using observation to collect data about a specific behavior and if participants know they are being observed, their behavior might change considerably. Another problem arises when you inform participants that their involvement in the research is voluntary: A certain number may choose not to participate. The researcher then does not know whether the results from the participants who agreed to participate are different from those who declined.

Sometimes—and these times are *not* frequent—the voluntary participation ethical standard may need to be modified. If this is necessary, you must clearly understand and explain the reasons. In particular, you must be careful that researchers do not use their power or authority to exploit the participants. Suppose a professor who is carrying out research on students' experiences of sexual harassment requests that all the students in her class complete a questionnaire that she estimates will take about 15 minutes. She states that participation is voluntary, but those who choose not to participate will be required to write a

---

THOUGHTS AND FEELINGS OF TEENAGE MOTHERS WHO HAVE HAD PREMATURE INFANTS
CONSENT FORM

PRINCIPAL INVESTIGATOR:
Dr. John Doe
Associate Professor, Department of Psychology
NEW MEXICO STATE UNIVERSITY
(505) 646-XXXX

DESCRIPTION:
I am interested in the thoughts and feelings of teenage mothers of premature infants. You, as the mother of a newborn premature infant, are the best person to describe these thoughts and feelings. This research study will involve one or two interviews with you, each lasting approximately 30 minutes. The interviews will be audio taped using a micro cassette recorder. The tapes will be typed out as word-for-word transcripts of the interviews. The tapes will then be erased.

CONFIDENTIALITY:
Your name will not be attached to your interview responses. Your name and any other identifiers will be kept in a locked file that is only accessible to me or my research associates. Any information from this study that is published will not identify you by name.

BENEFITS:
The results of this study may benefit other teenage mothers of premature infants by influencing the health care they receive. There will be no direct benefit to you from participating in this study.

RISKS:
It is possible that the discussion of thoughts or feelings about the birth of your baby might make you feel sad or uncomfortable. However, there are no other known risks to you.

CONTACT PEOPLE:
If you have any questions about this research, please contact the Principal Investigator at the phone number listed above. If you have any questions about your rights as a research subject, please contact the Office of the Vice Provost for Research at New Mexico State University at (505) 646-0000.

VOLUNTARY NATURE OF PARTICIPATION:
Your participation in this study is voluntary. If you don't wish to participate, or would like to end your participation in this study, there will be no penalty or loss of benefits to you to which you are otherwise entitled. In other words, you are free to make your own choice about being in this study or not, and may quit at any time without penalty.

SIGNATURE:
Your signature on this consent form indicates that you fully understand the above study, what is being asked of you in this study, and that you are signing this voluntarily. If you have any questions about this study, please feel free to ask them now or at any time throughout the study.

Signature _____

Date _____

A copy of this consent form is available for you to keep.

Site Sathis

Figure 8.4   ***A form for obtaining participants' informed consent***

five-page research paper. This clearly would be a form of coercion, with the professor using her authority to force participation. A similar situation can be envisioned with a social work researcher requiring the participation of individuals who are dependent upon the social worker for services. The decision to forgo the participant's consent must be carefully considered to ensure that no blatant coercion is occurring.

Another way of viewing the issue of the subject's consent is to modify our perspective on the distinction between researcher and participant. The relationship between researcher and participant can be seen as egalitarian rather than viewed, as it has been traditionally, as a relationship in which researchers wield power and authority over subjects. When an even footing is adopted, the question of the participant's consent becomes a nonissue. Instead, researchers make their research skills accessible to participants, participants become active contributors in the research, and both gain from being involved. Emphasizing the egalitarian relationship between researcher and participant is one way of incorporating this connectedness into research methodology. This type of relationship can be created by using sampling methods such as the key informant, the focus group, and the community forum, in all of which community members have an opportunity to serve both as participants and as contributors. An egalitarian relationship between researcher and participant is a characteristic of participatory research, as discussed in previous chapters.

When evaluating individual practice, the way the research is presented to the client is important and can affect the researcher-participant relationship. If you present the research as something special, different, or separate from practice, then the client will see it that way and often resist being involved (or used) in a research project. But if you stress the integration between research and practice and point out how the client will benefit from feedback on the relative effectiveness of the intervention, then you will be more accurately depicting the whole idea of evaluating practice. In addition, you will be engaging in a true partnership with the client, benefiting all involved.

Breaking down the distinction between researcher and participant has other advantages apart from the issue of the participant's consent. First, it addresses the concern that research is not always responsive to the needs of oppressed groups. When a partnership between researcher and participant is created, responsiveness is more assured. Second, the validity of the research may be enhanced.

The more traditional relationship between researcher and participant, which emphasizes separateness, may result in a greater likelihood of the participant's giving invalid responses out of a lack of understanding of the researcher's intent. This problem is avoided by building the partnership. Third, this approach seems to be particularly compatible to social work practice, where emphasis is placed on establishing a relationship with the client.

Creating an egalitarian relationship between participant and researcher thus seems a reasonable approach to adopt and one that offers several advantages. As a final note, however, we should add that in practice an egalitarian relationship can sometimes be difficult to achieve. Srinivasan and Davis (1991) commented on this in an article reporting on the organization of a women's shelter. This study, incidentally, is a good example of the application of feminist research principles. In the article Davis states:

> Although my intent was to establish egalitarian relationships with all participants in the study, I was not always successful in this regard. The staff readily accepted and treated me as another volunteer, but the residents had more difficulty accepting me as an equal. The residents were skeptical about why I was there. (p. 41)

HUMAN DIVERSITY ISSUES IN SAMPLING

Unfortunately, the social science literature prior to the early 1970s does not provide many examples of studies with heterogeneous samples. For example, Holmes and Jorgensen (1971) found that subjects were males twice as often as females, a ratio even higher than the ratio of college student subjects to noncollege student subjects. In addition to these samples being homogeneous, they were generalized to the population as a whole—populations that included noncollege graduates, women, and other underrepresented groups. These generalizations should never be made because the samples simply were not representative of the populations.

A classic example of this problem is presented by Kohlberg's study of the development of morality. In his initial study, he selected a sample of Harvard male graduates (1969). Based on this study, Kohlberg developed a model and theory of moral development that he used as a template to assess the moral development of *all* individuals. Moreover, as a result of applying this model to women, he concluded that women often did not reach the higher level of moral development and were, therefore, deficient morally. Later, Gilligan (1977) challenged these conclusions and studied moral development in a sample of women. She proposed alternative moral developmental stages for women, concluding that women were not deviant or deficient in their moral development but simply followed a different course.

Similar assumptions and erroneous generalizations have been made relating to minority populations. White middle-class samples have been studied, and the findings have been generalized and presented as the norm by which to evaluate minorities. Such improper generalizations are not always made by the researchers themselves but by others who draw assumptions from the findings and apply them to other groups.

Historically, such generalizations have been made about the effectiveness of social programs. If a program is demonstrated to be ineffective with an underrepresented urban sample, it may be concluded that consequently the program would be ineffective with all underrepresented groups. It is critical that we recognize diversity within different groups. Program ineffectiveness with some urban groups does not mean program ineffectiveness with other groups or with rural communities.

The danger of improper generalizations can in part be avoided if research consumers enhance their knowledge. This includes you! Researchers, as discussed in the previous section, can also help by being explicit about the limitations of their sampling method. It is often easier, however, to be critical of existing studies than to avoid such pitfalls in our own research. The erroneous assumptions that Kohlberg made seem almost obvious now, but that is because we have an increased sensitivity to gender issues. Additionally, there is an increasing awareness of ethnic and racial diversity when applying research methods. Be cautioned that other dimensions of diversity are less evident. For example, ageism and homophobia are still pervasive in our culture, even among social workers. Diversity issues in sampling go beyond consciously including or excluding a particular group.

Recognizing Diversity Within Groups

According to Deren et al. (1997), while Hispanics are overrepresented in AIDS cases in the United States, there is a dearth of information regarding the potential differences in drug and sex risk behavior among Hispanic subgroups. Thus, Deren et al. conducted a study on HIV-related risk behaviors among three groups of female Hispanic prostitutes in the United States in an effort to produce findings needed to develop culturally appropriate prevention programs. These subgroups included 77 Dominican women recruited in Washington Heights, NY; 151 Mexican women recruited in El Paso, TX; and 48 Puerto Rican women recruited in East Harlem, NY. Ethnographic interviews were conducted with a subgroup of participants to examine the cultural meaning of risk behaviors, and structured interviews with other participants were conducted to describe demographic characteristics and levels of behaviors. The results reflect a need for prevention efforts and interventions to be based on knowledge of differences related to geographic and cultural factors.

Gender in Sampling

Carpenter and Platt (1997) studied the impacts of the changing health care delivery system on the professional identity of clinical social workers, specifically the fit between personal and professional values. Acknowledging past research, which has used predominantly female samples, the authors in this study obtained a sample with equal numbers of male and female social workers. The findings clarified that there were no gender differences in the description of values. The sense of strain between the two values varied according to workplace setting.

SUMMARY

Key concepts in sampling are representativeness, generalizability, and information richness. The two different types of sampling strategies are probability and purposive methods. Probability sampling includes simple random sampling, systematic random sampling, stratified random sampling, and cluster sampling. Purposive sampling includes typical case, criterion sampling, focus groups, key informants, community forum, quota sampling, snowball sampling, and availability sampling.

When conducting sampling in an agency, sampling methods may need to be modified. Ethical issues include accurate reporting of the sampling method and the subject's consent. Human diversity issues relate to whether the sampling represents diverse populations adequately.

STUDY/EXERCISE QUESTIONS

1. A local agency has asked you to help them conduct a survey to determine whether the city needs an elder day care facility. The population of the city is 65,000. About 20% of the city's population lives below the poverty level. All persons over the age of 60 would be eligible for the center.

    a. Define the population.

    b. Will probability sampling be possible? If not, why not? If so, what method would you use?

    c. Discuss the pros and cons of each of the following suggestions made by various members of the board of the agency:

        (i) Interview elders who frequent the local shopping mall early in the morning for exercise.

        (ii) Mail questionnaires to members of the local branch of the American Association of Retired Persons (AARP).

        (iii) Conduct a telephone interview using the telephone directory as a sampling frame.

2. Review an issue of *Social Work,* and answer these questions about the research articles.

    a. What was the sampling method used?

    b. What are the limitations with each of the sampling methods?

    c. Were these limitations made explicit in the articles?

INFOTRAC COLLEGE EDITION

1. Search for a research study on gays and lesbians and describe the sampling approach used. Was there any discussion in the study about the consent of the participants?

2. Search for *random sampling*. According to these articles, what are some of the difficulties of implementing random sampling?

REFERENCES

Artz, S. (1998). Where have all the school girls gone? Violent girls in the school yard. *Child & Youth Care Forum, 27* (2), 77–109.

Biggerstaff, M. A., Morris, P. M., & Nichols-Casebolt, A. (2002). Living on the edge: Examination of people attending food pantries and soup kitchens. *Social Work, 47* (3), 267–278.

Carpenter, M. C., & Platt, S. (1997). Professional identity for clinical social workers: Impact of changes in health care delivery systems. *Clinical Social Work Journal, 25* (3), 337–350.

Delgado, M. (1997). Interpretation of Puerto Rican elder research findings: A community forum of research respondents. *Journal of Applied Gerontology, 16* (3), 317–332.

Deren, S., Shedlin, M., Davis, W. R., Balcorta, S., Beardsley, M. M., Sanchez, J., Jarlais, D. D., & Clatts, M. C. (1997). Dominican, Mexican, and Puerto Rican prostitutes: Drug use and sexual behaviors. *Hispanic Journal of Behavioral Sciences, 19* (2), 202–214.

Ensign, J. (2000). Reproductive health of homeless adolescent women in Seattle, Washington, USA. *Women & Health, 31* (2/3), 133–151.

Garcia, J. A., & Floyd, C. E. (2002). Addressing evaluative standards related to program assessment: How do we respond? *Journal of Social Work Education, 38* (3), 369–383.

Gilligan, C. (1977). In a different voice: Women's conceptions of self and of morality. *Harvard Educational Review, 47,* 481–512.

Holmes, D. S., & Jorgensen, B. W. (1971). The personality and social psychologists study men more than women. *Representative Research in Social Psychology, 2,* 71–76.

Hughes, M. J. (1997). An exploratory study of young adult black and Latino males and the factors facilitating their decisions to make positive behavioral changes. *Smith College Studies in Social Work, 67* (3), 401–414.

Johnson, G. D., Formichella, C., Thomas, J. S., Bhaumik, D., Degruy, F. V., Riordan, C. A. (1998). Stress and distress among Gulf of Mexico shrimp fishermen. *Human Organization, 57* (4), 404–410.

Johnson, H. C., Renaud, E. F., Schmidt, D. T., & Stanek, E. J. (1998). Social workers' views of parents of children with mental and emotional disabilities. *Families in Society, 79* (2), 173–187.

Kohlberg, L. (1969). *Stages in the development of moral thought and action.* New York: Holt, Rinehart & Winston.

Lackey, J. F., & Moberg, D. P. (1998). Understanding the onset of intercourse among Urban American Adolescents: A cultural process framework using qualitative and quantitative data. *Human Organization, 57* (4), 491–501.

Lindsey, E. W. (1998). Service providers' perception of factors that help or hinder homeless families. *Familes in Society, 79* (2), 160–172.

Linhorst, D. M., Hamilton, G., Young, E., & Eckert, A. (2002). Opportunities and barriers to empowering people with severe mental illness through participation in treatment planning. *Social Work, 47* (4), 425–435.

National Institutes of Health, U.S. Department of Health and Human Services (2002). *Human participant protections education for research teams.* Washington, DC: NIH.

Prindeville, D. M. (2002). A comparative study of Native American and Hispanic women in grassroots and electoral politics. *Frontiers, 23* (1), 67–91.

Rittner, B., & Dozier, C. D. (2000). Effects of court ordered substance abuse treatment in child protective services cases. *Social Work, 45* (2), 131–140.

Srinivasan, M., & Davis, L. V. (1991). A shelter: An organization like any other. *Affilia, 6* (1), 38–57.

Zimmerman, R. K., Mieczkowski, T. A., Mainzer, H. M., Medsger, A. R., Raymund, M., Ball, J. A., & Jewell, I. K. (2001). Effect of the vaccines for children program on physician referral of children to public vaccine clinics: A pre-post comparison. *Pediatrics, 108* (2), 297–308.

Leslie Parr

Collecting the Data

■

ow that you have decided on the research design and the way participants will be selected, you need to decide how you will gather the information or data. Do you go out and interview people directly? Do you use forms and questionnaires to collect information, or do you need to observe?

In generalist practice, you must also decide how information will be collected, after defining and conceptualizing the problem. This information is referred to in both practice and in research as **data** (singular **datum**), and they are collected using a **measuring instrument**, or data collection method. These methods include questionnaires, observation, logs and journals, interviews, scales, and secondary data. All these will be described in this chapter.

As a generalist social worker, you may or may not be the person who collects the data. The data collection plan and perhaps even the data collection itself may have already been implemented. Even if you don't direct the collection of the data, and certainly if you are responsible for collecting the data, you will need to know what instruments are used and under what circumstances.

This chapter will include a discussion of the following topics:

- quantitative and qualitative data
- ways of collecting data
- who collects the data
- combining data collection methods
- determining reliability and validity
- the agency and data collection
- ethical issues in collecting data
- human diversity issues in collecting data

QUANTITATIVE AND QUALITATIVE DATA

As discussed in Chapter 1, the positivist and interpretist approaches tend to involve the collection of different types of data. The former emphasizes the collection of quantitative data, hence the term *quantitative*, and with the latter the emphasis is on qualitative data, hence the term *qualitative*. Strictly speaking, though, *quantitative* and *qualitative* refer to the type of data rather than to an entire research approach. Sometimes studies using the positivist/quantitative approach will collect partly or completely qualitative data, and sometimes the interpretist/qualitative approach will involve the collection of some quantitative data. So using the data collection type to describe the entire research approach can be misleading. The correct distinction between the two research approaches is that the positivist/quantitative approach uses a more deductive method of knowledge building, whereas the interpretist/qualitative approach adopts more of an inductive strategy.

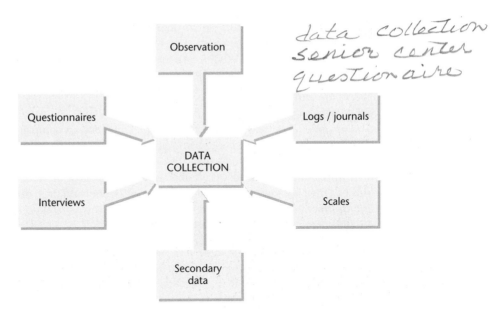

data collection
senior center
questionaire

Figure 9.1   **Methods of data collection**

WAYS OF COLLECTING DATA

Six major methods of collecting data, or measuring instruments, will be described in this section (see Figure 9.1): interviews, questionnaires, observation techniques, logs and journals, scales, and secondary data. All these methods can include both qualitative and quantitative data, except logs and journals, which are generally qualitative, and scales which are quantitative.

At this point, note that you can either construct your own data collection instrument using one or more of the methods listed here, or use an already existing measure. Whenever possible, use an existing measure, particularly if it is standardized. A standardized instrument is uniform throughout. It includes items uniformly administered and scored according to an agreed-upon procedure. A standardized instrument is convenient to use and has established reliability and validity, two measurement concepts discussed at the end of this chapter.

As they are described, each of the six methods will be assessed for **neutrality** and **applicability**. Patton (2001) proposed the term *neutrality* as an alternative to either *objectivity* or *subjectivity*. Objectivity is one of the central premises of the quantitative approach. As discussed in Chapter 1, however, objectivity is virtually impossible to achieve, and even the quantitative researcher admits it is a problematic term. Qualitative research is more concerned with the subjective experiences of the subjects in the study. *Subjective*, however, is also a problematic term, with negative connotations implying bias

A Structured Interview

Caetano and Raspberry (2000) conducted structured interviews with a sample of 250 whites and 250 Mexican Americans admitted to a DUI treatment program to obtain data on drinking patterns and DSM-IV alcohol and drug dependence among whites and Mexican Americans. Trained interviewers completed the interviews which averaged one hour in length. Results of the interviews indicated that while whites drank most frequently, followed by U.S.-born Mexican Americans, the amount of alcohol usually consumed is higher for Mexican Americans born in Mexico. The findings demonstrated that rates of alcohol and drug dependence in DUI treatment programs are higher than the rates in the general population. Additionally, among white, U.S.-born Mexican Americans, and Mexican Americans born in Mexico, patterns of alcohol consumption vary dramatically.

and relevance only to specific subjects. *Neutrality* appears to be a more useful term and is defined by Patton as characterizing research in which "the researcher does not seek out to prove a particular perspective or manipulate the data to arrive at predisposed truths" (p. 55).

Patton suggests adopting the term *empathetic neutrality* for the qualitative approach. Here, though, we maintain that *neutrality* is a useful term for both the quantitative and qualitative perspectives.

The other criterion by which the data collection methods will be discussed in the next section is applicability. The applicability of a measuring instrument is whether or not it is appropriate and suitable for a particular type of problem. For example, observation would typically not be a useful method to employ if we were collecting information on child abuse, but it would be suitable for collecting information on child behavior problems. Each data collection method will be described, along with a discussion of both its strengths and weaknesses in terms of neutrality and its relative applicability for the kinds of research questions we encounter as generalist social workers.

Interviews

As a generalist social work student, you are already quite skilled at conducting interviews. Interviews are structured, semistructured, or unstructured. Often the questions in all three types may be similar, but the interviews are distinguished based on how they are conducted.

Structured Interviews

In a **structured interview**, the interviewer knows in advance the questions to ask, and in many cases the interviewer is simply administering a verbal questionnaire. Often this questionnaire is already developed by agency workers.

A Semistructured Interview

Chermack et al. (2000) utilizes semistructured interviews to examine the gender differences of family history of alcoholism. The researchers compared family history of alcoholism with family history of violence on childhood conduct problems and on adult problems of alcohol, drugs, and violence. The participants included 110 men and 103 women identified as having alcohol-related problems. These participants were recruited within 30 days of entry into a treatment program for substance abuse dependence. Structural equation modeling analyses indicated that there are gender differences with regard to the influence of family history of alcoholism and family history of violence and how those factor into the development of childhood and adult behavior issues. The study clearly demonstrates that family history of violence is a significant risk factor for future problems with drugs and alcohol.

Semistructured Interviews

In a **semistructured** interview, the interviewer has more freedom to pursue hunches and can improvise with the questions. Semistructured interviews often use interview schedules consisting of the general types of questions to ask, but they are not in a questionnaire format. Sometimes semistructured interviews are referred to as open-ended interviews.

Unstructured Interviews

Completely **unstructured interviews** can also be used. This type of interview is similar to a conversation except that the interviewer and interviewee know that an interview is being conducted and that the interviewee is privy to information of interest to the interviewer.

Neutrality

Although structured and semistructured interviews are more neutral than unstructured interviews—because asking specific questions minimizes some bias—in general, the neutrality of interviewing is limited. We know that we respond differently to different people depending on how we are approached. The answer to an interviewer's question will be influenced by several factors: the interviewer's age, gender, ethnicity, and dress; the context in which the interviewer approaches the interviewee; the manner in which the interviewer speaks; and so forth. In addition, these characteristics will not have a constant effect on all the interviewees. Instead, each interviewee will respond differently to these characteristics depending on previous experiences, and there is no way of knowing exactly how these responses differ. This is referred to as the **reactive effect**: the interviewer influences the interviewee, and the interviewee responds in a particular way, which will then have a feedback effect on the interviewer. With the quantitative approach, the reactive effect can be a serious limitation and can jeopardize the data collection method's objectivity, which as you will remember is important when using the quantitative approach.

If you are using the qualitative approach, reactivity is not necessarily a problem, because the approach involves recognition that the relationship between the researcher and the subject exists and enhances the quality of the data and can even create the data. Using the interpretive/qualitative approach, the researcher and subject explore the topic together, each contributing to the process and each working in different ways.

Thus, when using the qualitative approach, you must acknowledge that objectivity will be lost. Neutrality is still important, however. In fact, qualitative researchers often state "up front" the type of relationship they strive for with their subjects. Gregg (1994) in her study of pregnancy stated:

> I continued (quite consciously) to refrain from developing friendships with the women during the course of the study, even though this sometimes seemed artificial and contrived. I did not want them to feel they had to continue with the study or to feel that they were obliged to reveal things to me out of loyalty or friendship . . . . When I ran into someone I had interviewed, we would say hello, I would ask her how she was, and we would go on. These encounters were awkward for me. (p. 55)

Some of the problems undermining the neutrality of interviews can be overcome by training the interviewers. They can be given an explicit protocol or format that they are required to follow. As a generalist social worker, you may be required to conduct interviews of this type. Also, audio recordings allow the interviews to be reviewed. Recordings can sometimes inhibit the interviewees, however, distorting their responses.

The advantage of interviews is that they allow ambiguous questions to be clarified. This opportunity does not exist when questionnaires are administered, particularly by mail. In those cases, the respondents interpret the question in their own way, which may be different from the intention of the researchers when they developed the questions.

Interviewing also has a positive effect on the **response rate**, the proportion of people who respond to the questions in either a questionnaire or interview. We have all been asked to participate in research—on the telephone, on the street, or through the mail. Sometimes we agree, and sometimes we refuse to participate.

For researchers, a problem arises when many people refuse to participate, because these people might turn out to be different from those who do. For example, if you send out 100 questionnaires asking about people's experiences of childhood sexual abuse, but only 25 people respond—all of whom state they were not abused as children—you have no way of knowing whether the nonrespondents were all abused and were reluctant to disclose this on their questionnaire, or were not abused and decided not to respond, or were distributed between abused and not abused. Because you do not know, you have to be cautious and assume that the results may well be biased. Interviews, however, generally obtain a high response rate. This is particularly true for face-to-face interviews, less so for telephone interviews.

Nevertheless, the high response rate of face-to-face interviews is not always assured. The response rate does not depend only on the method of data collection; other factors include the characteristics of the subjects, the purpose and nature of the research question or project, and the characteristics and training of those applying the data collection instruments.

One form of interviewing involves focus groups. These were described in Chapter 3 as a means of helping to develop the research question and in Chapter 8 as a sampling method; they can also be used as a way of collecting data.

Applicability

Interviewing may be preferred to other techniques in the following circumstances:

- You are interested in a high response rate.

- You want to gather in-depth information. Interviewing is one of the main methods for collecting qualitative data and is a key data collection method in many qualitative studies, where the focus is on collecting information that discloses the richness of the participant's, or informant's, experience.

- Anonymity is not of primary importance. If your research involves a sensitive issue—such as the incidence of spousal abuse in a community—and the community is relatively small, anonymity may be important, and interviewing would not be an appropriate data collection method. People are less reluctant to share such sensitive information with strangers.

- Time and money are of no great object. Interviews are time-consuming, particularly if you are interested in getting responses from a large geographic area. In addition, interviewers often need to be trained. Consequently, this data collection method is expensive. If the budget is low and the sample large, interviewing would not be the data collection method of choice.

- The respondent is not comfortable with writing or is illiterate.

Questionnaires

In general, questionnaires have many advantages that interviews do not have; at the same time, they lack the strengths of interviews. There are several types of questionnaires.

Mailed Questionnaires

Mailing questionnaires is a popular method of distributing questionnaires. Agencies often use this method to survey their clients as part of a program evaluation or needs assessment.

Face-to-Face Questionnaires

Face-to-face questionnaires may be administered much as structured interviews are. Structured interviews can be thought of as verbally administered questionnaires.

A Mailed Questionnaire

Fogel and Ellison (1998) mailed surveys to a random sample of 230 directors of field education at accredited social work programs to determine the prevalence of sexual harassment for B.S.W. students in their field settings. Reminder postcards were sent to those who did not respond within the previously requested three weeks. Eighty-eight surveys were returned, and responses indicated that sexual harassment in B.S.W. field settings is relatively common.

A Face-to-Face Questionnaire

Hines and Graves (1998) examined the behaviors related to AIDS protection and contraception among African-American, Hispanic, and white women. Trained interviewers collected the data through face-to-face interviews that took place in the respondents' homes. The respondents had the option of having the interview conducted in Spanish and were asked questions on AIDS-related behaviors and attitudes. The results indicated that during their most recent sexual encounter, a significant number of all the women and their partners did not use any form of protection.

Group Questionnaires

Group questionnaires are administered to groups. For example, if you are interested in getting feedback on a foster parent training session, you might administer questionnaires to the entire group at one time.

Bilingual Questionnaires

In many communities and with certain populations, **bilingual questionnaires** are essential.

Web Surveys

An increasingly popular method of conducting surveys using a questionnaire is with **Web surveys**. Although at this time they are used primarily for marketing and for specific member satisfaction and member needs assessments, they are likely to grow in use in the future, and will be used more often in social service settings. Web surveys offer a number of advantages in that they are easy to complete and submit, and the data can be automatically organized and analyzed. There is specific software available for the design and implementation of these surveys, and they include procedures for protecting the confidentiality of the respondents.

A Group Questionnaire

Greene, Causby, and Miller (1999) studied fusion, or the closeness of the relationship, in lesbians. They collected data from lesbians who attended a March on Washington for Lesbians and Gays. Surveys were distributed the morning of the march, and the researchers waited for the participants to complete them. A comparison group of heterosexual women from an introductory communication class completed the surveys outside of class in lieu of a short written assignment. The study showed no differences between lesbian and heterosexual women's levels of fusion, and it revealed that fusion was strongly related to satisfaction and dependence.

A Bilingual Questionnaire

Marx (1999) examined motivational characteristics associated with volunteering in the health and human services field. A face-to-face questionnaire was administered in English and when necessary in Spanish. The sample was derived from a representative national sample of 2,719 adult Americans. Marx found that volunteers in health and human services, as compared with other fields, volunteered to "gain a new perspective on things" and were more likely to be motivated by altruistic reasons. The author advises managers in social work to educate their volunteers about the broader significance of their assignments.

Neutrality

Questionnaires are relatively neutral. Interviewer bias is absent, and the responses are clear and usually unambiguous. The neutrality of the responses, however, depends a great deal on the care with which the questionnaire has been constructed. Ambiguities can be minimized by stating questions as clearly and simply as possible. For example, avoid questions containing double negatives, such as "Do you disapprove with the refusal to build a day care center in your neighborhood?" Also avoid double-barreled questions or two questions in one, such as "How many children under the age of 12 do you have, and do you have problems with child care?"

In addition, avoid leading and biased questions that indicate to the respondent the way in which you want the question answered. For example, "There is a great deal of community support for the new youth center; are you in favor of it?" Also, ask only questions respondents are capable of answering, in that they have some knowledge of the issue being researched. Try not to ask questions about future intentions; instead focus on the present. Finally, in an effort to maintain maximum neutrality, avoid response sets—in other words, don't phrase a series of questions in such a way that the answers will probably all be the same (for example, all yes or all no), because people tend to become set in a certain way of responding.

Just as interviews generally have high response rates, questionnaires—particularly those that are mailed—have low response rates. You can take some precautions to help improve the response rate, though. Such precautions include taking care with the questionnaire's directions, length, structure of the questions, content and order of the questions, format of the questionnaire, cover letter, and follow-up.

Directions   You need to give the respondents to the questionnaire clear directions. This is particularly important with mailed questionnaires. If you need a checkmark placed in a box, say so. If you need a sentence response, say so.

Length   Make the questionnaire as short as possible and eliminate unnecessary questions. When constructing a questionnaire, for each question ask yourself, "How is this question relevant to my research question?" If you cannot come up with a good answer, drop the question.

Structure of the Questions   Questions can be structured in two ways: closed-ended and open-ended. A **closed-ended question** gives the respondent a limited number of categories to use as answers. For example:

Name those who help you with child care:

> _____ parents
>
> _____ older children
>
> _____ other relatives
>
> _____ day care center
>
> _____ family day care/neighbor
>
> _____ friend
>
> _____ coworker
>
> _____ other

These are easy for the researcher to understand once the questionnaire is returned, but it is important to ensure that all possible categories are included for the respondent. Closed-ended questions result in quantitative data.

An **open-ended question** leaves it up to the respondent to create a response. No alternatives are given. For example:

*What kinds of improvements would you suggest the day care center make in this next year?*_____

Open-ended questions can be intimidating to respondents, and they may be put off by them, but this type of question ensures that respondents can answer in ways that accurately reflect their views—that is, they are not forced to respond using the researcher's categories. Open-ended questions are particularly useful when you do not know a great deal about the subject that you are investigating. They also provide a way of collecting qualitative data.

New Mexico State University
School of Social Work
MSC 3SW
Box 30001
Las Cruces, New Mexico 88003

We are carrying out a study on stress in the workplace and you have been randomly selected from a list of all employees at the university. Your answers will assist the university in planning programs to support its employees. This is the only survey you will be sent.

We would very much appreciate your filling out this brief survey; it should take only about five minutes to complete. Please return the survey in the enclosed addressed envelope.

Your participation in this research is entirely voluntary.

Please do not write your name on the survey as all the responses are completely confidential and anonymous. Your return of the survey indicates your willingness to participate in the study.

If you would like to receive the results from this survey, or have any questions, please e-mail me at cmarlow@nmsu.edu, or send me a note using the address above, or call me at 555-4984.

Thank you.

Christine Marlow, Ph.D.
Professor and Principal Investigator of the Employee Survey

Figure 9.2   **Example of a cover letter**

The Content and Order of the Questions   One strategy for increasing the response rate is to limit sensitive and very personal questions, or if they have to be included to embed them within the questionnaire. You also need to be careful about the ordering of opinion questions; these should be asked first, before the factual questions, otherwise the factual questions may influence the opinions. For example, if you are interested in assessing the need for respite care for foster parents, ask questions about need first, then follow with such questions as the number of foster children they have living with them and demands on the foster parents' time. People like to state their opinions; they are not as interested in demographic questions such as gender and educational level. Instead of starting the questionnaire with these questions, place them at the end.

Format and Appearance of the Questionnaire   The response rate can also be enhanced by the overall packaging of the questionnaire. Make sure it is free of typographical and spelling errors. Ensure that the layout is clear and uncluttered. Make it inviting to complete.

Cover Letter   If you are mailing the questionnaire, include a **cover letter** that briefly describes the purpose of the study and encourages the person to respond. An example of a cover letter is shown in Figure 9.2.

Table 9.1   **Checklist for constructing questionnaire and interview questions**

_____ The questions are short.	_____ Consent has been given to answer the questions.
_____ There are no double-barreled questions.	_____ Anonymity and confidentiality have been assured.
_____ The questions are clear and focused.	If mailed (snail or e-mail):
_____ There are no sensitive questions.	_____ A cover letter or explanation of the research is included.
_____ There are no leading questions.	_____ The questionnaire is clearly formatted.
_____ The respondents are capable of answering the questions.	_____ The questionnaire is short.
_____ The questions are focused on the present.	_____ There are mostly closed-ended questions.
_____ There are no questions containing double negatives.	_____ There is a return date.
_____ The response categories are balanced.	_____ A stamped, addressed envelope is included or return e-mail address clearly specified.
_____ The questions are in a language that can be understood by the respondent.	

The cover letter should include how confidentiality will be maintained (confidentiality is discussed later in this chapter). You may want to include a small incentive, such as a dollar bill, coupons, or a pen. This can increase the return rate by 10% to 15%. Of course, the person should never be coerced to respond. Always include a self-addressed, stamped envelope, ideally using an individual postage stamp rather than a bulk mailing stamp. This makes the request appear more personal and hence the participant may be more likely to respond.

Follow-Ups   Second mailings can enhance the response ratio of mailed questionnaires by about 10% to 15%, but of course they add to the cost of the project. Ideally, two follow-ups should be used. When the initial responses drop off, the first follow-up letters should be sent, and then later send another letter along with another copy of the questionnaire.

A checklist for constructing a questionnaire or an interview schedule is given in Table 9.1.

Even with a carefully designed and administered questionnaire, response rates can be low. As we discussed in relation to interviews, facts other than the structure of the instrument or the way it is administered can influence the

Observation

Trussell (1999) conducted a limited ethnographic study on street children in Ciudad Juarez, Mexico. Data were collected by means of observation. Trussell recorded behaviors, activities, and conversations and noted the physical environment. Observations and interviews were completed in approximately 130 hours of fieldwork time over a four-month period in a park (Parque de Leon) that is frequented by children who live and work in the streets. From the observations, Trussell concluded that varying levels of distrust, hostility, and aggression exist between street children and gangs, police, and the general public.

response rate. These factors include the topics and variables included in the research itself.

Applicability

Questionnaires can be used in preference to other data collection techniques when:

- a high response rate is not a top priority
- anonymity is important
- budgets are limited (although extensive mailings of questionnaires can be expensive)
- the respondents are literate

Observation Techniques

Not all phenomena can be measured by interviews or questionnaires. Examples of these types of phenomena include illegal behavior or children's behavior. If we are interested in a child's behavior in the classroom, interviewing or administering a questionnaire to the child would probably not elicit objective responses. As a social work student, you probably realize that observation is an integral part of social work practice, and you have already learned to be a good observer. Observation can be structured or unstructured.

Structured Observation

When behaviors are known and categorized prior to the observation, and the intention is to collect quantitative data, **structured observation** is the method of choice. In this method, behaviors are categorized prior to the observation according to their characteristics, including their frequency, direction, and magnitude. These categories can then be quantified.

Take the example of trying to measure a child's inattention in the classroom. First, inattention needs to be clearly defined, perhaps as talking with other children without the teacher's permission. Frequency would be the number of occasions during a specified period of time (for example, one hour) that the child talked with other children without permission. Duration would be the length of time the child talked. Magnitude would be how loudly the child talked within a specified period of time. Clearly, selection of the method of observation depends on what behavior is being measured, how the behavior is defined, and how often it occurs.

Unstructured Observation

When little is known about the behaviors being observed, or when an interpretive approach is adopted and the goal is to focus primarily on collecting qualitative data, unstructured observation is used. This strategy for collecting data is known as **participant observation**. Participant observers can adopt different roles.

At one extreme, the participation takes precedence over the observation. In other words, the researcher fully participates in the activity under study. The advantage of this approach is that a level of understanding of the phenomena under study can be gained that would be impossible to gain through other means. For example, studying the stress experiences of a child protective social worker might be best understood by "becoming" a CPS worker for a period of time and recording the experiences. Without this participation by the researcher, the workers may never disclose to the researcher the kinds of stresses they are experiencing. Of course the disadvantage of this approach is that the line between researcher and participant becomes blurred, and roles confused, making even an interpretive approach difficult to undertake. It also often involves a lengthy time commitment, not always an option to the researcher.

At the other extreme, the participant observer may observe only and not engage in the activities of the group. Clearly this approach is useful when studying illegal activities such as drug dealing. The disadvantage is that often the observation is for a short period of time and the knowledge gained about the activity therefore may be limited.

Whether observation or participation is emphasized, there is an ethical question of how much the participants are informed about the researcher's intentions. This is particularly the case when the role is as more of a participant. Does the researcher disclose to the other workers why she is adopting this role? If she does, wouldn't this then jeopardize the validity of observations? This is a difficult ethical dilemma and was discussed in the last chapter and needs to be considered carefully when participant observation is used.

Neutrality

Observation varies in its neutrality. The degree of neutrality depends a great deal on the type of observation, the level of researcher training, and the control for reactivity.

Type of Observation Generally, structured observation is more neutral than unstructured observation, because in structured observation the behaviors are

Participant Observation

One of Grey's (1999) means of collecting data included participant observation. The focus of the study is a large meatpacking plant in Iowa that experienced annual turnover of approximately 8%. In addition to participant observation, Grey used observation of community institutions, ethnographic interviews, and focus groups in an effort to garner greater understanding of the significantly high turnover rate. Two themes emerged from the study. One is that tension exists between the plant's predominant ethnic groups of Anglos and Latino immigrants. Additionally, poor (perceived) working conditions led to injuries and worker exhaustion.

defined beforehand. With unstructured observation, behaviors are not so clearly defined. In addition, in unstructured observation, the observer's involvement in the behavior can further bias the observation.

The Level of Training   The more training the observers receive regarding the procedures to be followed for the observation, the greater the neutrality. Often, particularly in structured observation, the categories are not immediately apparent, no matter how much care was taken in their development. Observers may need to be instructed in what is meant by, for example, asking for the participant's opinion.

Control for Reactivity   Reactivity, or the reactive effect, is the problem of subjects changing their behavior in some way as a result of the observer's observing them. (This effect was discussed earlier with regard to interviewing.) Reactivity can in part be controlled by using one or more of the following four strategies: videotapes, one-way mirrors, time with observer, and participant observation. A videotape recorder can be used to record behavior, but this may further inhibit the subject.

Second, sometimes one-way mirrors can be used, although we must be sure to obtain consent from those being observed. A third method for controlling reactivity is for the observer to spend some time with the subject so that the subject can become more comfortable with the observation. For example, if you want to observe classroom behavior, sit in the classroom for some time before you actually make the observation. Finally, we can overcome some reactivity effects with participant observation.

One further comment regarding neutrality is that observation need not always be visual. Sometimes enough information can be gained by listening to audio recordings. Maybe you have already used this method of observation as a means of improving your practice. Remember that because you are then without the nonverbal part of the interaction, neutrality can decrease, with the possible misinterpretation of the communication.

A Log

Voss et al. (1999) interviewed thirty-two Lakota elders, educators, leaders, and mental health providers to ascertain their views on traditional ideas of help and healing. The researchers hypothesized that ancient traditions of help and healing can serve as an alternative model for understanding social work theory. During the course of interviewing the thirty-two individuals, a log was kept of observations and conversations between the researchers and participants. Findings from the study indicated that the traditions of help and healing were closely linked to the ceremonial life of the tribe. Additionally, findings demonstrate a revival of traditional healing practice among the Lakota people.

Applicability

Observation can be used in preference to other data collection techniques when behaviors are difficult to measure using other techniques, and observers and funds are available for training.

Logs and Journals

Sometimes logs, journals, or diaries can be used to collect data. These could be considered forms of self-observation but really warrant a separate discussion from observation. Logs, journals, or diaries—like observation—can be structured or unstructured. There are two types. First, there are records kept by the researcher to record the process of their research. Keeping such a journal or log helps the researcher track their progress, or the lack of it, on a project. It can help them identify barriers and successes that may guide the present project and possibly future projects. A second type of log or journal is one kept by a social worker or client or other participant in the project that provides data for the research. The client may record his or her own behavior, or the social worker may record the client's behavior or their own. In Figure 9.3, the social worker is assessing her feelings and reactions to a home visit by recording them in a journal.

This log is unstructured and can allow for a stream-of-consciousness type of data collection; often these types of data are valuable in an interpretive study. Note that these types of journals can also be used by social workers to provide feedback for their practice. When they are used for this purpose they are referred to as process recordings. Logs can also be used to collect quantitative data. Service logs are of this type, where the entries involve checking or noting numbers next to categories of behavior or activities.

Neutrality

Neutrality of logs and journals can be fairly limited, particularly if they are not structured or guided in some way. Neutrality can be enhanced by the use of more

---

SOCIAL WORKER'S JOURNAL RECORD OF A HOME VISIT TO A CLIENT
Thursday, February 15

Tonight I visited Art A. again. The house looked dark when I pulled up, and I felt kind of uneasy. I went through all the safety precautions I had learned previously and then went to the door and knocked. My stomach felt jittery. Finally, after several minutes, I heard footsteps inside and Art opened the door. He looked kind of disheveled and I sensed that he was upset about something, but he asked me very politely to come in and sit down. The house was so dark! I asked him to turn on some lights, and I sat near the door, just in case. Something just didn't feel right. Then it hit me—his dog Spike hadn't barked when I knocked and that dog was his constant companion. I didn't want to ask him about Spike because I was sure it was bad. I felt a lump forming in my throat. What a great social worker I am! I'm supposed to be calm, cool, and collected! I guess if I didn't empathize though, I wouldn't have been there in the first place. Sure enough, Spike was dead—he'd been run over by a car.

CLIENT'S LOG OF DRINKING BEHAVIOR
Monday

10:00	I took my break at work and had a couple of sips of George's beer (he brings it in his lunch pail).
12:00	Drank 2 beers with lunch.
5:00	Stopped after work at Charlie's Grill and had 3 beers and 2 or 3 shots of whiskey, which my friends bought for me.
7:00	Jack Daniels before dinner (on the rocks).
8:00	3–4 beers watching the Broncos whip the Cowboys.
11:00	Went to buy cigs and stopped at Fred's bar, had a couple of beers.
1:00	Had a shot of whiskey before bed to help me get to sleep.

Figure 9.3   ***Examples of journal and log recordings***

structured journals and logs so that the client or worker responds to specific questions. It is also helpful to encourage the client to record behaviors as soon as they occur rather than to rely too much on retrospective documentation.

Applicability
Logs and journals can be used in preference to other data collection techniques when detailed personal experiences are required from subjects and subjects are literate.

Scales

Most variables are not clear-cut and cannot be contained in one question or item; instead, they are composed of a number of different dimensions or factors. Level of functioning, marital satisfaction, and community attitudes all are of this complex type. Composite measures consisting of a number of items are called **scales**. Scales can be used in interviews and questionnaires—sometimes even in structured observation—and they are important when you need to collect quantitative data.

Standardized scales are a type of scale that is uniform and tested extensively. Usually, published scales are accompanied by information about what they are intended to measure and with what type of population. Sometimes you may need a scale to measure a specific variable—for example, child well-being or aggression. Whenever possible, as with other types of data collection methods, try to use existing scales; they can eliminate considerable amounts of work. There are some drawbacks to using existing scales. They may not be designed to measure the variables in your study. For example, a family coping scale would not be appropriate for measuring family cohesion. The other problem is the temptation to design research around a standardized instrument—for example, changing your study to look at family coping rather than at family cohesion.

Developing Scales

If you are confronted with developing a scale, you will need to identify sources of scale items. These sources can include your own existing knowledge about the topic of the scale, the literature, people who are knowledgeable about the topic, and the people who are the focus of the research. The following steps need to be taken when developing scales:

1. Develop or locate more scale items than you think you will need.
2. Eliminate items that are redundant or unclear.
3. Pretest the remaining items for validity or reliability (see discussion below), and eliminate those that do not pass the test.
4. Repeat step 3 as many times as necessary to reduce the number of items to the required number.

Selecting the Scale Items   Each statement is considered for its content validity (see discussion later in this chapter). For example, if you are constructing a scale measuring adoptive parental attachment to adoptive child, the items should all relate to attachment in some form. For example, an item relating to the employment history of the biological parents would probably add little to the scale of level of attachment between the adoptive parents and the child.

Apart from the validity and the range of variation, items also need to be assessed based on their unidimensionality. In other words, the items need to relate to and measure only one variable, otherwise the scale becomes muddled. As a part of this process it is important to distinguish between different variables and different aspects of the same variable. Again, with the attachment example, attachment contains a number of dimensions including emotional and physical.

All the items should be connected to one another or correlate. This can be done by carrying out a pretest.

As you can tell by now, the construction of scales is not an easy process. In addition, certain types of scales have very specific requirements. A discussion of the different types of scales follows.

Types of Scales

The most common form for social science research is the **Likert Scale**. The respondent is shown a series of statements and is then asked to respond using one of five response alternatives, for example, "strongly agree," "agree," "no opinion," "disagree," "strongly disagree," or some variant of these.

Likert scales are designed to prevent certain kinds of response patterns, i.e. the statements vary in form so that the literal answers cannot always be the same. For example, in the F-COPES example, effective coping would not always be demonstrated by a "strongly agree" response.

Another type of scale is the **Thurstone Scale**. These are constructed using equal distance intervals. They are rigorously pretested, but can be used to generate interval level data (refer to Chapter 4) and hence allow the data to be more rigorously analyzed, as we will discuss in later chapters. Both Thurstone and Likert scales require at least 20 or more items to be included.

Another type of scale is the **Semantic Differential (SD) Scale**. This includes a format that presents the respondent with a stimulus, for example an event or a person, that is rated on a scale using opposite adjectives. Unlike the Likert and Thurstone scales, SD scales only require 4 to 8 adjective pairs to provide reliable results.

The last type of scaling in our discussion is the **Guttman Scale**. This type of scale ensures that a measurement is truly unidimensional and that the items on the scale are progressive, usually relating to the intensity of the variable under study. Generally they are organized with the "easy" items first and the "harder" ones later. A variation of this type of scale used to enhance both social work practice and research is called the target problem scale.

Target problem scales are a means to track changes in a client's target behavior. This type of scale is particularly useful when actual outcomes are difficult to identify. The scale involves identifying a problem, applying an intervention, and then repeatedly rating the extent to which the target problem has changed. One such target problem scale is shown in Figure 9.4. This example includes a global improvement scale that summarizes the amount of change that took place in the target problem.

Before finishing this section on scales, a mention should be made of rapid assessment instruments. A **rapid assessment instrument** (RAI) is a standardized series of structured questions or statements administered to the client to collect data in practice evaluations, and many include various types of scales. Rapid assessment instruments are short, easy to administer, and easy to complete. The Multi-Problem Screening Inventory (MPSI) (Hudson, 1990) is an example. The MPSI can be used in conjunction with practice to collect data on several variables, including generalized contentment and marital satisfaction. These scales are computerized.

TARGET PROBLEM (rated by client)	TARGET PROBLEM RATING					GLOBAL IMPROVEMENT
	Degree of Severity				Degree of Change	
	Session #				Month	
	1	2	3	4		
Difficulty in talking about feelings	ES	ES	S	S	S	3
Getting to work on time	ES	S	S	NVS	NP	5
Fear of leaving house in daytime	ES	S	S	NVS	NP	5
			TOTAL		13 / 3 = 4.3	
						Somewhat to a lot better

Severity Scale
NP = No problem
NVS = Not very severe
S = Severe
VS = Very severe
ES = Extremely severe

Improvement Scale
1 = Worse
2 = No change
3 = A little better
4 = Somewhat better
5 = A lot better

The global improvement rating is obtained by totaling the change scores and dividing by the number of target problems. This yields a number that reflects the client's overall improvement on all problems.

Figure 9.4   **Example of a target problem and global improvement scale for one client**

Neutrality

Scales are designed to be as neutral as possible, particularly those that are standardized.

Applicability

Scales are useful in studies where the emphasis is on collecting quantitative data. They are also useful for measuring multifaceted concepts. Scales are helpful when there is not a great deal of time available for data collection.

Secondary Data

Secondary data are data collected for purposes other than the present research. They may be data collected for another research project or data that were not collected with research in mind at all.

Secondary Data Use

Anderson and Gryzlak (2002) used secondary data analysis of TANF (Temporary Assistance for Needy Families) "leaver" studies from 12 states with large TANF caseloads. In the data analysis, the researchers focused on the employment and earning experiences of leavers in addition to TANF recidivism and use of support services. Findings indicated that while 55–65% of individuals leaving TANF found employment, the average earning fell below the poverty line. Additionally, support services are often underused as TANF leavers do not know their eligibility. Anderson and Gryzlak suggest that social workers must focus attention on advocacy efforts and improve existing policies.

Using Case Records as Data

Lewis, Giovannoni, and Leake (1997) assessed placement outcomes two years after prenatally drug-exposed children had been placed in foster care. The authors compared the data with the two-year outcomes of not prenatally drug-exposed children who had also been placed out of their homes. Retired social workers of the Department of Children and Families reviewed the agency records on each infant enrolled in the study. Findings indicated that two-thirds of the drug-exposed children and more than half of the children not drug-exposed were still in care at two years.

We use secondary data all the time in generalist practice—by consulting case records written by others and by referring to agency statistics when writing up reports. In fact, case records provide an important secondary data source for agency-based social worker research. Other sources of secondary data include U.S. census data and the numerous reports generated by state and federal government, including historical documents.

Agencies—both private and public—are creating data banks in increasing numbers and storing information about their operations, including the number of clients served, types of target problems, outcomes, staffing patterns, and budgets. Information can also be obtained on crime rates, child abuse and neglect rates, and so forth.

These types of data are particularly useful when conducting a needs assessment. Two strategies can be adopted using secondary data in a needs assessment: **rates under treatment** and social indicators. The rates-under-treatment approach uses existing data from agencies to determine the needs of a community. The problem with this approach is that use of existing services may not, in fact, reflect unmet needs.

Using Historical Data

Stuart (1999) examined social work's ability to link client systems and social welfare policy from a historical perspective, noting that this aspect has characterized the profession since the 19th century. In the article he discusses how social workers developed social survey methods as a way of understanding their clients' environments during the Progressive Era, drawing extensively upon historical data.

Rates Under Treatment

Nixon, Phillips, and Tivis (2000) examined the nature of substance abuse in nonreservation-residing American Indians who received inpatient treatment. The study sought to describe the alcohol use histories and family histories of nonreservation-residing American Indians in treatment. In addition, the study was implemented to provide comparative data and rates of treatment between American Indian and non-American Indian people. The participants consisted of 533 (13.6%) self-identified American Indians; 2,580 (67%) European Americans; 634 (16.5%) African Americans; and 95 (2.9%) Hispanic or "other." Results revealed a notable similarity in rates of treatment between treatment-seeking American Indians and the other ethnic groups.

The **social indicators** approach selects demographic data from existing public records to predict a community's needs. Existing statistics relating to people's spatial arrangement and facilities in a community, housing patterns, crime patterns, and so on can help us determine where, for example, to place a community center.

It is also possible to use **vignettes** in collecting data. These are hypothetical situations either drawn from a source or developed by the researcher (in which case the vignettes are not strictly secondary data) for the purpose of eliciting certain responses from the participants in the study.

Indirect Sources

Indirect sources refer to information that can be used for research but that was initially collected for some other purpose. Indirect sources include case records, newspapers, and other media reports. For example, we may be interested in studying an agency's attitudes toward the developmentally disabled, so we consult case records on this topic. The most common way of dealing with indirect sources is to subject it to **content analysis**. Content analysis is a method of

Using Vignettes to Collect Data

Savaya (1998) used vignettes to collect data examining the effects of economic need and self-esteem on the attitudes and use of professional services by Arab women. The vignettes simulated potential help-seeking situations, and at the end of each one a hypothetical professional family counseling service was presented.

Each woman in the study was asked to respond to one vignette. Findings indicated that self-esteem was associated with the women's help-seeking behavior, but not their attitudes, and only when economic need was not taken into account. When economic need was accounted for, the effect on self-esteem disappeared. These findings suggest that more attention needs to be focused on economic need and less on a "threat to self-esteem" model to explain underutilization of professional services.

coding communication to a systematic quantifiable form. It will be discussed further in Chapters 10 and 11.

Neutrality

When using secondary data, we need to be aware that sometimes these data have limited neutrality. Indirect sources can often be particularly biased because they were not initially collected for research purposes. For example, there may be gaps in a record that we are using. In addition, because records were made for a purpose other than ours, information relating to our research question may be missing. For example, if we were gathering information on agency attitudes toward the developmentally disabled, that information might be missing from case records.

Direct sources are more neutral, but the researcher needs to verify the exact form of the questions that were initially asked. The form of questions asked later by the secondary researcher may be different; we need to know what this difference is. For example, you may be interested in the number of juveniles with a previous record of substance abuse who were seen by the local juvenile probation office. Your focus may be on alcohol use, whereas the data collected did not distinguish between alcohol and other types of substance abuse. When using secondary data, you cannot assume that the first researcher's questions were similar to your own.

Applicability

Secondary data can be used when these data are available (this is not always the case). Secondary data also can be applied when the definition of the secondary data variables and the form of the questions are the same (or similar) to yours; if not, you must at least be aware of the differences. Secondary data can be helpful when a needs assessment is required and the budget is limited. Secondary data can yield much information when you are interested in conducting a historical study—for example, the history of an agency or of the way a particular problem has been addressed in the past.

Using Multiple Measures

Schoenberg (2000) investigated the nutritional risk of African-American elders. She combined two data collection methods from two separate studies. In the first study she examined the prevalence of nutritional risk through telephone surveys with 1,126 older adults. In the second study she used nearly 200 in-depth interviews to illustrate the findings from the survey. She explained her reason for combining these methods: "First, the survey is capable of revealing the nutritional risk patterns . . . in-depth interviews are necessary to illuminate the pathways behind these patterns" (p. 235).

WHO COLLECTS THE DATA

As with the other decisions to be made concerning data collection, the decision about who should collect the data depends greatly on the type of research question asked. We tend to think of the researcher as the only person who should collect the data, as when interviewing or administering a questionnaire.

Apart from the researcher, the client or subject can also collect the data. Journals or diaries can be used in this way. Questionnaires can be self-administered; mailed questionnaires are the obvious example. Clients can also observe and record their own behavior using scales or checklists. Engaging the client in the data collection process is particularly valuable in conducting single-system studies, and as we saw in Chapter 7 they can provide opportunities for feedback on changes in the client's behavior.

Reactivity effects were discussed earlier. The reactivity effect can also be a problem when the client collects data on his or her own behavior or uses **self-monitoring**. This reactivity can be quite strong, resulting in self-monitoring being used as an intervention device. Kopp (1988) presented an interesting review of the literature on how self-monitoring has been used both as a research tool and as a practice tool in social work.

COMBINING DATA COLLECTION METHODS

Methods and instruments can and should be used in conjunction with one another. As mentioned earlier in the chapter, both qualitative and quantitative data can be collected. In addition, a number of different methods can be used in the same study (see Table 9.2).

Combining measures can enrich your study and help to ensure that you are tapping a maximum number of dimensions of the phenomenon under study. Using a number of data collection methods is sometimes called triangulation. Other forms of triangulation include using a number of different theories,

Table 9.2   *Characteristics of data collection methods*

	Unstructured interviews	Mailed question-naire	Participant observation	Standardized observation	Logs	Face-to-face administered standardized scales
High response rate	yes	no	n/a	yes	maybe	yes
Anonymity assured	no	yes	no	no	no	no
Low reactivity effects	no	yes	maybe	maybe	yes	yes
Illiterate subjects	yes	no	yes	yes	no	no
Semilegal or illegal behavior	no	maybe	maybe	no	no	no
Large sample or limited funds	no	yes	no	no	no	yes
In-depth, "thick description"	yes	no	yes	no	yes	no

researchers, or research methods—for example, a mix of quantitative and qualitative approaches. Triangulation, particularly in qualitative studies, can help enhance the validity of findings.

DETERMINING RELIABILITY AND VALIDITY

Before a measuring instrument is used in the research process, it is important to assess its reliability and validity. This is important regardless of whether a qualitative or quantitative approach is used, although the way in which they are assessed does vary according to the approach and according to whether the data are qualitative or quantitative. Quantitative data collection instruments—particularly scales and highly standard interview, questionnaire, and observation schedules—lend themselves most easily to the tests for reliability and validity presented here. Standardized scales are always accompanied by the results of validity and reliability tests.

Open-ended, qualitative instruments, however, are more difficult to assess for reliability and validity. The principles presented here, if not the specific tests themselves, can still be used as guidelines with open-ended instruments to improve their validity and reliability.

Reliability

Reliability indicates the extent to which a measure reveals actual differences in the phenomenon measured, rather than differences inherent in the measuring instrument itself. Reliability refers to the consistency of a measure. To illustrate, a wooden ruler is a reliable measure for a table. If the ruler were made of elastic, however, it would not provide a reliable measure, because repeated measures of the same table would differ with the ruler's expansion and contraction. If a client is chronically depressed and you measure the degree of depression at two points in time, the instrument is reliable if you get close to the same score each time, provided the level of depression has in fact not changed. Clearly you need to establish the instrument's reliability before you can determine true changes in the phenomena under study.

As generalist social workers, you need to assess the extent to which the data collection instrument is reliable. There are two major ways to assess the instrument's reliability: assessing sources of error and assessing the degree to which the instrument's reliability has been tested. Each of these will be discussed in turn.

Sources of Error

When assessing the reliability of an instrument, you need to determine whether there is evidence of certain sources of error. The following are four major types of error: unclear definition of variables, use of retrospective information, variations in the conditions for collecting the data, and structure of the instrument.

Unclear Definitions of Variables

As we saw in Chapter 4, variables can be difficult to define because many social work terms tend to be vague. If a variable is not clearly operationalized and defined, its measurement lacks reliability: The possible outcome can be interpreted differently by different social workers. The wording of questions in questionnaires often creates problems with unclear definitions of variables. A question might be phrased in such a way that two individuals interpret it differently and provide two different answers, even though the actual behavior they are reporting is the same. For example, people might be asked, "Do you often use public transportation in the city?" In responding, people may interpret *often* in different ways. Interpretive studies where the variables are not necessarily clearly defined and operationalized clearly pose a particular challenge. Extensive use of interviews in these types of studies overcomes some of the problems, because the unstructured data collection method allows exploration of the concepts to take place. If the variable described by the respondent is unclear, the respondent can be asked to elaborate and define. The definition comes from the subjects, rather than from the researcher.

Use of Retrospective Information

Retrospective information is gathered through subject recall, either by a questionnaire or by an interview. These data are almost inevitably distorted. Moreover, sometimes subject recall is hampered because of the nature of the topic under study—as you might expect if you were investigating an adult's experience of childhood sexual abuse, for example. Case records are one form of retrospective data collection, and they are consequently subject to considerable error. Case records usually reflect the idiosyncratic recording practices of the individual social worker. The worker will select out certain aspects of the case for recording, resulting in impaired reliability.

Variations in Conditions for Collecting the Data

When interviews are used to collect data, interview conditions can also affect reliability. The subject may respond differently depending on whether the interviewer is male or female. (This is the reactive effect we discussed earlier.) Similar problems may arise from the ethnicity and age of the interviewer. Where the interview is conducted may also cause disparities in responses. Even with questionnaires (for example, mailed questionnaires), lack of control over the conditions under which they are administered can result in low reliability.

Structure of the Instrument

Certain aspects of the data collection method itself may enhance or decrease reliability. An open-ended questionnaire that requires that responses be categorized and coded can present reliability problems.

Testing Reliability

In addition to identifying the sources of error in an instrument, we can also assess the extent to which the instrument's reliability has been tested. As generalist social workers, you will need to be able to understand what reliability tests, if any, others have conducted. In addition, you may be able to use these tests on some of the instruments you develop.

Reliability is determined by obtaining two or more measures of the same thing and seeing how closely they agree. Four methods are used to establish the reliability of an instrument: test-retest, alternate form, split half, and observer reliability.

Test-Retest

Test-retest involves repeatedly administering the instrument to the same set of people on separate occasions. These people should not be subjects in the actual study. The results of the repeated administrations are then compared. If the results are similar, reliability of the instrument is high. A problem associated with this method of testing reliability is that the first testing has influenced the second.

For example, during the second testing the individuals may be less anxious, less motivated, or less interested, or they may simply remember their answers from the first test and repeat them. In addition, they may have learned from the first testing, particularly with attitude questions. To avoid these problems, measuring instruments that are strongly affected by memory or repetition should not be tested for reliability using this method.

Alternate Form

With **alternate form** tests, different but equivalent forms of the same test are administered to the same group of individuals—usually close in time—and then compared. The major problem with this approach is in the development of the equivalent tests, which can be time-consuming. This approach also involves some of the problems associated with the test-retest method.

Split Half

With the **split half method**, items on the instrument are divided into comparable halves. For example, a scale could be divided so that the first half should have the same score as the second half. This testing method looks at the internal consistency of the measure. The test is administered and the two halves compared. If the score is the same, the instrument is probably reliable. A major problem with this approach is ensuring that the two halves are equivalent. Equivalency is problematic with instruments other than scales.

Observer Reliability

Observer reliability involves comparing administrations of an instrument used by different observers or interviewers. For this method to work, the observers need to be thoroughly trained; at least two people will code the content of the responses according to certain criteria.

Each of these methods of testing for reliability involves comparing two or more results. Usually, this comparison uses some kind of **correlation coefficient**. This is a statistic that measures the extent to which the comparisons are similar or not similar—that is the extent to which they are related or correlated. The concept of correlation will be discussed in more detail in Chapter 12. For our purposes now in assessing reliability, the correlation coefficient can range from 0.0 to 1.0, the latter number reflecting a perfect correlation, or the highest level of reliability possible. Generally, a coefficient of .80 suggests the instrument is reasonably reliable. Table 9.3 summarizes the criteria that can be used to assess an instrument's reliability.

Instruments with High Reliability

The scales included in the Multi-Problem Screening Inventory developed by Hudson (1990) all have test-retest and split half reliability correlation coefficients of at least .90. The scales were developed for a variety of behaviors, including child problems, guilt, work problems, and alcohol abuse.

Table 9.3   ***Criteria for assessing the reliability of measuring instruments***

1	Is the variable clearly defined?
2	Is retrospective information avoided?
3	Are there controlled conditions under which the data are collected?
4	Is the question format closed?
5	Are reliability tests used? If so, is the correlation coefficient greater than 0.5?

If the answer is yes to most of these questions, then the instrument is probably reliable.

Validity

The **validity of a measuring instrument** reflects the extent to which you are measuring what you think you are measuring. Validity is different from reliability. To take the example used previously, if a wooden ruler is used to measure the dimensions of a table, it is a reliable and valid instrument. If you use the ruler to measure ethnicity, however, the instrument maintains its reliability, but it is no longer valid. You would not be measuring ethnicity but some other variable (for example, height), which has no relationship to ethnicity as far as we know.

Validity is not as straightforward as reliability because there are different types of validity, and each one is tested in a different way. The three main types of validity are criterion validity, content validity, and construct validity. Each type of validity relates to different aspects of the overall validity of the instrument, and each addresses different dimensions of the problem of ensuring that what is being measured is what was intended to be measured. These types of validities will be discussed along with the ways in which each can be tested.

Validity testing can be quite complex, and sometimes entire articles in the social work literature are devoted to testing the validity of specific instruments. Fries et al. (2001) validated a pain scale in nursing home subpopulations, and Gupta (1999) examined the reliability and validity of the Caregiver Burden Scale. As generalist social workers, you will need to understand what type of validity testing has been carried out and in some cases test instruments you have developed.

Criterion Validity

Criterion validity describes the extent to which a correlation exists between the measuring instrument and another standard. To validate an instrument developed to assess a program that helps pregnant teenagers succeed in high school, a criterion such as SAT scores might be used as a comparison. Similarities in scores would indicate that criterion validity had been established.

Reporting Reliability

Teare et al. (1998) investigated maternal family satisfaction following youths' return home from an emergency-crisis shelter. The study utilized several instruments and reported their reliability. The Inventory of Parent and Peer Attachment, for example, had a three-week test-retest reliability coefficient of .93 for the parent attachment measure. Results of the study indicated that higher ratings of family satisfaction were related to greater maternal problem-solving skills and less conflict within the family.

Content Validity

Content validity is concerned with the representativeness of the content of the instrument. The content included in the instrument needs to be relevant to the concept we are trying to measure. For example, the content validity of an instrument developed to measure knowledge of parenting skills could be obtained by consulting with various experts on parenting skills—perhaps social workers who run parenting groups and a professor at the department of social work. They could then point out areas in which the instrument may be deficient. Clearly, content validity is in part a matter of judgment and is dependent upon the knowledge of the experts who are available to you.

Construct Validity

Construct validity describes the extent to which an instrument measures a theoretical construct. A measure may have criterion and content validity but still not measure what it is intended to measure. Construct validity is the most difficult kind to establish, because as we mentioned earlier many research variables are difficult to define and are theoretically vague. Constructs used in social work include aggression, sociability, and self-esteem, to name a few. With construct validity, we are looking at both the instrument and the theory underlying it. The instrument must reflect this theory.

For example, in testing the construct validity of an instrument to measure aggression in preschoolers, the associated theoretical expectations need to be examined by referring to the literature and research on the topic. One explanation that may be found is that the highly aggressive children will not be achieving well in the classroom. If the instrument does not reflect this dimension of the topic, the instrument probably does not have construct validity. IQ tests provide an example of a measure with low construct validity. IQ tests were created to measure intelligence. Since their development, however, it has become apparent that they measure only one dimension of intelligence—the potential to achieve in a white middle-class academic system. Other dimensions of intelligence remain untapped by IQ tests, resulting in their limited validity for measuring intelligence.

Table 9.4   ***Criteria for assessing the validity of quantitative measuring instruments***

1	Was the instrument tested for criterion validity?
2	Was the instrument tested for content validity?
3	Was the instrument tested for construct validity?
4	Is the variable defined as clearly and concretely as possible?

If the answer is yes to most of these questions, then the instrument is probably valid (that is, if the findings from the tests support the validity of the instrument).

One way of more fully ensuring construct validity is to define the construct using small, concrete, observable behaviors (Duncan and Fiske, 1977). Such definition helps us to avoid some of the wishy-washiness associated with many constructs used in social work practice. For example, if both the verbal and nonverbal behaviors of preschoolers are recorded, and certain patterns of these behaviors become apparent in those children previously labeled aggressive, you can be more fully assured that your label does in fact have construct validity.

Once you are familiar with this information on validity and the ways it can be tested, you are then in a position as a generalist social worker to assess the validity of the measuring instruments you read about or that you propose to use. Table 9.4 presents a checklist that can be used to assess the validity of instruments.

Feedback

Feedback is an important way of testing the validity of qualitative data, particularly when the intent of the research may well be to define and to elaborate on these concepts. However, data must be understandable and relevant to the participants in the research. The participants should be allowed to verify the data. This feedback can be carried out both formally (for example, through focus groups or community meetings) or informally (for example, through meetings and informal gatherings with the participants).

Note that often in the collection of qualitative data, responsibility for validating the data lies directly with the researcher rather than being assured through the use of prescribed methods, such as a criterion validity check. Therefore it is even more important for the researcher to act responsibly and ethically.

THE AGENCY AND DATA COLLECTION

As generalist social workers, you often do not have much of a choice when it comes to selecting a data collection method. You may be asked to help develop a questionnaire for a needs assessment, in which case the decision about the data collection has already been made.

Because of time and money constraints, some of the more complicated and time-consuming data collection techniques—such as lengthy questionnaire and scale construction, participant observation, and extensive interviews—cannot be considered by the generalist social worker engaged in research. Instead, consider using rapid assessment instruments, case records, and self-observation (by the client) as much as possible.

It should not be forgotten, however, that generalist social workers can be key players in the data collection process. After all, it is they who have access to critical data, both directly from the clients and indirectly from the agency records. Thus the challenge for generalist social workers becomes to explore the opportunities offered in the agencies for data collection and research by either undertaking research themselves or by encouraging their agencies to explore research possibilities.

ETHICAL ISSUES IN COLLECTING DATA

When collecting data for a research study, we need to be concerned about three ethical issues: potential harm to the subjects, anonymity and confidentiality, and justification of the research.

Harm to the Participants

Clearly, we need to avoid harming the participants in any way. The NASW Code of Ethics (1999) states:

- Social workers engaged in evaluation or research should carefully consider possible consequences and should follow guidelines developed for the protection of evaluation and research participants. Appropriate institutional review boards should be consulted.

- Social workers engaged in evaluation or research should protect participants from unwarranted physical or mental distress, harm, danger, or deprivation.

  As simple as these mandates may seem, on closer examination these things are easier said than done. When asking questions in whatever form—whether interviewing or using a questionnaire—you are often requiring participants to examine and assess their own behavior. Questions relating to childhood abuse may be painful for the respondent. Other questions which are difficult to answer concern income and the ability to pay for a proposed service.

Consequently, assessing the extent of discomfort for the participant can be difficult. The **Institutional Review Boards** (IRBs) discussed in Chapter 8 make this assessment for you. All federally funded research and research conducted at universities require the proposed research to be reviewed by IRBs. If you complete a project as a part of your research class, then your proposal will need to be reviewed by your university's IRB. During the review process, the researcher must answer specific questions regarding potential harm to participants and complete an application for review by the board. This sounds like a big undertaking, and some studies undergo a thorough and lengthy review, but the intent is important—to protect the participants in the research from any type of harm. Many studies however, including those usually undertaken by undergraduates and masters students in the social sciences, qualify for an exemption from full review. This shortens the process considerably and usually approval can be gained in just a few days.

Exempt studies include:

- those conducted as a normal part of research on educational practices
- research using educational tests with confidentiality protection
- use survey or interview methods on public behavior with protection of confidentiality
- using existing data without violating confidentiality
- research federal demonstration projects
- survey or interview data when the respondents are elected or appointed officials or candidates for public office

Exemptions are generally not available when certain vulnerable populations are included in the study, for example children and prisoners, or when there is deception of the participants or they are subject to unusual situations, particularly those that involve any type of harassment or discomfort.

Small agencies not receiving federal funding do not require IRB review, so in this situation you need to be careful that your research is ethically sound. Always seek opinions of others on this issue.

Anonymity and Confidentiality

Both anonymity and confidentiality help participants avoid harm. The NASW Code of Ethics (1999) states:

> Social workers engaged in evaluation or research should ensure the anonymity or confidentiality of participants and of the data obtained from them. Social workers should inform participants of any limits of confidentiality and when any records containing research data will be destroyed.

Anonymity means that the researcher cannot identify a given response with a given respondent. It was mentioned previously that an interview can never be anonymous, and when identification numbers are put on questionnaires to facilitate follow-up and increase the response rate, anonymity is also jeopardized. Ensuring anonymity reassures the subjects and can also enhance the objectivity of the responses. For example, if you are asking questions about deviant behavior, the respondent is more likely to give a response that accurately reflects the behavior if anonymity can be assured.

Confidentiality means that the researcher knows the identity of the respondents and their associated responses but ensures nondisclosure of this information. Obviously, confidentiality becomes particularly critical when conducting interviews, for which anonymity is impossible to ensure. The principle of confidentiality should be explained to respondents either verbally or in a cover letter accompanying the questionnaires. Do not confuse confidentiality and anonymity; they are different and are both extremely important.

Justification of the Research

The NASW Code of Ethics (1999) states:

> Social workers should never design or conduct evaluation or research that does not use consent procedures, such as certain forms of naturalistic observation and archival research, unless rigorous and responsible review of the research has found it to be justified because of its prospective scientific, educational, or applied value and unless equally effective alternative procedures that do not involve waiver of consent are not feasible.

Informed consent was discussed in Chapter 6. Using data that are not collected directly from the participants (such as client records and other secondary data) does not exempt the researchers from another ethical responsibility: ensuring that the research is needed and justified.

HUMAN DIVERSITY ISSUES IN COLLECTING THE DATA

Awareness and knowledge of human diversity issues during the data collection stage of the research process are important. Some of the central issues to which we need to pay attention are the selection of the data collection method for diverse populations; the relevance to diverse populations of the content of the data collection method; and the application of the data collection method to diverse populations.

Selection of Data Collection Methods for Diverse Populations

The extent to which data collection methods may or may not be applicable to certain groups within a population needs to be considered. Some groups may be uncomfortable with the notion of being administered a questionnaire or being interviewed; you need to be sensitive to the ways in which different cultural groups might regard different methods.

Gilligan's (1982) analysis of the development of men's and women's resolutions of moral conflicts concluded that women develop a mode of thinking that is "contextual and narrative" and that their understanding is based on the individual in the context of their relationship with others. This way of thinking is contrasted with men's, which is seen as focusing on autonomy and separation from others. Some authors (such as Davis, 1986) have suggested that women's different ways of thinking require different approaches to research—in particular different data collection techniques. The more traditional approach emphasizes the abstract and formal and lends itself to quantification and the use of the positivist approach, whereas the alternative approach, with its emphasis on

Methodological Issues in Conducting Research with Diverse Groups

Gibbs and Bankhead-Greene (1997) described the methodological issues involved in conducting research with inner-city African-American youth. The study investigated the impact of the verdict and the subsequent civil disturbances in the Rodney King police brutality case. A number of civic, religious, and professional leaders in an African-American community in Los Angeles were contacted for suggestions on how to proceed with the study. The researchers collected both qualitative and quantitative data using focus groups and face-to-face interviews with both community leaders and youth. The authors discussed throughout the article the importance of carefully considering the research methods used in this type of study.

connection, lends itself more easily to an interpretive approach and its associated qualitative data.

Relevance to Diverse Populations of the Content of the Data Collection Method

In addition to the appropriateness of a particular data collection instrument, taking account of human diversity requires considering the content of that instrument and its appropriateness to the group under study.

Certain words or phrases—whether in interview or questionnaire form, whether conducted under the auspices of a feminist or traditional research approach—may be interpreted by the respondent in a different way from that intended by the researcher. In many cases, this divergence of interpretations may result from the researcher's lack of understanding or insensitivity to the cultural group that is being studied. For example, some groups may interpret questions about mothers as including mothers-in-law. Serious validity problems can result because the researcher is thinking of *mother* in one sense and the subject is defining *mother* differently. Reliability problems also arise.

Another perhaps less obvious problem might occur when conducting, for example, a research project concerned with methods and problems of disciplining children. You would need to acknowledge the methods and problems experienced by gay and lesbian parents (unless we purposefully *intend* to exclude them) in addition to those of heterosexual parents, because some of the problems gay and lesbian parents encounter might be different. Consequently, you would need to include questions relevant to this group so as not to exclude problems such parents might be experiencing and thus jeopardize the validity of your findings.

Earlier, we discussed the usefulness of rapid assessment instruments and other instruments that have already been developed. Check to see whether the instruments you use have been used with diverse populations and whether their reliability and validity have been tested with these groups.

Validating an Instrument with Diverse Populations

A study by Fries et al. (2001) was implemented to validate a pain scale for the Minimum Data Set (MDS) assessment instrument. The study also sought to examine prevalence of pain in major nursing home subpopulations. Using Automatics Interaction Detection, the MDS pain items and derivation of the scale was performed against the Visual Analogue Scale (VAS). Results showed that the four-group scale was highly predictive of VAS pain scores and thus valid in detecting pain.

Many of these issues are an extension of the discussion in Chapter 3 about the need to include relevant variables in the study. You must account for all the relevant variables but also be aware of human diversity issues in phrasing or constructing the data collection instrument.

Application of the Data Collection Method to Diverse Populations

Even if the data collection method and the structure and content of this method are sensitive to the needs of diverse populations, the way in which the instrument is administered may not be.

For example, you may be carrying out a needs assessment for socially isolated, recently immigrated Asian women. To obtain valid and reliable information, you would need to include questions relevant to this population, and to ensure that the interviews are conducted so that they elicit the required information. This necessitates the use of people who are sensitive to the population under study as interviewers, administrators of questionnaires, and observers. For example, with the Asian women, an interviewer would need to be familiar with this group's language, gender role, and intergenerational role expectations to engage the subject in the interview and to obtain valid and reliable data.

SUMMARY

Quantitative approaches create categories of the phenomenon under study and assign numbers to these categories. Qualitative approaches examine the phenomenon in more detail. Data collection methods include interviews, questionnaires, observation, logs and journals, and secondary data. Scales can measure complex variables. There are several techniques for checking the reliability and validity of data collection methods.

When collecting data in an agency, data collection methods that are compatible with the practice need to be used. Ethical issues include considering potential harm to the subjects and confidentiality and anonymity. When considering human diversity issues, the selection, relevance, and application of the data collection method need to be considered.

STUDY/EXERCISE QUESTIONS

1. Develop a questionnaire to assess the campus needs (such as parking, day care, and so on) of students in your class. Include both open-ended and closed-ended questions.

    a. How do you decide what questions to include?

    b. How would you administer the questionnaire?

2. Have another student in the class critique your questionnaire and comment on its reliability and validity.

3. Search for a suitable instrument to measure adolescents' self-esteem.

    a. Report on its validity and reliability.

    b. Are there any groups for which the instrument may not be reliable or valid?

4. Your agency has asked you to participate in planning a program for adults with a history of childhood sexual abuse.

    a. How would you collect data that would demonstrate the need for such a program?

    b. How would you ensure confidentiality?

5. Design a structured interview to assess the satisfaction of clients who have recently finished receiving services from a family service agency.

    a. Conduct this interview with a classmate.

    b. Would other methods of data collection be more reliable or valid in this case?

6. Design a way of observing a Head Start student who is reported to be disruptive in the classroom.

    a. How would you check the validity and reliability of this method?

INFOTRAC COLLEGE EDITION

1. Search for *"participant observation."* Could another data collection method have been used in this study?

2. Search for *"secondary data"* and examine two of the articles that used secondary data as their primary source of data. What limitations about the data were cited by the authors?

3. Search for *institutional review boards* and review three of the concerns/issues raised by the authors in how institutional review boards can both help and hinder research.

REFERENCES

Anderson, S. G., & Gryzlak, B. M. (2002). Social work advocacy in the post-TANF environment: Lessons from early TANF research studies. *Social Work, 47* (3), 301–315.

Caetano, R., & Raspberry, K. (2000). Drinking and DSM-IV alcohol and drug dependence among white and Mexican-American DUI offenders. *Journal of Studies on Alcohol, 61,* 420–426.

Chermack, S. T., Stoltenberg, S. F., Fuller, B. E., & Blow, F. C. (2000). Gender differences in the development of substance-related problems: The impact of family history of alcoholism, family history of violence and childhood conduct problems. *Journal of Studies on Alcohol, 61,* 845–852.

Davis, L. V. (1986). A feminist approach to social work research. *Affilia, 1,* 32–47.

Duncan, S., & Fiske, D. (1977). *Face-to-Face Interaction.* Hillsdale, NJ: Erlbaum.

Fogel, S. J., & Ellison, M. L. (1998). Sexual harassment of BSW field placement students: Is it a problem? *The Journal of Baccalaureate Social Work, 3* (2), 17–29.

Fries, B. E., Simon, S. E., Morris, J. N., Flodstrom, C., & Bookstein, F. L. (2001). Pain in U.S. nursing homes: Validating a pain scale for the minimum data set. *The Gerontologist, 41* (2), 173–180.

Gibbs, J. T., & Bankhead-Greene, T. (1997). Issues of conducting qualitative research in an inner-city community: A case study of black youth in post-Rodney King Los Angeles. *Journal of Multicultural Social Work, 6, 1* (2), 41–57.

Gilligan, C. (1982). *In a different voice.* Cambridge, MA: Harvard University Press.

Greene, K., Causby, V., & Miller, D. H. (1999). The nature and function of fusion in the dynamics of lesbian relationships. *Affilia, 14* (1), 78– 97.

Gregg, R. (1994). Explorations of pregnancy and choice in a high-tech age. In C. Riessman (Ed.), *Qualitative studies in social work research.* Newbury Park, CA: Sage.

Grey, M.A. (1999). Immigrants, migration, and worker turnover at the hog pride pork packing plant. *Human Organization, 58* (1), 16–26.

Gupta, R. (1999). The revised caregiver burden scale: A preliminary evaluation. *Research on Social Work Practice, 9* (4), 508–520.

Hines, A. M., & Graves, K. L. (1998). AIDS protection and contraception among African American, Hispanic and white women. *Health and Social Work, 23* (3), 186–194.

Hudson, W. (1990). *The multi-problem screening inventory.* Tempe, AZ: Walmyr Publishing.

Kopp, J. (1988). Self-monitoring: A literature review of research and practice. *Social Work, 24* (4), 8–21.

Lewis, M. A., Giovannoni, J. M., & Leake, B. (1997). Two-year placement outcomes of children removed at birth from drug-using and non-drug-using mothers in Los Angeles. *Social Work Research, 21* (2), 81–90.

Marx, J. D. (1999). Motivational characteristics associated with health and human service volunteers. *Administration in Social Work, 23* (1), 51–66.

McCubbin, J. L., & Thomson, A. I. (Eds.) (1991). *Family assessment inventories for research and practice.* Madison, WI: University of Wisconsin.

National Association of Social Workers. (1997). NASW Code of Ethics. *NASW News, 25,* 25.

Nixon, S. J., Phillips, M., & Tivis, R. (2000). Characteristics of American-Indian clients seeking inpatient treatment for substance abuse. *Journal of Studies on Alcohol, 61* (4), 541–547.

Patton, M. (2001). *Qualitative research and evaluation methods* (5th ed.). Newbury Park, CA: Sage.

Savaya, R. (1998). Associations among economic need, self-esteem, and Israeli Arab women's attitudes toward and use of professional services. *Social Work, 43* (5), 445–454.

Schoenberg, N. E. (2000). Patterns, factors, and pathways contributing to nutritional risk among rural African American elders. *Human Organization, 59* (2), 234–244.

Stuart, P. (1999). Linking clients and policy: Social work's distinctive contribution. *Social Work, 44* (4) 335–347.

Teare, J. F., Peterson, R. W., Authier, K., Schroeder, L., & Daly, D. L. (1998). Maternal satisfaction following post-shelter family reunification. *Child & Youth Care Forum, 27* (2), 125–138.

Trussell, R. P. (1999). The children's streets—An ethnographic study of street children in Ciudad Juarez, Mexico. *International Social Work, 42* (2), 189–199.

Voss, R. W., Douville, V., Little Soldier, A., & White Hat, A. (1999). Wo'Lakol Kiciyapi: Traditional philosophies of helping and healing among the Lakotas: Toward a Lakota-centric practice of social work. *Journal of Multicultural Social Work, 7* (1/2), 73–93.

Leslie Parr

Organizing the Data

Sometimes you get so caught up in designing a project and in planning the data collection that once the data are in hand, you may wonder what to do with it all. The three types of research discussed in this book—practice evaluation, program evaluation, and needs assessment—all have the potential to overwhelm you with data.

This chapter is concerned with organizing the data once they are collected. This stage bridges the gap between data collection and data analysis. In generalist practice, data organization and data analysis are equivalent to analyzing resource capabilities in practice.

How the data are analyzed depends to a great extent on whether they are qualitative or quantitative. As discussed in Chapter 1, quantitative data are the result of fitting diverse phenomena into predetermined categories. These categories are then analyzed using statistical techniques. Qualitative data, on the other hand, produce a mass of detailed information in the form of words rather than numbers. Such data must be subjected to forms of analysis that will help make sense out of these words. These different kinds of data also require different strategies for their organization before they can be analyzed.

This chapter includes the following topics:

- organizing quantitative data
- organizing qualitative data
- the agency and organizing the data
- ethical issues in organizing the data
- human diversity issues in organizing the data

ORGANIZING QUANTITATIVE DATA

You work for a public agency that provides assistance to foster care families. Your supervisor has just asked you to develop a mail questionnaire for all foster families in the area served by the agency, to identify their unmet needs.

There are 300 foster families in your area. You send out a two-page questionnaire to all 300 families and receive 150 back. These questionnaires contain a considerable amount of valuable data for your agency. These data are in raw form, however, and as such they are not very useful to you. Imagine trying to tally answers to 30 questions for 150 questionnaires by hand—a time-consuming and tedious process. This mass of quantitative data can be analyzed using statistical procedures, which can be further facilitated through the use of the computer.

You need to be thinking about how the data will be organized as early in the research process as possible. This is especially important when you use a questionnaire to collect data, because the way questions are structured can influence the way data can ultimately be organized. Organizing quantitative data involves coding the data and using statistical software in preparation for analysis.

Coding the Data

Referring to the foster family questionnaire, the first step to transferring the information from the questionnaire to the computer is to code it. **Coding** involves organizing the collected information so that it can be entered into the computer. Coding is accomplished in three steps: (1) converting the responses to numerical codes; (2) assigning names to the variables; and (3) developing a code book.

Converting the Responses to Numerical Codes

In the foster care example, one question on the questionnaire is: "How many times in the last month were you contacted by a worker in the agency?" The response to this type of question is straightforward; it simply entails entering the number reported into the computer. Note that this response is at the ratio level of measurement and reflects the absolute magnitude of the value (see Chapter 3). The level of measurement determines the type of statistical analysis that we can perform. With ratio data, you have a great deal of latitude in that responses can be manipulated in a variety of ways: They can be added, subtracted, multiplied, and divided. They represent real numbers and are not strictly codes.

When you look at the other types of questions and their responses, however, often the number that is assigned to the response is a code, and there is a certain amount of arbitrariness in its assignment. This is the case with data at the nominal and ordinal levels of measurement. For example, the questionnaire might read: "How would you gauge your overall level of satisfaction with the services our agency provides? (Circle the most applicable response.)

   very satisfied   satisfied   somewhat satisfied   not satisfied

This information can be entered more easily if you assign numeral codes to each of the possible responses—for example:

   very satisfied   1

   satisfied   2

   somewhat satisfied   3

   not satisfied   4

Note that the level of measurement of this variable is ordinal. The numbers are ranked, but the distance between the numbers is not necessarily equal. Thus our use of these numbers in statistical analysis will be more limited than it was for those in the previous question. Note that this satisfaction question constitutes one variable with four different possible responses or values, coded 1 to 4.

Another question on the questionnaire is this: "Specifically, which services could be expanded to meet any of your needs more to your satisfaction? Please check all that apply."

   _____ Individual counseling

   _____ Family counseling

   _____ Training—preparation for foster child

   _____ Other, please specify: _____

For this question, more than one response could be checked. The easiest way to deal with this type of question is to divide it into three subquestions or three variables, rather than one. The three subquestions would be about individual counseling, family counseling, and training. A number would be assigned (1 or 2) according to whether the respondent checked or did not check each item. Note that here we are dealing with variables that are at the nominal level of measurement. The numbers have been assigned arbitrarily to the responses, and they are not ranked in any way.

		numerical code
individual counseling	checked (yes)	1
	not checked (no)	2
family counseling	checked (yes)	1
	not checked (no)	2
training	checked (yes)	1
	not checked (no)	2

Another characteristic of this question that demands special attention is the "other" item, which directs respondents to write in an answer. One solution is to categorize the response to this subquestion or variable into finite (countable) groups (for example, individual services, group services, information and referral, and so on) and then assign numbers to each of these groups. Alternately, the data can be fitted into existing categories. We need to be careful not to lose the meaning intended by the respondent. An alternate strategy is to treat answers to this item as qualitative data. After all, this is essentially a qualitative mode of collecting data, in that it is attempting to seek information from the subject's perspective rather than to impose previously constructed categories on the subject's behaviors. Organization of qualitative data will be discussed later in this chapter.

Whatever type of question/answer you are coding, two guidelines need to be followed: The coding categories should be mutually exclusive and exhaustive. When categories are mutually exclusive, a given response can be coded in one way only for each variable. That is why in the last example the question needed to be treated as several variables to accommodate the fact that more than one yes response was possible.

The codes should also be exhaustive; in other words, all the data need to be coded in some way. Coding is a tedious task in research. Do not omit coding some responses because you think you will not need them in the analysis. (If this is the case, the questions should not have been asked.) Moreover, it is difficult to perform coding later and to add to the data set once data analysis has begun. So, although it can be tiresome, coding must be done with care. Any mistakes lead to a misrepresentation of the results.

Assigning Names to the Variables

It is too cumbersome to enter the entire question into the computer. Also, the computer cannot read questions in this way. Consequently, the variables themselves need to be coded or named so that they can be understood by the computer.

This means translating the questions into words that are of a certain length—for example, usually no more than seven characters. Generally, the first character has to be a letter; it cannot be a numeral. It is useful to pick a variable name that relates to the question. Say the question was this: "How would you gauge your overall level of satisfaction with the services our agency provides?" A possible variable name could be SATISFY. For the question that asked about individual counseling, family counseling, and training services, these three variables could be denoted SERVICE1, SERVICE2, and SERVICE3.

Developing a Code Book

The code book is used to record how responses are coded and how each variable is named. The code book provides a reference for you and other researchers who would need to know or remember to what the codes originally referred. Sometimes, particularly on smaller projects, a code book may not be needed because the codes can be included on the questionnaire. When designing the questionnaire, bear this in mind; it can save work later. In the last example, you would need to note in the code book that the code for a yes response to the question about expanding individual counseling, family counseling, and/or training services is 1; for a no response, the code is 2.

The next step is to enter the information into the computer. To do this, you need a statistical software package.

Using Statistical Software

Statistical software can be used to make data analysis a simple and efficient task. Data are collected and then organized to be entered into the computer and analyzed by the statistical software, producing statistical results. Many statistical programming packages are available, such as SPSS.

Many of the programming principles are similar, whatever particular software you use. Some software is more user-friendly than others. For all of them, the following general steps are followed:

1. Data are usually entered in rows (although some statistical packages do not require this). Columns are assigned to variables. The first few columns are usually assigned to the ID number of the questionnaire or interview schedule. In the previous example, if 150 questionnaires were returned, three columns will be needed for the ID number to cover the ID numbers 001 to 150. The next variable, SATISFY, needs only one column because the codes range only from 1 to 4.

2. Names can be given to each of the variables. There are usually restrictions on the form and length of these variable names.

3. The program is run choosing from the menu of commands. Each command refers to a specific statistical test. You can also use the commands to recode the data—for example, to convert ratio level data into categories at the nominal level, or to give instructions concerning what to do about missing data.

4. You will receive **output** from running the program. The output will appear on the screen, or you can produce hard copy that contains the results of the statistical analysis.

To gain familiarity and confidence with this software, check out university computer centers. They usually provide workshops and instruction in the use of specific software packages. If you plan to do statistical analysis using a computer, these workshops, which are usually free to students, can be helpful.

ORGANIZING QUALITATIVE DATA

Organizing qualitative data can be even more overwhelming than organizing quantitative data, simply because of the nature of this type of information.

Quantitative data by definition are pieces of information that fit into certain categories, which in most cases have been previously defined. Consequently, organizing the data is a matter of ensuring that the data are correctly assigned to the categories and are in a form that the computer can read. On the other hand, qualitative data, once collected, are usually completely uncategorized, to capture as much in-depth information as possible. Analysis becomes a much more complex process.

Use of the computer is not confined to quantitative data, but is equally useful for organizing and analyzing qualitative data. Using any current writing and editing software allows different types of files to be maintained and cross-referenced with minimal effort.

In addition, software packages such as ETHNOGRAPH and NUDIST are designed specifically for analyzing qualitative data. Weitzman and Miles (1995) have compiled a good listing of qualitative software.

Before you start collecting data, it is a good idea to decide what software you will be using. Then you will be able to organize your field notes and codes accordingly.

Four different elements involved in the organization of qualitative data will be described: note keeping, organizing files, coding notes, and identifying gaps in the data.

Note Keeping

As discussed in Chapter 9, the primary mode of collecting qualitative data is through observation or interviewing. Much note keeping is involved. Sometimes, particularly in the case of participant observation or informal interviewing, these notes are haphazard. Consequently, one of the first steps is to organize and rewrite these field notes as soon as possible after you have taken them. Rewriting the notes will help jog your memory, and the result will be more detailed, comprehensive notes. Bernard (1994), an anthropologist, suggested five basic rules in the mechanics of note taking and managing field notes:

Field Notes

Travis et al. (1999) conducted a study with the objective of achieving a better understanding of community development in South Africa. The study was descriptive and attempted to analyze interventions in the three distinct communities of Cato Crest, Bhambayi, and Ndwedwe. The study was also exploratory in nature as the researchers were foreigners and thus needed to gain an understanding of the perceptions regarding the intervention strategies. The participants interviewed for the study were selected by a convenience sampling based on their work in community development. Instruments employed included interview guides, note taking, and a recording device to maintain the field notes.

1. Don't put your notes in one long commentary; use plenty of paper and keep many shorter notes.

2. Separate your note taking into physically separate sets of writing.
   - Field jottings—notes actually taken in the field. These provide the basis of field notes.
   - Field notes—write-ups from your jottings.
   - Field diary—a personal record of your experience in the field, chronicling how you feel and how you perceive your relations with others in the field.
   - Field log—a running account of how you plan to spend your time, how you actually spend it, and how much money you spend.

3. Take field jottings all the time; don't rely on your memory.

4. Don't be afraid of offending people when you are taking field jottings.

   (Bernard made an interesting point about this: Being a participant observer does not mean that you *become* a fully accepted member of the group, but rather you *experience* the life of your informants to the extent possible.) Ask permission to take notes; usually it will be given. You can also offer to share your notes with those being interviewed.

5. Set aside some time each day to write up your field notes.

When collecting qualitative data, you can **transcribe** interviews (write down verbatim the contents of a recording of the interview). Transcriptions are extremely time-consuming; it takes six to eight hours to transcribe a one-hour interview. Sometimes, in the case of process recordings (discussed in Chapter 7), you can complete a shorthand transcription, writing down the main interactions in sequence. This results in something more complete than field notes but less detailed than a full transcription.

Of course, there may be occasions when the transcription is necessary and central to the study. For example, Marlow (1983) transcribed from a videotape a

Using a Transcription

Haight et al. (2001) conducted case-based research to study the behaviors of mothers and children during foster care visitations. In this study, nine mothers and their 24-month-old to 48-month-old children were videotaped during their 1-hour long visitations. Following the visits, the mothers participated in in-depth, audiotaped interviews. The videotaped interactions between parent and child and the audiotaped interviews with the mothers were transcribed verbatim to capture verbal behaviors in addition to a description of nonverbal behaviors such as actions, gestures, and facial expressions.

behavior therapy interview to look at the relationship between nonverbal and verbal behaviors. The transcription included small behaviors—for example, intonation and slight movements of the hands and facial features. Descriptions can give some important, detailed information that can enrich our understanding of client and worker experiences.

Organizing Files

Your rewritten field notes will form your basic or master file. Always keep backup copies of these notes as a precautionary measure. As you proceed with data collection, you will need different types of files or sets of notes. Generally, at a minimum you will need five types of files: descriptive files, methodological files, biographical files, bibliographical files, and analytical files.

The descriptive file includes information on the topic being studied. In the case of a program evaluation, this file would include information on the program itself, its history, its development, and so forth. Initially, this file will contain most of your notes.

The methodological file or set of notes deals with the techniques of collecting data. It gives you the opportunity to record what you think has improved or damaged your interviewing and observation techniques.

The biographical file includes information on individuals interviewed or included in the study. For example, it might include information about clients, the director, and so on.

The bibliographical file contains references for material you have read related to the study. This file is similar to the type of file you might keep when completing a research term paper.

Finally, the analytical file provides the beginnings of the analysis proper. It contains notes on the kinds of patterns you see emerging from the data. For example, when interviewing the clients of a family service agency, you may have detected the relationship between their perceptions about the benefits of the program and the specific type of problem they brought to the agency. Consequently, you may start a file labeled "Benefit-Problem." Your analytical set of notes will initially be the smallest file. Further discussion on the analysis of qualitative data will be in Chapter 11.

Do not forget to cross reference your files. Some materials in the "Benefit-Problem" file pertaining to a particular client may need to be cross-referenced with a specific biographical client file. A note in each will suffice. This preparation and organization will help the analysis later on.

Coding Notes

In addition to cross-referencing the five main types of notes, additional coding will help when you come to the analysis stage. As you write up the field notes, use codes for categorizing the notes. These codes can be recorded at the top of each page of notes or in the margin and can be either numbers or letters. Don't forget, though, to keep a code book just as you would for quantitative data.

Obviously, these codes will vary in their precision and form depending on the purpose of the study. In a program evaluation, the codes may refer to the different channels of authority within the organization, the different types of clients served, or any other aspect of the program that is of concern in the evaluation.

In a practice evaluation where you may be monitoring the application of an intervention, codes can be used to categorize the content of the interview or meeting. A description of how this coding is carried out is included in Chapter 11.

Identifying Gaps in the Data

Throughout the organization of the data, you need to keep notes on gaps in the data or missing information. Keeping track of gaps is not so necessary in a quantitative study when decisions pertaining to data collection are made early in the study. With a qualitative study, however, you often do not know what data need to be collected until well into the project, when new insights and ideas relating to the study become apparent.

THE AGENCY AND ORGANIZING THE DATA

The central message here is to make optimal use of current software. If your agency does not have easy access to current software for analyzing data, lobby for it.

ETHICAL ISSUES IN ORGANIZING THE DATA

Two ethical issues are involved in data organization—one for each type of data: quantitative and qualitative. For quantitative data, ethical issues are minimized because most decisions about how to handle the data have been made prior to the organization stage of the research. The major problem is how to deal with the "other" responses.

As mentioned before, you can create categories for these responses, or they can be fitted into existing categories. In adopting the latter approach, you need to be careful to preserve the integrity of the data and to put the data into categories that are appropriate and do not simply reflect your preferences.

Ethical issues relating to the organization of qualitative data are more pervasive. At each stage you must be careful that your biases do not overtly interfere. For example, when compiling field notes from your field jottings, ensure that your field notes and compilation reflect as closely as possible your observations in the field and are not molded to fit your existing or developing hypothesis. This is a difficult process because one of the underlying principles governing the interpretive approach (which usually involves qualitative data) is that objectivity is not the overriding principle driving the research. Instead, the researcher recognizes the role of subjectivity and that the nature of the data is in part a product of the relationship between the researcher and the participant.

When coding the notes, be aware of this subjectivity issue. If you doubt your objectivity, you may want to consult with someone who can examine part of your notes or your coding scheme and give you some feedback. What you are doing here is conducting a reliability check, which in itself can serve the purpose of ensuring that the research is being conducted in an ethical manner.

HUMAN DIVERSITY ISSUES IN ORGANIZING THE DATA

The primary human diversity issue parallels the ethical issues concerning quantitative data that were just discussed. When ambiguous data are categorized, such as responses to "other" questions, attention needs to be paid to ensuring that the categorization adequately accounts for the various human diversity issues that may be involved in the responses.

Human diversity issues arise in different stages in the organization of qualitative data. Field notes need to reflect any human diversity elements, although this depends on from whom you are getting your information. The coding also needs to tap this dimension. And you may wish to pay particular attention to whether or not human diversity issues were addressed when trying to determine whether gaps exist in your data. For example, in collecting data on clients' perceptions of the services they are receiving from a family service agency, it may be important to ask clients about how significant their social worker's ethnicity is to them or whether they feel that their social worker and the agency are sensitive to cultural differences.

SUMMARY

Organizing quantitative data includes coding the data and identifying statistical software packages. Organizing qualitative data also involves identifying appropriate software, in addition to note keeping, organizing the files, coding the notes, and identifying gaps in the data. Ethical and human diversity issues include ensuring that the integrity of the data is preserved.

STUDY/EXERCISE QUESTIONS

1. The agency in which you are employed has no computers available to the social workers. As a means of lobbying for computers, draw up a list of the ways in which the computer could be used for research and practice in the agency.

2. Construct a questionnaire of about five items to find out students' attitudes on combining research with practice. Administer the questionnaire to five students in the class.

   a. Create a code book.

   b. Enter the data in a computer using statistical software.

3. Interview five students in the research class about their attitudes on combining research with practice. How would you organize these data?

INFOTRAC COLLEGE EDITION

1. Search for *transcription*. Describe a study that transcribed the data.

REFERENCES

Bernard, H. R. (1994). *Research methods in cultural anthropology.* Newbury Park, CA: Sage.

Haight, W. L., Black, J. E., Workman, C. L., & Tata, L. (2001). Parent-child interaction during foster care visits. *Social Work, 46* (4), 325–335.

Marlow, C. R. (1983). *The organization of interaction in a behavior therapy interview.* Unpublished doctoral dissertation. Chicago, IL: University of Chicago.

Travis, R., McFarlin, N., van Rooyen, C. A. J., & Gray, M. (1999). Community development in South Africa. *International Social Work, 42* (2), 177–187.

Weitzman, E. A., & Miles, M. B. (1995). *Computer programs for qualitative data analysis.* Newbury Park, CA: Sage.

Analysis of Qualitative Data

With Colin Collett van Rooyen, M.Soc.Sc.

Working with qualitative data can initially appear overwhelming! For the new qualitative researcher, Mason (2002) suggests that the almost reflexive "impulse to impose some form of organization and order to your data" (p. 8) simply adds to the feeling of being overwhelmed. No matter how you collect qualitative data—through interviews, open-ended questionnaires, or personal logs—the amount of data and its apparent lack of order can become an unnecessary stressor. However, this need not be so, because there are systems for organizing and managing the data in ways that allow the producer and consumer of the data to interact with it in a meaningful way.

This chapter describes ways that qualitative data can be analyzed. The primary focus of this chapter will be on analyzing data in qualitative/inductive studies. Although qualitative studies will be the focus, some of the techniques and approaches discussed can also be used to analyze the qualitative data collected as part of primarily quantitative studies.

This chapter discusses the following topics:

- Comparing qualitative and quantitative data analysis
- Planning the analysis of qualitative data
- Identifying categories in qualitative data analysis
- Interpreting qualitative data
- Validating qualitative data
- Writing qualitative reports
- The agency and qualitative analysis
- Ethical issues in qualitative analysis
- Human diversity issues in qualitative analysis

COMPARING QUALITATIVE AND QUANTITATIVE DATA ANALYSIS

Analysis of qualitative data and analysis of quantitative data differ in a number of important ways, and these differences will be discussed in this section (see Table 11.1). Quantitative data analysis will be considered in full in the following chapter. The common conception is that qualitative data analysis is "easier" than quantitative, mostly because quantitative data are analyzed using statistical procedures, and we all know that statistics are something we want to avoid, right? Wrong, as we will see in the next chapter. Actually, we will see that qualitative data analysis has its own difficulties, different from those confronted during statistical analysis but nonetheless equally if not more challenging. Let us now look at these differences.

First, the distinctions among data collection, data organization, and data analysis are much more difficult to define when the data are qualitative. Data analysis can often begin before data collection is completed, and this initial analysis can often influence further data collection. Thus when a study involves

Table 11.1　　**Comparing quantitative and qualitative data analysis**

Quantitative analysis	Qualitative analysis
Data collection, organization, and analysis are discrete steps	Data collection, organization, and analysis are often conducted simultaneously
Structured statistical tests are used	Unstructured methods of analysis are used
The goal of the analysis is to establish statistical significance	The goal of the analysis is to identify patterns in the data
Data are "separated" for analysis	Data are kept in context for analysis
Deductive process of analysis	Inductive process of analysis

primarily qualitative data the research process becomes more fluid and circular. Obviously this flexibility can provide important insights and discoveries throughout the project, but on the other hand the lack of structure places considerable responsibility on the researcher to make decisions that are not guided by the research process itself.

Second, the methods of analysis themselves are also much less structured than they are with quantitative data. As a result, qualitative data analysis is much more challenging and at times difficult to complete successfully. Many decisions are left to the researcher's discretion. This raises important issues surrounding the impact of the researcher's values on the research. As we discussed in Chapter 1, the qualitative approach focuses less on capturing an "objective" reality and more on the "subjective" experience. However, despite the emphasis on subjectivity, there needs to be an awareness of one's own values as a researcher and their possible impact on the data analysis. This is more difficult to maintain than at first it may appear.

A third way that qualitative and quantitative data analyses differ is that the primary mission in the analysis of qualitative data is to look for patterns in the data, noting similarities and differences. Various techniques can be used to identify these patterns. In quantitative analysis the emphasis is on establishing the statistical significance of the findings based on probability theory.

Fourth, one of the goals of quantitative data analysis is to "separate" the data and to place it in discrete groups, the "cleaning" referred to in the last chapter. With qualitative data it is important to keep the data in context (Neuman, 2003). Understanding the context within which an action took place and through which meaning was developed is central to the qualitative research process. Information interpreted or presented that is devoid of contextual content is thus seen as information that is lacking in ability to convey meaning and may present an event or situation in a distorted manner. Contextual analysis is central to qualitative research. Data must always be presented in context by referring to the specific situations, time periods, and persons around which the identified pattern occurred.

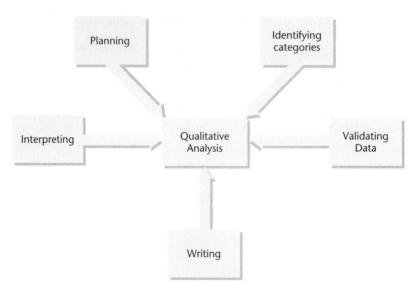

Figure 11.1 **Dimensions of qualitative analysis**

Fifth, qualitative data analysis tends to be inductive rather than deductive as discussed earlier in this text. Quantitative data is often used to test hypotheses derived from theoretical constructs. With qualitative analysis, careful observation leads to the description of connections and patterns in the data that can in turn enable us to form hypotheses and develop them into theoretical constructs and theories. These theories evolve as the data are collected and as the process of interim analysis takes place. In this way, and given the cognizance afforded to contextual issues, the findings are grounded in real life patterns—hence the term *grounded theory* is also used to refer to qualitative data analysis (Glaser and Strauss, 1967).

In this chapter four steps in the analysis of qualitative data will be discussed. These steps include planning the analysis; identifying categories; looking at relationships; and validating the data (see Figure 11.1).

PLANNING THE ANALYSIS OF QUALITATIVE DATA

Organizing both qualitative and quantitative data was discussed in the last chapter. With qualitative data this involves note keeping, including transcribing, organizing the files, coding the data, and identifying gaps in the data. The next step, and the one considered here, is to set up a plan for the data analysis. This is important, because as we discussed earlier in this chapter, there are not as many prescribed rules or steps to follow as with quantitative analysis.

The first step is to read over all the transcribed material so that you get a sense of the data as a whole. As you proceed, take down some brief notes and jot

down some beginning ideas. For example, you may see in a st
living with HIV, that the women mention "abandonment" fai.
and that when they talk about support "friends" are mentioned freq

This leads us to the second important component of this planning
you have not done so already you need to start a research journal. This ide
introduced initially in Chapter 9 as a part of the data collection process. In the
journal you record the process of the study and record ideas and insights. For
example, you might note that when abandonment is mentioned it is often done
in the context of a discussion of family. Make a note of this. Remember context
is important. Don't worry about systematically recording observations at this
point, as later in the analysis you will need to be more systematic. Here the concern is with noting insights and things that "jump out at you" from the data.

The journal not only helps you to "remember" your ideas as they occur to
you, but it also provides an "audit trail" (Tutty, Rothery, and Grinnell, 1996). An
audit trail is used if and when an outside person is brought in to review your
work and to make sure there are not any serious problems or flaws with the
analysis. This is particularly important with a qualitative study because of the
lack of the clear, precise, and regulated rules to guide the analysis.

IDENTIFYING CATEGORIES IN QUALITATIVE DATA ANALYSIS

As mentioned earlier, qualitative studies generally use an inductive rather than a
deductive approach. Patterns emerge from the data rather than being developed
prior to collection. The data are organized, classified, and edited into an accessible package. The researcher begins to sift out pieces of data that are considered
relevant to the aims of the study and codes and categorizes these data as a means
of developing themes. Hence your next step in the analysis of the data is to start
creating these categories and coding them.

Tutty, Rothery, and Grinnell (1996) suggest that there are two levels of
coding and categorizing in qualitative data analysis, and the following guide follows their recommendations.

The **first level of coding** involves identifying meaning units and fitting
them into categories and assigning codes to these categories. This happens as
you read and reread the data. This is time-consuming and involves five tasks:

1. *Identifying the important experiences or ideas in the data or "meaning units,"* i.e.
   finding out what pieces of data fit together. Eventually they will develop
   into patterns that will provide the core of your interpretation (the next
   step). The meaning units can be thought of as the building blocks of the
   analysis. A unit can be a word, a sentence, or part of a sentence or a paragraph, or more. This is the part of the analysis where you have to be aware of
   your possible biases and interests in the research. For example, in the example of women with HIV, one type of meaning unit might be those relating to
   the women feeling alone and helpless, another might relate to their feelings
   of sadness about their children.

2. *Fitting the meaning units into categories and assigning category names* to groups of similar meaning. This stage is quite challenging because you have to decide how the meaning units interrelate with one another. There is no set number of categories that you will end up with; the more you have, the more complex the study. Also remember that these categories can change as you progress with the analysis. For example, possible categories in the women and HIV study may include: feelings of abandonment and helplessness; ways in which the women are gaining control of their lives; feelings of sadness about their children; approaches to their treatment; types of family support; concerns about children's welfare; and relationships with spouses. However, you later decide that "ways in which they are gaining control of their lives" in fact includes two main meaning units: "ways of maintaining their health" and "seeking supports outside the family." Later you may find more.

3. *Assigning codes or a form of shorthand to the categories.* This is fairly straightforward; the codes are made up of one or two letters. For example, F for types of family support, H for ways of maintaining their health.

4. *Refining and reorganizing coding.* Before moving on to the next stage of analysis, review your work and do not hesitate to make changes. As you become more and more familiar with the data, your confidence in making the right kinds of decisions about the analysis will increase.

5. *Deciding when to stop.* One way of determining an ending point is that when you interview new participants their responses fit easily into the existing categories.

First-level coding is fairly concrete; you are identifying properties of data that are clearly evident rather than undertaking interpretation.

The **second level of coding** is more abstract and involves interpreting the data. Here you identify similarities and differences between the categories as a first step in finding relationships. This involves two tasks:

1. *Retrieving meaning units from each of the interviews into categories,* preferably using a computer program designed for this purpose or simply cutting and pasting using writing software. At this level you are beginning to compare data across respondents.

2. *Comparing and contrasting categories,* the goal being to integrate the categories into themes. For example, you may decide that "concern about children's welfare" and "feelings of sadness about children" comprise one theme: "relationships between mothers and their children." Relationships between categories can be based on similarity of content (the above example) or they can be based on time (i.e. one category always precedes another) or on causality. This latter type of relationship is difficult to establish, though (remember all the conditions needed to establish causality?) as we will see later when the analysis is validated. Once a theme is identified you assign a code to it (as you did with the categories).

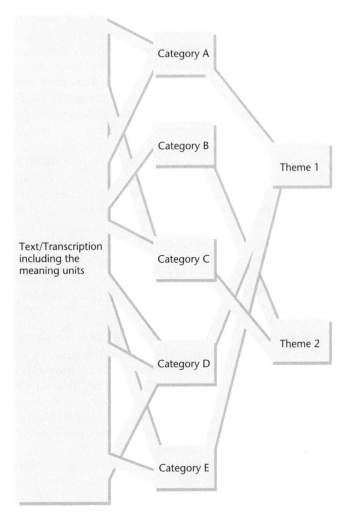

Figure 11.2 **Stages in the analysis of qualitative analysis**

Types of Categories

At this point it is important to note that categories can be conceptualized as two types: indigenous categories and researcher-constructed categories (see Figure11.2). You need to decide at the point of collecting the data which of these approaches you will be using.

Indigenous Categories

Indigenous categories, which use the **emic** approach, identify the categories used by those observed or adopt the natives' point of view. In many ways, this approach is compatible with the practice skills of building rapport and developing empathy so that the worker can see the world from the client's point of view.

Indigenous categories are constructed from data collected using the **frame elicitation technique**. Frame elicitation involves asking or posing questions in such a way that you find out from the research participants what they include in a particular topic or category. An approach that works well for community needs or strengths assessments is to ask subjects what kinds of strengths community members already have that will help resolve identified community challenges.

For example, if you are interested in finding ways in which the community can better deal with its physically challenged citizens, you can ask: "What kinds of services for the hearing impaired can community members offer?" Categories of responses are then elicited from the respondents rather than from the researcher. To identify overlapping areas of different responses, the researcher can ask whether one category of response is the same as or part of another category.

Using our example, the question would be framed thus: "Is afterschool care the same as respite care?" Such questions elicit data with which you can construct a taxonomy of services from the respondent's perspective.

Another example of this process was one used by Main (1998), who studied a group of South African health workers' understandings of community participation. Main went to great lengths to ensure that the research participants defined the categories of their responses. Through a group process participants were able to identify common responses and develop their own categorizations of "community participation." Through the use of frame elicitation, questions were posed by Main that helped to clarify the participant's explanations rather than a "once-removed" researcher imposing his or her own categories.

You need to be aware of a number of issues when constructing taxonomies or categories in this way. First, inter-informant variation is common, that is different informants may use different words to refer to the same category of things. Second, category labels may be fairly complex, consisting of a phrase or two rather than simply a word or two. Third, for some categories, informants may have no label at all. Fourth, the categories overlap.

Where possible, the use of group processes for data gathering may allow for clarity and identification of different terminology for similar concepts. Groups, however, are not always ideal because group dynamics themselves can impact on the process. Once these issues have been considered, however, indigenous categories can be useful to the generalist social worker. You can be assured that the case is being presented from the client's perspective and is not being interpreted inappropriately by the researcher. This allows for a level of integrity in the results that creates a sense of trustworthiness and credibility, important components in qualitative research.

The use of indigenous categories is essential to the specific qualitative approach called *phenomenology*. The details of this approach (see Patton, 2001) will not be discussed here except to note that it is concerned with answering the question: "What is the experience of this phenomenon for these people?" To capture this experience, the researcher should use indigenous categories.

Using Indigenous Categories or Themes

Krumer-Nevo (1998) listened to the stories of three mothers from multi-problem families regarding their perceptions of their stressful situations and methods of assistance available to them. After recording their responses, the author derived categories, based on the language they used, which accurately portrayed their experiences. "The way distress and obtaining help are experienced are keys to understanding the central conflicts of the speaker, her central sensitivities, and the code of her interpretative system."

Researcher-Constructed Categories

Parsons (2001) studied empowerment-based practice in two groups—one for welfare recipients and one for domestic violence victims. She analyzed the data using previously decided on categories: the presenting situation or problem; the environment; and the practice strategy. Themes were organized within these categories—for example in the category "presenting situation," the themes were isolation; depression; alienation; needing community, commonality, and support; and seeking relationship and mutuality.

Researcher-Constructed Categories

Researcher-constructed categories are categories that researchers apply to the data. Studies using researcher-constructed categories can be considered qualitative as long as the study follows the major principle of qualitative research—namely, that data are considered in context rather than through rigidly imposed categories. The researcher makes informed decisions, based on her or his knowledge of the field of study and about the types of responses that may emerge. The specific aims and objectives of the study will also influence the process of category construction and the resulting themes.

Content Analysis

Content analysis is a type of qualitative analysis that involves researcher-constructed categories. The content of interviews and documents is coded, i.e. put into researcher constructed categories, and then inferences are made based on the incidence of these codes.

The emphasis of content analysis is on description, and content analysis is less concerned with looking at relationships between categories and themes. This approach was first mentioned in Chapter 9 in discussion of the use of secondary data. Content analysis can be performed on transcribed recorded interviews,

Content Analysis

Grise-Owens (2002) conducted content analysis of the *Journal of Social Work Education* over the two-year period of 1998–1999. Sixty-five articles were included in the content analysis. The author notes that five themes of subtle and systemic sexism emerged from the works in the journal. These themes included: Discrepancies in pronoun usage; sexist language; inconsistent attention to gender as a variable or construct; and inattention to gender as a framework in understanding topics. Findings of the content analysis showed that the majority of articles in the *Journal of Social Work Education* were either "inattentive to gender or that the consideration of gender was inconsistent" (p. 152). Grise-Owens recommends replication of the study to assess if the themes are prevalent in other journals, too.

process recordings on a case, published articles in newspapers or journals, and so forth.

Alter and Evens (1990) suggested six steps for content analysis:

1.   Select the constructs of interest and define them clearly.

2.   Select a unit of analysis (word, sentence, phrase, theme, and so on) to be coded.

3.   Define the categories. They should be mutually exclusive and fairly narrow.

4.   Test this classification scheme on a document/recording.

5.   Revise if reliability is low, and test again until an acceptance level of reliability is achieved.

6.   Code the text of interest and do a category count.

Allen-Meares (1984) discussed the important role that content analysis can have in social work research. An early example of content analysis is provided by Hollis (1972), who used coding typology. Hollis was interested in describing and understanding the communications that take place in social casework interviews.

Interviews were transcribed and coded line by line using the following codes: U—unclassified; A—sustainment; B—direct influence; C—exploration, description, ventilation; D—person-situation reflection; E—pattern-dynamic reflection; F—developmental reflection. Interviews could then be understood depending upon the frequency of the different types of communication. These codes were developed specifically for casework practice; thus, different categories would need to be developed to do content analysis on generalist practice interviews.

Although content analysis is often used in social work research it has a number of problems. First, the validity of codes, like any other researcher-constructed category, may be an issue. Second, the coding of the text can be unreliable if it is done by only one coder. Intercoder reliability should be established, which often means training the coder. Third, the coding almost inevitably involves lifting concepts out of context, which essentially negates much of the value of qualitative research.

INTERPRETING QUALITATIVE DATA

This is probably the most exciting stage in qualitative analysis, at the heart of what you are trying to accomplish. Interpretation involves looking at the relationships between variables and concepts. Tutty, Rothery, and Grinnell's (1996) discussion of qualitative analysis identifies two steps in this process: first, developing classification systems, and, second, developing hypotheses and theories.

Developing Classification Systems

Different strategies can be used for interpreting the data:

Cluster Diagrams

Author diagrams involve drawing circles for each theme and arrange them in relation to one another, some may overlap and some may stand alone. Make larger circles for the themes that are most important. This is a good approach if you are a visual learner!

Matrices

Data can also be displayed and analyzed in a table or **matrix**. If we use the earlier example of the Zulu *isangoma* and his or her interactions with the client, we may develop a table or matrix that could look something like the table presented in Table 11.2.

This table allows the researcher to organize data in a way that they are easily accessible, have some structure, and allow the identification of relationships. In our hypothetical example, the system that the researcher has used allows easy access to positive, negative, and neutral responses and also helps attempts to link clients to types of responses.

Counts

You can use **counts** to track the occurrences of the meaning units, categories, or themes without your study becoming quantitative. It gives another dimension to the analysis and also helps you to detect any biases that might have influenced your handling of the data. This is often the approach taken in content analysis.

Metaphors

Metaphors can be useful when you are thinking about relationships within the data. An example of a metaphor is the one used by Gregg (1994) when she studied the perceptions of women and their pregnancies. She used the term "a little bit pregnant" to depict the women's thinking about a future pregnancy, their perception that it in fact began, in their eyes, before the actual conception.

Table 11.2   **Matrix of client questions and isangoma responses**

Client questions	Positive response	Negative response	Neutral response
"Will I be wealthy one day?"	Client A: "Yes, you have worked hard and you will be rewarded."	Client B: "You will continue to struggle in this life."	Client E: "Wealth is not important, what is more important is that you and your family are healthy."
	Client C: "How can you ask me this? It is clear that you will be wealthy, the ancestors say this."	Client D: "Wealth is not important to you so you will never be rich, but you will be happy."	Client F: "This is not something that I can speak about— maybe you need to consult a bank manager on this."
"Can you cure me of HIV?"	Client A: "I can make medicine from herbs that can cure you of any illness."	Client C: "No, there is no cure of that disease—but you will have money to make your life good."	Client D: "Often people ask me that question, but I do not know the true answer as they do not return to me to tell me how the herbs have worked."
	Client B: "You may struggle with wealth but you will be cured of this illness."	Client E: "There is nothing that I can do to stop you from getting ill."	Client F: "This I cannot answer—it depends on many things that are beyond my work."

Missing Links

It may be that two categories or themes seem to be related, but in fact there may be a third variable linking them; this is referred to as a **missing link**.

Contradictory Evidence

Contradictory evidence must always be accounted for and not simply ignored. This evidence can be used to help validate data and will be discussed later in this chapter.

Developing Hypotheses and Theories

Qualitative research is primarily concerned with developing hypotheses, rather than with testing them. Part of qualitative and interpretive analysis, however, does involve speculation about causality and linkages. One way of representing and presenting causality is to construct **causal flowcharts**. These are visual representations of ideas that emerge from studying the data, seeing patterns, and seeing possible causes for phenomena. We have been using causal flowcharts in this text to illustrate some of the research methods. Often, causal flowcharts consist of a set of boxes connected by arrows. The boxes contain descriptions of states (attitudes, perceptions, ages, and so on), and the arrows show that one state leads to another. See Figure 11.3 for an example of a causal flowchart.

The development of hypotheses and causal statements should be firmly rooted in the data and not imposed on the data or overly influenced by the researcher's theoretical biases. If a researcher uses a category previously defined theoretically, the qualitative nature of the research can be ensured by the nature of the data collection methods and the manner in which those data are used either to support or to refute the categories. The context of the data must be taken into full consideration. The researcher should try to avoid the linear thinking associated with quantitative analysis. A strength of qualitative analysis is its potential for revealing contextual interrelationships among factors and their circular and interdependent natures.

VALIDATING QUALITATIVE DATA

Validation of qualitative data requires rather different processes than validation of quantitative data. Processes for validation of qualitative data include consideration of rival or alternative hypotheses, negative cases, triangulation, preservation of the context of the data, and establishing your own credibility.

Rival or Alternative Hypotheses

After a hypothesis has been developed and proposed, **rival or alternative hypotheses** need to be explored and compared to the proposed hypothesis. Rival hypotheses can emerge from the literature or from the data. The rival

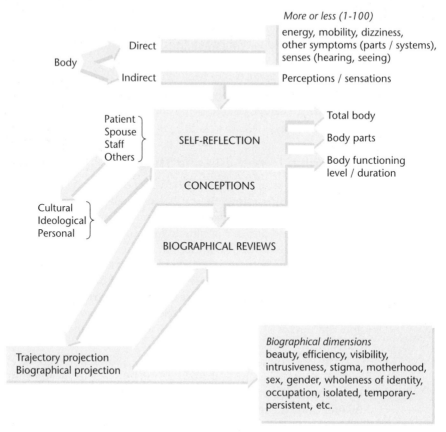

Figure 11.3   **An example of a causal flow chart**

Source: From *Basics of qualitative Research* by A. Strauss and J. Corbin, 1998, Thousand Oaks, CA: Sage Publications, p. 240. Reprinted by permission of Sage Publications.

hypotheses and the proposed hypothesis are both tested by looking at the data and considering which hypothesis appears to most closely reflect the data. In some cases, more than one hypothesis appears to be supported.

Negative Cases

Patterns in data emerge when researchers look at what occurs most often. Almost always, however, there are exceptions, or **negative cases**, that do not fit the patterns. These need to be examined and explained.

When you encounter a case that does not fit your theory, ask yourself whether it is the result of (1) normal social variation, (2) your lack of knowledge about the range of appropriate behavior, or (3) a genuinely unusual case.

Triangulation Using Different Data Sources

Varga (2002) used multiple data sources to investigate abortion experiences among female and male Zulu adolescents in KwaZulu/Natal, South Africa. Additionally, the study explored methods of pregnancy termination and the role of abortion in young people's sexual experiences. To elicit as much rich information as possible, Varga used a variety of data sources including focus groups, narrative workshops, role playing, involved surveys, and in-depth interviews. Varga suggested that "the methodological triangulation used offers the opportunity for alternative theoretical and methodological approaches to research on abortion-related issues" (p. 283).

Force yourself to think creatively on this issue. As Bernard (1994) stated: "If the cases won't fit, don't be too quick to throw them out. It is always easier to throw out cases than it is to reexamine one's ideas, and the easy way out is hardly ever the right way in research" (p. 321).

Triangulation

Triangulation involves the use of different research approaches to study the same research question. The most usual method of triangulation is to collect different kinds of data, such as interviews and observations, which may include both qualitative and quantitative data. Another approach is to have different people collect and analyze the data or to use different theories to interpret the data.

Using triangulation may result in what appears to be conflicting information. Such conflicts do not automatically invalidate the proposed hypothesis. Instead, such conflicts may simply indicate that new and different information has been acquired, adding another dimension to our understanding of the phenomenon being studied.

Preserving the Context of the Data

One central purpose of qualitative data analysis is that the data are kept in context. This contextualization provides a greater level of assurance that the findings are not distorted. The context of each response needs to be considered. Additionally, it is important to recognize the limitations of the sampling method used, for these limitations can affect the external validity of the findings. Generally, sampling methods are purposive in interpretive studies. The context of the findings is limited; to put it another way, the findings have limited generalizability.

The Limited Context of the Findings

Pettys and Balgopal (1998) studied the multigenerational conflicts that Indo-American immigrants experience. Interviews with 30 Indo-American families, some including grandparents, revealed the natures of the major conflicts, the role of grandparents, and the coping strategies these families used. The authors identified several areas in which this study is limited: the small sample size, the economic profile of the families interviewed (i.e. middle and upper-middle classes), the non-Brahman identity of the families (vs. Brahman identities, which are different), and the fact that all of the families were from South India, which tends to be more conservative than other regions of India.

Establishing Your Own Credibility

Because qualitative analysis depends so much on the researcher rather than on the methods, it is essential that you are extremely careful about your records. Keeping an accurate research journal is critical. In it you can document the process and record any particular biases you think you might have.

WRITING THE QUALITATIVE REPORT

A qualitative report can be written using different approaches. Although research writing is the focus of Chapter 13, some of the different types of qualitative studies will be discussed here. These types include case studies, analytical studies, and ethnographies. Bear in mind that there is considerable overlap among these different types.

Case Studies

A **case study** may be about the "case" of an event, an individual, or an institution, or any other phenomenon that is identifiable in itself. The narrative can be **chronological** or **thematic** (or both) but it is generally primarily descriptive. For example, case study may take the form of an account that describes the life of the participant since the day she heard of her HIV positive test result—touching on important events since that day. This would constitute a chronological narrative. A thematic narrative would use the themes that emerged through the organization of the data as the framework for presentation.

Analytical Studies

An **analytical study** is more concerned with looking at the relationships between variables (as discussed previously). In other words, it is more explanatory. It might involve a needs assessment or a program evaluation. The Parsons (2001) study is an example of a program evaluation.

A Case Study

Cooper and Lesser (1997) explored how race affects the helping process in their description of a cross-racial therapy session between a white female worker and an African-American woman. The authors describe approaches taken by the worker and proposals as to what she could have done differently. They examine issues of biculturalism, identity development, and the effects of cross-racial counseling through the case material.

An Analytical Qualitative Study

Parsons (2001) carried out a qualitative study of two groups, a domestic violence survivors group (DVS) providing personal support and a group of welfare recipients who had formed a coalition to change welfare policies. Both were empowerment focused. The two groups reported some different experiences that helped them change and also many common experiences. Although the welfare recipients group did not join the group for personal change, they reported that it did have that effect. Similarly, the DVS group did not join the group to gain awareness of the social problem of domestic violence, but they reported that this knowledge was important for their change. Overall the results provide important information for optimizing the effectiveness of empowerment-based groups.

Ethnographies

One particular type of qualitative report is an **ethnography**. As described in Chapter 9, ethnography is a description of a culture. Usually, ethnographic interviewing is used, which involves collecting "stories" from individuals about the study topic. Ethnography is also regarded as a specific approach to qualitative research (see Patton, 2001, for a presentation of the different approaches to qualitative research). Historically, ethnography was the domain of anthropology. Anthropologists rely on participant observation to produce ethnographic studies or monographs of cultures.

Social workers have recognized the value of this approach in describing the different cultures with which they are involved—for example, the culture of homelessness or of gangs. In anthropology, ethnographies are often long and detailed, but social work researchers have produced mini-ethnographies. Note that ethnographies (both full-length and short ones) can also be a useful resource for social workers and can help acquaint them with the cultures with which they work.

An Example of an Ethnography

An interesting example of an ethnography is provided by Gordon (2002) who while teaching an undergraduate course, "Race, Culture, and Class," involved some of her students who were gang members in an ethnographic study of gangs. Data included personal essays and the results of students interviewing gang members. A number of themes emerged from the data including separation from family; separation from other students; masking of self; and hesitancy to ask for assistance. The results provided an understanding of the "culture" of the college experience for former gang members, including their educational perceptions and aspirations.

THE AGENCY AND QUALITATIVE ANALYSIS

Qualitative data and its subsequent analysis can be invaluable to the generalist social worker. By its nature, it is compatible with practice. We interview as part of our practice, and we keep logs as part of our practice. Both are important sources of qualitative data.

One preconception about qualitative analysis is that it is not as complex as quantitative analysis and does not require as sophisticated skills as does quantitative analysis. One goal of conducting qualitative research in an agency setting is to dispel this notion, both to enhance the credibility of qualitative studies and to earn the time and support necessary to conduct qualitative data analysis thereby producing reports that can make a meaningful contribution to the agency.

ETHICAL ISSUES IN QUALITATIVE ANALYSIS

There are ethical issues in the analysis of qualitative data that you don't encounter in the analysis of quantitative data. Quantitative analysis is protected by the nature of statistical analysis and the rules that govern the statistical significance of findings. Without this kind of objective guide, the interpretation and analysis of qualitative data depend a great deal more on judgment; thus, the possibility that ethical standards might be violated increases.

Personal, intellectual, and professional biases are more likely to interfere with qualitative data analysis, despite the existence of validation controls. For example, sometimes it can be tempting to ignore negative cases, implying that there is more agreement than actually exists among the findings to make the proposed hypothesis or argument appear stronger. For example, a negative case may not have been examined because the researcher did not see it as an exception but in fact interpreted it as supporting the proposed hypothesis.

As discussed earlier, keeping a research journal can help to identify these possible biases. In addition, you may consider using "member checking" (Tutty,

Rothery, and Grinnell, 1996), getting feedback from the research participants, and asking them to confirm your conclusions.

HUMAN DIVERSITY ISSUES IN QUALITATIVE ANALYSIS

As with ethical issues, analysis of qualitative data provides more opportunities to ignore human diversity issues than does the analysis of quantitative data. Data can be analyzed and hypotheses generated that directly reflect the researcher's biases, which may reflect negatively on certain groups. Although such biases can also appear in quantitative research, they are more likely in qualitative research, and additional precautions need to be taken. Researchers conducting qualitative analysis should constantly use self-examination to determine whether they are perpetuating stereotypical or negative images of the participants in their studies. The purpose of the validation procedure is in part to ensure that stereotyping and other forms of bias do not occur.

Qualitative analysis can also be a great asset in ensuring that human diversity issues are recognized. The qualitative approach can provide a richer and fuller picture of the complexity of how certain groups are viewed and treated in the research.

Overcoming biases can be a difficult task, even with the use of careful qualitative strategies. Sometimes it is hard for us to identify biases in our thinking; even the definition of a bias can be problematic. As social workers we know that the environment and society in which we live profoundly affect the way we think, including the way we think about different groups. Our upbringing and social environment may result in our unconscious exclusion of certain groups. This effect provides the foundation for **discourse analysis**.

Discourse analysis focuses on ways in which all analyses are embedded in the researcher's biographical and historical location. It looks at the structure and sequencing of utterances in social exchanges, rather than their storytelling as such (Gubrium and Holstein, 2000). For example, men and women's conversations may be analyzed to assess relative power and control, and their relationship to gender.

This perspective relates to the discussion in Chapter 1 concerning the difficulty of achieving true objectivity and the impact of values on how science is conducted.

SUMMARY

The primary mission in qualitative data analysis is to look for patterns in the data while maintaining a focus on the importance of the study's context. There are a number of differences that distinguish qualitative from quantitative data analysis. There are two levels of coding involved in the identification of categories stage. The two different types of categories are indigenous and researcher constructed. Interpreting the data involves cluster diagrams, matrices, counts, metaphors, missing links, and contradictory evidence. Qualitative data are validated through the construction of rival or alternative hypotheses, constructing negative cases, triangulation, preserving the context of the data, and establishing your own credibility.

Qualitative reports can be written using content analysis, case studies, analytical studies, or ethnographies.

Although qualitative data analysis is naturally compatible with social work practice, the myth persists that it is unduly time-consuming, unsophisticated, and nonproductive. Researchers in agency settings have the responsibility of dispelling this myth. Indeed, most of them are, at times unknowingly, gathering and analyzing qualitative data and are thus well placed for dispelling the myths that exist. Because qualitative data are less structured than quantitative data, it is important to ensure that personal, intellectual, and professional biases do not interfere with the process or that steps are taken to minimize the extent to which they might interfere. It is also important that diverse and minority groups are recognized at this stage of the research process, and, indeed, throughout the process.

STUDY/EXERCISE QUESTIONS

1. Conduct an interview with a fellow student, gathering information on what he or she considers to be his or her family's culture.

   a. Use the indigenous category approach discussed in this chapter.

   b. Compare your findings with others in the class.

   c. Is it possible to propose a hypothesis based on these findings?

   d. How would you validate your findings?

2. Carry out a content analysis on ethics and research using issues of a social work journal. Note that you will need to define *ethics* and *research*, and specify the number and type of journal. What conclusions can you draw from your findings?

INFOTRAC COLLEGE EDITION

1. Search for *content analysis* and for two articles. Describe the codes that were used to analyze the data.

2. Search for *ethnography*. Selecting one article, present a rationale for using this approach for the phenomena under study. Would another research approach have yielded a greater understanding?

REFERENCES

Allen-Meares, P. (1984). Content analysis: It does have a place in social work research. *Journal of Social Science Research 7*, 51–68.

Alter, C., & Evens, W. (1990). *Evaluating your practice*. New York: Springer.

Bernard, H. R. (1994). *Research methods in cultural anthropology*. Newbury Park, CA: Sage.

Cooper, M., & Lesser, J. (1997). How race affects the helping process: A case of cross racial therapy. *Clinical Social Work Journal, 25* (3), 323–335.

Glaser, B. G., & Strauss, A. L. (1967). *The discovery of grounded theory strategies for qualitative research.* New York: Aldine de Gruyter.

Gordon, A. (2002). From gangs to the academy: Scholars emerge by reaching back through critical ethnography. *Social Justice, 29* (4), 71–81.

Grise-Owens, E. (2002). Sexism and the social work curriculum: A content analysis of the *Journal of Social Work Education. Affilia, 17* (2), 147–166.

Gubrium, J. F., & Holstein, J. A. (2000). Analyzing qualitative approach practice. In N. L. Denzin and Y. S. Lincoln (Eds.), *Handbook of qualitative research* (2nd ed.), 487–508. Thousand Oaks, CA: Sage Publications.

Hollis, F. (1972). *Casework: A psychosocial therapy.* New York: Random House.

Krumer-Nevo, M. (1998). What's your story? Listening to the stories of mothers from multi-problem families. *Clinical Social Work Journal, 26* (2), 177–194.

Main, M. P. (1998). Community participation: A study of health workers' perceptions. Unpublished Master's Dissertation. Durban, South Africa: University of Natal.

Mason, J. (2002). *Qualitative researching.* London: Sage Publications.

Neuman, W. L. (2003). *Social research methods: Qualitative and quantitative approaches.* Boston: Allyn and Bacon.

Parsons, R. (2001). Specific practice strategies for empowerment-based practice with women: A study of two groups. *Affilia, 16* (2), 159–179.

Patton, M. Q. (2001). *Qualitative evaluation and research methods.* Newbury Park, CA: Sage.

Pettys, G. L., & Balgopal, P. R. (1998). Multigenerational conflicts and new immigrants: An Indo-American experience. *Families in Society,* July–August, 410–432.

Tutty, L. M., Rothery, M. A., & Grinnell, R. M. (1996). *Qualitative research for social workers.* Boston: Allyn and Bacon.

Varga, C. A. (2002). Pregnancy termination among South African adolescents. *Studies in Family Planning, 33* (4), 283–299.

Leslie Parr

Analysis of Quantitative Data

■

This chapter describes how quantitative data can be analyzed. As discussed in Chapter 1, these are data that can be counted or quantified. The analysis stage of the research process makes some sense out of the information collected. This research stage is comparable to the analyzing resource capabilities stage in practice. This stage in research often elicits considerable anxiety. This text attempts to describe and explain statistics in as straightforward a manner as possible.

Meaning can be derived from quantitative data in two ways. One is through the use of **descriptive statistics**, which summarizes the characteristics of the sample or the relationship among the variables. During this process, you want to get as full a picture as possible of the data. A number of different statistical techniques allow you to do this, including frequency distributions, measures of central tendency, variability, and association. You can also use **inferential statistics**, which are techniques for determining whether generalizations or inferences about the population can be made using the data from your sample. Inferential statistics involve using statistical tests to evaluate hypotheses. This approach can also be used for data derived from practice evaluations. Both descriptive and inferential statistics will be discussed in this chapter.

The focus of this chapter is twofold. First, it focuses on understanding which statistics are useful for which purpose. Some statistics are simply inappropriate and meaningless when used with certain types of data. This approach to statistical understanding prepares you to become an informed and observant consumer of research—a critical role for the generalist social worker. Using findings for practice involves understanding and interpreting statistical analysis of the data in various studies. A second focus of this chapter is how to run different statistical tests using statistical software. Many different statistical software packages are available, all of which use similar procedures. A sample disc of data is included with this text.

This chapter discusses the following topics:

- frequency distributions
- measures of central tendency
- measures of variability or dispersion
- measures of association
- sources of error, hypotheses, and significance levels
- types of statistical tests
- statistics and practice evaluations
- descriptive statistics and practice evaluations
- the agency and quantitative analysis
- ethical issues and quantitative analysis
- human diversity issues and quantitative analysis

FREQUENCY DISTRIBUTIONS

As discussed in Chapter 4, each variable possesses values. The variables' names, along with their values, are entered into the computer as described in Chapter 10. One of the first things you need to do in statistical analysis is to get an idea about how these values are distributed for each variable. To do so, you use **frequency distributions**. These are descriptions of the number of times values of a variable occur in a sample.

For example, say you have collected data on the need for a day care center on a local university campus. Let's assume that 25 students with preschool children were interviewed. Each of these students represents one observation, or case; this is equivalent to a unit of analysis. The variables included number of preschool children, ethnicity, expressed need for day care on campus, and miles from campus. The ethnic groups are represented by codes: 1 for white non-Hispanic; 2 for Hispanic; and 3 for African American. Expressed need for day care on campus is coded on a 4-point scale, with the number 4 representing greatest need, and 1 the least need. The number of preschool children in a family and the distance in miles from campus are represented by the actual numbers of children and miles. We could present the data as in Table 12.1.

Simply reviewing this table does not make it easy to understand what the data look like. Several frequency distributions can be constructed for the previous example: one for the variable ethnicity (see Table 12.2), one for expressed need for day care (see Table 12.3), and one for number of preschool children (see Table 12.4). One can also be constructed for miles from campus (see Table 12.5); rather than list each distance separately, however, you can categorize values to make data more readable. Try to use categories that make some intuitive or theoretical sense. You also need to ensure that categories are of the same size.

For example, you might use categories such as "less than 5 miles," "5–9 miles," "10–14 miles," and "15 miles and more." By grouping data points into categories in this way, of course, some information is inevitably lost.

Sometimes frequency distributions can be displayed as graphs or charts. Chapter 13 discusses how to do this. An example of a frequency distribution from a published article is displayed in Table 12.6. This table presents some of the results of a study carried out by Markward, Dozier, and Colquitt (1998) who studied the substance-abuse child-abuse association seen in abused women. The authors found a significant association between child abuse and substance abuse by parents of abusers. Note that both raw numbers (n) and percentages (%) of the backgrounds of the abused women and their abusers are presented.

MEASURES OF CENTRAL TENDENCY

Another important perspective on data is the location of the middle of the distribution, or the average value. There are three different types of averages, each determined in a slightly different way. These three types are mode, median, and mean.

Table 12.1   **Data on four variables by each observation**

Observation number	Number of children	Ethnicity	Need for day care	Miles from campus
1	2	1	3	2
2	1	1	4	1
3	1	3	4	10
4	1	1	4	23
5	1	2	3	4
6	1	1	3	2
7	2	2	4	1
8	2	1	3	1
9	1	2	2	6
10	3	1	4	40
11	2	1	3	2
12	1	2	1	1
13	1	1	2	3
14	2	1	4	7
15	2	1	4	8
16	1	3	4	9
17	1	1	3	15
18	2	1	4	12
19	1	2	1	23
20	2	1	1	1
21	2	1	4	2
22	1	2	4	1
23	2	1	4	3
24	1	1	4	1
25	2	1	3	6

Mode

The **mode** is the value possessed by the greatest number of observations. In Table 12.2, non-Hispanic white is the mode for ethnicity because this category or value occurred most often. In Table 12.3, "great need" is the mode for expressed need for day care, and in Table 12.5, "less than 5 miles" for distance

Table 12.2 **Frequency distribution of ethnicity**

Label	Value	Frequency	%
non-Hispanic white	1	17	68
Hispanic	2	6	24
African American	3	2	8
	Total	25	100

Table 12.3 **Frequency distribution of need for day care**

Label	Value	Frequency	%
No need	1	3	12
A little need	2	2	8
Some need	3	7	28
Great need	4	13	52
	Total	25	100

Table 12.4 **Frequency distribution of number of preschool children in the household**

Value	Frequency	%
1	13	52
2	11	44
3	1	4
Total	25	100

Table 12.5 **Frequency distribution of miles from campus**

Value	Frequency	%
Less than 5 miles	14	56
5–9 miles	5	20
10–14 miles	2	8
15 miles and over	4	16
Total	25	100

Table 12.6   **Abuse in backgrounds of abused women and abusers**

Type of abuse	n	%	n	%
Childhood abuse	96	.55	96	.62
Adult sexual abuse	92	.48	–	–
Childhood sexual abuse	93	.42	93	.15
Alcohol abuse	92	.24	95	.84
Drug abuse	91	.23	92	.59
Abuse in family of origin	73	.62	68	.62
Parental substance abuse	70	.53	67	.64

Notes: n = number out of 100 sheltered women reporting abuse in their own backgrounds and those of their abusers.

Source: From "Association between substance abuse and child maltreatment in the context of woman abuse," by M. J. Markward, C. D. Dozier, and C. Colquitt, 1998, *Aretê, 22* (2), 1–11. Reprinted by permission of the publisher.

from campus. The mode can be used regardless of the level of measurement. It can be used for ethnicity (a nominal level of measurement), expressed need for day care (an ordinal level of measurement), and for miles from campus (a ratio level of measurement). In contrast, other measures of central tendency and other statistics discussed in this chapter (measures of variability and measures of association) are restricted in terms of the levels of measurement that they can use.

Median

The **median**, another type of average, can be used only with ordinal, interval, and ratio level data. The median is the value at which 50% of observations are above it and 50% of observations are below it. The median is thus the value that divides the distribution in half.

The median cannot be used for nominal levels of measurement because it has meaning only with ranked data. Nominal data cannot be ranked, and consequently it cannot be determined whether cases lie above or below a particular nominal value. Numbers are often assigned to nominal data, but these numbers do not have any inherent meaning. We cannot rank, say, the values of ethnicity in any order from highest to lowest, and thus we cannot determine the middle or median value. The median is a popular measure of central tendency primarily because it is not influenced by extreme values that can be a problem with the mean (see the following section). In addition, the median is more stable than the mode, although less stable than the mean. Salaries are often described using the median. (See Appendix B for the formula for the median.)

A Study Using the Mean

Cook, Selig, Wedge, and Gohn-Baube (1999) explored social, environmental, and psychological barriers that interfere with early and regular use of prenatal health services. The researchers developed a 24-item Access Barriers to Care Index (ABCI) and interviewed low-income adult women who were hospitalized on the post-partum unit of a large medical center. The women were asked to rate each barrier from 2 to 5, 2 being slightly difficult and 5 being extremely difficult. The researchers reported the means and standard deviations among the answers for each item, or barrier, of the ABCI. Results showed that barriers involving family and friends significantly increased the odds of receiving inadequate care. Other important barriers were those related to the health care system and intrapersonal issues.

Mean

The **mean**, the third type of measure of central tendency, is even more restrictive in the level of measurement that can be used. It can be computed only from interval and ratio levels of measurement (although some people will argue that it can also be used with ordinal level data). The mean is a result of summing the values of observations and then dividing by the total number of observations. The mean miles from campus for our participants in the needs assessment (Table 12.1) is 7.36 miles. (See Appendix B for the formula for the mean.)

The major strength of the mean is that it takes into consideration each value for each observation. Extreme values, however, either high or low, can distort the mean, particularly if sample size is relatively small. Let's look at the example of miles from campus again but substitute one high value (60 miles) for a middle range value (6 miles). The mean now becomes 9.52 (238/25 = 9.52), a two-mile difference in the mean as a result of one observation. The mean is the most stable measure of central tendency, however, and in addition is the prerequisite for the computation of other statistics.

In summary, to determine which measure of central tendency to apply, you need to consider how you are going to use the information. For example, means are appropriate when you are interested in totals. If you know the national average is 2.3 children per family, then you can guess that a town of 100 families would have about 230 children. If you know that the mode is 1 child per family, then any family you choose at random will probably have 1 child. The reason the average household income is often reported as the median rather than the mean is that often we are interested in an individual comparison of our own financial situation to other normal-range incomes. The mean is inflated by the few unusual persons who make millions. Mean income, however, is more useful in comparing different countries' gross national product (GNP).

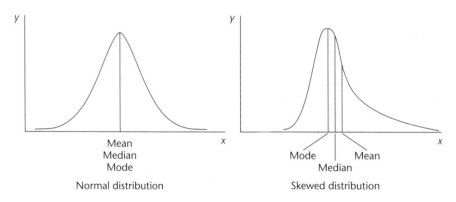

Figure 12.1 **Normal and skewed distributions**

Visual Distribution of Data

Data from a frequency distribution can sometimes be presented as a chart enabling the data, particularly measures of central tendency, to be assessed visually. If the data are evenly or symmetrically distributed, the chart will take on the shape of a bell or a **normal distribution**. The properties of a normal distribution are as follows:

1. The mean, median, and mode have the same score value.
2. It is symmetrical: The right half of the distribution is the mirror image of the left half.
3. Most scores are concentrated near the center.

The assumption that a distribution is normally distributed underlies many inferential statistical tests, which will be discussed later in this chapter. If distributions have most scores concentrated at one end of the distribution rather than at the middle, this is referred to as a **skewed distribution** (see Figure 12.1). Consequently, the mean, median, and mode are going to be different. Displaying data in this form can be useful in gaining a visual and almost intuitive sense of how the data are distributed. There will be further discussion of charts and tables in Chapter 13.

MEASURES OF VARIABILITY OR DISPERSION

Another dimension for describing data is the extent to which scores vary or are dispersed in distribution. Figure 12.2 depicts three distributions. They have the same measure of central tendency, but they differ in the extent to which they are spread out, or in their variability.

Like measures of central tendency, measures of variability differ, with each one more appropriate in some situations than in others. Two types of measures of variability are discussed here: the range and the standard deviation.

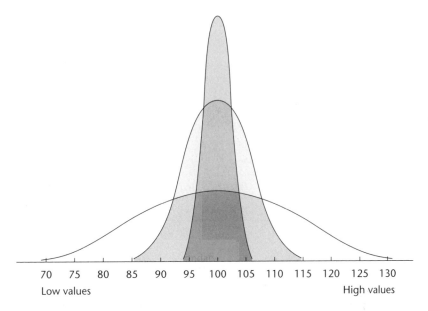

70 75 80 85 90 95 100 105 110 115 120 125 130

Low values   High values

Figure 12.2 ***Three distributions with the same measure of central tendency but different variabilities or dispersions***

Range

The **range** is the easiest measure of variability to compute and to understand: It is simply the distance between the largest or maximum value and the smallest or minimum value. The range is computed by subtracting the lowest value from the highest value. The range can be used only with interval and ratio levels of data because it assumes equal intervals.

The problem with the range is its extreme instability. Different samples drawn from the same population may have very different ranges. Consequently, the range does not give you a reliable view of what the variability is in the population. The range for the miles from campus variable in Table 12.1 is 39 (40 minus 1). If you changed either the highest or lowest score to an extreme value, the range would be dramatically affected.

Standard Deviation

The **standard deviation** is a measure that averages together each value's distance from the mean. Calculating the standard deviation involves the following steps:

1. Calculate the mean.
2. Measure the distance of each score from the mean.
3. Square these distances (to eliminate negative values).

Table 12.7   **Descriptive statistics for each discipline variable**

Discipline items	Never happened N(%)		M	SD	Mdn	Range
Explained	55	(6)	4.84	1.68	6.00	0–6
Time out	187	(19)	3.34	2.17	4.00	0–6
Shook child	846	(85)	.28	.77	.00	0–6
Hit child on bottom with a hard object	705	(71)	.72	1.33	.00	0–6
Gave child something else to do	164	(16)	3.36	2.11	4.00	0–6
Shouted, yelled at child	133	(13)	3.70	1.98	4.00	0–6
Hit child with fist or kicked	986*	(99)	.02	.19	.00	0–4
Spanked child on bare bottom with hand	364	(36)	1.78	1.82	1.00	0–1
Grabbed child around neck and choked	993*	(99)	.01	.08	.00	0–6
Swore, cursed at child	738	(74)	.79	1.51	.00	0–6
Hit child as hard as could over and over	994*	(99)	.01	.12	.00	0–2
Threatened to send child away/kick out	933*	(93)	.16	.68	.00	0–6
Burned or scalded child on purpose	999*	(100)	.001	.03	.00	0–1
Threatened to spank or hit child	381	(38)	2.20	2.18	2.00	0–6
Hit child with a hard object	950*	(95)	.13	.63	.00	0–6
Slapped child on hand, arm, or leg	487	(49)	1.40	1.75	1.00	0–6
Grounded/removed privileges	215	(22)	3.10	2.07	3.00	0–6
Pinched child	939*	(94)	.15	.71	.00	0–6
Threatened child with a knife or gun	999*	(100)	.001	.03	.00	0–6
Threw or knocked child down	992*	(99)	.01	.16	.00	0–4
Called child dumb or lazy	822	(82)	.52	1.24	.00	0–6
Slapped child on face, head, or ears	936*	(94)	.13	.58	.00	0–6

Note: N = 1,000 per variable. Items in the table are listed in the order in which they appear in the survey.

*Variable with less than 10% endorsement by participants, therefore the variable was dropped from further analysis.

Source: From "Predicting abuse-prone parental attitudes and discipline practices in a nationally representative sample," by S. Jackson, R. A. Thomson, E. H. Christiansen, R. A. Coleman, J. Wyatt, C. W. Buckendahl, B. L. Wilcox, R. Peterson, 1999, *Child Abuse and Neglect, 23* (1), 15–29. Reprinted by permission of Elsevier Science.

4. Add the squared differences from the mean.

5. Divide by the *n*, thus calculating a mean of the differences from the mean.

6. Take the square root of the result.

(See Appendix B for the formula for the standard deviation.)

Because the standard deviation uses the mean and is similar to the mean in many respects, it can be used only with interval and ratio level data. The standard deviation is the most stable of the measures of variability, although it, too, because it uses the mean, can be affected by extreme scores.

Table 12.7 displays the results of a study by Jackson and colleagues (1999) that examined factors that place parents at risk of abusing their children by predicting parents' use of discipline practices and attitudes that may bias parents to "abuse proneness." The means, standard deviations, ranges, and medians of the variables are displayed.

MEASURES OF ASSOCIATION

Up to this point we have been looking only at **univariate measures**, which measure one variable at a time, and we have been trying to develop a picture of how that one variable is distributed in a sample. Often, though, we want to measure the relationship between two or more variables; such measures are, respectively, **bivariate** and **multivariate measures**.

Often, when carrying out a program evaluation, you are interested in the relationship between two or more variables. For example, you may want to study the effect of a special program for high school students on their self-esteem. You would need to look at the relationship between the independent variable (the special program) and the dependent variable (self-esteem). Or you may wish to compare the dependent variables of an experimental and control group—that is outcomes from two different programs. To do so, you need to use bivariate statistics.

Similarly, in needs assessments, sometimes you are interested in examining the relationship among variables. For example, in investigating a community's need for a YMCA/YWCA, you want to know how many people express this need and the characteristics of these individuals—ages of their children and so forth. Here the two variables are expressed need and ages of children.

Multivariate analysis involves examining the relationships among more than two variables. This text does not discuss this type of analysis, but you should be able to find plenty of statistics texts and courses on this topic.

Two bivariate measures of association are discussed in this section: cross-tabulation and correlation.

Cross-Tabulation

Cross-tabulation is probably the most widely used bivariate statistic because it is simple to use and extremely versatile. Cross-tabulations are also known as **contingency tables**. Cross-tabulations may be used with any level of measurement.

CHORE		Count Row % Column % Total %	FLEX		Row total
			Yes	No	
Low participation	1		75 83.3 65.8 53.6	15 16.7 57.7 10.7	90 64.3
Medium participation	2		15 83.3 13.2 10.7	3 16.7 11.5 2.1	18 12.9
High participation	3		24 75.0 21.1 17.1	8 25.0 30.8 5.7	32 22.8
Column total			114 81.4	26 18.6	140 100.0

Figure 12.3   Cross-tabulation of two variables: FLEX and CHORE

If interval and ratio (and sometimes ordinal) levels of measurement are used, however, they must be collapsed into a smaller number of categories (the meaning of *smaller* here is discussed a little later).

An example of a cross-tabulation, shown in Figure 12.3, is from a study that examined the workplace service needs of women employees. This particular contingency table looks at the relationship between how the women perceived their husband's participation in household chores (CHORE) and their need for flexible work hours (FLEX).

Generally, the dependent variable (in this case, the need for flexible work hours) is displayed in columns, and the independent variable (husband's participation in chores) is displayed in the column totals, and percentages are written at the end of each row and column, respectively.

CHORE has three values (low, medium, and high participation), and FLEX has two values (yes, a need; no, no need). Consequently, we have what is called a 3 by 2 (3 values by 2 values) contingency table, with 6 cells or boxes. If the variables had more values, the table would be larger. You need to be careful that the table is not too large; we also cannot let the number of cases in any of the cells get too low (5 or fewer), because then there are problems in the use of inferential statistics. (Inferential statistics will be discussed later in this chapter.) Sometimes

Table 12.8   **Self-esteem scores and number of weeks in the program (n = 10)**

Client ID	Self-esteem score	Number of weeks in program
1	8	1
2	10	2
3	12	3
4	14	4
5	16	5
6	18	6
7	20	7
8	22	8
9	24	9
10	26	10

several values need to be combined to reduce the number of values and to reduce the size of the table. As a result, the number of cases in each cell increases.

Let's continue reading the table. The top number in each cell refers to the number of cases. In the top left-hand cell in Figure 12.3, the number of cases is 75. The second number is the row percentages—that is, for the percentage of women who stated their husbands were low participants in household chores, 83.3% requested flexible work hours. The third number in the cell is the column percentage: In our example, this represents the percentage of women who requested flexible work hours—65.8% reported low participation of their husbands in household chores. The bottom number in the cell is the total percentage. In other words, the number of cases in the cell, 75, is 53.6% of the total number of cases. The total number of cases can be found in the lower right-hand corner. In Figure 12.3, this number is 140 and, as is recorded immediately below 140 in the cell, represents 100% of cases. You can go through and read each of the cells in this manner. To the extreme right are the row totals and percentages, and at the bottom of the table, the column totals and percentages. Note that the labels on the table help guide your interpretation.

The availability of percentages allows you to compare groups of unequal size. A sense of association can be gained by comparing these percentages. For example, a slightly lower proportion of those reporting high participation of their husbands in household chores requested flexible work hours (75%) than those who reported medium and low participation (83.3% for both). Is this difference big enough to signify a relationship between the variables, or is it simply chance? This question is answered later in this chapter.

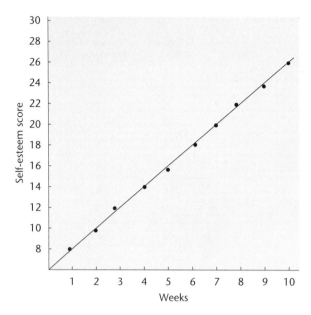

Figure 12.4   **Scattergram showing a perfect positive correlation**

Correlation

Correlation is another common way of looking at the relationship between variables, which can be used only with interval and ratio level data. In our example of a study investigating the impact of a program directed at increasing the adolescent participants' self-esteem, it was hypothesized that the number of sessions adolescents attended would have an impact on their level of self-esteem, measured on an equal interval scale. Ten adolescents were tested on their level of self-esteem before and after the program (see Table 12.8).

These data can then be plotted on a chart called a **scattergram** (Figure 12.4). The horizontal axis (X) represents the client's length of time in the program, and the vertical axis (Y) represents the difference in the client's level of self-esteem before and after participation in the program.

In Figure 12.4, the line connecting the dots is perfectly straight. In this case, there is a **perfect correlation** between the two variables: When one variable increases or decreases, the other does so at the same rate. A perfect correlation rarely occurs; usually you find that the dots do not perfectly follow the line but are scattered around it. The direction of the relationship can vary. Figure 12.4 demonstrates a **positive correlation** between the number of sessions attended and the level of self-esteem. As the number of sessions attended increased, so did the level of self-esteem. A **negative correlation** can also occur; this is depicted in Figure 12.5. Here the high values of one of the variables, self-esteem, are associated with the low values of the other variable, the number of sessions attended.

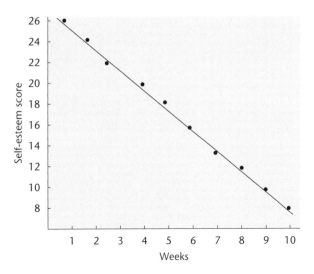

Figure 12.5 **Scattergram showing a perfect negative correlation**

The extent to which data points are scattered gives us an indication about the strength of the relationship between the two variables. There is a formula to precisely measure the strength of this relationship; again, it involves inferential statistics and will be discussed in the next chapter.

The line passing through the dots is used to predict certain values. This prediction involves **regression analysis**, which will be discussed later in this chapter.

SOURCES OF ERROR, HYPOTHESES, AND SIGNIFICANCE LEVELS

Sources of Error

Throughout the research process, there are possibilities for error in our conclusions. Errors can come from three different sources, and each source of error can be addressed by specific strategies.

First, a measurement error may affect data collection; this possibility can be assessed by checking the reliability and validity of the data collection instrument (see Chapter 9 for a discussion). Second, other variables might be responsible for the relationship, and they need to be controlled. Variables can be controlled by the research design or, as we discussed in the last chapter, statistically. The third source of error is chance. Chance has to do with sampling variability, as was discussed in Chapter 8. A randomly drawn sample and a population may differ because of chance. The role of chance factors can be assessed through the use of inferential statistics, which relies on probability theory. (The specific statistical tests involved are described later in this chapter.) These three sources of error and the strategies for their assessment are illustrated in Figure 12.6.

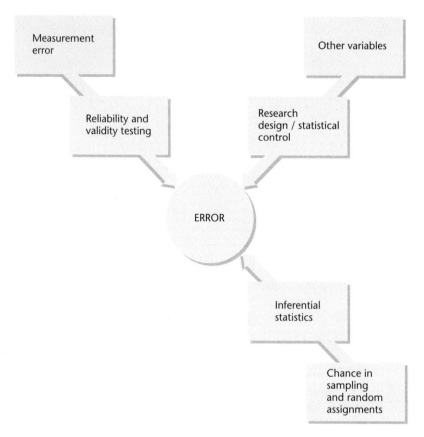

Figure 12.6   ***Sources and corrections for error***

Types of Hypotheses

A hypothesis suggests that two or more variables are associated in some way.

There are two types of hypotheses. First, the **two-tailed** or **nondirectional hypothesis** simply states that there is an association between two or more variables but predicts nothing about the nature or the direction of the association. One such example would be the hypothesis that gender has an impact on the likelihood of hospitalization for depression.

A **one-tailed** or **directional hypothesis** specifies that the variables are associated and the nature or direction of the relationship or association—whether it is positive or negative. For example, we might hypothesize that women are more likely than men to be hospitalized for depression.

The state of prior knowledge drawn from the literature and from theory will in part determine whether one-tailed or two-tailed hypotheses are developed. Remember that when developing hypotheses you do need to draw on existing knowledge; hypotheses should not be based on impulse or initial impressions.

		What the "real" relationship is between the variables.	
		True	False
Researcher decision about the relationship between the variables	Fail to reject null hypothesis	Correct decision	Type II error
	Reject null hypothesis	Type I error	Correct decision

Figure 12.7   ***Type I and Type II errors***

A type of hypothesis that is central in inferential statistics is the **null hypothesis**, which is derived from either the one-tailed or two-tailed hypothesis. The null hypothesis states there is no association between the variables. The null hypothesis is formulated only for testing purposes. Using our previous example of a one-tailed hypothesis, the null hypothesis would be that women are not more likely than men to be hospitalized for depression or that there is no relationship between gender and hospitalization. Statistical analysis then allows the null hypothesis to fail to be rejected. If the null hypothesis is not rejected, then it is concluded that no relationship exists between the variables. On the other hand, if the null hypothesis is rejected, there does appear to be a relationship between the variables that is not a result of chance.

This process may seem unnecessarily complicated. The concept of the null hypothesis is important, however, because it reminds us that statistical tests are intended to determine to what extent a relationship is caused by chance, rather than whether or not the hypothesis is true.

Sometimes decision errors can be made in either failing to reject or rejecting the null hypothesis. These two errors are referred to as Type I and Type II errors. Type I error is the rejection of the null hypothesis and the false conclusion that a relationship exists between the variables when in fact no "real" relationship does exist. Type II error is the failure to reject the null hypothesis and so the failure to identify any "real" relationship between the variables (see Figure 12.7). Obviously these errors can present some serious problems.

A statistical test's ability to correctly reject a null hypothesis is referred to as **statistical power**. The test's power is also greater the higher the level of measurement—that is tests using ratio level data will be more powerful than those using nominal level data. Also, note that as with larger sample size, as discussed in Chapter 8, our sampling error is reduced. Similarly, the sample size has an effect on the power of the statistical test. As the sample size increases, the power of the statistical test also increases. Findings can be generalized more confidently from a large sample, even if the relationship does not appear strong between the variables.

Significance Levels

When data are first examined it is not possible to draw clear conclusions based on the findings. For example, in the question relating to gender and hospitalization for depression, the results may disclose that of the people hospitalized for depression, 55% were women versus 45% men. Just looking at these results does not disclose whether this 10% difference between the men and women is simply chance or the effect of the program or some other variable. A statistical test must be used for this purpose.

A finding is statistically significant when the null hypothesis is rejected and the probability that the result is attributable to chance in the sample or population (or, in other words to sampling error) falls at or below a certain cutoff point. This cutoff point has been established by statistical convention to be .05. In other words, if a relationship occurs by chance no more than 5 times out of 100, the null hypothesis is rejected. In this case, it is unlikely that the relationship is based on chance, and the hypothesis acknowledges that the variables named in it are having an impact on the outcome. Sometimes the significance level is set at lower levels (for example, .01) or, under special circumstances, higher levels (.10). The important thing to remember is that the significance level is set prior to the statistical testing.

The observed level of significance is signified by $p < .05$ (or $p < .01$), and any level below .05 (or .01) is regarded as statistically significant. Establishing statistical significance at the .05 level or less does not mean there is a proven relationship between the variables but rather that there is only a 5% probability that the relationship is a result of chance occurrence. Avoid stating that a hypothesis has been proved. A more accurate statement is that the hypothesis is statistically significant at the .05 level.

It is important to distinguish between significance levels and the confidence levels discussed in Chapter 8. Both involve probability, but confidence levels relate to how closely the samples match the actual population, while significance levels relate to the outcomes of statistical tests and how much the findings are chance or a "real" relationship between the variables being analyzed.

TYPES OF STATISTICAL TESTS

Before discussing specific statistical tests we will describe the common steps you need to take. They are as follows:

1. Identify the appropriate test and identify its formula.

2. Enter the raw data into the formula and compute the statistical score. (The formulas for the statistical tests can be found in Appendix B.)

3. Compute the degree of freedom, which is related to the size of the sample and the power of the test.

4. Use the probability tables (see Appendix C) to assess the probability level and statistical significance of the statistics score.

Table 12.9 ***Types of statistical tests and some conditions for use of correlational analysis***

	T-test	ANOVA	Correlation coefficient	Chi-square analysis
Comparing means of two populations	Yes	No	No	No
Comparing means of more than two populations	No	Yes	No	No
All variables at interval/ratio level of measurement	No	No	Yes	No
One variable only at interval/ratio level of measurement	Yes	Yes	No	No
All variables at ordinal/nominal level of measurement	No	No	No	Yes

These steps are completed rapidly and accurately by whichever statistical software you may be using. Generally, the statistics score and its statistical significance are reported.

In this section we describe the most common statistical tests encountered in the social work literature and those needed for the analysis of most of your data. Four tests will be discussed: t-tests, analysis of variance (ANOVA), correlational analysis (including regression analysis), and chi-square analysis.

Each test is appropriate only under certain conditions. When selecting a test, you need to consider four factors: first, the structure of the null hypothesis; second, the need to use certain tests only with certain levels of measurement; third, the size of the sample; fourth, the distribution of the responses—whether or not the distribution is normal. A summary table of the tests and their conditions for use is presented in Table 12.9.

T-Tests

Conditions of Use

The t-test is used under the following conditions:

1. You are interested in testing a null hypothesis to find whether two groups have the same mean.
2. The dependent variable is at the interval level of measurement at least (although some argue that the ordinal level of measurement is acceptable), and the other variable (usually the independent variable) is at the nominal level of measurement.
3. The sample size can be small.
4. The observations are independent.

The Use of T-Tests in the Literature

Saulnier (1997) studied the effectiveness of social group work on the alcohol problems and marginalization of lesbians. Participants chose their own goals and identified personal and environmental factors that contributed to their use of alcohol. Discussion took place within a feminist perspective. A pretest and a posttest measured alcohol consumption and frequency of drunkenness. Using a t-test, the pretest and posttests were compared, and the differences were statistically significant for both of the dependent variables. These findings were supplemented by qualitative data.

These conditions often occur in social work. Many program evaluation designs include comparison groups. Each group that is compared represents a value at the nominal level of measurement. Program evaluations often measure the outcome or dependent variable (for example, the number of months an individual has held a job, or the score on a standardized test) at the interval or ratio level. The null hypothesis in such a program evaluation could be that the intervention had no effect; in other words, the two groups had similar outcomes or mean scores. Just on the basis of probability, though, outcomes are likely to be different. The t-test discloses whether this difference could be chance. Similarly, you would want to use this test when comparing two groups such as males and females, urban and rural residents, or married and unmarried people, and looking at their differing outcome variables. This type of t-test is known as an independent samples t-test or a groupwise comparison t-test.

Another type of t-test is the paired samples or pairwise comparison t-test. Also commonly used in social work research, the paired samples t-test compares two means at different points in time for the same sample. For example, such a test might compare academic and cognitive scores for children at the beginning of a Head Start program with their scores at the end of a year.

The degrees of freedom for the t-test is accomplished by subtracting 2 from the *n* (the total number of participants in both groups).

Analysis of Variance (ANOVA)

Conditions of Use

The analysis of variance statistical test (ANOVA) is used under these conditions:

1. You are interested in testing a null hypothesis to find whether or not the means in more than two groups are the same.
2. The dependent variable is at least the interval level of measurement, and the other variable, usually the independent variable, is measured at the nominal level.

The Use of ANOVA

Secret and Green (1998) used analysis of variance (ANOVA) to test their hypothesis that there would be differences in the psychological well-being, social well-being, and husbands' participation in family activities among three groups of mothers: those with full-time professional/managerial jobs, those with full-time, working class/blue-collar jobs, and those who were unemployed. The authors found that women with professional/managerial jobs and women who were unemployed scored higher on all four well-being scales than did women with working class/blue-collar jobs; however, time spent by husbands in family activities was found to be greater for women with working class/blue-collar jobs than for women with professional/managerial jobs and for unemployed women.

3. The sample size can be small.

4. The observations are independent.

Sound familiar? The t-test is in fact a special case of ANOVA, and the conditions of the use of ANOVA are consequently similar to those of the t-test, except that ANOVA is used to compare more than two groups. The ANOVA results in an *F*-test statistic.

ANOVA is useful if, for example, you are comparing the outcomes of three or more programs in different parts of the state and the outcome is being measured at the interval level or above.

Correlational Analysis

Conditions of Use

The correlation coefficient gives an indication of the strength of the correlation between two variables. It is used under the following conditions:

1. You are interested in testing the null hypothesis to find out whether two variables are not correlated.

2. Both variables are at the interval level of measurement or a higher level.

3. A normal distribution of responses is not required.

Earlier in this chapter we discussed the use of the scattergram to look at the relationship between two variables. This relationship was described as a correlation. The correlation coefficient examines the strength and direction of the relationship between two variables and discloses whether the relationship is statistically significant. The correlation coefficient statistic is represented by *r*, also referred to as the Pearson *r*. The coefficient is in the range of −1.0 to +1.0. The −1.0 represents a perfect negative correlation, and +1.0 represents a perfect positive correlation.

Correlational Analysis

Zunz (1998) explored whether protective factors that contribute to resiliency in other populations could be applied to human service managers facing job-related burnout. The study examined several previously identified protective factors, three additional protective factors, and four social support measures as they correlated to burnout measures. Among the findings, for example, protective factors were negatively correlated with emotional exhaustion and depersonalization and positively correlated with personal accomplishment. Because there were several correlations detected, data from the study could be used to provide concrete, proactive suggestions for interventions that might prevent burnout.

The degrees of freedom for the Pearson *r* is simply the *n*. You need to remember that the *r* statistic is simply looking at the strength and relationship between two variables; under no circumstances is it to be used to imply causation. Level of self-esteem and performance on an aptitude test for social work might be highly correlated but this does not mean that one causes the other; the other conditions of causality also need to be met (see Chapter 3).

Multiple Regression Analysis

Multiple regression analysis is another statistical test that like the ANOVA allows us to look at the relationship between more than two variables. It uses as a base the correlation coefficient and looks at the overall correlation between different independent variables and an interval or ratio level of measurement dependent variable. The multiple correlation coefficient is represented by *R* and explains the proportion of variation explained by the entire set (rather than just one) of independent variables. Multiple regression analysis also computes the standardized regression coefficient or beta weight, which allows the relative contribution and statistical significance of each independent variable to be assessed, while controlling for the others. In this way the contribution of each variable to predicting a particular outcome can be evaluated both in terms of the direction and the amount of change.

For example, we know that scores on various academic tests (e.g., SAT/ACT) are related to parents' educational level, ethnicity, and parental income, among other factors. Regression analysis allows us to assess the contribution of each of these independent variables to test scores. A regression coefficient of +2 points on the ACT for the variable "years of parents' education" indicated that one more year of parents' education is worth 2 more points on the ACT (assuming that the other independent variables are held constant).

Multiple regression analysis can become quite complex, and more details are beyond the scope of this text. However, you can see that it is an important test

Regression Analysis

Erwins, Casper, and Buffardi (1998) surveyed 1,675 parents of preschool-aged children. They used regression analysis to determine that parents were more satisfied with child care that was provided by relatives or au pairs in the home than by either center-based care or home care providers. There was no significant difference found in parental satisfaction of the latter two forms of child care. Regression analysis also allowed the data to reveal that child care satisfaction was a good predictor of work/family balance for both mothers and fathers.

in contributing to our understanding of how certain variables contribute to and can predict changes in a dependent variable or outcome.

Chi-Square Analysis

Conditions of Use

Chi-square analysis is one of the most widely used statistical tests in social work research, in part because it is a test that can be used with the ordinal or nominal levels of measurement.

The chi-square is used under these conditions:

1. You are interested in testing the null hypothesis to find whether there is no relationship between two variables.

2. The variables are both measured at the nominal or ordinal level. Although chi-square can be used with data at any level of measurement, often at the interval or ratio level of measurement the data will need to be collapsed into categories.

Earlier in this chapter, cross-tabulation was discussed as a way of describing the relationship between two variables measured at the nominal or ordinal level. With cross-tabulation, we are eyeballing or estimating the relationship. The chi-square statistic can be applied to cross-tabulation to give us a more accurate reflection of the significance of the relationship between two variables. Chi-square analysis assesses the extent to which the frequencies in our cross-tabulation, called the **observed frequencies**, differ from what we might expect to observe if the data were distributed in the cross-tabulation according to chance. These chance frequencies are called the **expected frequencies**. The more the actual or observed frequencies vary from the expected frequencies, the more likely it is that there is an association between the two variables.

The chi-square statistic is represented by χ^2. The degrees of freedom for the chi-square are related to the number of cells rather than to the n (see Table 12.10). They are computed using the following formula: df = (r − 1) (c − 1)

t = number of rows
c = number of columns

Chi-Square Analysis

Krahé, Scheinberger-Olwig, Waizenhofer, and Koplin (1999) studied the link between childhood sexual abuse and revictimization in adolescence. A sample of adolescents between the ages of 17 and 20 completed the Sexual Experiences Survey that was used to measure unwanted sexual contacts in adolescence and whether the girls had experienced childhood sexual abuse. Nearly 9% of the respondents indicated childhood sexual abuse, and 8.5% reported uncertainty of childhood sexual abuse. Both of these groups of girls were more likely to report unwanted sexual contacts in adolescence than girls who did not report childhood sexual abuse. Girls who reported childhood sexual abuse also had higher levels of sexual activity, which implies that childhood sexual abuse can be a risk factor for adolescent sexual victimization.

Exercise caution when using chi-square analysis. If the sample is too small or if one or more of the cells has an expected value of less than 5, chi-square should not be used.

QUANTITATIVE ANALYSIS AND PRACTICE EVALUATIONS

It is also possible to use statistical techniques with the results from single-system studies. Before describing some of these techniques, a distinction needs to be made between three types of significance, which can be encountered in the analysis of group data but often are more relevant in single-system studies: These types of significance are practical or clinical, visual, and statistical. **Practical** or **clinical significance** is attained when the specified goal of the intervention has been reached. For example, the goal of an intervention may be to increase a child's school attendance from 50% to 90%. Anything below this goal may not be of practical significance, even though that figure may be higher than what is needed for statistical significance. This distinction between practical and statistical significance is also relevant to the analysis of group data, not just single-system data.

Chapter 7 discussed the importance of visual presentation of the data from single-system studies. If the results look significant, this is known as **visual significance**. As with practical significance, there can be some discrepancy between visual significance and statistical significance. Occasionally, visual significance may not represent statistical significance; we may be looking for even a very slight visual trend.

Some researchers argue that statistical analysis cannot be conducted on data from single-system studies (Campbell and Stanley, 1966) because of the completely different nature of single-system and group data. Another potential problem with using inferential analysis with single-system data is that often we find that outcome scores are related to one another. This relationship, called **autocorrelation**, occurs when scores are related, so that if we know what happened in the past, we

Table 12.10 ***Association between child abuse and substance abuse by parent of abusers (n = 100)***

	Child Abuse	
Substance Abuse by Parent of Abusers	Yes	No
Yes	18	19
No	2	10

Note: n = 49.
$p \le .05$, $\chi^2 = 3.84$

Source: From "Association between substance abuse and child maltreatment in the context of woman abuse," by M. J. Markward, C. D. Dozier, and C. Colquitt, 1998. *Aretê, 22* (2), 1–11. Reprinted by permission of the publisher.

can predict what will happen in the future. Autocorrelation can result in misleading findings and can complicate any statistical analysis.

In recent years, however, attempts have been made to accommodate these potential problems involved in analyzing single-system data. For example, Bloom, Fischer, and Orme (1995) described methods to manage and interpret autocorrelation in some detail.

The three following analytical procedures will be discussed: celeration line approach, standard deviation approach, and relative frequency approach.

Celeration Line Approach

This approach for analysis of single-system data was developed by Gingerich and Feyerherm (1979). It involves connecting the midpoints of the two values of baseline data with a line and projecting this line into the intervention period. The line may either accelerate or decelerate depending upon its direction—hence the term **celeration line**. If a certain proportion of the data are on the desired side of the celeration line, then an estimate can be made of the statistical significance using tables. Details of this method can be found in Bloom, Fischer, and Orme (1995).

The celeration line approach has the advantage of not being influenced by autocorrelation, but it is subject to a number of limiting conditions. These include the fact that the number of observations in the baseline and intervention phases should be approximately the same. Second, celeration lines cannot be used when the baseline is bounded—that is when the line reaches either the maximum or the minimum. In these cases, the line obviously cannot be extended into the intervention phase. See Figure 12.8 for a visual representation of the celeration line.

Standard Deviation Approach

This approach is based on the standard deviation, which measures the dispersion of scores around the mean (see Chapter 12). With this approach for analyzing data of single-system studies, if the possible intervention mean is more than two standard deviations from the baseline mean then there is a statistically significant

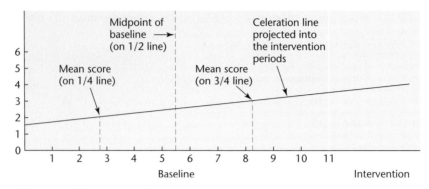

Figure 12.8   **Celeration line approach**

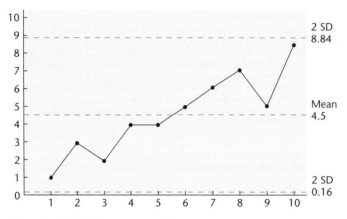

Figure 12.9   **Standard deviation approach**

change. Figure 12.9 illustrates this procedure. See Bloom, Fischer, and Orme (1995) for details of how to compute this approach. This simple procedure can be used for almost any number of data points. This approach cannot be used with data that are autocorrelated, however, unless the adjustments mentioned earlier are made (see Bloom, Fischer, and Orme, 1995).

Relative Frequency Approach

This approach assumes that typical behavior is represented by the middle two thirds of the baseline behavior. The proportion of scores that fall outside this range during the intervention period is calculated, and the proportion is located on a probability table. The value from the probability table is the estimate of statistical significance of the change. See Bloom, Fischer, and Orme (1995) for details on the computations involved in this approach. The relative frequency procedure is illustrated in Figure 12.10.

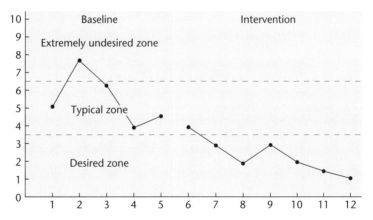

Figure 12.10   ***Relative frequency approach***

As with the celeration approach, the number of observations in the baseline and intervention period should be approximately the same. Autocorrelation can interfere with interpretation of results using this approach.

THE AGENCY AND QUANTITATIVE ANALYSIS

Although reports from the outcomes of agency-based research studies may contain descriptive and inferential statistics, often more in-depth analysis is missing. This is probably a result of two factors: first, the human tendency to focus on practical over statistical significance; second, the lack of statistical and statistical software knowledge.

The focus on practical significance is understandable in an agency setting. Often, this practical significance can be thought of as political significance. If an agency is carrying out a program evaluation, the agency may not be concerned with whether the results are statistically significant but rather with whether the goals of the program have been met. Demonstrating statistical significance could enhance practical findings considerably, however, and therefore strengthen the agency's case.

Unfortunately, lack of statistical and statistical software knowledge in agency settings is all too common. This overview of statistics has given you some basic knowledge that you can build on by enrolling in statistics courses or by exploring the many available statistics texts. If you still feel at a loss when confronted with analysis of your data, seek consultation. Universities often have statistical consultants, or you can look in your community for someone with statistical know-how. If you are writing a grant or research proposal, budget in the cost of a statistical consultant. Whenever possible, bring in the consultant early in the project's planning stage.

As we have seen, the type of analysis you carry out is contingent upon other aspects of the research process—the levels of measurement, design, and sample size.

Thus, utilizing the consultant from the start will help the data analysis itself. Statistical consultation groups also exist on the Internet.

ETHICAL ISSUES AND QUANTITATIVE ANALYSIS

One major ethical issue in the use of statistical analysis is ensuring that the correct—that is the appropriate—statistic and statistical test is being used to present and analyze the data. In addition, you must avoid distorting the data to fit any preconceived ideas. Beware of leaving out data that do not support your hypothesis—this is completely unethical. Accurate reporting of the methods you use and the results you obtain is the backbone of good science. Only in this way can we replicate studies and add to the knowledge base of social work. The NASW Code of Ethics (1999) states: "Social workers should report evaluation and research findings accurately. They should not fabricate or falsify results and should take steps to correct any errors later found in published data using standard publication methods."

Another issue is the importance of recognizing that statistical significance is not a concrete entity or property of a particular set of data. The presence of statistical significance may or may not indicate strong relationships and depends on a number of factors, many of which we have already discussed, including sample size, type of question being asked, and the influence of other factors. Consequently, we need to be careful in how we present results and in how we draw conclusions when referring to statistical significance.

Weinbach (1989) stated: "If practitioners are to make intelligent and informed discussions regarding whether a finding is meaningful for them, they must know more than just whether a relationship between variables is statistically significant" (p. 35). He stressed the importance of responsible reporting of results, including a statement of the sample size and whether this size falls within the usual size range for which the test is best suited. Such reporting would help the reader assess the appropriateness of the particular test for the research.

The strength of the relationship should be presented as clearly as possible—as a percentage difference or an actual correlation. Weinbach concluded: "The ethical researcher who invites replication and feels comfortable in the use of statistical testing should not object to any of these requirements" (p. 35).

HUMAN DIVERSITY ISSUES AND QUANTITATIVE ANALYSIS

In categorizing values—for the purpose of constructing frequency distribution tables or for cross-tabulations—care must be taken that differences between groups of individuals are respected. The number of subjects in some minority groups is sometimes small, and there is a temptation to collapse these groups into one. In doing so, however, we may lose critical information about human diversity.

Consequently, it is important to devise a means to retain this information. One strategy would be to add a qualitative or interpretive dimension to your study. In addition, care must be taken in how you interpret and understand statistical findings however clearly and responsibly they are reported. Occasionally, findings can seduce us into believing that something is related to something else when actually the findings are partial or otherwise open to question. You must be careful that these results are used responsibly and that they have acknowledged their potential bias against certain groups. As we have discussed throughout this book, the sources of these biases can exist at each stage of the research process.

SUMMARY

Descriptive statistics summarize the characteristics of a sample. Frequency distributions are descriptions of the number of times the values of a variable occur in a sample. The measures of central tendency are the mode, median, and mean. Data can be distributed in a normal or bell-shaped curve or in a skewed pattern. Measures of variability are the range and the standard deviation. The measures of association are cross-tabulation and correlation.

One possible source of error in research is chance. The role of chance factors can be assessed with inferential statistics and the use of probability theory. Hypotheses can be two-tailed, one-tailed, or null. A finding is statistically significant when the null hypothesis is rejected and the probability that the finding will occur by chance falls at or below a certain cutoff point. The ability of a statistical test to correctly reject a null hypothesis is the power of the test.

Statistical tests include t-tests, ANOVA, correlational analysis, regression analysis, and chi-square analysis. Techniques for analyzing the results from single-system studies include the celeration line approach, the standard deviation approach, and the relative frequency approach.

STUDY/EXERCISE QUESTIONS

1. Look for articles in social work journals that use
   a. the mean/median or mode
   b. the standard deviation
   c. correlation
   d. cross-tabulations

2. One of the Study/Exercise Questions in Chapter 10 asked you to develop a questionnaire for measuring student attitudes on combining research and practice, to administer the questionnaire, and to construct a code book. Construct a frequency distribution table for two of the variables included in this questionnaire.

3. Find an article in a social work journal that uses a single-system design. Are the data presented visually? Are the results clear as a result of this visual presentation?

INFOTRAC COLLEGE EDITION

1. Search for *standard deviation* and examine how this is used to describe the data in at least three articles.

2. Search for *correlation* and examine how this is used to describe the data in at least three articles.

REFERENCES

Bloom, M., Fischer, J., & Orme, J. (1995). *Evaluating practice: Guidelines for the accountable professional* (2nd ed.). Boston: Allyn and Bacon.

Campbell, D. T., & Stanley, J. C. (1966). *Experimental and quasi-experimental designs for research.* Chicago: Rand McNally.

Cook, C. A. L., Selig, K. L., Wedge, B. J., & Gohn-Baube, E. A. (1999). Access barriers and the use of prenatal care by low-income, inner-city women. *Social Work, 44* (2), 129–139.

Erdwins, C. J., Casper, W. J., & Buffardi, L. C. (1998). Child care satisfaction: The effects of parental gender and type of child care used. *Child & Youth Care Forum, 27* (2), 111–123.

Gingerich, W., & Feyerherm, W. (1979). The celeration line technique for assisting client change. *Journal of Social Service Research, 3,* 99–113.

Jackson, S., Thomson, R. A., Christiansen, E. H., Coleman, R. A., Wyatt, J., Buckendahl, C. W., Wilcox, B. L., & Peterson, R. (1999). Predicting abuse-prone parental attitudes and discipline practices in a nationally representative sample. *Child Abuse & Neglect, 23* (1), 15–29.

Krahe, B., Scheinberger-Olwig, R., Waizenhofer, E., & Kolpin, S. (1999). Childhood sexual abuse and revictimization in adolescence. *Child Abuse & Neglect, 23* (4), 383–394.

Markward, M. J., Dozier, C. D., & Colquitt, C. (1998). Association between substance abuse and child maltreatment in the context of woman abuse. *Aretê, 22* (2), 1–11.

Saulnier, C. F. (1997). Alcohol problems and marginalization: Social group work with lesbians. *Social Work with Groups, 20* (3), 37–59.

Secret, M., & Green, R. G. (1998). Occupational status differences among three groups of married mothers. *Affilia, 13* (1), 47–68.

Weinbach, R. W. (1989). When is statistical significance meaningful? A practice perspective. *Journal of Sociology and Social Welfare, 16* (1), 31–37.

Zunz, S. J. (1998). Resiliency and burnout: Protective factors for human service managers. *Administration in Social Work, 22* (3), 39–54.

Leslie Parr

Research Writing

You've analyzed the research results, and in front of you are several computer printouts or, in the case of qualitative data, masses of notes and coded material. Inevitably, there comes a time when you need to write up your research results. Writing the research report is necessary both for you—particularly when you are evaluating your own practice—and for others. In fact, for needs assessments and program evaluations, the writing of the report is a critical research stage; as a generalist social worker, you may be more involved in this stage than any other. In addition, you may be asked to assist with developing research proposals, often as part of larger grant proposals. As a student, you will need to write up research reports, and, in a graduate program, a thesis or dissertation. You may decide to submit an article, based on a completed research project, for publication in one of the many professional journals in social work or a related field.

Writing about research is the focus of this chapter. The two basic types of research writing—proposal writing and reporting research results—are analogous to similar steps in practice: first, the writing of an assessment and intervention plan; and second, the reporting of the results of the intervention.

This chapter discusses the following:

- general principles of research writing
- the research proposal
- the research report
- disseminating the report
- the agency and research writing
- ethical issues in research writing
- human diversity issues in research writing

GENERAL PRINCIPLES OF RESEARCH WRITING

Four general principles of research writing are addressed here: knowing your audience; using appropriate citations and references; the structure of the report or proposal; and, finally, the process of writing.

Knowing Your Audience

One of the basic principles of writing, research or otherwise, is to identify your audience. The content and style of the written product should vary according to your intended readers. For example, in writing a research proposal for a needs assessment to establish a date rape prevention program on a university campus, clarify from the outset to whom the proposal is directed—the university administration, a local chapter of NASW, or some other audience.

Obviously, audiences are very different. The university administration might need considerable information about the phenomenon of date rape and a discussion of its potential impact on student recruitment, whereas the NASW chapter might require more emphasis on the social and psychological costs of the problem, such as date rape's impact on women's self-esteem.

Your intended audience influences the content of your proposal or report and the style you adopt. If writing for the university administration, your writing style would be more formal than if you were writing a report for a group of parents in the community.

Referencing Sources of Information

When you are writing any type of report that refers to work by other authors, whether quoting them directly or through indirect reference, it is critical that you appropriately cite your sources of information. Although you can use a number of different referencing styles, the one most widely used in social work literature is the American Psychological Association (APA) referencing method. This is the style used in this book.

The *Publication Manual of the American Psychological Association,* 5th ed. (2001) is the guidebook for APA style. This book contains a great deal of information; therefore, only a few examples follow:

Quotations from a Source

She stated: "The stressors and homophobia that affect lesbian, gay and bisexual youth emphasize the need for our youth-serving agencies to improve their outreach to, and work with, this population" (Curtin, 2002, p. 287).

Referencing Citations in the Text

Siegel (2003) used a longitudinal study to examine adoptive parents' perceptions of their infants' open adoptions.

Referencing Citations from Electronic Sources

Often electronic sources do not provide page numbers. If paragraph numbers are visible, then use them rather than page numbers. Use the ¶ symbol or abbreviation para. For example:

As Waller and Patterson (2002, ¶ 2) state: "In Dine tradition, helping one another is a way of life."

If neither page numbers nor paragraph numbers are available, cite the heading and the number of the paragraph (¶) following the heading. For example:

"In response to these findings, the health care system needs to develop new strategies to make comprehensive reproductive health services more available to Black and other minority women to ensure that these women are able and willing to use these services" (Saftlas, Koonin, and Atrash, 2000, Discussion section, ¶ 10).

These citations in the text, whether direct quotes or ideas, are then listed in a bibliography. The sources are listed alphabetically by author, using the following format:

Journal articles

1. One author:

Prindeville, D. M. (2000). Promoting a feminist policy agenda: Indigenous women leaders and closet feminism. *The Social Science Journal, 37* (4), 637–645.

2. Two authors, journal paginated by issue:

Finn, J. L., & Jacobson, M. (2003). Just practice: Steps toward a new social work paradigm. *Journal of Social Work Education, 39* (1), 57–79.

Books

Murdoch, J., & Price, D. (2002). *Courting justice: Gay men and lesbians vs. the Supreme Court.* New York, NY: Basic Books.

Articles or Chapters in Edited Books

Guendelman, S. (2003). Immigrant families. In M. A. Mason, A. Skolnick, & S. D. Sugarman (Eds.), *All our families* (pp. 244–264). New York: Oxford University Press.

Reports

National Institute on Drug Abuse (1992). *Socioeconomic and demographic correlates of drug and alcohol use* (DHHS Publication No. ADM 92-1906). Washington, DC: U.S. Government Printing Office.

Note that lower case is used quite extensively in the APA style. Guffey (1997) presents in her article the different ways that electronic sources can be cited. The article is full of examples and can be accessed by InfoTrac. Also refer to Szuchman and Thomlison (2000) who specifically discuss APA style and social work.

The Structure of the Proposal or Report

This section outlines some general principles relating to the structure of the report. (The specifics of the content of both the proposal and the report are discussed in the following section.) Again, the APA manual is useful because it contains details about referencing sources and describes each component of the report or proposal. In general, these conventions should be followed:

- ■ *Title*   Use a clear and concise title.

- ■ *Authorship and sponsorship*   Credits should be inclusive. Don't forget anyone!

- ■ *Abstract*   An overview of the contents of the report or proposal is provided in the form of an abstract to prepare the reader for what follows. Abstracts are often included at the beginning of journal articles.

- ■ *Appendices*   Sometimes the report may include material that is relevant but too bulky to include in the text of the proposal or report. These materials are then included as appendices. Common materials to place in the appendices are the data collection instruments and statistical tables that do not relate directly to the findings.

■ *Bibliography and referencing*   As was discussed in the previous section, be sure to cite all your sources appropriately.

Remember that your report or proposal should maintain a consistent style. For instance, if you use the APA style for references, you should also use this manual's instructions on how to structure titles and abstracts.

The Process of Writing

Research reports and proposals should be written as clearly and as concisely as possible. This is not the place for flamboyant writing. Remember that you want others, possibly from very diverse backgrounds, to read and understand the results of your research. A long and convoluted report may cloud comprehension of the findings and could also discourage some members of your potential audience from even trying to read the report. Be as straightforward in your writing as possible. The following suggestions can help you to achieve this clarity:

■ Keep a research log to facilitate the process of the report or proposal writing as well as the process and development of the research itself. A research log is an informal but systematic record of ideas and progress relating to the research. Once the research is completed, it may be difficult to remember exactly why one research strategy was adopted over another or what doubts there were about a particular approach. The research log can help jog the memory.

■ Prepare an outline (details will be discussed in the next section). You may not end up following your outline exactly, but that's OK. The idea is to at least have a rough idea in your mind and on paper of how the report or proposal is structured. The outline helps to prevent a written product that wanders from one topic to another.

■ Write a first draft, then revise and revise and revise, if necessary. Do not expect your first draft to be anything like the final one.

■ Ask colleagues, faculty, or students to read early drafts and to give their comments. Do not be afraid of criticism at this point. Generally, the more input you receive, the higher the quality of the written product. Have your readers comment on structure, content, style, grammar, and spelling.

■ Have someone proof the final copy—primarily for grammar and spelling.

THE RESEARCH PROPOSAL

A **research proposal** is a paper proposing the undertaking of a specific type of research. This is often necessary to obtain permission and funds to conduct the study.

Writing the proposal can also directly assist the researcher in conceptualizing the research. By systematically thinking through each step of the research process, as is required in the research proposal, the researcher can gain new insights and clarifications regarding the research itself.

The format required for a research proposal varies depending upon the specific conditions under which the proposal is being written. These include the following:

- The funding agency may provide application forms that specify the information being requested.

- The funding agency may request a letter of intent, which requires the researcher to describe the proposal briefly. The funding source, based on this letter, may or may not ask the researcher to submit a full-fledged proposal.

- Sometimes funding agencies send out requests for proposals (RFPs) that specify what they are interested in funding and how proposals should be submitted.

Taking these conditions into consideration, generally a standard outline is used for writing research proposals. The different components include these:

- statement of the research topic
- literature review
- research questions and hypotheses
- research design
- sampling strategy
- data collection
- data analysis
- administration and budget
- credentials of the researcher and other relevant personnel

These outlines tend to have a quantitative or positivist bias. Although it could be argued that the outline could also accommodate an interpretive or qualitative study, many funding agencies are, in reality, still primarily interested in more traditional approaches. As discussed in Chapter 1, however, researchers are increasingly adopting a number of different methods of inquiry, which will eventually influence the format and expectations of RFPs.

Each step of the outline has been explained sequentially in this book. A few items should be clarified, though. First, the literature review varies according to what type of research is being proposed (as was also discussed in Chapter 4). In the case of a program evaluation, this section would report why the program is being evaluated and would include findings from the evaluations of similar programs. For a needs assessment, this section would include a description of prior research that has reported on the extent of the social problem to be investigated. Some of this information could be found in the social work literature, and it may also be found in various government document depositions or in agencies' archives. The literature review for a less applied study—for instance, looking at the impact on a child's self-image of one parent being physically challenged (a possible thesis topic)—would be different. Here the literature review would include a discussion of the various theories that have suggested a relationship may exist between these variables, and may report similar research and their findings. This information could be found in the social work and social science literature in university libraries.

In the data collection section, you are generally required only to state the method you will use to collect data. For example, if the data collection requires the development of an instrument—such as an interview schedule or a questionnaire—typically this does not need to be completed for the proposal, but you will need to state what types of variables you will be including. If you plan to use scales or other instruments that have already been developed, then you would include these in an appendix to the proposal.

The data analysis section clearly cannot be discussed in any detail in the proposal except to indicate which statistical tests or other forms of analysis will be used. The presentation of the results section should include a discussion of how and to whom the results will be presented. The budget section should itemize all expenses, including supplies, personnel costs, mailing costs, computer costs, and so forth. Finally, you usually need to summarize your credentials as they relate to the project and to include a curriculum vitae.

THE RESEARCH REPORT

As with the research proposal, the organization of the research report depends in part upon the demands of the agency or the funding source. In general, however, this outline is followed:

- statement of the research topic
- literature review
- research questions and hypotheses
- research design
- sampling strategy
- data collection method(s)
- results
- discussion
- limitations
- recommendations for future research
- implications for practice

These sections apply whether you are reporting on a practice evaluation, needs assessment, or program evaluation study and regardless of whether the study employs a primarily quantitative or qualitative approach.

Reporting Results

Harrison, Boyle, and Farley (1999) determined the effectiveness of a 12-week family-based intervention for troubled children. Psychological, social, and demographic data on 176 parents and 160 children receiving weekly skills and relationship training were analyzed. Significant improvements were found in family cohesion, family conflict, family time together, time spent in community, mental health of parents, and parenting style. The results were presented in tables. Table 13.1 shows the results from the parenting discipline findings.

Obviously, the report outline is similar to the proposal. In fact, if you have a well-structured and well-informed proposal, the research report will be much easier to complete. Some differences do exist between the proposal and the report. The report includes four additional sections: the results of the study, a discussion of the findings, the limitations of the study, and suggestions for future research.

Results Section

Use power point

Regardless of your audience and the type of research, the focus of your report will be on the results. How results or findings are reported depends on whether the study has adopted a quantitative or qualitative approach, and reference will be made to this distinction throughout the following sections. Reporting findings often involves the use of tables, graphs, and pie charts. These visual representations are particularly useful for presenting quantitative data. In the following section, we will describe some forms visual representations can take.

Tables

Statistical tables are the most common form of reporting quantitative findings and are essentially types of frequency distributions. Several principles should guide the presentation of the data. First, clearly display the data and do not clutter the table with unnecessary details. Second, make the table as complete as possible, usually including both raw numbers and percentages (percentages facilitate comparison). Third, provide a summary of the statistical tests at the bottom of the table when appropriate. Finally, clearly label the table, including footnotes where appropriate.

Graphs

Graphs are an alternative or a supplement to tables that present the data more visually. Similar guidelines apply to graphs as apply to tables. One drawback of graphs is that they lack the detail of tables; but their advantage is that they present

Table 13.1 **The percentage of parents who endorsed five different discipline approaches**

Subscale	Low-SES national norm	Homeless (n = 42)	Matched sample* (n = 41)	Comparison sample (n = 40)
Global self-worth				
M	2.66–3.24	3.17	2.99	3.05
SD	.44–.85	.63	.64	.63
Scholastic				
M	2.61–2.95	2.84	2.81	2.92
SD	.56–.86	.65	.68	.72
Social				
M	2.56–3.00	2.79	2.91	2.79
SD	.47–.92	.67	.69	.65
Athletic				
M	2.47–3.21	2.94	2.81	2.82
SD	.54–.88	.71	.77	.68
Physical appearance				
M	2.62–3.16	3.16	2.84	2.76
SD	.58–.94	.63	.74	.66
Behavior				
M	2.75–3.32	3.00	2.87	3.04
SD	.34–.72	.55	.73	.59

Note: SES = socioeconomic status.

* Students with low SES who were geographically mobile.

Source: From "Evaluating the outcomes of family-based intervention for troubled children: A pretest/posttest study," by R. S. Harrison, S. W. Boyle, & O. W. Farley, 1999, *Research in Social Work Practice, 9* (6), 640–655.

a visual image of the data that makes the results apparent at a glance. Graphs are particularly useful in presenting data from practice evaluation studies. Some of the principles of graphing were discussed in Chapter 7.

Various types of graphs can be used. The **line graph** connects various data points with lines. These types of graphs are used extensively for the evaluation of individual practice.

Another type of graph is the bar graph. **Bar graphs** are useful visual means of displaying data at the nominal level of measurement.

Pie Charts

A final type of pictorial or visual presentation of data is the **pie chart**. Pie charts can be used when we want to show the relative contributions of each value to the whole variable. Pie charts are particularly useful for displaying a budget. If too many values need to be included, however, pie charts can look cluttered

Using Bar Graphs

In a study by Valentine et al. (1998), bar graphs were used to display the extent to which doctoral students in social work are prepared for teaching. These bar graphs are displayed in Figure 13.1.

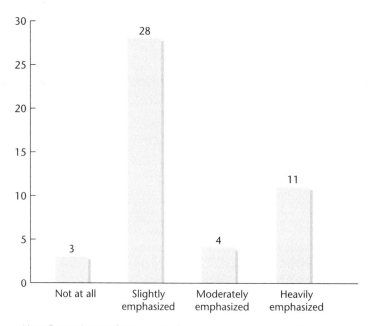

Note: Due to incomplete answers, five responses were unusable.

Figure 13.1   ***Emphasis on preparation for teaching in doctoral programs (n = 46)***

Source: From "Preparing social work doctoral students for teaching: Report of a survey," by D. P. Valentine, S. Edwards, D. Gohagan, M. Huff, & P. Wilson, 1998, *Journal of Social Work Education*, 34 (2) 273–282.

and be confusing. Figure 13.2 is an example of pie charts used in the Ziesemer, Marcoux, and Marwell (1994) study. The chart shows the proportion of the samples in student functioning risk categories. Computer programs can generate graphs and charts, often in different colors. Remember when constructing these visual aids that the goal is to make the data more accessible and clearer to the reader.

Apart from reporting the results using visual aids, the other part of presenting findings is to describe them in writing. This description need not be extensive and can simply consist of translating the findings as straightforwardly as possible. When describing the findings, it is important to avoid interpreting the data; simply report the information and, when necessary, the statistical tests and their results.

Reporting Results from a Quantitative Study

Cook et al. (1999) designed a quantitative study to determine which social, environmental, and psychological issues were most likely to serve as a barrier in the use of prenatal health services. Low-income adult women hospitalized on the postpartum unit were provided with the 24-item Access Barriers to Care Index (ABCI), which was developed by the researchers. The survey instrument consisted of a five-point Likert-type scale. The authors' presentation of the results followed the usual format for reporting the results of a positivist or quantitative study. First, the authors showed the participants' responses using a table (Table 13.2):

Table 13.2   **Severity and prevalence of access barriers to prenatal health care (N = 115)**

Type of barrier	Difficulty		Frequency	
	M	SD	N	%
Embarrassed about pregnancy	3.7	1.4	6	5.2
Heard bad things about clinic	3.5	2.1	2	1.7
Didn't want people to know was pregnant	3.5	1.3	12	10.4
Didn't like care received at clinic	3.4	1.5	8	7.0
Didn't trust health care system	3.3	1.6	7	6.1
Personal problems of family or friends	3.3	1.2	19	16.5
Clinic had no evening or weekend hours	3.2	1.2	25	21.7
Transportation	3.1	1.2	30	26.1
Not sure wanted this baby	3.1	1.3	21	18.3
Didn't think prenatal care was important	3.0	1.4	4	3.5
People in personal life wouldn't help get to clinic	3.0	1.1	11	9.6
Cost of transportation	3.0	1.2	21	18.3
No child care	2.9	1.1	24	20.9
Long waiting time at clinic	2.9	1.2	40	35.1
Depressed or unhappy about pregnancy	2.8	1.0	51	44.3
Afraid something wrong with baby	2.8	1.1	28	24.3
Own personal problems	2.8	1.1	24	20.9
Clinic too crowded	2.8	1.2	28	24.6
Own alcohol or drug use	2.8	0.5	4	3.5
Too tired	2.7	1.1	34	29.5
Couldn't schedule timely appointments	2.7	0.9	19	16.5
Couldn't leave work or school	2.6	1.1	15	13.0
Clinic too far away	2.5	1.0	25	21.7
People in personal life stopped from going to clinic	2.4	0.9	5	4.3
Didn't like going to clinic	2.3	0.5	6	5.2
Didn't need care because felt fine	2.3	0.5	4	3.5
No place to live	1.2	0.8	10	8.7
Didn't want to tell clinic staff that wasn't taking medications	1.1	0.6	10	8.7

*Extent that barrier caused difficulty in obtaining prenatal care with scale ranging from 2 = slightly difficult to 5 = extremely difficult.

Source: From "Access barriers and the use of prenatal care by low-income, inner-city women," by C. A. Cook, K. L. Selig, B. J. Wedge, E. A. Gohn-Baube, 1999, *Social Work, 44* (2), 129–139.

Reporting Results in a Qualitative Study

Johnson (1999) reports on interviews with 25 women who had previously lived in an emergency shelter. The team of interviewers conducted the interviews using a personal narrative approach so that the women's experiences would be told within the context of their lives. The research disclosed that the onset of homelessness was different for working and nonworking women and that the women obtained different perspectives on their problems from living in the shelter. Homelessness was viewed as part of a process of solving worse problems. Substantive themes emerged such as "Initial Reactions," "New Perspectives on Problems," "Help in Dealing with Problems," and "Leaving Harmful Relationships." Several quotes were included in the article. The following is one made by Emily, a 31-year-old Puerto Rican: "Just specifically being homeless with no place to turn to—nowhere—it's given me something totally different about life. As a woman you have to fight for your rights—for what you believe in. You've got to see the positive things about the bad things that are happening. You got to use that, you know. There's nothing wrong with being in a shelter. It showed me that I will never go back and I will never be in that position. I will never look at the world the same way I looked at it before. Life is not a joke, marriage is not a joke, having children is not a joke." (p. 53)

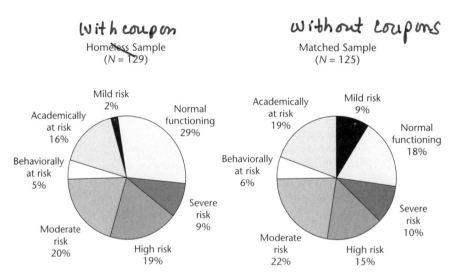

Figure 13.2 **Proportion of samples in student functioning risk categories**

Source: From "Homeless Children: Are They Different from Other Low-Income Children?" by C. Ziesemer, L. Marcoux, and B. E. Marwell, 1994, *Social Work, 39* (6). Copyright © 1994 National Association of Social Workers, Inc. Reprinted with permission.

Reporting Quantitative and Qualitative Results

Lopez (1999) studied a fictive kin system called *compadrazgo* (co-parenthood) among 39 Latinas. The system encourages the sharing of childrearing responsibilities among the parents and the acquired godparents. Quantitatively, the author reports on the mean and standard deviations among responses to 20 statements on the respondents' experiences with their closest *comadre* (co-mother). Qualitatively, the study included open-ended questions that asked the respondents why they selected nonfamily members to serve as *comadres* and to make additional comments on the *compadrazgo* system itself. One woman stated: "We selected our compadres because we know how they would bring our children up if we were not around. Religious, moral, sensitive, and caring persons, they are the type of model persons, and we know they would take (the children) in as their own." (p. 37)

A Discussion Section from a Quantitative Study

Yick and Agbayani-Stewart (2000) conducted a study with 289 Chinese-American and 138 white students to determine the perceptions of and experiences with dating violence and gender role beliefs. Students were self-administered three scales which took approximately 15–20 minutes to complete. Findings showed that 20% of Chinese-American students and 31.3% of white students had experienced some form of physical violence. Additionally, Chinese-American students appeared more likely to provide contextual justification for the use of dating violence. After presenting the results, the authors used a discussion section to address and examine the issues of definitions of dating violence, contextual justification of dating violence, experiences in dating violence, relationship between perceptions of and experiences with dating violence, and the relationship between gender role beliefs and perceptions of and experiences with dating violence.

Sometimes studies include both qualitative and quantitative results. The quantitative results might be presented followed by a description of the qualitative findings. A discussion section would then integrate the two.

Discussion Section

Unlike a research proposal, a research report always contains some kind of discussion section. The discussion section follows and is closely linked to the results section, and it provides an explanation of the results. This section is important

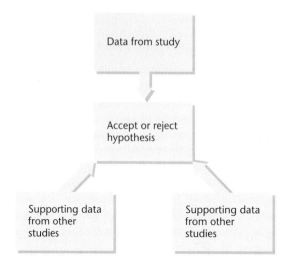

Figure 13.3   **Structure of the discussion section of a research report**

whether you are discussing the results of an evaluation of your own practice, a needs assessment, or a program evaluation.

The findings are related to the hypotheses (if there are any) and to the theoretical premise of the study itself. Part of this process involves comparing your research findings to findings from comparable research in the literature and pointing out similarities and differences in the results and conclusions. In this way, you can make connections among various empirical findings, thereby providing collective support and evidence for theories (see Figure 13.3).

In qualitative studies, the distinction between describing the results and discussing the findings can be fuzzy. In part, this fuzziness may result from our attempt to provide an insightful description of the phenomenon under study. We still need to make a careful distinction between the description and the interpretation.

Limitations Section

By now it should be evident that no research is perfect. Flaws and limitations may result from the nature of the question that is being asked, but often—and particularly in social work research—these imperfections simply reflect the social and political context of the studies. For example, random assignment into the experimental and control groups is not always feasible, as discussed in Chapter 6. Sometimes there simply is not time to carry out in-depth interviews with as many people as you would like. In reporting the limitations, go through the research process and point out the drawbacks of the method at each stage. Some

A Discussion Section from a Qualitative Study

Worth, Reid, and McMillan (2002) presented a study based on interviews with twenty New Zealand men who represented eleven gay couples. Using in-depth unstructured interviews, they discussed issues of monogamy, trust, and sexual behavior negotiations in their relationships. Worth et al. used actual excerpts from the interviews in their paper to identify and incorporate recurring themes from the interview. In their discussion, they state:

> Gay men's notions of intimacy within a relationship are constructed within a heterosexualized world. Same-sex relationships are not sanctioned legally and socially in the same way as opposite-sex relationships, and gay couples cannot escape the impact of this general lack of social and legal validation. Edwards suggests that 'gay relationships are often imbued with a sense of difference that can potentially create a psyche so convinced of its isolation that relationships are put under a particular stress and intensity' (Edwards, 1994). This stress can be evidenced in the way gay men's relationships are regarded within the gay community itself. Several of our respondents spoke of feeling unsupported by the wider gay community in their attempt to maintain a monogamous long-term relationship. (p. 252)

A Limitations Section

Drumm, Pittman, and Perry (2001) offered a qualitative study that identified the emotional needs of female Kosovar refugees in southern Albania in May 1999. This date was about one month following their flight from Kosovo. This qualitative study was completed at the request of the Adventist Development and Relief Agency (ADRA) to assess the emotional needs of refugees in its care. Fifty-three Kosovar refugees were interviewed individually while fifty-six other refugees were enrolled in focus groups. While this study was important in ascertaining many of the emotional needs of the refugees to better serve them, there were also numerous limitations of this study. Such limitations included language barriers, variations in translator effectiveness, and a relatively small sample size. The authors reported:

> In spite of the appropriate precautions, there were some difficulties. First, the interpreters differed in their proficiency both in English and in communication with the Kosovar refugees. For the two Albanian interpreters, the dialects were different enough that they had difficulty communicating with confidence. Second, it appeared that some of the Kosovar participants distrusted the Albanian interpreters. . . . Another limitation was the small sample size. We were only able to spend one day in the refugee camps, and although we contacted more than 100 participants, more in-depth work is needed to gain a comprehensive view of the refugees' emotional needs. (p. 473–474)

common limitations have been discussed in previous chapters, but here is a summary of these problems:

- *Problems associated with the research strategy or approach* The study's approach—descriptive, explanatory, qualitative, quantitative—needs to be made explicit, and the approach's drawbacks need to be acknowledged.

- *Limitations of the sampling method* Nonprobability sampling will result in limited generalizability of the findings; but probability sampling may not yield information-rich cases.

- *Limited response rate* A response rate of less than 50% limits generalizations even if probability sampling is used.

- *The reliability and validity of the data collection methods* These need to be specified.

- *The problems associated with internal and external validity* Validity problems can occur when the research is explanatory (rather than descriptive) and often result from the lack of a comparison group, particularly one that has been randomly assigned. These problems need to be acknowledged.

- *The problems associated with the interpretation of the results* It is important to point out that interpretations are just that, interpretations; other people may interpret the results rather differently. Interpretive problems may arise with either statistical tests or qualitative data.

Obviously, there are other limitations, which will be explored further in the next chapter. The ones presented here provide a general guideline to follow when writing the limitations section of your report, paper, or article.

The extent to which you discuss limitations depends on your audience. You must devote at least a paragraph to addressing these issues. If you are writing up the results of a needs assessment or a program evaluation, the limitations section can be minimal. But if your audience is more knowledgeable about research, you must provide a more extensive limitations section.

Recommendations Section

The next section of the report consists of recommendations for further study and explicitly states the questions that have arisen from the research itself.

Implications for Practice

An implications for practice section is critical to many reports and central when the research is a needs assessment or a program evaluation. After all, these implications are a central purpose of the research.

The order and structure of these last few sections can vary. Often the discussion section includes the implications for practice section, the limitations section, and the suggestions for further research section.

Recommendations for Further Research Section

Mowbray, Oyserman, Bybee, and MacFarlane (2002) examined the effects of mental illness on parenting. They used a large urban-based sample of women with serious mental illness. Of the participants, seventy percent were women from ethnic minority groups, and all of the participants had care responsibility of at least one minor child. Data from the Diagnostic Interview Schedule modules indicated that diagnosis had a small but significant negative effect on parenting attitudes and behaviors. The authors suggested that the results of this study will be useful in consideration of parenting among mothers with serious mental illness, but note that additional research with a larger sample size and diversity in ethnicity is necessary. The authors state:

> Future research clearly needs to move beyond much of the published litera-
> ture, which has primarily involved white, middle-class, intact families. To assess
> the generalizability of the findings reported here, additional subpopulations
> (for example, Latinas, Asian Americans) should be included. Multisite studies
> with even larger samples could simultaneously examine race-ethnic group
> membership along with age and socioeconomic status. Future research
> should also look at the possibility that race-ethnicity matters not only in its
> effects on diagnosis obtained using standard instruments but also in other
> important clinical variables of interest . . . (p. 238)

An Implications for Practice Section: Program Evaluation

Block and Potthast (1998) discuss a program, *Girl Scouts Beyond Bars,* that enhanced regular prison visits between daughters and their prison-residing mothers. The program supported the mother-daughter relationships and eased some of the problems caused by incarceration. The authors suggest several implications for child welfare professionals based on program results. The professional has responsibilities to help maintain contact between the parent who is incarcerated and her children, to provide resources to the family, to develop permanency plans, and/or to facilitate reunification. The professional can do this by communicating with the mothers, supporting regular visits by the children, and encouraging qualifying children and mothers to become involved in available programs. At the organizational level, child welfare agencies are encouraged to establish linkages with visiting programs, such as the *Girl Scouts Beyond Bars* program, in their communities.

An Implications for Practice Section: Needs Assessment

Cook, Selig, Wedge, and Gohn-Baube (1999) studied the social, environmental, and psychological barriers that interfere with the early and regular use of prenatal services by low-income, inner-city women. The authors suggested the following initial screening of the women to identify those most at risk: targeting the highest risk group, particularly when resources and staff are in short supply; mail and telephone reminders of appointments; on-site child care; and community outreach, including home visiting.

DISSEMINATING THE REPORT

Disseminating or distributing the research report is an essential prerequisite to incorporation of research into practice. The dissemination of a report can take several forms: Reports can be orally presented; distributed internally in written form; and published in journals.

Oral Presentation

You may be required to present your research results orally at a community meeting, at a meeting of the agency's board of directors, or to legislators. In the case of practice evaluations, usually the results are discussed more informally with the client and others who might be involved. When presenting orally at a formal meeting, keep the following items in mind:

- Know how much time you have to give the report and stick to this time. Rehearsing your presentation will help.

- Allow time for questions and discussion. Know in advance how much time will be allocated for discussion.

- Use visual aids (overheads, slides, and so on) and handouts (containing a summary of the results and perhaps some charts and scales) when appropriate.

- Try not to become defensive about the research if someone criticizes it during discussion or question time. Simply answer the questions as clearly and as straightforwardly as possible. You should already be aware of the limitations and have thought them through, but you may have missed some.

Distributing Written Reports Internally

The appearance of the report is important even if it is only to be distributed in-house. The term *in-house* can encompass anything from a small agency to a large government department. Be sure that the original report is clear and will reproduce good copies; it can be frustrating to read a report that has been poorly copied. Make sure that everyone who is meant to receive the report actually does.

Publishing the Report

You should strive to publish whenever possible. Publications undoubtedly give the professional the best access to research findings. Social work journals are making a conscious effort to solicit and publish articles written by practitioners. As a practitioner, you have important contributions to make that can be different from those of academicians.

There are some ways to assess whether or not your report has potential for publication. Consider the following:

- Is it investigating a problem that has received little attention in the past in the research literature? Many journals devote entire issues to research on a newly explored topic.

- Does it have a new slant or perspective on a problem? For example, there may have been many program evaluations on the effectiveness of parent training on reducing the incidence of child abuse and neglect. But if your agency has a program that serves a large number of Puerto Rican clients and you have been involved in evaluating the program, you might have excellent material for publication if none has previously been published on this type of intervention with this particular client group.

- Is it an innovative research method or combination of methods?

Use participatory principles in disseminating the report. Petersen, Magwaza, and Pillay (1996) used the following methods:

> The participants decided that the results of the epidemiological study needed to be made accessible to the community via pamphlets which could be distributed in the community as well as an audiotape which could be played at the district hospital. On a more regional and national level it was decided that the results needed to be made accessible to other communities experiencing violence via the media such as the national/public radio as well as an article published in a black national Sunday newspaper. The participants agreed to distribute the pamphlets to the parents of the pre-school children. Due to the lack of community resources, the researchers were requested to ensure that the other above-mentioned tasks were carried out. (p. 71)

If you are considering publishing, you should know that different journals are interested in different types of articles. To get a sense of who is interested in what, refer to the *NASW Guide to Social Work Authors*. This gives information on many journals and lists their specific requirements in terms of length of article, reference style, number of copies, and so on.

THE AGENCY AND RESEARCH WRITING

Very often the agency for which you are completing the research will give you specific requirements on how to write the report. Usually, an in-house report on a program evaluation or needs assessment will focus on the results section. A needs assessment may also concentrate on the implications of the findings for practice. If you are writing the report for publication and wider distribution, you may want to emphasize the methods section over the results and devote some attention to a discussion of how the results support or reject previous research. This will enable other researchers to replicate or augment your study.

As a generalist social worker employed in an agency, you will most often write reports on individual cases. These are also research reports if you used some type of evaluation as part of your practice. So start now—combine research and practice and contribute to social work knowledge.

Also, don't forget that another important way in which you can contribute is to give presentations at conferences. For example, your state NASW chapter probably holds conferences every year and strongly encourages practitioners to contribute.

ETHICAL ISSUES IN RESEARCH WRITING

Two major ethical issues arise in research writing. The first issue is appropriately referencing material that is included in a report. The second is confidentiality of results. We will discuss each of these issues in turn.

Referencing Appropriately

Existence of Previous Work

Whenever research is being planned and conducted, it is imperative that you consult other work that has been completed in the target area. For example, you may have been asked by your supervisor to conduct a needs assessment for an after-school program in your community. You are excited about the opportunity to show off some of your newly acquired research skills. But the next day an ex-classmate calls you from a neighboring city; after you tell her about your assignment, she tells you she has just finished conducting such a study in her community.

You are tempted to ignore this piece of information and continue with your own plans because that way you could do your survey alone and collect the credit. Ethically, however, you need to acknowledge your friend's information as useful assistance in the development of your needs assessment; perhaps you may even be forced to recognize that there is no need for this type of study in your community at this time.

Citing References Appropriately

Given that you do decide to use information from your friend's study, it is imperative that you give her credit for her work. This applies to a study published locally as a report, as well as to more widely distributed publications. Recognizing others' contributions can present dilemmas. It would be impossible to credit everyone who has contributed to our intellectual and professional development.

In the case of specific research endeavors, however, you must recognize the contributions of others; otherwise, you may be guilty of plagiarism.

Confidentiality of Results

Just as confidentiality needs to be ensured during the data collection phase, you also need to preserve confidentiality when writing and disseminating the report. Subjects' identities should not be disclosed without their permission. Confidentiality may be problematic in qualitative reports with extensive quotes that inadvertently reveal the subject's identity. It is also an issue with practice evaluations.

The NASW Code of Ethics (1999) states:

- Social workers engaged in the evaluation of services should discuss collected information only for professional purposes and only with people professionally concerned with this information.

- Social workers who report evaluation and research results should protect participants' confidentiality by omitting identifying information unless proper consent has been obtained authorizing disclosure.

Another related issue is copyright. Copyright law applies to both published materials and in-house reports. Be sure to check on the restrictions that might pertain to distribution and publishing before you disseminate a report more widely.

HUMAN DIVERSITY ISSUES IN RESEARCH WRITING

Three human diversity issues are involved in research writing. First, you must ensure that bias against certain groups is not contained in the report. Second, you should avoid using exclusive language. Third, you must consider to whom the results are being disseminated.

Bias Against Certain Groups

Be careful to exclude biases in the writing that tend to stereotype groups. You are less at risk for this if you paid careful attention to human diversity issues throughout the research process. Then you simply ensure the data are accurately presented and equitably and nonjudgmentally discussed.

Exclusive Language

The issue of exclusive language involves acknowledging our differences and avoiding sexism. Although the predominant use of the male pronoun as a generic pronoun is becoming increasingly less acceptable, we do need to ensure that nonsexist terms are employed consistently. This involves the appropriate use of male, female, and plural pronouns and the use of terms that are gender neutral, such as *chair* instead of *chairman*.

We also need to ensure that terms do not reflect ethnic or cultural biases or a lack of sensitivity to human diversity. Use a descriptor of a cultural group that is recognized by the group itself. For example, using the term *Mexican American* in New Mexico to refer to Hispanics could be offensive to some individuals who view themselves as Spanish Americans with minimal connections to Mexico. Accuracy often requires that we not lump different groups of people together under one label.

Disseminating the Results

The final human diversity issue relating to research writing is the question of who should receive the results. There is a growing argument in favor of giving the findings to the participants included in the research rather than just to the practitioners and other researchers. This is of course critical when conducting participatory or action research.

This does not necessarily entail making the entire research report available to the participants, particularly if it is extensive or excessively technical. Instead, a smaller report can be written specifically for those participating in a needs assessment or program evaluation, in which the results could potentially influence an entire community. One advantage of practice evaluations is that the results are routinely shared with the client (usually verbally).

Advocates of the feminist perspective point out that sharing the results with the participants is another dimension of how "the researcher and subject can work in different ways to explore a 'truth' that they mutually locate and define" (Davis, 1986). This form of disseminating the results of the research characterizes the participatory and consensual style attributed to feminist approaches in research and in administrative style and social work practice. Disseminating the results this way does not jeopardize the confidentiality of the results any more than disseminating the results in a more "traditional" manner, as individual responses are not disclosed to the participants.

Giving participants access to findings is also being increasingly viewed as an issue for underrepresented groups in that the research results can be empowering to subjects. Historically, underrepresented groups have participated in research but have reaped no benefits from it.

Apart from making the results accessible to the participants, researchers need to pay more attention to repaying the participants. Of course, in social work research, the results of needs assessments, program evaluations, and practice evaluations all directly contribute to the development or improvement of interventions designed to assist those who are studied.

Sometimes, though, benefits can be extended further—for example, by returning a proportion of the royalties from book sales to the community or by paying participants for the time they spend being interviewed.

SUMMARY

Four general principles of research writing are to know your audience, to use appropriate citations and references, to structure your research report or proposal correctly, and to write the report as clearly and as concisely as possible. The research proposal is a paper proposing a specific type of research. The funding

agency may have requests for proposals (RFPs) that list the prc
ested in funding and how the proposals should be submittec
proposal, the research report should follow an outline structu
research topic, theoretical framework, research questions an
collection methods, sampling strategy, research design, results
tions, recommendations for future research, and implications for practice.
Reports may be presented orally, distributed internally (in-house), or published.

In an agency, generalist social workers are involved in writing formal reports
and proposals and case reports. The ethical issues involved in research writing
include appropriately referencing material and ensuring confidentiality of the
results. Human diversity issues of concern in research writing are eliminating
stereotyping of certain groups, avoiding exclusive language, and disseminating
results to subjects.

STUDY/EXERCISE QUESTIONS

1. Request sample grant applications from organizations in your city or state
   that fund research efforts related to social work. Share these in class and discuss their similarities and differences.

2. Select a social work journal article and critique it, using the structure of a
   research report presented in this chapter as a guide.

3. Select research articles from social work journals that contain tables or charts.

   a. Do they clearly illustrate the results of the research?

   b. What changes would you make to improve them?

REFERENCES

American Psychological Association (2001). *Publication manual of the American
Psychological Association* (5th ed.). Washington, DC: APA.

Block, K. J., & Potthast, M. J. (1998). Girl scouts beyond bars: Facilitating parent
child contact in correctional settings. *Child Welfare, LXXVII* (5), 561–578.

Cook, C. A., Selig, K. L., Wedge, B. J., & Gohn-Baube, E. A. (1999). Access barriers and the use of prenatal care by low-income, inner-city women. *Social
Work, 44* (2), 129–139.

Davis, L. V. (1986). A feminist approach to social work research. *Affilia, 1,* 32–47.

Drumm, R., Pittman, S., & Perry, S. (2001). Women of war: Emotional needs of
ethnic Albanians in refugee camps. *Affilia, 16* (4), 467–487.

Guffey, M. E. (1997). Formats for the citation of electronic sources in business
writing. *Business Communication Quarterly, 60* (1), 59.

Harrison, R. S., Boyle, S. W., & Farley, O. W. (1999). Evaluating the outcomes of
family-based intervention for troubled children: A pre-test post test study.
Research in Social Work Practice, 9 (6), 640–655.

Johnson, A. K. (1999). Working and nonworking women: Onset of homelessness within the context of their lives. *Affilia, 14* (1), 42–77.

Lopez, R. A. (1999). *Las Comadres* as a social support system. *Affilia, 14* (1), 24–41.

Mowbray, C., Oyserman, D., Bybee, D., & MacFarlane, P. (2002). Parenting of mothers with a serious mental illness: Differential effects of diagnosis, clinical history, and other mental health variables. *Social Work Research, 26* (4), 225–241.

National Association of Social Workers (1999). NASW Code of Ethics. *NASW News, 25,* 24–25.

Petersen, I., Magwaza, A. S., & Pillay, Y. G. (1996). The use of participatory research to facilitate a psychological rehabilitation programme for child survivors of violence in a South African community. *Social Work/ Maatskaplike Werk, 32* (1), 67–74.

Szuchman, L., & Thomlison, B. (2000). *Writing with style: APA style for social work.* Belmont, CA: Brooks/Cole Publishing.

Valentine, D. P., Edwards, S., Gohagan, D., Huff, M., Pereira, A., & Wilson, P. (1998). Preparing social work doctoral students for teaching: Report of a survey. *Journal of Social Work Education, 34* (2), 273–282.

Worth, H., Reid, A., & McMillan, K. (2002). Somewhere over the rainbow: Love, trust and monogamy in gay relationships. *Journal of Sociology, 38* (3), 237–255.

Yick, A. G., & Agbayani-Stewart, P. (2000). Dating violence among Chinese American and white students: A sociocultural context. *Journal of Multicultural Social Work, 8* (1/2), 101–129.

Ziesemer, C., Marcoux, L., & Marwell, B. E. (1994). Homeless children: Are they different from other low-income children? *Social Work 39* (6).

Library and Internet Resources

Compiled by Joe Buenker, M.S.
Assistant Librarian
Arizona State University West, Library (Phoenix, AZ)

A. Recommended Resources Provided by Academic Libraries [66]

1. Getting Started: Overview Sources for Contemporary Social Issues [10]

2. Library of Congress Subject Headings: Beyond Keyword Searching

3. Dictionaries and Handbooks [12]

4. Encyclopedias [11]

5. Special Populations [8]

6. Statistical Sources [9]

7. Journal Articles: Tools for Identifying Periodical Literature [16]

B. Recommended "Free" World Wide Web Resources [298]

1. Social Work Gateways or Metasites [2]

2. Social Work's Professional Organizations [18]

3. Consumer Health Information [5]

4. Datasets and Statistics [17]

5. Indexes and Databases [7]

6. Associations and Organizations [134]

7. United States Government Agencies and Information [64]

8. Significant Journal Titles and Their Homepages [52]

Note: The number of sources listed and annotated or summarized in sections A and B are listed in brackets at the end of the section title.

Even though far more free Web sources are identified than are library sources, students are strongly encouraged to begin **all of their research** at their academic library. The Internet/Web is a great supplemental search tool, but it has not (and will not) surpass the abilities of academic libraries to supply quality information, instruction, and research assistance.

For additional information (and more extensive listings) about social work research, please see the ASU West Library "Social Work Research" guide:

- http://www.west.asu.edu/library/research/reference/social_work/

A. RECOMMENDED LIBRARY RESOURCES

A1 Getting Started: Overview Sources for Contemporary Social Issues

The following is a list of 8 actively published book series and 2 government information periodicals or serials that discuss significant social topics. Many of these sources and their individual titles are likely to be in the collections of academic libraries. To ascertain if a library has these resources, perform a title or series title search of the library's catalog.

Book Series

The American family. Santa Barbara, CA: ABC-CLIO.
   http://www.abc-clio.com/products/browseseries.aspx?seriesid=23
Contemporary issues. Amherst, NY: Prometheus Books.
   http://www.prometheusbooks.com/
Contemporary world issues. Santa Barbara, CA: ABC-CLIO.
   http://www.abc-clio.com/products/browseseries.aspx?seriesid=8
Controversial Issues in . . . Boston, MA: Allyn and Bacon/Longman.
   http://www.ablongman.com/
Current Controversies. San Diego, CA: Greenhaven Press.
   http://www.galegroup.com/greenhaven/
Springer Series on Social Work. New York, NY: Springer Publishing Company.
   http://www.springerpub.com/store/SSSW.html
Taking Sides: Clashing Views on Controversial Issues . . . Guilford, CT: Dushkin Publishing Group.
   http://www.dushkin.com/online/contentsmain.mhtml
Teaching social work values (series). Alexandria, VA: Council on Social Work Education.
   http://www.cswe.org/publications/pubsbyseries.htm

Government Information Periodicals

Congressional digest. Washington, DC: Congressional Digest Corp.
   http://www.congressionaldigest.com/cdm/cdm.htm
CQ Researcher. Washington, DC: Congressional Quarterly, Inc.
   http://library.cqpress.com/cqresearcher/

A2 Library of Congress Subject Headings

When performing literature searches beginners often rely exclusively on results gained from keyword searches. When using library catalogs and journal article indexes/databases, however, you will achieve much more relevant results when you realize that these resources have controlled or standard vocabularies built into their structure.

To optimize the power and flexibility of a library catalog, you will want to review the results from your keyword search so that you can identify the most relevant records. Note the subject headings (academic libraries typically use the Library of Congress Subject Headings [LCSHs]) for these relevant titles, and write them down. The good news is that almost all academic libraries use the LCSH classification system. So when you have learned how to effectively search your library's catalog, you will not have much difficulty if/when you need to search other university's catalogs.

With your list of LCSHs, perform a subject search of the catalog—instead of the keyword search—and you will normally retrieve better and more useful results.

Also, take advantage of the search limits offered by catalogs and library indexes. Common limits include limiting by language of publication, type of materials (book or video recording, etc.), and the range of publication years of interest to you.

A quick note about Library of Congress Subject Headings and social work: The phrase "social work" is not recognized as an official LCSH, but when you enter a subject search of "social work" most academic library catalogs will direct you to the preferred LCSH—which is "social service."

It is not uncommon for a 500-page book to receive only 4–5 subject headings. This is because the LCSHs are often broad or general concepts—such as "social service." With searching experience, however, you will learn that part of the power of library catalogs comes from the use of what are called subheadings. Subheadings are indicated by double-dashes in catalogs, and in the examples below you can see that in addition to the general subject of "social services," there are also subject headings that point to the more focused and specific topics of "Social Service—Moral and Ethical Issues" and "Social Service—United States—History."

Examples of Library of Congress Subject Headings for Social Service

Social Service
    Handbooks, manuals, etc.
    Library resources
    Literature
    Methodology
    Moral and Ethical Issues
    Psychological aspects
    Research
    Research Methodology
    Statistical Methods
    Teamwork
    United States
    United States—History
    Vocational Guidance

Additional Subject Headings for Social Work Issues

Adolescence—Encyclopedias

Adolescent psychology—
Encyclopedias

African American social workers

African Americans—Statistics

Aged—Economic conditions

Aged—Encyclopedias

Aged—Government Policy

Aging—United States—Encyclopedias

AIDS (Disease)—Encyclopedias

Alcoholism—Encyclopedias

American Sign Language—Dictionaries

Asian Americans—Statistics

Charities—United States

Child abuse—Dictionaries

Child development—Encyclopedias

Child psychology—Encyclopedias

Child Sexual Abuse

Child welfare

Child Welfare Workers

Children—Health and hygiene

Council on Social Work Education

Demographic surveys

Deviant behavior—Encyclopedias

Disability studies—Handbooks,
manuals, etc.

Drinking of alcoholic beverages—
Encyclopedias

Drug abuse—Encyclopedias

Family—United States—Statistics

Gays—Bibliography

Gerontology—Encyclopedias

Health services administration

Helping behavior

Hispanic Americans—Economic
conditions

Hispanic Americans—Statistics

Household Surveys—United States

Human Services—research

Indians of North America—Population

Indians of North America—Statistics

Interviewing in Child Abuse

Lesbians—Bibliography

Medical care—Dictionaries

Medical Social Work

Military Social Work

Minority aged—Care

Minority aged—Counseling of

Minority aged—Health and hygiene

Minority aged—Services for

National Association of Social Workers

Old age

Pacific Islander Americans—Statistics

People with disabilities—
Rehabilitation

Psychiatric Social Work

Psychiatry—Dictionaries

Public health

Public welfare

Racism in Social Services

Retirees

School Social Work

Social case work

Social history—Encyclopedias

Social problems

Social reformers

Social sciences

Social sciences—Dictionaries

Social sciences—Methodology

Social sciences—Research

Social sciences—Statistical methods

Social service—Dictionaries

Social service—Moral and ethical aspects

Social service—Research

Social service—Research—Methodology

Social service—United States

Social service—United States— Dictionaries

Social service—Vocational guidance—United States

Social Work Education—United States—History

Social Work with African Americans

Social Work with Alcoholics

Social Work with Bisexuals

Social Work with Children

Social Work with Criminals

Social Work with Gays

Social Work with Juvenile Delinquents

Social Work with Lesbians

Social Work with Minorities

Social Work with Narcotic Addicts

Social Work with People with Disabilities

Social Work with People with Social Disabilities

Social Work with Teenagers

Social Work with the Aged

Social Work with the Homeless

Social Work with the Terminally Ill

Social Work With Women

Social Work with Youth

Social Workers

Social workers—Professional ethics

Social workers—United States

Social workers—United States— Statistics

Sociology

Sociology of disability

Spanish Americans—Statistics

Statistics—Methodology

Substance abuse—Encyclopedias

Transsexuals—Services for

United States—Census

United States—Economic conditions

United States—Politics and government

United States—Population—Statistics

United States—Social conditions— Encyclopedias

United States—Social conditions— Statistics

United States—Social life and customs

United States—Social policy

United States—Statistics

United States—Statistics, Vital

United States Census—21st, 1990

United States Census—22nd, 2000

United States—Population

Violence—United States

Violence in the workplace

Violent crimes—United States

Women—Crimes against

Women Social Workers

Youth—Services for

A3 Dictionaries & Handbooks

Typically the most recently published subject-specific dictionaries owned by a library are kept in that library's reference collection. Items shelved in reference collections normally are not available for checkout because they are intended for quick consultation and are likely to be of value to many researchers.

More and more students are relying almost exclusively on Web-based information sources—meaning that most never consider the possible uses of print reference materials. Librarians identify materials in the reference collection based on the needs of their local clients (students, faculty, and community users) and the potential value of the title. Items in reference collections are typically current, comprehensive, written by scholars, published by leading academic publishing groups, and—perhaps most important—**exist only in print format**.

Get to know your library's reference collection and ask a reference librarian to provide you with an overview of the social sciences section.

Barker, Robert L. (2003). *The social work dictionary,* 5th ed. Washington, DC: NASW Press.

Designed to document the development of the profession and to represent the growing and divergent body of social work terminology, this source promotes better communication and understanding and with its thousands of definitions, and is a standard for social workers and human services professionals. Emphasis is given to the brief interpretation of significant words, concepts, diversity, individuals, laws, organizations, historical events, and values. It also includes an alphabetical listing of acronyms frequently used by social workers; a timeline of important events in social work and social welfare; the NASW Code of Ethics; contact information for state boards regulating social work, and contact information for NASW state chapter offices.

Note: The most recent NASW Code of Ethics is freely available online from:
http://www.naswdc.org/pubs/code/
or http://www.socialworkers.org/pubs/code

Calhoun, Craig (Ed.) (2002). *Dictionary of the social sciences*. New York, NY: Oxford University Press.

Designed to overcome the differences in social sciences vocabulary to bring researchers together, and to make meaningful communication between researchers and the general public easier to achieve, this source includes 1,800 entries—each ranging from between 50–500 words. Emphasizes those fields that focus on social phenomena and human relations and provides biographical information on nearly 300 important social scientists/theorists. Goes beyond providing mere definitions by linking concepts with theories and their historical development and includes an extensive bibliography.

Colman, Andrew M. (2001). *A dictionary of psychology*. New York, NY: Oxford University Press.

Provides easily understood definitions of the most important and difficult words that students are likely to encounter while researching the field of psychology. Terminology includes psychology, psychiatry, neuroanatomy, neurophysiology, psychopharmacology, statistics, and psychoanalysis. The appendices feature a list of phobias and an extensive list of more than 700 abbreviations and symbols commonly used in psychology and related fields.

Hamilton, Neil A. (2002). *American social leaders and activists*. New York, NY: Facts on File, Inc.

Presents brief biographical information on more than 250 of the most important social reformers in America's post-Civil War history. Major categories include abolitionists, antiwar protestors, civil rights workers, labor organizers, peace advocates, socialists, and temperance crusaders. Includes a subject index, entries for individuals who promoted or extended African-American, American Indian, Latino, and Puerto Rican viewpoints, and profiles two social workers: Grace Abbott and Dorothy Day.

National Association of Social Workers (2003). *Social work speaks: National association of social workers policy statements [2003–2006]*, 6th ed. Washington, DC: NASW Press.

Contains 63 public and professional policy statements related to 18 topic areas: adolescents, aging, behavioral health, child welfare, community, discrimination and equity issues, education, employment, ethnicity and race, families and children, family planning, gender issues, health, macro issues, political action, social work professional statements, substance abuse and violence. Each statement consists of a background review, an issue statement, a policy statement, and a list of references.

Roberts, Albert R., & Greene, Gilbert J. (Eds.) (2002). *Social workers' desk reference*. New York, NY: Oxford University Press.

Organized into 14 parts, this single volume includes nearly 150 chapters written by the leading social work practitioners and faculty in the United States and Canada and emphasizes the use of interventions that are supported by empirical evidence. Designed to be a comprehensive reference for theories, practice issues, client assessment, treatment plans, therapeutic techniques, and case management, this source contains numerous references to relevant literature and concludes with a glossary, and both a name index and a subject index. This is an essential resource for all students of social work and will be a valuable tool for years to come.

Schwandt, Thomas A. (2001). *Dictionary of qualitative inquiry*, 2nd ed. Thousand Oaks, CA: Sage.

Provides practical introductory definitions of vocabulary related to philosophical and methodological concepts and, to a lesser degree, those terms dealing with the technical aspects of methods and procedures related to qualitative inquiry. Each of the approximately 300 terms has its own list of recommended resources. Includes some evaluation or criticism of the discussed concepts and concludes with a bibliography of significant secondary sources.

Shahrokh, Narriman C., & Hales, Robert E. (Eds.) (2003). *American psychiatric glossary*, 8th ed. Washington, DC: American Psychiatric Publishing.

Provides concise definitions for approximately 1,500 of the most commonly used words to describe psychiatric disorders and symptoms. Includes a list of commonly used abbreviations (primarily for the names of associations and organizations), a table of psychiatric drugs, a table of commonly abused drugs, a list of legal terms, a list of neurological deficits, a table of psychological tests, a list of research terms, and an outline of the schools of psychology. Emphasis is given to medical and legal terms.

Tennant, Richard A., & Brown, Marianne Gluszak (1998). *The American sign language handshape dictionary*. Washington, DC: Clerc Books/Gallaudet University Press.

This source organizes ASL signs by 40 basic one or two handshapes for easy identification which makes it a highly valuable tool for people interested in learning ASL and for situations when you know what a shape looks like but can't recall its meaning. Includes an introduction to deaf culture, the structure of ASL, illustrations of more than 1,600 signs and an index of English vocabulary for all included signs.

Timmereck, Thomas C. (1997). *Health services cyclopedic dictionary*, 3rd ed. Sudbury, MA: Jones and Bartlett Publishers.

Provides brief definitions of terms related to health care, health services, health care administration, and public health; it is not intended to be used as a replacement to medical dictionaries. Includes more than 15 appendices.

Trattner, Walter I. (Ed.) (1986). *Biographical dictionary of social welfare in America*. New York, NY: Greenwood Press.

Provides a single-volume source of information for the 300 most influential people in American social welfare history. Begins by defining social welfare and detailing criteria for exclusion [preference was given to doers—not individuals who were solely thinkers or givers—and no living persons were included], presents the 300 entries in alphabetical order and concludes with a subject index. Each biographical essay includes a brief bibliography and the appendix also includes a chronology of significant events in the history of American social welfare.

Vogt, W. Paul (1999). *Dictionary of statistics and methodology: A nontechnical guide for the social sciences*, 2nd ed. Thousand Oaks, CA: Sage Publications.

Provides an alphabetically arranged reference source for better understanding statistical concepts and methodological terms related to the study of social and behavioral sciences. Contains nearly 2,000 entries written in plain English, focuses on concepts—not calculations or mathematical formulas—and concludes with a brief list of recommended readings.

A4 Encyclopedias

As with dictionaries and handbooks, the most current and comprehensive encyclopedia sets are often shelved in the library's reference collection.

Libraries continue to spend a great deal of money on these resources, and unfortunately, many students either don't appreciate the value of the information contained in edited encyclopedia sets or don't understand the function of an academic reference collection.

Again, ask a reference librarian to recommend a few quality encyclopedias when you are in the beginning phases of a research project. Encyclopedias will provide great overviews. Take the time to page through the table of contents of an encyclopedia and browse through the index and appendices (normally at the back of the book). These pieces of information are of great value but are too detailed to include in the brief space allotted for catalog records.

Albrecht, Gary L., Seelman, Katherine D., & Bury, Michael (Eds.) (2001). *Handbook of disability studies*. Thousand Oaks, CA: Sage Publications.
Provides an interdisciplinary and international examination of the historical and cultural development of disabilities studies, organized into three parts: the shaping of disability studies as a field; experiencing disability; and disability in context. Aimed at students and researchers, disabled people, and those interested in social welfare policies, the book seeks to broaden the understanding of disabilities studies and to stimulate its advancement. Each chapter provides an overview, a detailed analysis of issues in disabilities studies, an extensive list of references, and questions for shaping future research and practice. The chapter "The Relationship between Disabled People and Health and Welfare Professionals" is particularly relevant.

Borgatta, Edgar F., & Montgomery, Rhonda J. V. (Eds.) (2000). *Encyclopedia of Sociology,* 2nd ed. New York, NY: Macmillan Reference USA.
Considered to be the definitive encyclopedia for the study of sociology, this 5-volume set contains approximately 400 in-depth original essays written by expert scholars. Each essay concludes with a list of related essays or and a detailed bibliography. The essays provide detailed historical overviews and attempt to predict future developments or trends in the research area.
Essays include: Aging and the Life Course; Childhood Sexual Abuse; Drug Abuse; Education and Development; Ethics in Social Research; Ethnicity; Family Violence; Human Rights/Children's Rights; Juvenile Delinquency; Public Policy Analysis; Race, Social Work, Statistical Inference, and Statistical Methods.

Breslow, Lester (Ed.) (2002). *Encyclopedia of public health*. New York, NY: Macmillan Reference USA.
This 4-volume set includes more than 900 alphabetically arranged entries related to the preservation, protection, promotion, and restoration of health for all of a community's people. All entries were written and signed by a leading expert, and most of the entries include see-also references and brief bibliographies. Provides entries for all major ethnic groups, census data, careers in public health, diseases, drug abuse, environmental health, ethical practice guidelines, inequalities in health care, nutrition, and population demographics. Concludes with a collection of significant historic public health statements, an annotated bibliography, a subject and name index, and a categorization of the 900 entries into 15 major subject areas: administration and agencies of public health; communicable diseases; noncommunicable diseases and conditions; injuries and violence; oral health; international health; statistics for public health; environmental health; behavioral and community health services; personal health

services; history, philosophy, and ethics of public health; nutrition; laboratory services; and public health and the law.

Carson-Dewitt, Rosalyn (Ed.) (2001). *Encyclopedia of drugs, alcohol and addictive behavior.* New York, NY: Macmillan Reference USA.
This 4-volume source examines the global impact of drugs, alcohol, and addictive behavior and details how they affect economic, educational, family well-being, legal, political, psychological, public health, and social issues.

Cayton, Mary Kupiec, Gorn, Elliott J., & Williams, Peter W. (Eds.) (1993). *Encyclopedia of American social history.* New York, NY: Charles Scribner's Sons.
This 3-volume set includes 180 scholarly entries arranged into 14 thematic parts: Periods of Social Change; Methods and Contexts; The Construction of Social Identity; Process of Social Change; Ethnic and Racial Subcultures; Regionalism and Regional Subcultures; Space and Place; Patterns of Everyday Life; Work and Labor; Popular Culture and Recreation; Family History; Social Problems, Social Control, and Social Protest; Science, Medicine, and Technology; and Education and Literacy. The essays average 10–15 pages in length and provide historical overviews of time periods, ethnic and geographic groups, and various other aspects of American life and culture. Each essay contains a bibliography and the set contains a master index.

Clark, Robin E., Clark, Judith Freeman, & Adamec, Christine (Eds.) (2001). *The encyclopedia of child abuse,* 2nd ed. New York, NY: Facts on File.
Features more than 500 alphabetically arranged entries on the prevention, recognition, treatment, and understanding of child abuse—including emotional, psychological, and sexual as well as neglect concerns. Emphasizes the educational, legal, medical, mental health, political, and sociological issues related to child abuse and provides a great deal of state and national statistics. The appendices also include detailed lists of relevant child welfare and child protection agencies and centers.

Dell Orto, Arthur E., & Marinelli, Robert P. (Eds.) (1995). *Encyclopedia of disability and rehabilitation.* New York, NY: Macmillan Reference Library USA.
Designed to assist persons involved in rehabilitation processes by providing relevant information on mental, organic, and physical disabilities, this source includes more than 150 signed articles. It begins by defining the terms disability and rehabilitation and then presents the articles in alphabetical order. Focus is given to definition of terms and procedures, assistive technology, the workplace, and psychosocial adjustment to disabilities. Each article includes a bibliography, and when appropriate, see-also references for related articles. Articles of note include: aging; Americans with Disabilities Act; disability law and social policy; ethics; minorities; reasonable accommodation; and social work practice in rehabilitation.

Ekerdt, D. J. (Ed.) (2002). *Encyclopedia of aging.* New York, NY: Macmillan Reference USA.

This 4-volume set was designed to make the scientific and scholarly study of human age, aging, and the aged accessible to general readers. Containing more than 400 articles, each written by an expert, it focuses on issues relating to bioethics, biology, economics, history, law, medicine, psychology, public policy, religion, and sociology. Areas of special relevance include medical ethics, end of life issues, social theories of aging, selected population groups, social services, and United States government role. Each article includes cross-references to other relevant articles and contains a bibliography.

Gitterman, Alex (Ed.) (2001). *Handbook of social work practice with vulnerable and resilient populations*, 2nd ed. New York, NY: Columbia University Press.
29 chapters focused around clients' "life conditions" and "life circumstances and events." Designed to expose social workers to strategies for providing relevant and empowering client services; coverage includes AIDS, substance abuse, mental health, chronic physical illness and disability, learning disabilities, adolescent pregnancy, child abuse, foster care, crime victims, bereavement, suicide, homelessness, and gay and lesbian persons.

Maddox, George L. (Ed.) (2001). *Encyclopedia of aging: A comprehensive resource in gerontology and geriatrics,* 3rd ed. New York, NY: Springer Publishing.
Edited by the former president of the American Society of Gerontology, this two-volume set includes approximately 600 alphabetically arranged articles. The set is highly interdisciplinary—covering biology, medicine, nursing, psychology, psychiatry, sociology, and social services—and is the result of the efforts of numerous prominent scholars. Articles range from one to five pages and include cross-referencing to other relevant articles. Includes a subject index and the second volume contains an extensive references section.

National Association of Social Workers (1995). *Encyclopedia of social work*, 19th ed. Richard L. Edwards, Editor-in-Chief. New York, NY: NASW.
This 3-volume set includes a detailed subject index, nearly 300 topical essays, more than 140 biographical entries, 80 readers' guides on major topics, numerous appendices, and emphasizes issues of ongoing relevance in the provision of social work services. It is responsive to global political and technological changes and devotes more coverage to women and persons of color who had a significant impact on social work and social welfare. Each entry includes an overview, a detailed analysis, a conclusion, a list of references, suggested resources for further reading, and a list of related entries.
This is the definitive encyclopedia for social work.

National Association of Social Workers (1997). *Encyclopedia of social work*, 19th ed., 1997 supplement. Richard L. Edwards, Editor-in-Chief. New York, NY: NASW.
This update to the 19th edition includes 30 new topical essays and 14 biographical profiles.

National Association of Social Workers (2003). *Encyclopedia of social work*, 19th ed., 2003 supplement. Richard L. Edwards, Editor-in-Chief. New York, NY: NASW.

A5 Special Populations

The study and inclusion of diversity and disability continue to gain importance across universities, and the social work profession—far from falling behind on these issues—has been one of the leading groups of practitioners and researchers engaged in these areas. As the United States and the world begin to come to grips with an aging population living longer, geriatric and gerontological issues promise to play an increasingly important role for social workers.

Appleby, George Alan, & Anastas, Jeane W. (1998). *Not just a passing phase: Social work with gay, lesbian, and bisexual people.* New York, NY: Columbia University Press.
Prepares social workers for more effective and informed engagement by providing an overview of everyday life for gays, lesbians, and bisexuals. Stresses individual, interpersonal, organizational, social and institutional interventions and provides approaches for working with issues of acceptance, addiction, disease, identity, mental health, oppression, shame, and violence.

Burlingame, Virginia S. (1999). *Ethnogerocounseling: Counseling ethnic elders and their families.* New York, NY: Springer Publishing Company.
Notes the increasing need to deviate from the predominantly Anglo/European models of elderly services and presents gerocounseling strategies and techniques for work with ethnic minority groups. Contains numerous case histories and explores the psychological, social, and spiritual influences of each group's culture on an individual member's late life decisions. Concludes by encouraging practitioners to "Treat others as they would like to be treated."

Martin, Elmer P., & Martin, Joanne M. (2002). *Spirituality and the Black helping tradition in social work.* Washington DC: NASW Press.
Documents the importance of spirituality for pioneering Black caregivers and social workers in their efforts to promote their cultural survival and advancement, and emphasizes the neglected attention given to Black spirituality in the social work literature. Corrects misunderstandings about the origins and evolution of the Black helping tradition and summarizes the African-American struggle for racial justice and equality. Considers how spirituality can be used to prevent negative life outcomes for contemporary young African Americans.

Martin, James I., & Hunter, Ski (2001). *Lesbian, gay, bisexual, and transgender issues in social work: A comprehensive bibliography with annotations.* Alexandria, VA: Council on Social Work Education.
A 12-chapter bibliography of more than 600 references to English-language journal articles, book chapters, and books published between 1993 and 2000 that relate to work with GLBT clients. Written by the co-chairs of the CSWE Commission on Sexual orientation and Gender Expression, the source provides 1–2 sentence summaries for approximately 160 of the included references. The number of references appearing in a chapter

appear in parentheses after the title name: overview (57); anti-GLBT oppression (41); life course development (52); selected life course arenas (165); health (64); mental health (19); alcohol & drug addiction (12); intimate partner violence (27); practice issues (114); policy issues (19); research issues (17); and social work education issues (20).

Newhill, Christiana E. (2003). *Client violence in social work practice: Prevention, intervention, and research.* New York, NY: Guilford Press.

Begins with a discussion of violence in society and workplaces in general and then focuses on the incidence and prevalence of client violence toward social workers. Addresses the different types of client violence and how to assess risk, and provides strategies for intervening with a violent client. Discusses the emotional and physical impact of client violence and offers models for developing safety plans and violent incident report forms.

Schneider, Robert L., Kropf, Nancy P., & Kisor, Anne J. (Eds.) (2000). *Gerontological social work: Knowledge, service settings, and special populations,* 2nd ed. Belmont, CA: Brooks Cole/Thomson Learning.

Organized by knowledge, service settings and special population categories, this text is designed to encourage educators to expand and integrate instructional content on aging into their curriculums in order to produce a new generation of well-trained gerontological social workers. Presents health and psychological data about elderly populations, discusses relevant social policies and the role of the social worker, and concludes by examining especially vulnerable client populations.

Stout, Karen D., & McPhail, Beverly (1998). *Confronting sexism and violence against women: A challenge for social work.* New York, NY: Longman.

Argues that American law, the English language, and societal attitudes contribute to discrimination and violence against women and recommends interventions or strategies for prevention and change. Uses a feminist perspective to discuss issues related to reproductive freedom, pornography, sexual harassment, battery, and rape.

Wykle, May L., & Ford, Amasa B. (Eds.) (1999). *Serving minority elders in the 21st century.* New York, NY: Springer Publishing.

Designed around discussions of physical health, mental health and community care, and with a focus on strategies for accommodating the unprecedented growth in America's minority elderly population, this text offers approaches and intervention strategies for working with aged African Americans, Asian Americans, Native Americans, and Mexican Americans.

A6 Statistics: National and Group-Specific

*Students are encouraged to consult the Web sites listed with the U.S. Census Bureau (alphabetically placed in the "Us") in the "Recommended Web Resources—Government Information" section of this appendix for identifying the most relevant Web-based census data and search tools.

Becker, Patricia (Ed.) (2002). *A statistical portrait of the United States: Social conditions and trends*, 2nd ed. Lanham, MD: Bernan Press.

Provides a detailed overview of recent social change in the United States; focusing primarily on the last 30 years and with special emphasis given to developments since the 1990s. The 13 chapters are: population characteristics; households and families; social conditions; labor force and job characteristics; housing; income, wealth, and poverty; education; crime and criminal justice; health; leisure, volunteerism, and religiosity; voting; environment; and government. Each chapter includes summary statistics, graphics depicting trends over time, and bibliographic references for further reading. Overall there are more than 150 figures and 80 tables presented.

Chadwick, Bruce A., & Heaton, Tim B. (1999). *Statistical handbook on the American family,* 2nd ed. Phoenix, AZ: Oryx Press.

Provides a detailed examination of American family life in late 20th and early 21st century America by using data from federal and state government agencies, relevant journals, and public opinion polls. Presents brief written overviews of the nine broad subject areas and includes 340 relevant tables, charts, and illustrations. Subject areas are: marriage; quality of marriage and family life; divorce and separation; children; sexual attitudes and behaviors and contraceptive use; living arrangements and kinship ties; working women, wives, and mothers; demographic and economic context; and child care. Concludes with a bibliography and a subject index.

Gall, Susan B., & Gall, Timothy L. (Eds.) (1993). *Statistical record of Asian Americans*. Detroit, MI: Gale Research Inc.

Though dated and short on 1990 Census data, this is perhaps the most comprehensive commercially published source for demographic information on Asian Americans. Chapters include: attitudes and opinions; business and economics; crime, law enforcement, and civil rights; domestic life; education; employment and occupations; health; housing; immigration; income, spending, and wealth; the military; population and vital statistics; public life; and religion. Includes a bibliography and nearly 1,900 statistical tables, but again does not present a complete or current profile of Asian Americans.

Ginsberg, Leon (1995). *Social Work Almanac,* 2nd ed. Washington, DC: NASW Press.

Using mostly governmental statistics and data, provides an overview of the major American social issues and social programs of the 1990s. Includes nearly 300 tables, more than 60 figures, and descriptions of how the information affects the practice of social work. Organized into 9 chapters: basic demographic data on the population of the United States; children; crime, corrections, and delinquency; education; health and mortality statistics; mental illness and developmental disabilities; older adults; social welfare, economic assistance, housing, and homelessness; and social work: professional issues.

Hornor, Louise (Ed.) (2002). *Black Americans: A statistical sourcebook*. Palo Alto, CA: Information Publications. [annual]

A one volume statistical reference source of information relating to Black Americans; the majority of information presented was drawn from U.S. Census Bureaus publications. Includes a glossary, subject index, and nearly 200 statistical tables. Chapter titles are Demographics & Characteristics of the Population; Vital Statistics & Health; Education; Government, Elections & Public Opinion; Crime, Law Enforcement, & Corrections; The Labor Force, Employment & Unemployment; Earnings, Income, Poverty & Wealth; and Special Topics.

Hornor, Louise (Ed.) (2002). *Hispanic Americans: A statistical sourcebook*. Palo Alto, CA: Information Publications. [annual]

A one volume statistical reference source of information relating to Hispanic Americans; information presented was gathered from governmental sources. Includes a glossary, subject index, and nearly 200 statistical tables. Chapter titles are Demographics & Characteristics of the Population; Vital Statistics & Health; Education; Government, Elections & Public Opinion; Crime, Law Enforcement, & Corrections; The Labor Force, Employment & Unemployment; Earnings, Income, Poverty & Wealth; and Special Topics.

Reddy, Marlita A. (Ed.) (1995). *Statistical record of Native North Americans,* 2nd ed. Detroit, MI: Gale Research, Inc.

Provides a compilation of statistics on the first inhabitants of North America by using state and federal government data, and information from tribal governments and other relevant organizations. Includes a guide to the chapters and the overall contents, chapter references, a final bibliography, and a comprehensive keyword index. Chapter titles: history; demographics; the family; education; culture and tradition; health and health care; social and economic conditions; business and industry; land and water management; government relations; law and law enforcement; and Canada.

Smith, Jessie Carney, & Horton, Carrell P. (1997). *Statistical record of Black America,* 4th ed. Detroit: Gale.

Last published in 1997, this source contains a list of references, a subject index, and nearly 1,000 statistical tables. The chapter titles are: Attitudes, Values, and Behavior; Business and Economics; Crime, Law Enforcement, and Legal Justice; Education; Health and Medical Care; Housing; Income, Spending, and Wealth; Labor and Employment; Miscellany; Politics and Elections; Population; Social and Human Services; Sports and Leisure; The Family; and Vital Statistics.

United Nations Children Fund. *The state of the world's children 2003*. Geneva, Switzerland: UNICEF.

Full-text available at http://www.unicef.org/publications/pub_sowc03_en.pdf

An annual report of the economic and social indicators of child well-being worldwide. Includes maps, statistical tables and photographs and artwork by children.

A7 Journal Articles: Tools for Identifying Periodical Literature

Most journal indexes, even if they are also published in print format, are now available online (Web-based format). Web availability of journal indexes, however, is a relatively new development in research—with most libraries switching from print and or CD-ROM indexes in the mid to late 1990s. Some journal indexing tools still exist only in print format and many of the CD-ROM or Web versions are not comprehensive—meaning they do not duplicate all of the entries that were published in the print versions of indexes prior to the conversion to CD-ROM and later Web formats.

There are more than 150,000 actively published journals, magazines, and newspapers. Each journal index has a group of persons responsible for determining what type of materials they will index (books chapters, journal articles, Ph.D. dissertations, conference presentations, Web sites, etc.) and for journals, which of the thousands of possibly relevant titles will be indexed by their tool. Because there are so many journal titles published and on so many different topics, there is no single search tool for identifying articles related to a topic or keyword from all available journal titles. This is why there are hundreds of different databases to choose from.

Some of the periodical indexes listed below are available only as subscriptions. Your library may provide on-site and off-campus access to some of these titles and a few of them are made freely available by the publisher or content producer to all Web users.

Abstracts in social gerontology: Current literature on aging (1990 to date).
   * For product details see
   http://www.sagepub.com/journal.aspx?pid=27
Ageline (1978 to date).
   * For product details and free access to the database, see
   http://research.aarp.org/ageline/
CIJE (*Current index to journals in education*) (1969 to date).
   * For free access to the database, see
   http://www.ericfacility.net/extra/pub/sjisearch.cfm
Contemporary Women's Issues (1992 to date).
   * For product details, see
   http://www.gale.com/
Criminal justice abstracts (1977 to date).
   * For product details, see
   http://www.sagepub.com/journal.aspx?pid=253
   **Available in print and full text format.
   Former title: *Crime and delinquency literature* (1970–1976).
ERIC (*Educational Resources Information Center*) *Database* (1966 to date).
   * For free access to the database, see
   http://www.eduref.org/Eric/

* For product information, see
http://www.eduref.org/Eric/Help/dbfaqs.shtml
*** *ERIC* includes CIJE, ERIC Digests, and RIE documents.

ERIC Digests (1992 to date).

* For free access to the database, see
http://www.ericfacility.net/ericdigests/
** For free access to pre-1992 documents from *ERIC Digests,* see
http://www.ericfacility.net/ericdigests/index/edopre92.html

PAIS international in print (1991 to date).

* For product details, see
http://www.pais.org/pdf/paisintl.pdf and
http://www.pais.org/products/
** Former titles: *Bulletin of the Public Affairs Information Service* (1915–1968);
Public Affairs Information Service Bulletin (1969–1985); *PAIS Bulletin* (1986–1990).

PsycInfo (1967 to date).

* For product details, see
http://www.apa.org/psycinfo/products/psycinfo.html
** Former titles: *Psychological Abstracts (1927–1966); PsycLIT* [CD-ROM]
(1974–late 1990s).

RIE (Resources in education) (1975 to date). Washington, DC: Government Printing Office.

* Former title: *Research in education (1966–1974).*

Sage family studies abstracts (1979 to date). Newbury Park, CA: Sage Publications.

* For product details see
http://www.sagepub.com/journal.aspx?pid=141
**Available in print and full-text format.

Social sciences fulltext (1974 to date). New York, NY: H. W. Wilson.

* For product details see
http://www.hwwilson.com/databases/socsci.htm
** Previous titles: *Social sciences index*

Social service abstracts. Bethesda, MD: Cambridge Scientific Abstracts.

* For product details see
http://www.csa.com/csa/factsheets/socserv.shtml

Social work abstracts (1994 to date). Silver Spring, MD: National Association of
Social Workers.

* Former titles: *Abstracts for Social Workers (1965–1977); Social Work Research
& Abstracts (1977–1993)*

Sociological Abstracts (1952 to date). San Diego, CA: Sociological Abstracts.

* For product details see
http://www.csa.com/csa/factsheets/socioabs.shtml

Violence and abuse: Current literature in interpersonal violence.

* For product details see
http://www.sagepub.com/journal.aspx?pid=55

B.   RECOMMENDED "FREE" WORLD WIDE WEB RESOURCES

B1 Social Work Gateways or Metasites

Social Work and Social Services Web Sites
    http://gwbweb.wustl.edu/websites.html
    From the George Warren Brown School of Social Work, Washington University in St. Louis (St. Louis, MO).

World Wide Web Resources for Social Workers
    http://www.nyu.edu/socialwork/wwwrsw
    This site was created to facilitate social workers' access to quality online information and is cosponsored by the New York University Shirley M. Ehrenkranz School of Social Work and the Division of Social Work and Behavioral Science, Mount Sinai School of Medicine.

B2 Social Work's Professional Associations

Academy of Certified Social Workers
    http://www.socialworkers.org/credentials/credentials/acsw.asp

American Board of Examiners in Clinical Social Work
    http://www.abecsw.org/

Association for Gerontology Education in Social Work
    http://www.agesocialwork.org/

Association for the Advancement of Social Work with Groups
    http://www.aaswg.org

Association of Baccalaureate Social Work Program Directors
    http://www.bpdonline.org/

Association of Oncology Social Work
    http://www.aosw.org

Association of Social Work Boards
    http://www.aswb.org

Clinical Social Work Federation
    http://www.cswf.org

Council on Social Work Education
    http://www.cswe.org

Diplomate in Clinical Social Work
    http://www.socialworkers.org/credentials/credentials/dcsw,asp

Institute for the Advancement of Social Work Research
    http://www.iaswresearch.org/

National Association of Deans and Directors of Schools of Social Work
    http://www.cosw.sc.edu/nadd/

National Association of Social Workers (NASW)
    http://www.naswdc.org
    http://www.socialworkers.org/

NASW Code of Ethics
http://www.naswdc.org/pubs/code/
or http://www.socialworkers.org/pubs/code

National Network for Social Work Managers
http://www.socialworkmanager.org/

North American Association of Christian Social Workers
http://www.nacsw.org

Qualified Clinical Social Worker
http://www.socialworkers.org/credentials/credentials/qcsw.asp

School Social Work Association of America
http://www.sswaa.org

Society for Social Work and Research
http://www.sswr.org/

Society for Social Work Leadership in Health Care
http://www.sswlhc.org/

B3 Consumer Health Information

Centers for Disease Control: Health Topics A–Z
http://www.cdc.gov/az.do

Health Resources and Services Administration: Topics A–Z
http://www.hrsa.gov/ConsumerEd/

National Institutes of Health: Health Information
http://health.nih.gov/

United States Department of Health and Human Services, Substance Abuse and
Mental Health Administration, Office of Applied Studies
http://www.samhsa.gov/oas/topics.cfm

B4 Datasets and Statistics

American Sociological Association (2003). *The Importance of Collecting Data and
Doing Research on Race.* [paper]
http://www.asanet.org/media/asa_race_statement.pdf

Centers for Disease Control, National Center for Health Statistics. *Linked Birth
and Infant Death Data Set.*
http://www.cdc.gov/nchs/linked.htm

Centers for Disease Control, National Center for Health Statistics. *National
Death Index.*
http://www.cdc.gov/nchs/r&d/ndi/ndi.htm

Centers for Disease Control, National Center for Health Statistics. *National
Maternal and Infant Health Survey.*
http://www.cdc.gov/nchs/about/major/nmihs/abnmihs.htm

Centers for Disease Control, National Center for Health Statistics. *National Mortality Followback Survey.*
http://www.cdc.gov/nchs/about/major/nmfs/nmfs.htm

Centers for Disease Control, National Center for Health Statistics. *State and Territorial Data.*
http://www.cdc.gov/nchs/fastats/

Centers for Disease Control (CDC) National Prevention Network.
http://www.cdcnpin.org/

Jackson, Richard, Howe, Neil, & Center for Strategic International Studies (2003). *The Aging Vulnerability Index: An Assessment of the Capacity of Twelve Developed Countries to Meet the Aging Challenge.*
http://www.csis.org/gai/aging_index.pdf

National Institutes of Health & Health Resources and Services Administration. *Combined Health Information Database (CHID Online).*
http://chid.nih.gov/

Surveys and Data Collection Systems from the National Center for Health Statistics
http://www.cdc.gov/nchs/express.htm

United States Department of Health and Human Services. *Gateway to Data and Statistics.*
http://hhs-stat.net/

United States Department of Health and Human Services, Office of the Assistant Secretary for Planning and Evaluation (2000). *Trends in the Well-Being of America's Children and Youth.*
http://aspe.hhs.gov/hsp/00trends/

United States Department of Health and Human Services, Public Health Services, Health Resources and Services Administration, Bureau of Health Professions. *A National Agenda for Geriatric Education: White Papers.*
http://bhpr.hrsa.gov/interdisciplinary/gecagenda.html [index page]
Chapter 11: The State of the Art of Geriatric Social Work Education and Training
ftp://ftp.hrsa.gov/bhpr/interdisciplinary/gecwhite/11socialwork.pdf

United States Department of Health and Human Services, Substance Abuse and Mental Health Administration. *Drug Abuse Warning Network (DAWN).*
http://dawninfo.samhsa.gov/

United States Department of Health and Human Services, Substance Abuse and Mental Health Administration, Office of Applied Studies. *Drug and Alcohol Services Information System (DASIS).*
http://www.oas.samhsa.gov/dasis.htm

United States Department of Health and Human Services, Substance Abuse and Mental Health Administration, Office of Applied Studies. *National Survey on Drug Use and Health (NHSDA).*
http://www.oas.samhsa.gov/nhsda.htm

United States Department of Health and Human Services, Substance Abuse and Mental Health Administration, Office of Applied Studies. *Substance Abuse and Mental Health Statistics*.
http://www.samhsa.gov/oas/oasftp.cfm

B5 Indexes and Databases

Ageline
http://research.aarp.org/ageline/

Cochrane Collaboration [Evidence-Based Health Care]
http://www.cochrane.org

ERIC [*Educational Resources Information Center*]
http://www.eduref.org/Eric/

NCJRS (*National Criminal Justice Reference Service*)
http://www.ncjrs.org/search.html

PILOTS Database [Electronic Index to Traumatic Stress]
http://www.ncptsd.org/publications/pilots/

Project CORK [Authoritative Information on Substance Abuse]
http://www.projectcork.org/

PubMed [The MEDLINE database and more]
http://www.ncbi.nlm.nih.gov/entrez/

B6 Associations and Institutes

Alliance for Aging Research
http://www.agingresearch.org/

American Association of People with Disabilities
http://www.aapd.com/

American Association of Retired Persons
http://www.aarp.org/

American Council for the Blind
http://www.acb.org/

The American Geriatrics Society
http://www.americangeriatrics.org/

American Public Human Services Association
http://www.aphsa.org/

American Society of Addiction Medicine
http://www.asam.org/

American Society on Aging
http://www.asaging.org/

Assistive Living Facilities Association of America
http://www.alfa.org/

The CATO Institute
http://www.cato.org/

Center for Effective Public Policy
http://www.cepp.com/

Center for Health and Gender Equity (CHANGE)
http://www.genderhealth.org/

Center for Independent Living
http://www.cilberkeley.org/

Center for Law and Social Policy
http://www.clasp.org/

Center for Policy Research
http://www-cpr.maxwell.syr.edu/

Center for Prevention of Sexual and Domestic Violence
http://www.cpsdv.org/

Center for Research on Women with Disabilities
http://www.bcm.tmc.edu/crowd/

The Center for Social Gerontology
http://www.tcsg.org/

Center for the Study and Advancement of Disability Policy
http://www.disabilitypolicycenter.org/

Center for the Study and Prevention of Violence
http://www.colorado.edu/cspv/

Center for Violence Prevention and Control
http://www1.umn.edu/cvpc/

Child Welfare Institute
http://www.gocwi.org/

Child Welfare League of America
http://www.cwla.org/

Children of Aging Parents
http://www.caps4caregivers.org/

The Children's Defense Fund
http://www.childrensdefense.org/

Crimes Against Children Research Center
http://www.unh.edu/ccrc/

Cross Cultural Health Care Program
http://www.xculture.org/

Department of Juvenile Justice and Delinquency Prevention
http://www.ncdjjdp.org/

Disability Social History Project
http://www.disabilityhistory.org/

Domestic Violence and Mental Health Policy Initiative
http://www.dvmhpi.org/

ERIC Clearinghouse on Disabilities and Gifted Education
http://ericec.org/

Family Violence and Sexual Assault Institute
http://www.fvsai.org/

Family Violence Prevention Fund
http://endabuse.org/

Gallaudet Research Institute
http://gri.gallaudet.edu/

The Gerontological Society of America
http://www.geron.org/

Global Aging Initiative
http://www.csis.org/gai/

The Grantsmanship Center
http://www.tgci.com/

Home and Community Based Services Resource Network
http://www.hcbs.org/

Hospice Association of America
http://www.hospice-america.org/

Hospice Education Institute
http://www.hospiceworld.org/

Human Rights Campaign: Working for Lesbian, Gay, Bisexual and Transgendered Equal Rights
http://www.hrc.org/

Human Rights Watch
http://www.hrw.org/

The Hunger Project
http://www.thp.org/

INCITE! Women of Color Against Violence
http://www.incite-national.org/

The Institute for Rehabilitation and Research
http://www.tirr.org

Institute for Social Science Research
http://www.sscnet.ucla.edu/issr/

Institute for Women's Policy Research
http://www.iwpr.org/

Institute for Youth Development
http://www.youthdevelopment.org/

Institute on Domestic Violence in the African American Community
http://www.dvinstitute.org/

International Child Resource Institute
http://www.icrichild.org/

International Gay and Lesbian Human Rights Commission
http://www.iglhrc.org/

International Society for Prevention of Child Abuse and Neglect
http://www.ispcan.org/

International Women's Rights Action Watch
http://iwraw.igc.org/

Inter-University Consortium for Political and Social Research (ICPSR)
http://www.icpsr.umich.edu/

Joint Center for Poverty Research
http://www.jcpr.org/

National Alliance for the Mentally Ill
http://www.nami.org/

National Association of Alcoholism and Drug Abuse Counselors
http://www.naadac.org/

National Association of Home Care and Hospice
http://www.nahc.org/

National Association of Professional Geriatric Care Managers
http://www.caremanager.org/

National Association of State Units on Aging
http://www.nasua.org/

National Center for Children in Poverty
http://www.nccp.org/

National Center for Health Education
http://www.nche.org/

National Center for Policy Analysis
http://www.ncpa.org/

National Center for the Dissemination of Disability Research
http://www.ncddr.org/

National Center on Elder Abuse
http://www.elderabusecenter.org/

[Sargent Shriver] National Center on Poverty Law
http://www.povertylaw.org/

National Child Welfare Resource Center for Family-Centered Practice
http://www.cwresource.org/

National Children's Alliance
http://www.nca-online.org/

National Clearinghouse for Alcohol and Drug Information
http://www.health.org/

National Coalition Against Domestic Violence
http://www.ncadv.org/

National Coalition for the Homeless
http://www.nationalhomeless.org/

National Committee to Preserve Social Security and Medicare
http://www.ncpssm.org/

National Council on Child Abuse and Family Violence
http://www.nccafv.org/

National Council on Crime and Delinquency
http://www.nccd-crc.org/

National Council on Independent Living
http://www.ncil.org/

National Council on the Aging
http://www.ncoa.org/

National Crime Prevention Council
http://www.ncpc.org/

National Data Archive on Child Abuse and Neglect
http://www.ndacan.cornell.edu/

National Families Caregivers Association
http://www.nfcacares.org/

National Federation of the Blind
http://www.nfb.org/

National Gay and Lesbian Task Force
http://www.ngltf.org/

National Hispanic Council on Aging
http://www.nhcoa.org/

The National Hospice and Palliative Care Organization
http://www.nhpco.org/

National Indian Council on Aging
http://www.nicoa.org/

National Latino Alliance for the Elimination of Domestic Violence
http://www.dvalianza.org/

National Low Income Housing Coalition
http://www.nlihc.org/

National Mental Health Association
http://www.nmha.org/

National Organization on Disability
http://www.nod.org/

National Rehabilitation Information Center
http://www.naric.com/

National Resource Center for Foster Care and Permanency Planning
http://www.hunter.cuny.edu/socwork/nrcfcpp/

National Resource Center for Information Technology and Child Welfare
http://www.nrcitcw.org/

National Resource Center for Youth Development
http://www.nrcys.ou.edu/nrcyd.htm

National Resource Center on Child Maltreatment
http://www.gocwi.org/nrccm/

National Rural Health Association
http://www.nrharural.org/

National School Safety Center
http://www.nssc1.org/

National Senior Citizens Law Center
http://www.nsclc.org/

National Sexual Violence Resource Center
http://www.nsvrc.org/

National Violence Against Women Prevention Research Center
http://www.vawprevention.org/

National Youth Advocacy Coalition
http://www.nyacyouth.org/

National Youth Gang Center
http://www.iir.com/nygc/

North American Council on Adoptable Children
http://www.nacac.org/

PFLAG: Parents and Friends of Lesbians, Gays, Bisexual and Transgendered Persons
http://www.pflag.org/

Partnerships Against Violence Network
http://www.pavnet.org/

Planned Parenthood Federation of America, Inc.
http://www.plannedparenthood.org/

Policy Information Exchange
http://www.mimh.edu/mimhweb/pie/

The Prejudice Institute
http://www.prejudiceinstitute.org/

Prevent Child Abuse America
http://www.preventchildabuse.org/

Prevention Institute
http://www.preventioninstitute.org/

The Project for Research on Welfare, Work, and Domestic Violence
http://www.ssw.umich.edu/trapped/

Public Citizen
http://www.citizen.org/

The Research Institute on Addictions
http://www.ria.buffalo.edu/

Safe Schools Coalition
http://www.safeschoolscoalition.org/safe.html

Saving Women's Lives
http://www.savingwomenslives.org/

SeniorNet
http://www.seniornet.org/

Social Science Data Analysis Network
http://www.ssdan.net/

Southern Poverty Law Center
http://www.splcenter.org/

Spaulding for Children (Special Needs Adoptions)
http://www.spaulding.org/

StopFamilyViolence.org
http://www.stopfamilyviolence.org/

Teen Victim Project (National Center for Victims of Crime)
http://www.ncvc.org/tvp/

Tolerance.org
http://www.tolerance.org/

United Nations
http://www.un.org/

United Nations Children's Fund (UNICEF)
http://www.unicef.org/

Urban Institute
http://www.urban.org/

Violence Policy Center
http://www.vpc.org/

Voices for America's Children
http://www.childadvocacy.org/

Volunteers of America
http://www.voa.org/

Wellesley Centers for Women
http://www.wcwonline.org/

Wisconsin Clearinghouse for Prevention Resources
http://wch.uhs.wisc.edu/

Women Watch
http://www.un.org/womenwatch/

Women's International League for Peace and Freedom
http://www.wilpf.org/

World Childhood Foundation
http://www.childhood.org/

World Health Organization
http://www.who.int/en/

World Institute on Disability
http://www.wid.org/

World Resources Institute
http://www.wri.org/

YOUTH.org
http://youth.org/

B7 United States Government Agencies and Information

State and Local Governments (Library of Congress list)
http://lcweb.loc.gov/global/state/stategov.html

Administration for Children and Families
http://www.acf.dhhs.gov/

Administration on Aging
http://www.aoa.dhhs.gov/

Americans with Disabilities Act Homepage
http://www.ada.gov/

Bureau of Justice Statistics
http://www.ojp.usdoj.gov/bjs/

The Catalog of Federal Domestic Assistance
http://www.cfda.gov/

Center for Substance Abuse Prevention
http://www.samhsa.gov/centers/csap/csap.html

Centers for Disease Control and Prevention
http://www.cdc.gov

Centers for Medicare and Medicaid Services
http://cms.hhs.gov/

Child Protective Services: A Guide for Case Workers
http://nccanch.acf.hhs.gov/pubs/usermanuals/cps/

The Children's Bureau
http://www.acf.dhhs.gov/programs/cb/

Corporation for National and Community Service
http://www.cns.gov/

Crimes Against Children Program
http://www.fbi.gov/hq/cid/cac/crimesmain.htm

FedStats
http://www.fedstats.gov/

FEMA: Federal Emergency Management Agency
http://www.fema.gov/

FirstGov.gov
http://www.firstgov.gov/

Forum on Child and Family Statistics
http://www.childstats.gov/

GovBenefits.gov
http://www.govbenefits.gov/

GPO Access (U.S. Government Printing Office)
http://www.gpoaccess.gov/

Health Resources and Services Administration
http://www.hrsa.gov/

Healthy People 2010
http://www.healthypeople.gov/

Indian Health Service
http://www.ihs.gov/

The Library of Congress
http://www.loc.gov/

Maternal and Child Health Bureau
http://www.mchb.hrsa.gov/

Medicare.gov
http://www.medicare.gov/

National Center for Complimentary and Alternative Medicine
http://www.nccam.nih.gov/

National Center for Education Statistics
http://nces.ed.gov/

National Center for Health Statistics
http://www.cdc.gov/nchs/

National Clearinghouse for Child Abuse and Neglect Information
http://nccanch.acf.hhs.gov/

National Health Information Center
http://www.health.gov/nhic/

National Institute on Deafness and Other Communication Disorders
http://www.nidcd.nih.gov/

National Institute of Mental Health
http://www.nimh.nih.gov/

National Institute on Aging
http://www.nia.nih.gov/

National Institute on Drug Abuse
http://www.nida.nih.gov/

National Institute of Justice
http://www.ojp.usdoj.gov/nij/

National Institutes of Health
http://www.nih.gov/

National Survey of Family Growth
http://www.cdc.gov/nchs/nsfg.htm

The National Women's Health Information Center
http://www.4woman.gov/

Occupational Outlook Handbook
http://www.bls.gov/oco/

Office for Victims of Crimes
http://www.ojp.usdoj.gov/ovc/

Office of Disability, Aging and Long-Term Care Policy
http://aspe.hhs.gov/daltcp/

Office of Disease Prevention and Health Promotion
http://odphp.osophs.dhhs.gov/

Office of Special Education and Rehabilitation Services
http://www.ed.gov/about/offices/list/osers/

Office of the Surgeon General
http://www.surgeongeneral.gov/

Reports of the Surgeon General
http://www.nimh.nih.gov/ResearchFunding/fedreport.cfm OR
http://www.surgeongeneral.gov/library/reports.htm

Social Security Online
http://www.ssa.gov/

Statistical abstract of the United States
http://www.census.gov/statab/www/

Substance Abuse and Mental Health Services Administration
http://www.samhsa.gov/

THOMAS: U.S. Congress on the Internet
http://thomas.loc.gov/

U.S. Administration on Aging
http://www.aoa.dhhs.gov/

U.S. Census Bureau
http://www.census.gov/

American FactFinder
http://factfinder.census.gov/

Current Population Survey
http://www.bls.census.gov/cps/

American Indian and Alaska Native Populations
http://www.census.gov/population/www/socdemo/race/indian.html

Asian and Pacific Islander Populations
http://www.census.gov/population/www/socdemo/race/api.html

The Black Population in the United States
http://www.census.gov/population/www/socdemo/race/black.html

Hispanic Population of the United States
http://www.census.gov/population/www/socdemo/race/hispanic.html

U.S. Congress
[See "THOMAS" above]

U.S. Department of Education
http://www.ed.gov/

U.S. Department of Health and Human Services
http://www.dhhs.gov/

U.S. Department of Housing and Urban Development
http://www.hud.gov/

U.S. Department of Justice
http://www.usdoj.gov/

U.S. Department of Veteran Affairs
http://www.va.gov/

U.S. National Library of Medicine
http://www.nlm.nih.gov/

U.S. Senate
http://www.senate.gov/

The White House
http://www.whitehouse.gov/

B8 Significant Journal Titles and Homepages

You can perform a journal title search from your library catalog to determine if your library has any holdings and/or an active subscription to the following social work-related journals. You will need to learn how to do this because very few journal indexes/databases are comprised entirely of full text. Most journal indexes offer full text for some journal titles (as arranged by the journal publisher and the database provider) and the percentage of journals in full-text can vary from almost zero to more than half. And there are also journal indexes that continue to just provide citations to the publication and an abstract or brief summary of the research.

Many libraries are increasingly providing full-text access to journal titles either through agreements with individual publishers or by licensing journal indexes/databases which offer full-text articles. Some libraries are noting if full-text for a journal is available directly within the journal title's catalog record, while other libraries have decided to either create a list of their full-text journals, magazines and newspapers or license another product and company to manage what could be thousands of titles and hundreds of databases for them. Either way, if you are not sure if your library has access to a journal title, ask a reference librarian.

To briefly return to the idea of Library of Congress Subject Headings (LCSHs), a good number of the below titles will be classified as either:

- Social Service—Periodicals
- Social Service—United States—Periodicals

Significant Journal Titles and Their Homepage Addresses
Sample:

ISSN	Journal Title (Year Publication Began–) Homepage for Journal
0965-2140	Addiction (1993–) http://www.blackwellpublishing.com/journal.asp?ref=0965-2140
0364-3107	Administration in Social Work (1977–) http://www.haworthpress.com/store/product.asp?sku=J147

0886-1099   AFFILIA: Journal of Women & Social Work (1986–)
            http://www.sagepub.com/journal.aspx?pid=133
0734-7324   Alcoholism Treatment Quarterly (1984–)
            http://www.haworthpress.com/store/product.asp?sku=J020
0091-0562   American Journal of Community Psychology (1973–)
            http://www.kluweronline.com/issn/0091-0562/
0005-7967   Behaviour Research and Therapy (1963–)
            http://www.elsevier.com/locate/brat/
0045-3102   The British Journal of Social Work (1971–)
            http://bjsw.oupjournals.org/
0145-2134   Child Abuse & Neglect (1977–)
            http://www.elsevier.com/locate/chiabuneg/
0738-0151   Child & Adolescent Social Work Journal (1984–)
            http://www.kluweronline.com/issn/0738-0151/
1356-7500   Child & Family Social Work (1996–)
            http://www.blackwellpublishing.com/journals/CFS/
1077-5595   Child Maltreatment (1996–)
            http://www.sagepub.com/journal.aspx?pid=15
0009-4021   Child Welfare (1948–)
            http://www.cwla.org/pubs/pubdetails.asp?PUBID=P101
1532-8759   Children & Schools: A Journal of Social Work Practice (2000–)
            http://www.naswpress.org/publications/journals/children/
            csintro.html
            Note: Continuation of *Social Work in Education*, 0162-7961 (1978–2000)
0190-7409   Children and Youth Services Review (1979–)
            http://www.elsevier.com/locate/childyouth/
0091-1674   Clinical Social Work Journal (1973–)
            http://www.kluweronline.com/issn/0091-1674/
1369-1457   European Journal of Social Work (1998–)
            http://www.tandf.co.uk/journals/titles/13691457.html
1044-3894   Families in Society: The Journal of Contemporary Human Services
            (1990–)
            http://www.alliance1.org/fis/
0197-6664   Family Relations: Interdisciplinary Journal of Applied Family
            Studies (1952–)
            http://www.blackwellpublishing.com/journal.asp?ref=0197-6664
0016-9013   The Gerontologist (1961–)
            http://gerontologist.gerontologyjournals.org/
0966-0410   Health and Social Care in the Community (1993–)
            http://www.blackwellpublishing.com/journal.asp?ref=0966-0410
0360-7283   Health & Social Work (1976–)
            http://www.naswpress.org/publications/journals/health/
            hswintro.html
1369-6866   International Journal of Social Welfare (1999–)
            http://www.blackwellpublishing.com/journal.asp?ref=1369-6866
            Note: Continuation of *Scandinavian Journal of Social Welfare* 0907-
            2055 (1992–1999)

0020-8728   International Social Work (1958–)
            http://www.sagepub.co.uk/journal.aspx?pid=105604

0140-1971   Journal of Adolescence (1978–)
            http://www.elsevier.com/locate/adolescence

1053-8712   Journal of Child Sexual Abuse (1992–)
            http://www.haworthpress.com/store/product.asp?sku=J070

0090-4392   Journal of Community Psychology (1973–)
            http://www.wiley.com/WileyCDA/WileyTitle/productCd-JCOP.html

1531-3204   Journal of Ethnic and Cultural Diversity in Social Work (2000–)
            http://www.haworthpress.com/store/product.asp?sku=J051
            Note: Continuation of *Journal of Multicultural Social Work*,
            1042-8232 (1991–2000)

1052-2158   Journal of Family Social Work (1995–)
            http://www.haworthpress.com/store/product.asp?sku=J039
            Note: Continuation of *Journal of Social Work and Human Sexuality*,
            0276-3850 (1982–1993)

0163-4372   Journal of Gerontological Social Work (1978–)
            http://www.haworthpress.com/store/product.asp?sku=J083

1049-2089   Journal of Health Care for the Poor and Underserved (1990–)
            http://www.press.jhu.edu/journals/journal_of_health_care_
            for_the_poor_and_underserved/

0091-8369   Journal of Homosexuality (1974–)
            http://www.haworthpress.com/store/product.asp?sku=J082

0047-2794   Journal of Social Policy (1972–)
            http://journals.cambridge.org/journal_JournalofSocialPolicy/

0148-8376   Journal of Social Service Research (1977–)
            http://www.haworthpress.com/store/product.asp?sku=J079

1043-7797   Journal of Social Work Education (1985–)
            http://www.cswe.org/publications/jswe/jswefront.htm

0265-0533   Journal of Social Work Practice (1983–)
            http://www.tandf.co.uk/journals/carfax/02650533.html

1533-256X   Journal of Social Work Practice in the Addictions (2001–)
            http://www.haworthpress.com/store/product.asp?sku=J160

1521-3668   Journal of Social Work Research and Evaluation (2000–)
            http://www.springerpub.com/store/home_jswre.html

0191-5096   Journal of Sociology and Social Welfare (1973–)
            http://www.wmich.edu/hhs/Newslettersjournals/jssw/

0884-1233   Journal of Teaching in Social Work (1987–)
            http://www.haworthpress.com/store/product.asp?sku=J067

1522-8835   Journal of Technology in Human Services (1999–)
            http://www.haworthpress.com/store/product.asp?sku=J017
            Note: Continuation of *Computers in Human Services*,
            0740-445x (1985–1998)

1049-7315   Research on Social Work Practice (1991–)
            http://www.sagepub.com/journal.aspx?pid=148

0037-7317   Smith College Studies in Social Work (1930–)
            http://www.smith.edu/ssw/smith.htm
            * Homepage does not appear to be regularly updated

0303-8300	Social Indicators Research (1974–)
	http://www.wkap.nl/journalhome.htm/0303-8300
0037-7961	Social Service Review (1927–)
	http://www.journals.uchicago.edu/SSR/home.html
0037-8046	Social Work (1956–)
	http://www.naswpress.org/publications/journals/social_work/ swintro.html
0953-5225	Social Work & Social Sciences Review (1990–)
	Published by Whiting & Birch (http://www.whitingbirch.com/) but no journal homepage.
0261-5479	Social Work Education (1981–)
	http://www.tandf.co.uk/journals/carfax/02615479.html
0098-1389	Social Work in Health Care (1975–)
	http://www.haworthpress.com/store/product.asp?sku=J010
1533-2985	Social Work in Mental Health (2002–)
	http://www.haworthpress.com/store/product.asp?sku=J200
1070-5309	Social Work Research (1994–)
	http://www.naswpress.org/publications/journals/research/ swrintro.html
0160-9513	Social Work with Groups: A Journal of Community and Clinical Practice (1978–)
	http://www.haworthpress.com/store/product.asp?sku=J009
1064-5136	Stress, Trauma and Crisis: An International Journal (2003–)
	http://www.tandf.co.uk/journals/titles/15434613.asp
	Note: Continuation of *Crisis Intervention and Time-Limited Treatment* 1064–5136 (1994–2003)

Statistical Formulas

Pearson *r*

$$r = \frac{e - \dfrac{(a)(b)}{N}}{\sqrt{\left[c - \left(\dfrac{a^2}{N}\right)\right]\left[d - \left(\dfrac{b^2}{N}\right)\right]}}$$

where r = Correlation coefficient
a = Sum of values of x
b = Sum of values of y
c = Sum of values of x^2
d = Sum of values of y^2
e = Sum of values of x and y
N = Number of cases

t-test

$$t = \frac{Ma - Mb}{\sqrt{\left(\dfrac{(Sa)^2 + (Sb)^2}{Na + Nb - 2}\right)\left(\dfrac{Na + Nb}{(Na)(Nb)}\right)}}$$

where t = t value

Na = Number of cases in Group A
Nb = Number of cases in Group B
Sa = Sum of squares of raw scores in Group A
Sb = Sum of squares of raw scores in Group B

Mean

$$\bar{x} = \frac{\sum X_1}{N}$$

where $\sum$ = scores added together
X_1 = score for subjects
N = number of subjects

Median

Given an ordered list of n values, the median equals the value at position $\frac{(n+1)}{2}$.
If n is odd, a single value occupies this position. If n is even, the median equals
the mean of the two middle values.

Standard Deviation

$$S = \sqrt{\frac{\sum (x-\bar{x})}{n-1}}$$

where S = sample standard deviation
n = sample population
$\bar{x}$ = sample mean
x = total scores

Chi-Square

$$\chi^2 = \sum \frac{(O-E)^2}{E}$$

where χ^2 = Chi-square value
O = Observed frequency
E = Expected frequency
$\sum$ = Sum of (for all cells)

$$E = \frac{(R)(C)}{(N)}$$

where E = Expected frequency in a particular cell
R = Total number in that cell's row
C = Total number in that cell's row
N = Total number of cases

Probability Tables

Critical values of chi-square

			Level of significance for a one-tailed test			
	.10	.05	.025	.01	.005	.0005
			Level of significance for a two-tailed test			
df	.20	.10	.05	.02	.01	.001
1	1.64	2.71	3.84	5.41	6.64	10.83
2	3.22	4.60	5.99	7.82	9.21	13.82
3	4.64	6.25	7.82	9.84	11.34	16.27
4	5.99	7.78	9.49	11.67	13.28	18.46
5	7.29	9.24	11.07	13.39	15.09	20.52
6	8.56	10.64	12.59	15.03	16.81	22.46
7	9.80	12.02	14.07	16.62	18.48	24.32
8	11.03	13.36	15.51	18.17	20.09	26.12
9	12.24	14.68	16.92	19.68	21.67	27.88
10	13.44	15.99	18.31	21.16	23.21	29.59
11	14.63	17.28	19.68	22.62	24.72	31.26
12	15.81	18.55	21.03	24.05	26.22	32.91
13	16.98	19.81	22.36	25.47	27.69	34.53
14	18.15	21.06	23.68	26.87	29.14	36.12
15	19.31	22.31	25.00	28.26	30.58	37.70
16	20.46	23.54	26.30	29.63	32.00	39.29

(continued)

Critical values of chi-square *(continued)*

			Level of significance for a one-tailed test			
	.10	.05	.025	.01	.005	.0005
			Level of significance for a two-tailed test			
df	.20	.10	.05	.02	.01	.001
17	21.62	24.77	27.59	31.00	33.41	40.75
18	22.76	25.99	28.87	32.35	34.80	42.31
19	23.90	27.20	30.14	33.69	36.19	43.82
20	25.04	28.41	31.41	35.02	37.57	45.32
21	26.17	29.62	32.67	36.34	38.93	46.80
22	27.30	30.81	33.92	37.66	40.29	48.27
23	28.43	32.01	35.17	38.97	41.64	49.73
24	29.55	33.20	36.42	40.27	42.98	51.18
25	30.68	34.38	37.65	41.57	44.31	52.62
26	31.80	35.56	38.88	42.86	45.64	54.05
27	32.91	36.74	40.11	44.14	46.94	55.48
28	34.03	37.92	41.34	45.42	48.28	56.89
29	35.14	39.09	42.69	46.69	49.59	58.30
30	36.25	40.26	43.77	47.96	50.89	59.70
32	38.47	42.59	46.19	50.49	53.49	62.49
34	40.68	44.90	48.60	53.00	56.06	65.25
36	42.88	47.21	51.00	55.49	58.62	67.99
38	45.08	49.51	53.38	57.97	61.16	70.70
40	47.27	51.81	55.76	60.44	63.69	73.40
44	51.64	56.37	60.48	65.34	68.71	78.75
48	55.99	60.91	65.17	70.20	73.68	84.04
52	60.33	65.42	69.83	75.02	78.62	89.27
56	64.66	69.92	74.47	79.82	83.51	94.46
60	68.97	74.40	79.08	84.58	88.38	99.61

Source: From Table IV of R. A. Fisher and F. Yates, *Statistical Tables for Biological, Agricultural, and Medical Research,* published by Addison Wesley Longman Ltd. Reprinted by permission of Addison Wesley Longman Ltd.

Code of Ethics, approved by the 1996 National Association of Social Workers (NASW) Delegate Assembly and revised by the 1999 NASW Delegate Assembly, Section 5.02 Evaluation and Research

(a) Social workers should monitor and evaluate policies, the implementation of programs, and practice interventions.

(b) Social workers should promote and facilitate evaluation and research to contribute to the development of knowledge.

(c) Social workers should critically examine and keep current with emerging knowledge relevant to social work and fully use evaluation and research evidence in their professional practice.

(d) Social workers engaged in evaluation or research should carefully consider possible consequences and should follow guidelines developed for the protection of evaluation and research participants. Appropriate institutional review boards should be consulted.

(e) Social workers engaged in evaluation or research should obtain voluntary and written informed consent from participants, when appropriate, without any implied or actual deprivation or penalty for refusal to participate; without undue inducement to participate; and with due regard for participants' well-being, privacy, and dignity. Informed consent should include information about the nature, extent, and duration of the participation requested and disclosure of the risks and benefits of participation in the research.

(f) When evaluation or research participants are incapable of giving informed consent, social workers should provide an appropriate explanation to the participants, obtain the participants' assent to the extent they are able, and obtain written consent from an appropriate proxy.

(g) Social workers should never design or conduct evaluation or research that does not use consent procedures, such as certain forms of naturalistic observation and archival research, unless rigorous and responsible review of the research has found it to be justified because of its prospective scientific, educational, or applied value and unless equally effective alternative procedures that do not involve waiver of consent are not feasible.

(h) Social workers should inform participants of their right to withdraw from evaluation and research at any time without penalty.

(i) Social workers should take appropriate steps to ensure that participants in evaluation and research have access to appropriate supportive services.

(j) Social workers engaged in evaluation or research should protect participants from unwarranted physical or mental distress, harm, danger, or deprivation.

(k) Social workers engaged in the evaluation of services should discuss collected information only for professional purposes and only with people professionally concerned with this information.

(l) Social workers engaged in evaluation or research should ensure the anonymity or confidentiality of participants and of the data obtained from them. Social workers should inform participants of any limits of confidentiality, the measures that will be taken to ensure confidentiality, and when any records containing research data will be destroyed.

(m) Social workers who report evaluation and research results should protect participants' confidentiality by omitting identifying information unless proper consent has been obtained authorizing disclosure.

(n) Social workers should report evaluation and research findings accurately. They should not fabricate or falsify results and should take steps to correct any errors later found in published data using standard publication methods.

(o) Social workers engaged in evaluation or research should be alert to and avoid conflicts of interest and dual relationships with participants, should inform participants when a real or potential conflict of interest arises, and should take steps to resolve the issue in a manner that makes participants' interests primary.

(p) Social workers should educate themselves, their students, and their colleagues about responsible research practices.

AB design   A single-system design in which there is a comparison between the baseline (A) and an intervention period (B).

ABAB design   A single-system design that is also known as a withdrawal or reversal design, where the AB design is duplicated to increase the validity of the results.

ABC design   A single-system design in which the baseline (A) is followed by one intervention period (B) and a second intervention period (C). Also known as successive intervention design.

Alternate form   A method of testing an instrument's reliability where different but equivalent forms of the same test are administered to the same group of individuals, usually close in time, and then compared.

Alternative hypothesis   Another term for a rival hypothesis.

Analytical study   An approach to writing a qualitative report that looks at relationships between variables.

Anonymity   A condition in which the researcher cannot identify a given response with a given respondent.

Applicability   Whether or not a measuring instrument is appropriate and suitable for a particular type of problem.

Applied research   Research that produces practical outcomes and is directed at solving problems encountered in social work practice.

Authority   Referring to outside sources of knowledge.

Autocorrelation   The relationship between the outcome or dependent variable scores in single-system studies.

Availability sampling (convenience sampling)   A nonprobability sampling method where available or convenient elements are included in the sample.

Bar graph   A visual means of displaying data at the nominal level of measurement.

Baseline   Repeated measurement before the introduction of the intervention that allows the comparison of target behavior rates before and after the intervention.

Baseline comparison   A strategy for comparing the equivalency between experimental and comparison groups where the comparison group is composed of cases handled prior to the introduction to the program.

Bilingual questionnaires   Questionnaires that include the questions and instructions in two languages.

Bivariate measure   A method of measuring the relationship between two variables.

Case studies   A description of the application of an intervention. Also an approach to writing a qualitative report.

Causal flowcharts   A visual means of representing causal connections of qualitative data.

Causality A principle that involves meeting three conditions: first, two factors are empirically related to one another; second, the cause precedes the effect in time; and third, the relationship between the factors cannot be explained by other factors.

Celeration line A means of predicting the dependent variable in single-system studies.

Chronological narrative An approach to writing a qualitative report that tracks a phenomenon through time.

Client satisfaction survey A design used to ask clients how they experienced or perceived a program.

Clinical significance (practical significance) Significance level that is achieved when the specified goal of the intervention has been reached.

Closed-ended question Questions that provide respondents with a fixed set of alternatives from which they choose.

Cluster diagram One method of developing a classification system in the analysis of qualitative data.

Cluster sampling A form of probability sampling that involves randomly sampling a larger unit containing the elements of interest and then sampling from these larger units the elements to be included in the final sample.

Coding A means of organizing and collecting information so that it can be entered into a computer.

Cohort groups A strategy for increasing the equivalency between experimental and comparison groups where the comparison groups move through an organization at the same time as those in the program being evaluated but do not receive program services.

Cohort studies Cohort studies examine specific subgroups as they change over time.

Community forum A public meeting or series of meetings where individuals are briefed on the issues and then asked for input—a form of purposive sampling.

Comparison groups Subjects who receive another type of intervention or who receive no type of bona fide intervention and who have not been randomly assigned. Comparison groups can be used to increase the internal and external validity of group designs.

Confidence level How often you would expect to find similar results if the research were repeated.

Confidentiality A state in which the researcher knows the identity of the respondents and their associated responses but guarantees not to disclose this information.

Construct validity A means of testing an instrument's validity; involves examining the extent to which an instrument measures a theoretical construct.

Contamination The difficulty of distinguishing between the experimental and comparison groups, because of either contact between the subjects of each group or no clear distinction between the program experiences of the clients in each group.

Content analysis A method of coding written communication to a systematic quantifiable form.

Content validity A method of testing an instrument's validity that involves ensuring that the content of the instrument corresponds to the concepts being measured.

Contingency table A measure of association, also known as cross-tabulation.

Contradictory evidence One method of developing a classification system in the analysis of qualitative data.

Control group   Subjects who do not receive the intervention being evaluated, and who have been randomly assigned.

Convenience sampling (availability sampling)   A nonprobability sampling method where available or convenient elements are included in the sample.

Copyright   Laws that apply not only to published material but also to in-house reports.

Correlation   A measure of association used with interval or ratio level data.

Correlation coefficient   A statistic that measures the extent to which the comparisons are similar or not similar, related or not related.

Cost-effectiveness study   Program costs compared to some measure of program output; a cost per unit is calculated.

Counts   One method of developing a classification system in the analysis of qualitative data.

Cover letter   Sent with a questionnaire to briefly describe the purpose of the study and the principle of confidentiality.

Criterion sampling   Selecting all cases that meet some criterion. A type of nonprobability sampling.

Criterion validity   The extent to which a correlation exists between the measuring instrument and another standard.

Cross-classification   A method of qualitative data analysis that creates categories by crossing one dimension or typology with another.

Cross-sectional design   A method of measuring behavior as it occurs at one point in time or over a relatively short period of time.

Cross-tabulation   A measure of association, also known as a contingency table.

Data (datum)   Information that is collected for research.

Deductive reasoning   A process of drawing conclusions from the general to the particular; opposite to the process of induction.

Dependent variable   The outcome variable that has been presumably affected by the independent variable.

Descriptive research   A process of recording and reporting phenomena; not primarily concerned with causes.

Descriptive statistics   A means of summarizing the characteristics of a sample or the relationship among the variables.

Developmental research (intervention research)   Research specifically focused on developing innovative interventions by actually using research to design the interventions, test their effectiveness, and modify them based on recommendations that emerge from testing.

Directional hypothesis (one-tailed hypothesis)   A hypothesis that specifies not only that there is an association between variables but also predicts whether the relationship is negative or positive.

Discontinuity   A difference in data levels between the baseline and intervention periods.

Discourse analysis   A way of understanding how the researcher's social context can influence how data are understood and analyzed.

Drifts   Trends that occur across the intervention and baseline periods.

Ecological fallacy   The danger of reaching conclusions in your study using a unit of analysis other than that used by the study.

Element   The item under study in the population and sample; in social work, a client system.

Emic   A system of organizing and developing categories of qualitative data that are derived from those being studied rather than being constructed by the researcher.

Empirically based practice   Social work practice based on specific findings from research.

Empiricism   Observation through the use of the senses.

Ethnography   A method of describing a culture or society.

Explanatory designs   Designs that examine the impact of the intervention on the target behavior, these designs are also called single-system designs or single-system studies.

Ex post facto design ("After the fact")   refers to designs where subjects already possess the independent variable of interest before the study begins.

Expected frequencies   Cross-tabulations that are what one might expect to observe according to probability.

Experience   A form of knowledge that includes firsthand, personal participation in events.

Experimental designs   Group research designs that randomly assign to the control group and experimental group.

Experimental group   In a program evaluation, the group that receives the intervention being evaluated.

Explanatory research   Studies directed at providing explanations of events to identify causes.

Exploratory research   A form of research that generates initial insights into the nature of an issue and develops questions to be investigated by more extensive studies.

External validity   The extent to which research results are generalizable to the wider population.

Face-to-face questionnaires   Questionnaires administered I person rather than by mail.

Feasibility studies (needs assessment)   Another term for a needs assessment.

Feedback   An important way of testing the validity of data from interpretive studies and making certain that the data are understandable to and relevant to the participants in the research.

Feminist research   An approach to research that argues that a relationship is formed between the researcher and participant, which results in the formation of a constructed reality between them.

First-level coding   This level of coding in qualitative data analysis involves identifying meaning units and fitting them into categories and assigning codes to these categories.

Focus group   A group formed to help develop the research question, or as a form of non-probability sampling.

Follow-up   A second and further follow-up mailings can enhance the response ratio of mailed questionnaires.

Formative program evaluation   An examination of the planning, development, and implementation of a program.

Frame elicitation   A means of framing questions to elicit from subjects what they include in a particular topic or category.

Frequency distribution   A description of the number of times the values of a variable occur in a sample.

Front-end analyses (needs assessment)   Another term for a needs assessment.

Generalist social work practice   A form of social work practice taught in B.S.W. programs that involves practice with different-size client systems and uses a number of different interventions and practice roles.

Generalization   The application of research findings to other situations.

Generalize   The ability to apply the findings from studying the sample to the population.

Group design   The effect of a variable or variables on another variable or variables for a number of different client systems or elements.

Group questionnaires   Questionnaires administered to groups rather than to individuals.

Guttman Scale   A type of scale that is unidimensional and the items on the scale are progressive, generally they are organized with the "easy" items first and the "harder" ones later.

History   A threat to the internal validity; those events that occur, other than the intervention, to affect the outcome.

History-treatment interaction   A threat to the external validity.

Human diversity   The whole spectrum of differences among people, including but not limited to gender, ethnicity, age, and sexual orientation.

Human subjects committees   Committees that review the ethical implications of research.

Hypothesis   A probability statement about the relationships among certain factors.

Independent variable   The presumed causal variable in a relationship.

Indigenous categories   Categories used in qualitative data analysis that incorporate the categories used by those observed.

Inductive reasoning   The use of observation to examine the particular and then develop a generalization to explain the relationship among many of the particulars; the opposite of deduction.

Inferential statistics   A means to determine whether an observed relationship is by chance or in fact reflects a relationship among factors; allows us to generalize the findings to the wider population.

Information-rich sampling (purposive sampling)   Picking cases from which you can learn about the issues central to the research question—the sampling method of choice in interpretive studies.

Informed consent   Subjects' permission, obtained after fully informing potential participants of their research role and the consequences of their participation.

Institutional review boards   Boards that review the ethical implications of research being conducted at that institution.

Instrumentation   A threat to internal validity; the way in which the variables are measured may change when measures are taken more than once.

Internal validity   The extent to which the changes in the dependent variable(s) are a result of the introduction of the independent variable(s) rather than other factor(s).

Interpretism   An approach to science that emphasizes the subjective, descriptive, inductive, and qualitative aspects of inquiry, also known as the qualitative approach to research.

Interval measures   Measures that classify observations into mutually exclusive categories in an inherent order and with equal space between the categories.

Intervention research (developmental research)   Research specifically focused on developing innovative interventions by actually using research to design the interventions, test their effectiveness, and modify them, based on recommendations that emerge from testing.

Intuition   A form of insight not based on specialized training or reasoning.

Key informant sampling   Picking someone in the community identified as an expert in the field of interest; a form of nonprobability sampling.

Level of measurement   The extent to which a variable can be quantified and subsequently subjected to mathematical or statistical procedures.

Likert scale   A common measurement scale consisting of a series of statements with five response alternatives.

Limited probability sample   A sample whose characteristics are compared with the characteristics of a sample drawn from a larger population, allowing some tentative generalizations of the findings to be made.

Line graph   A graph that uses a line to connect the data points.

Literature review   A resource for consulting with the written material relevant to the research problem.

Longitudinal design   A study that tracks behavior over a significant period of time.

Mailed questionnaires   Questionnaires distributed by mail rather than face to face.

Margin of error   Measure of the precision the researcher needs.

Matching   A strategy for increasing the equivalency of experimental and comparison groups; certain characteristics thought to be important impacts on outcomes are selected, and these characteristics are equally represented in each group.

Matrix   One method of developing a classificiation system in the analysis of qualitative data.

Maturation   A threat to internal validity; a change that is not a result of the intervention but of the subject's becoming more mature with the passage of time.

Mean   A measure of central tendency; the result of summing all values of the observations and then dividing by the total number of observations.

Measuring instrument   The method or means by which data are collected.

Median   A measure of central tendency; a value where 50% of the cases lie above the value and 50% of the cases lie below the value.

Metaphors   One method of developing a classification system in the analysis of qualitative data.

Missing links   (see Metaphors)

Mode   A measure of central tendency; the value possessed by the greatest number of observations.

Monitoring client progress   Examine and reflect on client progress; used in practice evaluation.

Monitoring interventions Examine and reflect on interventions used in practice evaluation.

Mortality A threat to internal validity; subjects dropping out of groups, resulting in a lack of equivalency between the groups.

Multiple baseline design A replication of the AB design where the same intervention is applied to two or more target problems, to two or more clients, or in two or more settings at different points in time.

Multivariate analysis Involves examining relationships between more than two variables.

Multivariate measure A method of measuring the relationship of two or more variables.

Needs assessment (feasibility studies and front-end analysis) Questions concerned with discovering the nature and extent of a particular social problem to determine the most appropriate type of response.

Negative cases A means of validating findings from qualitative research.

Negative correlation A relationship between two variables; as the values of one variable increase, the values of the other variable decrease.

Neutrality When the researcher does not seek a particular perspective to draw conclusions.

Nominal measures Measures that clarify observations into mutually exclusive categories with no ordering to the categories.

Nondirectional hypothesis (two-tailed hypothesis) A hypothesis that states there is an association between two or more variables but predicts nothing about the direction of that association.

Nonprobability sampling The process of selecting a sample where each element in the population has an unknown chance of being included in the sample.

Normal distribution A bell-shaped curve that is symmetrical; the mean, median, and mode are the same, and most of the scores cluster around the mean, median, and mode.

Null hypothesis A hypothesis that there is no association between the variables.

Objectivity The condition in which to the greatest extent possible the researcher's values and biases do not interfere with the study of the problem.

Observation A way of collecting information separate from philosophizing or speculating.

Observed frequencies Frequencies in a cross-tabulation derived from the sample.

Observer reliability The comparison of different administrations of the same instrument by different observers or interviewers.

One-group posttest-only design A type of quasi-experimental group design.

One-group pretest/posttest design A type of quasi-experimental group design.

One-tailed hypothesis (directional hypothesis) A hypothesis that specifies not only that there is an association between variables but also predicts whether the relationship is negative or positive.

Open-ended questions Questions that do not provide respondents with responses, leaving them free to formulate their own responses.

Operationalize A means of specifying the manner by which the variable is to be measured.

Ordinal measures Measures that classify observations into mutually exclusive categories with an inherent order.

Outcome analysis   Another term for summative program evaluation and assessment of whether or not goals and objectives are met.

Output   The final product obtained from submitting a computer program to the computer; this can be displayed on the **screen or as hard copy (printout).**

Overflow comparison groups   A strategy for increasing the equivalency of comparison and experimental groups where the comparison groups are those who are referred to a program but who cannot be served at that time.

Panel studies   Studies that look at the same set of people over time.

Participant observation   An observation method involving the observer's fully submerging himself or herself to become one of the observed group.

Participatory action research   An opportunity for the subjects' involvement in the research process—an approach to research that has several aims, all intended to empower participants.

Perfect correlation   A relationship between two variables where the values of each variable increase or decrease at the same rate as each other.

Pie charts   A visual representation of data used to show the relative contributions of each of the values to the whole variable.

Population   All possible cases that are of interest to the researcher.

Positive correlation   A relationship between two variables where, as the values of one variable increase, the values of the other variable also increase.

Positivism   An approach to science that adheres to the principles of objectivity, causality, deduction, collecting quantitative data, and producing generalizable results. Also referred to as the quantitative approach to research.

Posttest-only control-group design   A type of experimental design.

Power (statistical) The probability of correctly rejecting a null hypothesis.

Practical significance (clinical significance)   Significance level that is achieved when the specified goal of the intervention has been reached.

Practice evaluation   The type of research that assesses an individual social worker's practice.

Practice logs   A type of process recording where the practitioner keeps an ongoing record of their practice.

Preexperimental designs   Group designs that use comparison groups rather than control groups, or that use no type of comparison group or control group, and thus have limited internal and external validity.

Pretest/posttest comparison-group design   A type of preexperimental group design.

Pretest-posttest control-group design   A type of experimental design.

Probability sampling   The process of selecting a sample where each element in the population has a known chance of being included in the sample.

Process recording (process analysis)   A written record of what transpired with a client system.

Program evaluation   A type of research concerned with the assessment of a program's overall functioning.

Proportional stratified sampling   Another term for stratified random sampling.

Pure research   Research centered on answering questions about human behavior to satisfy intellectual curiosity with little concern for the practical benefits that might result.

Purposive sampling   Another term for nonprobability sampling.

Qualitative   The nonnumerical examination of phenomena focusing on the underlying meanings and patterns of relationships. Can denote a specific approach to research.

Quantitative   The creation of categories of phenomena under study prior to investigation and the assignment of numbers to these categories. Can denote a specific approach to research.

Quasi-experimental designs   Designs that eliminate more threats to internal and external validity than preexperimental designs, and use comparison groups rather than control groups, and thus still have limited internal and external validity.

Quota sampling   A nonprobability sampling method that includes a certain proportion of elements with specific characteristics in the sample.

Random assignment   The process by which every subject has an equal chance of being assigned to a control group or the experimental group.

Range   A measure of variability; the distance between the largest and the smallest value.

Rapid assessment instrument (RAI)   A standardized series of questions or statements to connect data in single-system studies.

Rates under treatment   A type of secondary data that uses existing data from agencies to determine the needs of the community.

Ratio measures   Measures that classify observations into mutually exclusive categories with an inherent order and equal spacing between the categories; the ratio measure reflects the absolute magnitude of the value (and has an absolute zero point).

Reactive effect (reactivity)   The degree to which the researcher's presence affects the behavior being observed.

Reductionism   The extreme limitation of the kinds and numbers of variables to be considered when explaining or accounting for broad types of behavior.

Regression analysis   A statistical analysis that allows an estimate of how much change in the dependent variable is produced by a given change in the independent variable or variables.

Regression to the mean   A threat to external validity; the tendency of test scores to regress to the mean.

Reliability   The extent to which a measure reveals actual differences in what is being measured, rather than differences that are inherent in the measuring instrument itself.

Replicate   To repeat a study to determine if the same results are found.

Representative sample   A sample that accurately represents the distribution of relevant variables in the population.

Researcher-constructed categories   Categories that researchers apply when analyzing qualitative data.

Research log   Informal but systematic records of ideas and progress relating to a research study.

Research methods   Means of systematically organizing observations and replicating studies.

Research proposal   A paper proposing to undertake a specific type of research.

Response rate   The proportion of the sample that responds to a questionnaire or interview.

Reversal design   A design that is the same as an ABAB single-system design.

Rival hypothesis   A means of validating findings when analyzing qualitative data (also referred to as an alternative hypothesis).

Sample   A group of subjects chosen from the population.

Sampling   A means of determining the subjects of the study.

Sampling error   The extent to which the values of a sample differ from those of the population.

Sampling frame   A list of all the elements in the population from which the sample is selected.

Scales   A measurement technique that combines a number of items into a composite score.

Scattergram   A means of plotting the relationships between two-interval or ratio-level data.

Science   A system for producing knowledge and the knowledge produced from that system.

Secondary data   Existing forms of information that have been previously collected.

Second level of coding   This level of coding in qualitative data analysis is more abstract than first-level coding and involves interpreting the data.

Selection   A threat to internal validity; the possibility that the group of people selected for one group will differ from those selected for the other group.

Selection-treatment interaction   A threat to external validity.

Self-monitoring   A process in which a client collects data on his or her own behavior.

Semantic Differential (SD) Scale   A type of scale that presents the respondent with a stimulus, for example, an event or a person, that is then rated on a scale using opposite adjectives.

Semistructured interview   An interviewing situation in which the interviewer is freer to pursue hunches and improvise in asking questions.

Simple random sampling   A form of probability sampling in which the population is related as a whole unit and each element has an equal chance of being included in the sample.

Single-subject design study   Also known as single-system studies.

Single-system design or study   The type of design used in practice evaluation.

Skewed distribution   A distribution in which most of the scores are concentrated at one end of the distribution rather than in the middle.

Slopes   Trends that occur in the data within the baseline or within the intervention period.

Snowball sampling   A form of nonprobability sampling that identifies some members of the population and then has those individuals contact others in the population.

Social indicators   A form of secondary data collection that involves selecting demographic data from existing records to predict a community's needs.

Solomon four-group design   A type of experimental group design.

Split half method   Items on the instrument are divided into comparable halves.

Standard deviation   A measure of variability that averages the distance of each value from the mean.

Standardized scales   Uniform scales that are tested extensively.

Static-group comparison design   A type of quasi-experimental group design.

Statistically significant   Characteristic of a finding when the null hypothesis is rejected and the probability that the result was due to chance falls at or below a certain cutoff point—usually 5%, or the .05 significance level.

Stratified random sampling   A form of probability sampling in which the population is divided into strata, and subsamples are randomly selected from each stratum.

Strengths needs assessment   A needs assessment that examines the strengths rather the deficits of a population.

Structured interview   An interviewing situation in which the interviewer knows ahead of time the questions to be asked and in many cases is simply verbally administering a questionnaire.

Structured observation   Behaviors are categorized prior to the observation according to their characteristics, including their frequency, direction, and magnitude. These categories can then be quantified.

Subjective   Reality as perceived by the subject; the researcher's biases and values are explicitly stated.

Successive intervention design   A design that is the same as the ABC single-system design.

Summative program evaluation   An assessment that determines whether goals and objectives have been met and the extent to which program efforts are generalizable to other settings and populations.

Survey research   Studies focusing on describing the characteristics of a group.

Systematic random sampling   A form of probability sampling in which every *n*th element of the sampling frame is selected for the sample.

Target problem scales   Scales used in single-system studies to track the changes in a client system's target behavior.

Task forces   Representatives of the agency or community, used to help formulate research questions.

Testing   A threat to internal validity; the effect the testing itself may have on the subject.

Test-retest   The repeated administration of the instrument to the same set of people on separate occasions.

Thematic narrative   An approach to writing a qualitative report that uses the themes identified in the data.

Theories   Scientific descriptions and explanations of logical relationships among phenomena.

Thurstone Scale A type of scale that is constructed using equally distant intervals.

Time series design   A type of quasi-experimental design in which a number of measurements are made both before and after the intervention.

Transcribe   The act of writing down verbatim a recording of the interview.

Treatment diffusion   The act of ensuring that there are no interferences during the course of the evaluation that may affect either the equivalence of the groups or the representativeness of the sample.

Trend studies   Multiple samplings from the same population over months or years to monitor changes or trends.

Triangulation   A means of validating findings from qualitative research.

Two-tailed hypothesis (nondirectional hypothesis)   A hypothesis that states that two or more variables are associated, but does not predict whether the association is negative or positive.

Type I error   An erroneous rejection of the null hypothesis—the conclusion that a relationship exists between the variables when no relationship in fact exists.

Type II error   An erroneous failure to reject the null hypothesis—a failure to identify a relationship between variables.

Typical case sampling   The most-often-used type of nonprobability sampling. Typical cases are sought using the literature, previous research, or consultation with relevant groups.

Unit of analysis   The situation or person who is the object of the study.

Univariate measures   Measures that examine variables one at a time.

Unstructured interviews   Interviews that are similar to conversations except that the interviewer and interviewee know that an interview is being conducted and the interviewee is privy to information of interest to the interviewer.

Unstructured observation   Observation that is used when little is known about the behaviors being observed and no categorization of the behaviors has been done before the interview.

Validity of a measuring instrument   The extent to which we are measuring what we think we are measuring.

Value   The quantitative measure attached to a variable.

Variable   Characteristic of a phenomenon; something that varies and subsequently has different values.

Vignettes   Hypothetical situations either drawn from a source or developed by the researcher for the purpose of eliciting certain responses from the participants.

Visual significance   A state that occurs when the visual presentation of results from a single-system study looks significant.

Web surveys   Data collection using a Web-based questionnaire.

Withdrawal design   A design that is the same as an ABAB single-system design.

TO THE OWNER OF THIS BOOK:

I hope that you have found *Research Methods for Generalist Social Work*, Fourth Edition useful. So that this book can be improved in a future edition, would you take the time to complete this sheet and return it? Thank you.

School and address:_____

Department:_____

Instructor's name:_____

1. What I like most about this book is:_____

_____

_____

2. What I like least about this book is:

_____

_____

3. My general reaction to this book is:

_____

_____

4. The name of the course in which I used this book is:

_____

5. Were all of the chapters of the book assigned for you to read?_____

   If not, which ones weren't?_____

6. In the space below, or on a separate sheet of paper, please write specific suggestions for improving this book and anything else you'd care to share about your experience in using this book.

_____

_____

_____

FOLD HERE

BUSINESS REPLY MAIL
FIRST-CLASS MAIL   PERMIT NO. 102   MONTEREY CA

POSTAGE WILL BE PAID BY ADDRESSEE

Attn: Lisa Gebo / Social Work Editor

BrooksCole/Thomson Learning
60 Garden Ct Ste 205
Monterey CA 93940-9967

FOLD HERE

OPTIONAL:

Your name:_____ Date: _____

May we quote you, either in promotion for *Research Methods for Generalist Social Work*, Fourth Edition, or in future publishing ventures?

Yes: _____   No: _____

Sincerely yours,

Christine Marlow